ACCLAIM FOR *Drew Gilpin Faust's*

# MOTHERS OF INVENTION

"Faust brings alive the voices and feelings of southern slaveholding women. . . . An engaging narrative that demonstrates how fully this devastating war was, in fact, a story of and by women as well as men."

—Elizabeth Fox-Genovese, author of
*Within the Plantation Household:*
*Black and White Women of the Old South*

"A captivating, richly researched, and elegantly written analysis of gender, race, and class at the crossroads of war and region by one of the finest historians of our generation." —Darlene Clark Hine, editor of
*The Encyclopedia of Black Women's History*

"Drew Faust provides a welcome and stunning contribution to Civil War history." —Evelyn Brooks Higginbotham,
Professor of Afro-American Studies,
Harvard University

"Faust re-creates a society in the depths of social, military, and economic disintegration, and shows its corrosive effect upon the morals and manners of white Southerners who were members of the elite."

—Bertram Wyatt-Brown,
*The New York Review of Books*

"A complex and poignant history. . . . Faust has brought back to life the women and girls whom the Confederate troops left behind."

—*Philadelphia Daily News*

"I read with unanticipated fascination, spellbound by the gathered voices, their passion and stamina, their gifts of introspection and observation."

—Josephine Humphreys,
*The New York Times Book Review*

# MOTHERS
# OF INVENTION

# MOTHERS
# OF INVENTION

*Women of the Slaveholding South
in the American Civil War*

## DREW GILPIN FAUST

*Vintage Books*
A Division of Random House, Inc.
New York

FIRST VINTAGE BOOKS EDITION, OCTOBER 1997

Library of Congress Cataloging-in-Publication Data

Faust, Drew Gilpin.
Mothers of invention : women of the slaveholding South in the American
Civil War / by Drew Gilpin Faust.
p. cm.
Includes bibliographical references and index.
ISBN 0-679-78104-8
1. United States—History—Civil War, 1861–1865—Women. 2. Women—
Confederate States of America—History. 3. Confederate States of Amer-
ica—History. I. Title.
[E628.F38 1997]
973.7'082—dc21  97-6670
CIP

Random House Web address: http://www.randomhouse.com/

Printed in the United States of America
10   9

*In Memory of*

Isabella Tyson Gilpin (1894–1983)

Catharine Ginna Mellick (1895–1989)

Catharine Mellick Gilpin (1918–1966)

# CONTENTS

# ILLUSTRATIONS

# PREFACE

When I was growing up in Virginia in the 1950s and 1960s, my mother taught me that the term "woman" was disrespectful, if not insulting. Adult females—at least white ones—should be considered and addressed as "ladies." I responded to this instruction by refusing to wear dresses and by joining the 4-H club, not to sew and can like all the other girls, but to raise sheep and cattle with the boys. My mother still insisted on the occasional dress but, to her credit, said not a negative word about my enthusiasm for animal husbandry.

*tomboy*

Looking back, I am sure that the origins of this book lie somewhere in that youthful experience and in the continued confrontations with my mother— until the very eve of her death when I was nineteen—about the requirements of what she usually called "femininity." "It's a man's world, sweetie, and the sooner you learn that the better off you'll be," she warned. I have been luckier than she in that I have lived in a time when my society and culture have supported me in proving that statement wrong.

My professional historical interest in the South grew out of those early years as well, for I lived in Harry Byrd's home county during the era of *Brown v. Topeka* and "massive resistance" to school desegregation, a time when even a young child could not be unaware of adult talk and worry about social transformations in the offing. It was not until I heard news about the *Brown* decision on the radio that I even noticed that my elementary school was all white and recognized that this was not accident. But I quickly penned a letter to President Eisenhower to say how illogical I thought this seemed in the face of the precepts of equality I had already imbibed by second grade. I confronted the paradox of being both a southerner and an American at an early age.

That I should become a historian, focus my scholarship on the South and the Civil War, and write a book on white women in the Confederacy seems almost overdetermined. That I should dedicate it to the memory of my mother and my two grandmothers—"ladies" who were at the same time the most powerful members of my family—seems entirely fitting. All three were, in fact, women deeply affected by war, though for them the homefront did not merge with battle the way it did for Confederate women. But my grandmothers sent husbands off to Europe in the First World War, and one lost an only brother in a volunteer flying mission over the English Channel. My mother was married in 1942 with less than a week's notice, and my parents were soon separated for eighteen months by my father's service overseas. The formal photographs of my father, uncles, and grandfathers that decorated the shelves and tables of my childhood pictured them in uniform. I grew up thinking all men were soldiers.

I have tried to write this book as if my mother and grandmothers were going to read it. After two decades as an academic historian, I sometimes fear I no longer can communicate in a manner that will engage a general reader, but the compelling nature and human drama of this war story have made me want to try. As a consequence, the scholarly reader will find most references to theoretical questions and historiographical debates in the endnotes rather than in the text. I have tried not to drown out the Confederate women's voices with my own.

In fact, a considerable portion of my interest in this subject has derived from the richness of language and expression in the voluminous collections of writing elite southern women left as their historical legacy. Because they were educated and because they often had leisure time for reflection, they created an extensive written record of self-justification as well as introspection and self-doubt. Although the history of elites has not been a particularly fashionable topic in recent years, I have been attracted to it by the opportunity to use such abundant and revealing sources to explore how military and social crisis can challenge power and privilege to define their essential nature. For the women as well as the men of the South's master class, the Civil War was indeed, as I am hardly the first to observe, a moment of truth.

The self-consciousness and eloquence of the Confederacy's elite women, preserved in diaries, letters, essays, memoirs, fiction, and poetry, have provided this study with documentation of extraordinary range as well as richness. Diaries written for the author's eyes alone, for her children, or for posterity must of course be interpreted differently from letters addressed to particular individuals, or novels produced within the constraints of popular contemporary genres, or reminiscences composed through a haze of reconstructed memories and changed circumstances. But the variety of material has ultimately worked to enhance my understanding through its diversity of forms and complementarity of perspectives.

Published editions of women's writing from the Civil War era grow more numerous every year and greatly aided me in my task. The most compelling part of my research, however, was my visits to more than two dozen manuscript repositories, concentrated in eleven southern states and the District of Columbia, but including a number of Yankee institutions as well. My debt to all those who assisted me at those libraries and archives is incalculable.

I have listened to the voices of more than 500 Confederate women. But my research extended well beyond the writings of the women themselves, for it was not just females who were worried about the changing nature of identity and of gender relations in the wartime South. White women's self scrutiny engaged them in an ongoing conversation with the larger society of which they were a part, in a process of negotiation about what womanhood would come to mean in circumstances of dramatic social upheaval. As a result, I have directed considerable attention to public discourse about gender and about woman's place in the new southern nation. Some of this discussion I have discovered in Confederate popular culture—in plays, novels, songs, and paintings. But I have also found it closely associated with political dimensions of southern life—in remarks by leading southern statesmen such as Jefferson Davis, in newspaper editorials, and even in public policy decisions.

Existing studies of Confederate politics and public life have paid almost no attention to the place of women, either as targets of policies or as influences on them. I hope to show in this book that not only did leaders of Confederate opinion and government talk about the proper place of white women in both the new nation and the war to secure its independence; they executed plans and passed legislation that had direct effects on women's lives. Whether or not Confederate leaders recognized these implications, Confederate women certainly did. In a nation rent by war and invasion, there are no private lives. Women's evaluations of the southern government's policies on conscription, relief, home defense, economic production, and slavery influenced and, I argue, in the end undermined women's support for continued war.

Public discussion and public actions affected as well the ways in which women revised their identities and reinvented themselves amidst warborn social transformation. The experiences of my own youth have not permitted me to forget how the disruption of prevailing public values can create the opportunity for new choices within the seemingly most private aspects of individual lives. Yet, as we shall see, the tenacious hold of traditionalism can combine ultimately to restrict these choices as well. This book is about the clash of old and new within the lives of a group that was at once the beneficiary and the victim of the social order of the Old South; it is about the paradox of being at once privileged and subordinated; it is about how people manage both to change and not change, about the relationship of such personal transformations to a larger world of society and politics. It is about the half of the Confederacy's master class that was female.

*Wellfleet, August 1994*

# ACKNOWLEDGMENTS

I have been working on this project long enough that nearly everyone I know has helped me in some way or other. Even people I have never met have kindly responded to inquiries about nineteenth-century clothing styles, provided me with unpublished primary material, helped me locate photographs, and offered critiques of particular sections or concepts. I am the grateful beneficiary of much generosity from friends and strangers alike. Lynn Hunt, Linda Kerber, Stephanie McCurry, Reid Mitchell, and Steven Stowe carefully read and commented on the entire manuscript. As reviewers for the University of North Carolina Press, Nancy Hewitt and Suzanne Lebsock provided me with a gratifying balance of criticism and support. My editor, Kate Torrey, had faith in the book even when I was not yet sure it would be a book at all. Ron Maner and Stephanie Wenzel paid careful and expert attention during its copyediting and production. Vernon Burton, Stephanie Cole, Kathy Fuller, Grace Elizabeth Hale, John Inscoe, Stephanie McCurry, Amy Murrell, Susan O'Donovan, Joel Perlman, Philip Racine, Leslie Rowland, Joan Severa, Jane Schultz, and Stephen Whitman offered invaluable assistance from their own works in progress. Graduate students Todd Barnett, Dana Barron, Nancy Bercaw, Brian Crane, Larry Goldsmith, and Max Grant helped with research and provided their own critical perspectives as well. Nancy's closely related dissertation work helped me to see within a textured local context many of the broader questions I had endeavored to frame. Rebecca Brittenham, John W. Chambers, Elizabeth Fox-Genovese, Eugene Genovese, Lori Ginzberg, Anne Jones, Winthrop Jordan, Jane Pease, George Rable, Janice Radway, Kathy Rudy, Charles Reagan Wilson, and Bertram Wyatt-Brown commented astutely on individual chapters. Philip Lapsansky of the Library Company of Philadelphia; Corinne Hudgins, Guy Swanson, and Tucker Hill of the Museum of the Confederacy; Kym Rice of Washington, D.C.; Lynda Crist and Mary Dix of the Papers of Jefferson Davis at Rice University; Ralph Elder of the Center for American History of the University of Texas; David Moltke-Hansen of the Southern Historical Collection; Frances Pollard of the Virginia Historical Society; Edwin Bridges of the Alabama Department of Archives and History; and Allen Stokes of the South Caroliniana Library all drew my attention to materials that proved invaluable. Lee Pugh of the interlibrary loan department of the University of Pennsylvania Libraries was unfailingly helpful and efficient, and Stephen Lehmann, humanities bibliographer, worked miracles to acquire crucial microfilm.

The University of Pennsylvania has for twenty years now supported my scholarship in countless ways, and I am grateful to administrators and department chairs past and present for facilitating the writing of this book. I owe my deepest appreciation to Sheldon Hackney, Michael Aiken, Hugo Sonnenschein, and Rosemary Stevens and to history department chairs Richard Beeman and Michael Katz.

The volume's endnotes may suggest how much travel this book required. Jessica Rosenberg and Charles Rosenberg tolerated it all, mostly with good humor and always with genuine enthusiasm for the project that made all those trips necessary. As always, Charles asked penetrating conceptual and editorial questions and read every word at least twice. As *Mothers of Invention* leaves my study to enter the wider world, he will, I am sure, be relieved to be surrounded by not quite so many women.

Part of Chapter 3 appeared in slightly different form as "Trying to Do a Man's Business" in *Gender and History*; part of Chapter 7 appeared in slightly different form as my introduction to *Macaria* (Baton Rouge: Louisiana State University Press, 1992). I am grateful for permission to reprint this work here.

I have not altered spelling or punctuation or noted misspellings with the intrusive *sic* in quotations from nineteenth-century sources, for I wanted to hold as much as possible to the fidelity of the original documents.

# MOTHERS
# OF INVENTION

Necessity & war is the mother of invention.
                                    —Clara Solomon, May 18, 1862

Will I ever have my dear husband at home any more or am I doomed to fight & buffet my way through this friendless world alone. God forbid indeed I do not think I could unless necessity were to make a different woman of me.
                                    —Julia Davidson, September 8, 1863

# All the Relations of Life

Just a little more than a year after the firing on Fort Sumter and the outbreak of armed conflict between North and South, Lucy Buck of Front Royal, Virginia, observed in her diary, "We shall never any of us be the same as we have been." The Civil War would replace the Old South with a new, slavery with freedom, and wealth with poverty. In transforming governments, economies, and society, the war necessarily challenged the very foundations of personal identity as well.[1]

White men and women of the antebellum South had defined and understood themselves in relation to a number of categories: race, which marked the difference between bound and free, superior and inferior; gender, which was designed to distinguish independent from dependent, patriarch from subordinate; and class, more subtle and more hidden in a society that rested within a democratizing America but present nonetheless in distinctions of wealth, power, education, and refinement, in claims to honor and gentility. Of course, white southerners acknowledged other identities as well; they might be Presbyterians or Baptists or Methodists, Louisianians or Virginians or South Carolinians, Whigs or Democrats, but none of these characteristics was so readily apparent or so socially or personally fundamental as the Old South's hierarchies of race, gender, and class. Southerners inevitably thought of themselves first in terms of blackness or whiteness and maleness or femaleness, for these attributes did not just shape identities but dictated life choices and aspirations. In the minds of white southerners, class was less rigid than these seemingly biological distinctions, yet this very fluidity made attention to social status and its shifts all the more imperative, for class identity had to be constantly asserted and claimed. Evident in skin color, dress, hairstyle, language, and prescribed behavior, race, class, and gender were both the markers and the principal determinants of power, as well as the stuff of self-definition.

When the Civil War convulsed southern society, when it overthrew slavery and undermined the wealth and political power of the planter elite, it necessarily threatened and transformed each of these interrelated hierarchies, instigating what one contemporary newspaper described as a "Stampede from the Patriarchal Relation" that had so firmly placed white men at the apex of the social pyramid. But perhaps just as significant as measurable shifts in social power was the challenge to the very categories that had defined and embodied that dominance. What did whiteness mean when it was no longer the all but exclusive color of freedom? What was maleness when it was defeated and impoverished, when men had failed as providers and protectors? What did womanhood involve once the notion of dependence and helplessness became an insupportable luxury? "We are passing through a great revolution," a correspondent wrote to the *Montgomery Daily Advertiser* in July of 1864. "The surface of society, like a great ocean, is upheaved, and all the relations of life are disturbed and out of joint." But the relations of life were more than just out of joint; they seemed incomprehensible. The upheavals of war created conceptual and emotional as well as social dislocations, compelling southerners to rethink their most fundamental assumptions about their identities and the logic of their places in the world.[2]

We have, as Americans, long been attentive to the discussion and debate that the Civil War generated about the meaning of freedom and its relationship to blackness or whiteness. This has, for example, been a central theme within the evolution of American constitutional law as well as the source of the uniquely significant place the war occupies in our national history and consciousness. In recent years historians have devoted increasing attention to the more individual dimension of this transformation, looking closely at the ways in which black southerners claimed and defined freedom, acting as agents of their own emancipation. But very little of the enormous scholarly and popular literature on the war has been devoted to the ways in which it disrupted assumptions about gender or to how those disruptions produced their own long-lived legacy. This book seeks to make a contribution to redressing that imbalance by exploring the meaning of the Civil War for one especially articulate and introspective group of women: those of the privileged and educated slaveowning class of the Confederate South, a group that has left to us in diaries, letters, and memoirs an extraordinary window into their experience and consciousness.[3]

Wars have frequently been seen as transformative of the status quo. But both the circumstances and the purposes of the Civil War made its impact unparalleled in the American experience. With armies—and death tolls—of previously unimagined magnitude, the Civil War inaugurated a new era in the history of warfare. In the Revolution, no more than 30,000 Americans were ever simultaneously under arms. Civil War armies numbered close to a million, and deaths exceeded 600,000. Almost all of this conflict and destruction took place on southern soil. The totality of warfare for the South, the extraordinarily high level of mobilization of both men and resources, and the enormous significance of the southern homefront as well as its frequent transformation into battlefront made the Civil War experience so direct and thus so significant for Confederate women. With a few exceptions along the Confederacy's borders, northern women were not subjected to the ravages of battle, nor were they called upon to make so essential a contribution to the war effort or to suffer the material deprivation imposed on southerners by the weakness of the Confederate economy.

The North, moreover, had inaugurated its reexamination of gender assumptions more than a generation earlier, as women's rights advocates began to destabilize traditional understandings of men's and women's roles. In the South, by contrast, emergent nineteenth-century feminism had by 1861 exerted almost no impact, and understandings of womanhood had remained rigidly biological and therefore seemingly natural and immutable. In the eyes of many of the South's defenders, this contrast was in itself evidence of the superiority of southern civilization and of the dangerous tendencies inherent in the northern way of life. "There is something wrong," regional apologist and proslavery advocate George Fitzhugh warned in 1854, with woman's "condition in free society, and that condition is daily becoming worse." Northern democratization, abolitionism, and feminism all seemed to represent a challenge to hierarchy that, Fitzhugh feared, would logically culminate in the overthrow of the institution of marriage. "The people of our Northern States, who hold that domestic slavery is unjust and iniquitous," he proclaimed, "are consistent in their attempts to modify or abolish the marriage relation." In the face of the struggle for women's rights under way in the North, Fitzhugh affirmed on behalf of his region that "woman . . . has but one right and that is the right to protection. The right to protection involves the obligation to obey. A husband, lord and master . . . nature designed for every woman." Just, he might have added, as nature had designed a master for every slave.[4]

A war that challenged the South's peculiar institutions of racial hierarchy would require a reconsideration of traditional notions of womanhood as well. From the very outset of conflict, the white South undertook an unprecedented exploration of the implications of gender, as it found itself vesting women with unaccustomed responsibilities for the survival of their families and their nation, then worrying, like the *Milledgeville Confederate Union*, about the "unsexed women" these changes appeared likely to create. A conflict that at first seemed to reaffirm and even strengthen traditional divisions between masculine and feminine by defining war as the glorious and exclusive domain of men soon produced widespread uncertainty about gender categories and identities. Increasingly, women found themselves—in the words of one Texas female—"trying to do a man's business" supporting households and families and managing slaves. In the face of the demands and unexpected horror of total war, long-cherished understandings of womanhood began necessarily to be redefined. For the South these warborn disruptions of female identity came, as the correspondent to the *Montgomery Daily Advertiser* suggested, with the suddenness and force of "the earthquake, the whirlwind and the storm."[5]

Within the context of this broader public discussion, however, Confederate women themselves were undertaking a more personal and individual reassessment of their place. Among the more than half-million white women who belonged to the slaveholding families of the Confederacy, this crisis of identity was particularly acute. The most privileged southern women were those who defined themselves and their status in relation to the slave institution on which their privilege rested, and they experienced the destruction of war as a dramatic social and consequently personal upheaval. As the women who benefited most from the South's class and racial arrangements, females in slaveholding families had the most to lose from warborn transformation. Rapidly shifting foundations of social power brought every dimension of these women's self-definition into question. With the departure of white men for battle and with the disintegration of slavery and the disappearance of prewar prosperity, prerogatives of gender, class, and race eroded; "all the relations of life" became simultaneously vexed and uncertain. Females of the southern elite began to recognize that their notion of womanhood had presumed the existence of slaves to perform menial labor and white males to provide protection and support. *Lady*, a term central to these women's self-conception, denoted both whiteness and privilege at the same time it specified gender; a lady's elite status had been founded in the oppressions of slavery, her notions of genteel womanhood intimately bound up with the prisms of class and race through which they were reflected.[6]

When elite women of the Confederate South confronted the new world spawned by war, they struggled to cope with the destruction of a society that had privileged them as white yet subordinated them as female; they sought to invent new foundations for self-definition and self-worth as the props of whiteness, wealth, gentility, and dependence threatened to disappear. The extent and the limits of their abilities to construct new selves were shaped by a profound sense of how much they had to lose.[7]

Like Lucy Buck, Confederate women understood that "we shall never . . . be the same as we have been." But how they would come to be different—and how different they would become—was not predetermined, nor was the process of change simply imposed upon them along with the other burdens of war. Articulate and educated, the elite white women of the South negotiated the meaning of these transformations as they responded to the hardships and deprivations they encountered. Their staunch commitment to many of the fundamental values and assumptions of their prewar world ultimately enabled them to contain much of the change war seemed destined to inaugurate. Inevitably shaped by the revolution they experienced, they nevertheless struggled to resist its full import by striving to impose their vision and their self-interest on the circumstances of a changed world. "Necessity," Confederate women repeatedly intoned, "is the mother of invention." The harsh realities of military conflict and social upheaval pushed women toward new understandings of themselves and toward reconstructions of the meanings of southern womanhood that would last well beyond the Confederacy's demise. But the pages that follow demonstrate that many women of the wartime South invented new selves designed in large measure to resist change, to fashion the new out of as much of the old as could survive in the altered postwar world of defeated Confederates, regional poverty, and black freedom.[8]

# CHAPTER ONE

# What Shall We Do?

## WOMEN CONFRONT THE CRISIS

As the nation passed anxiously through the long and uncertain months of the "secession winter" of 1860–61, Lucy Wood wrote from her home in Charlottesville, Virginia, to her fiancé, Waddy Butler. His native South Carolina had seceded just before Christmas, declaring itself sovereign and independent, but Virginia had not yet acted. Just a week before Lucy Wood's letter of January 21, her state's legislature had voted to call a secession convention, and Wood thought disunion was "fast becoming the order of the day." Yet these momentous events had already changed Lucy's life. Waddy Butler, preoccupied with new military obligations in service of what Wood pointedly called *"your* country," had been neglecting his intended bride, failing to write as frequently as she had come to expect. Affianced they still might be, but, Wood noted, they had become citizens of different nations, officially "foreigners to each other now."[1]

In January 1861 Lucy Wood was more bemused than genuinely troubled by this intrusion of grave public matters into her personal affairs, and she fully expected Virginia's prompt secession to reunite her with Butler in "common cause." But beneath the playful language of her letter lay an incisive perception. Waddy Butler's new life as a soldier would ultimately not just deprive his future wife of "hearing from you as often as I otherwise should," but would divide the young couple as he marched off to war and she remained home in a world of women. By removing men to the battlefield, the war that followed secession threatened to make the men and women of the South foreigners to one another, separating them into quite different wartime lives. As the sense of crisis mounted through the early months of 1861 and as political conflict turned into full-scale war, southern ladies struggled to make the Confederacy a common cause with their men, to find a place for themselves in a culture increasingly preoccupied with the quintessentially male concerns of politics and of battle. Confederate women were determined that the South's crisis must be "certainly ours as well as that of the men."[2]

## Public Affairs Absorb Our Interest

Like most southern women of her class, Lucy Wood was knowledgeable about political affairs, and her letter revealed that she had thought carefully about the implications of secession. Her objections to disunion, she explained to Waddy Butler, arose from her fears that an independent southern nation would reopen the African slave trade, a policy she found "extremely revolting." Yet as she elaborated her position, detailing her disagreements with the man she intended to wed, Wood abruptly and revealingly interrupted the flow of her argument. "But I have no political opinion and have a peculiar dislike to all females who discuss such matters."[3]

However compelling the unfolding drama in which they found themselves, southern ladies knew well that in nineteenth-century America, politics was regarded as the privilege and responsibility of men. As one South Carolina lady decisively remarked, "woman has not business with such matters." Men voted; men spoke in public; ladies appropriately remained within the sphere of home and family. Yet the secession crisis would see these prescriptions honored in the breach as much as the observance. In this moment of national upheaval, the lure of politics seemed all but irresistible. "Politics engrosses my every thought," Amanda Sims confided to her friend Harriet Palmer. "Public affairs absorb all our interest," confirmed Catherine Edmondston of North Carolina. In Richmond, Lucy Bagby crowded into the ladies' gallery to hear the Virginia Convention's electrifying secession debates, and women began customarily to arrive an hour before the proceedings opened each morning in order to procure good seats. Aging South Carolina widow Keziah Brevard confessed that she was so caught up in the stirring events that when she awoke in the night, "My first thought is 'my state is out of the union.' "[4]

Like Lucy Wood, however, many women thought this preoccupation not entirely fitting, even if irresistible. Few were as adamant in their opposition to women's growing political interest and assertiveness as Louisianian Sarah Morgan, who longed "for a place where I would never hear a woman talk politics" and baldly declared, "I hate to hear women on political subjects." But most ladies were troubled by feeling so strongly about matters they could only defensively claim as their rightful concern. "I wonder sometimes," wrote Ada Bacot, a young widow, "if people think it strange I should be so warm a secessionist, but," she continued more confidently, "why should they, has not every woman a right to express her opinions upon such subjects, in private if not in public?" The "Ladies of Browards Neck" Florida demonstrated a similar mixture of engagement and self-doubt when they united to address the "politicians" of their state in a letter to the *Jacksonville Standard*. Their positive views on secession, they assured their readers, were not frivolous or ill-founded but were supported in fact and argument. "And if any person is desirous to know how we come by the information to which we allude, we tell them in advance, by reading the newspapers and public journals for the ten years past and when we read we do so with inquiring minds peculiar to our sex." Rather than accepting their womanhood as prohibiting political activism or undermining the legitimacy of their political views, these Florida ladies insisted on the special advantages of their female identity, boldly and innovatively claiming politics as peculiarly appropriate to woman's sphere.[5]

Catherine Edmondston worried about the vehemence of her secessionist views because of the divisions they were causing in her own family. Before Lincoln's call for troops in April 1861, Edmondston's parents and sister remained staunch Unionists, although Catherine and her husband of fifteen years strongly supported the new southern nation. Edmondston found the resulting conflict very "painful" and was particularly distressed at having to disagree with her father. "It is the first time in my life that my judgment & feelings did not yeild to him." It was a "pity," she observed, that politics had become so heated as to "intrude into private life." Boundaries between what she had regarded as public and private domains were being undermined, as were previously unquestioned definitions of women's place within them. As war consumed the South, Edmondston would find that little space was left to what she called "private life." The private, the domestic, would become part of the homefront, another battlefield in what was by 1865 to become total war.[6]

In 1861, however, southern women still largely accepted the legitimacy of divisions between the private and the public, the domestic and the political, the sphere of women and the sphere of men. Yet they nevertheless resisted being excluded from the ever more heated and ever more engrossing political conflict that surrounded them. Women's politics in the secession crisis was necessarily a politics of ambivalence. Often women, like men, were torn about their decision to support or oppose secession. Few white southerners of either sex left the Union without a pang of regret for the great American experiment, and just as few rejected the newly independent South without a parallel sense of loss. "It is like uprooting some of our holiest sentiments to feel that to love [the Union] longer is to be treacherous to ourselves and our country," remarked Susan Cornwall of Georgia. As Catherine Edmondston explained, it seemed to her perfectly acceptable for a Confederate to "mourn over" the United States "as for a lost friend."[7]

But women's political ambivalence in the secession crisis arose from a deeper source as well: their uncertainty about their relationship to politics altogether. Admitting that they as women had no place in the public sphere, they nevertheless asserted their claims within it. Yet they acted with considerable doubt, with reluctance and apology, longing to behave as ladies but declining to stand aside while history unfolded around them. War had not yet begun, but southern women had already inaugurated their effort to claim a place and an interest in the national crisis.

## *Your Country Calls*

What one Alabama lady called the "unexpected proportions" of the Civil War would take most Americans North and South by surprise. Many southerners anticipated that the Union would not contest southern secession, and James Chesnut, former United States senator from South Carolina, confidently promised that he would drink all the blood spilled in the movement for independence. Yet as soon as their states seceded, southern men began to arm and drill, and expectations of military conflict at once thrilled and frightened the region's women. Looking back on those early days, one Virginia lady remarked that war had at first seemed like "a pageant and a tournament," but others wrote of "foreboding for the future" or of a "trembling fear" of what might be in store. Disunion troubled Julia Davidson for reasons entirely apart from divisions of politics. "I study about it sometimes," she wrote her husband, John, "and get The blues so bad I do not know what to do. God grant That all things may yet be settled without *bloodshed*." As an elderly widow living alone on a large plantation, Keziah Brevard feared not just military bloodshed but worried too about what she called the "enemies in our midst," the vulnerability of the South to slave uprisings.[8]

White southern women felt far freer than their men to admit—and even no doubt to feel—fears that, however unmanly, were entirely justified by the perilous circumstances facing the South. Women voiced apprehensions about war and anxieties about loss of particular loved ones, fears that masculine conventions of honor and courage would not permit men to express. From the outset this touch of realism tempered women's politics and women's patriotism; the culturally accepted legitimacy of women's private feelings and everyday obligations posed a counterweight to the romantic masculine ideology of war. Soon after the passage of the Ordinance of Secession, a South Carolina lady offered her womanly resolution of the inconsistency between these imperatives, explicitly privileging the personal over the political, loyalty to family over obligation to the state. "I do not approve of this thing," she declared. "What do I care for patriotism? My husband is my country. What is country to me if he be killed?" Kate Rowland of Georgia admitted that her "patriotism is at a very low ebb when Charlie comes in competition." When her husband joined the army, she had no ambition for him to garner fame and glory; instead she wished him to secure a post as far as possible from all fighting. "Charlie is dearer to me than my country, & I cannot willingly give him up," she confessed.[9]

The conflict between women's emergent patriotism and their devotion to the lives and welfare of their families became clear as southern men prepared for war. Very precise expectations of men's appropriate behavior in wartime enhanced many women's enthusiasm for the Confederacy. The romance of the military and the close association of manhood with honor, courage, and glory outweighed the reluctance many women felt to give up their loved

*Women watch the outbreak of war. "The House-Tops of Charleston during the Bombardment of Sumter."* Harper's Weekly, *May 4, 1861.*

ones, for they had come to believe that the very value of these men was inseparable from their willingness to sacrifice their lives in battle. A "man did not deserve the name of man if he did not fight for his country," Kate Cumming concluded. One lady of the Shenandoah Valley sent her son off to camp with a triumphant proclamation in the columns of the *Winchester Virginian*: "Your country calls. . . . I am ready to offer you up in defense of your country's rights and honor; and I now offer you, a beardless boy of 17 summers,—not with grief, but thanking God that I have a son to offer." Sarah Lawton of Georgia celebrated the opportunities she thought war would provide to make men more manly and to arrest what she regarded as men's failure to fulfill her expectations of them. "I think something was needed to wake them from their effeminate habits and [I] welcome war for that." Mary Vaught ceased speaking to those of her gentleman friends who had not enlisted, and a group of young women in Texas presented hoop-skirts and bonnets to all the men in the neighborhood who did not volunteer.[10]

But the call for soldiers deeply troubled many women, who anticipated that their husbands and sons might well meet death rather than glory on the battlefield. Alabama widow Sarah Espy was distressed by her son's determination to enlist. "I do not like it much," she wrote, "but will have to submit." Lizzie Ozburn of Georgia endured just a few weeks of army service by her husband, Jimmie, before herself arranging for a substitute to complete his term of enlistment. "Then if you don't come," she warned him, "you wont have any lady to come to when you do come."[11]

The conflicting imperatives of patriotism and protectiveness played themselves out dramatically in the ritualized moment of troop departures. Communities gathered en masse to wish the soldiers farewell and often to present them with uniforms or flags sewn by local ladies. Patriotic addresses were the order of the day, and the soldiers marched off, as one young member of the elite Washington Artillery described it, "pelted with fruit, flowers, cards & notes" from throngs of ladies. Ceremonies of colorful uniforms, waving banners, patriotic speeches, and martial music displayed all the romance of war as well as unbounded expectations of personal courage and glorious victory.[12]

The ebullience of the crowd, however, often came at the expense of considerable repression of feeling. Gertrude Thomas spoke of the "speech-less agony" with which she bade her husband good-bye, and Emily Harris seemed almost resentful that "It has always been my lot to be obliged to shut up my griefs in my own breast." When one woman burst into tears before two young soldiers, their mother chastised her, "How could you, let them see you crying? It will unman them." Men could evidently be men only with considerable female assistance.[13]

But often enough, women, especially younger ones, did break down. Sixteen-year-old Louisiana Burge described the reactions of her boarding school friends to the departure of a regiment from their Georgia town. Almost all the girls were weeping. "Em Bellamy spent nearly the whole evening in my room crying about the war and John T. Burr who leaves tonight. . . . Between her and cousin Emma Ward crying about Ed Gwinn I

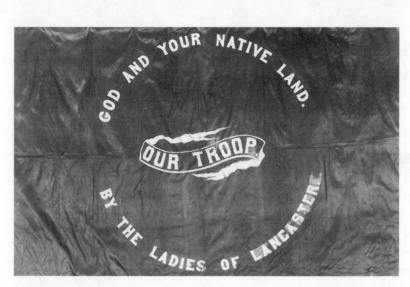

*A flag made for the Ninth Virginia Cavalry, Company D, by the ladies of Lancaster, Virginia. Courtesy of the Museum of the Confederacy, Richmond, Virginia. Photography by Katherine Wetzel.*

have had a time of it. . . . Ginnie Gothey's feelings have overcome her; she has gone to bed, sick with crying about Bush Lumsden who don't care a snap for her. Ridiculous! I can hear Susie Clayton screaming way down in her room."[14]

A seventeen-year-old bride loudly voiced her rejection of the masculine ethos of war for the feminine ideal of domestic love. "Oh Dan! Dan!" she sobbed, "I don't want to be proud of you. I just don't want you to get hurt! . . . I don't want fame or glory! I want you!" Catherine Edmondston, more mature as well as considerably invested in her new claims to a political identity and new sense of public responsibility, contrasted her behavior with the likes of this young bride. As her husband, Patrick, departed with his men, "The women, many of them wept, sobbed, nay even shreiked aloud, but I had no tears to shed then. With a calm, stern, determined feeling I saw them depart. The sentiment of exalted Patriotism which filled my heart found no echo in Lamentations, no vent in tears. He is gone, gone in the highest exercise of man's highest & holiest duty! . . . I would not have him here, would not have him fail in one duty, falter in one step."[15]

Catherine Edmondston's posture embodied the prescriptions of an emergent ideology of wartime womanhood. Confederate females could not privilege their personal needs above the demands of the nation. In the moment of crisis, country had to come before husband or son. If the South was to survive, women had to become patriotic, had to assume some of the political interests of men, and had to repress certain womanly feelings and expectations for the good of the Cause. Woman should cultivate a spirit of "self reliance," should practice "self denial," wrote Leila W. in a piece for the *Southern Monthly* that she entitled "Woman A Patriot." But, the essayist was careful to add, "we do not mean to say that she should become masculine."[16]

By the summer of 1861 the effort to create a new Confederate woman was well under way in the South's public press. Military manpower needs required a rationalization of female sacrifice and a silencing of women's direct interest in protecting husbands and sons. The nineteenth-century creed of domesticity had long urged self-denial and service to others as central to woman's mission, but war necessitated significant alterations—even perversions—of this ideology of behavior and identity. Women's self-sacrifice for personally significant others—husbands, brothers, sons, or family—was transformed into sacrifice *of* those individuals to an abstract and intangible cause.[17]

Redefining women's sacrifice in this manner created both logical and emotional difficulties for southerners, who endeavored to address and resolve these contradictions in extensive public discussion. Gender thus became an explicit subject of widespread debate. Songs, plays, poems, even official presidential pronouncements sought to enlist women of all classes in the work of filling the ranks. One popular theme urged young women to bestow their favors only on men in uniform. In a much reprinted song, a male songwriter assumed a female voice to proclaim, "I Would Like to Change My Name." This fictionalized heroine was searching for a husband,

> But he must be a soldier
> A veteran from the wars,
> One who has fought for "Southern Rights"
> Beneath the Bars and Stars.

A letter from "Many Ladies" to the *Charleston Daily Courier* in August 1861 warned cowards and slackers, "None but the brave deserve the fair." Even Jefferson Davis addressed the question of women's appropriate marital choice, declaring the empty sleeve of the mutilated veteran preferable to the "muscular arm" of "him who staid at home and grew fat."[18]

One song published early in the war acknowledged the clash between woman's traditional role and the conflict's new demands. From "stately hall" to "cottage fair," every woman rich or poor was confronted by her own "stormy battle" raging within her breast.

> There Love, the true, the brave,
> The beautiful, the strong,
> Wrestles with Duty, gaunt and stern—
> Wrestles and struggles long.[19]

Like male songwriters who addressed that theme, the "Soldiers Wife" who had penned the lyrics was certain that, like soldiers, women themselves would win "heart victories" over their emotions and in their "proudest triumphs" send their menfolk off to war. Stirring marches commemorated the scene of parting, with men striding nobly into the horizon while women such as Catherine Edmondston just as nobly waved handkerchiefs and cheered their departure. "Go fight for us, we'll pray for you. Our mothers did so before us." Popular songs and poems deplored the very behavior Edmondston had found so upsetting, urging women to repress their grief, lest they weaken soldiers' resolve. "The maid who binds her warrior's sash / And smiling all her pain dissembles" or "The mother who conceals her grief" accomplished woman's highest duty, a poem in the *Richmond Record* affirmed. Women, one newspaper proclaimed, had been offered a "glorious privilege" in the opportunity to contribute to the Cause by offering up their men. Yet popular expression acknowledged that women often harbored lingering doubt. A newspaper poem, "I've Kissed Him and Let Him Go," was among the frankest of such treatments.[20]

> There is some, I know, who feel a strange pride
> In giving their country their all,
> Who count it a glory that boys from their side
> In the strife are ready to fall,
> But I sitting here have no pride in my heart
> (God forgive that this should be so!)
> For the boy that I love the tears will still start.
> Yet I've kissed him and let him go.

Best was to feel right, so dedicated to the Cause that personal interest all but disappeared. Next best was to stifle lingering personal feeling. But the minimal requirement was to silence doubt and behave properly, even if right feeling proved unattainable. Catherine Edmondston and Gertrude Thomas both knew how they were expected to act, as did the Louisiana woman who confided to her diary, "How I do hate to give him up, but I suppose I have to be a martyr during this war."[21]

*Women prepare their men for war.* Equipment, 1861, *watercolor by William Ludwell Sheppard. Sheppard made sketches during the war but did not complete his watercolors until the turn of the century. Courtesy of the Eleanor S. Brockenbrough Library, Museum of the Confederacy, Richmond, Virginia.*

## Some Womanly Occupation

Only months into the conflict, women's behavior and identities had already become a matter for public discussion and private scrutiny. In considerable measure this debate arose from the needs of a state and a culture endeavoring to enlist women in its defense, and these imperatives would become ever more powerful as military struggle intensified during the next four years. But women themselves had very strong personal motives in undertaking this examination of female roles and opportunities in the new wartime world.[22]

From the start, war seemed to belong to the men. They, "more privileged," as Julia Le Grand explained, "are abroad and astir, making name and fortune and helping to make a nation." Women remained at home, seemingly useless, marginal to the stirring events of the day. "I am like a pent-up volcano," complained Le Grand. "I wish I had a field for my energies. I hate common life, a life of visiting, dressing and tattling, which seems to devolve on women, and now that there is better work to do, real tragedy and real romance and history weaving every day, I suffer, I suffer, leading the life I do." A young girl despaired to a friend that she was a "cipher," a zero, in the "great conflict. I am miserable when I think of it." "If I could only be of some use to our poor stricken country," she lamented.[23] In these painful feelings of uselessness lay the seeds of women's wartime transformation, a transformation grounded in demeaning sentiments of self-loathing directed against both their individual selves and the female sex. "What is the use of all these worthless women, in war times?" Sarah Morgan scornfully demanded.[24]

Numbers of women translated this contempt into a fantasy of becoming men, a desire to escape from a gender identity that had in peacetime seemed entirely acceptable. Being unable to fight made Sarah Morgan regret being a woman "for the first time in my life." Alice Ready, a young Tennessean, confessed to her diary, "I never before wished I was a man—now I feel so keenly my weakness and dependence. I cannot do or say anything—for it would be unbecoming in a young lady—How I should love to fight and even die for my country. . . . [W]hat a privilege I should esteem it, but am denied because I am a woman." Ready was surprised that "I am angry so much now and use so many harsh expressions." Her language, she feared, would in itself mark her as an unnatural woman in the eyes of returning veterans. Ready had previously regarded womanhood as simply implying difference. But now suddenly it dictated exclusion and deprivation, conditions that provoked her to rage, as they did many other southern women.[25]

Anger, in fact, became an emotional staple among females of the wartime South. Most often women identified it as a by-product of legitimate patriotism and self-consciously directed their fury against Yankee invaders and oppressors. But the true and unacknowledged sources of women's wartime rage were far more complex and diffuse. Ready's anger in the early months of conflict arose from frustration and resentment at the way in which war's exaltation of men and masculine virtues established a compelling logic of female inferiority. Numbers of other southern ladies turned newly discovered feelings of anger and futility against themselves as useless women. Sarah Morgan exemplified just such bitter self-loathing in her explanation of why she feared war's outcome. "The men . . . who are worth something," she wrote, "will die off in their prime; while we worthless women, of no value or importance to ourselves or the rest of the world, will live on, useless trash in creation."[26]

Inactivity and consequent feelings of unimportance were debilitating, yet few women knew where to turn. "I don't know how to be useful often times," Caroline Davis of Virginia remarked. "Oh! to see and be in it all," Kate Stone yearned. "I hate weary days of inaction. Yet what can women do but wait and suffer?" As Stone understood clearly after the departure of her brothers for the front, "We who stay behind may find it harder than they who go." Action was more than a matter of self-esteem, as, increasingly, it served as a means of managing anxiety. "How much heavier is the pressure of greif," Catherine Edmondston observed, "when there is nothing to be done but to look the dreadful fact steadily in the face, than when there is a need for *action*, for exertion, for thought of some kind." A Louisiana mother spoke a different tongue, but shared the same sentiments: "Les occupations sont . . . un grand remède."[27]

In the early months of 1861 Ada Bacot turned to a traditional outlet for women's energies as a remedy for her feelings of unworthiness. "Another day has passed & what have I accomplished[?] . . . I am too unworthy. . . . There is nothing left me but prayer," she resolved. Bacot began to see her religious devotions not as an end but as a means to a larger usefulness. Widowed in her twenties, she had in addition lost her only child, and she found herself in 1861 without any clear purpose in life. Yet as she contemplated the national crisis, she believed herself peculiarly equipped to deal with its demands. Her loss, she thought, had inured her to emotional suffering and privation, even though, she conceded, she had experienced no material hardship. She looked to war and upheaval as a divinely sent opportunity. "Now I can give myself up to my state, the very thought elevates me.

These long years I have prayed for something to do, perhaps my prayer is now being answered."[28]

"Something to do," "a field for my energies," "to live to some purpose," "to be in the heat and turmoil of it all"—women longed for a part in the crisis. A May 1861 letter from Vernon, Louisiana, to the *New Orleans Daily Picayune* expressed in a public forum the sentiments women across the South had been confiding to their diaries. The author, careful to write anonymously so as not to claim public attention unbecoming to her sex, explained that "the universal cry is 'what shall we do?' " "We wish merely," she explained, "some womanly occupation in which to vent our patriotism, in which to render real and substantial aid . . . in which we can work and act without," she reassured her readers, "moving from our feminine sphere." Could not, she entreated, some "inventive genius" define an appropriate role for southern women in wartime?[29]

It would not be an inventive genius, but thousands of southerners, male and female, who would in both deeds and words respond to the query posed by this "Daughter of the South." Newspapers and periodicals, sharing the letter writer's concern about the boundaries of the "feminine sphere," stressed the wartime relevance of woman's customary moral and spiritual role. "Can you imagine," asked the editors of the *Southern Field and Fireside*, "what would be the moral condition of the Confederate Army in six months without woman's influence?" The *Augusta Weekly Constitutionalist* confirmed in July 1861, "Great indeed is the task assigned to woman. . . . Not," the paper observed pointedly—and a bit defensively—"to make laws, not to lead armies, not to govern empires; but to form those by whom laws are made, armies led . . . to soften firmness into mercy, and chasten honor into refinement." John B. Minor echoed these public statements in an April 1861 letter to his cousin Mary Blackford. "It is the province of your sex," he declared, "in its weakness and its fears, vastly to influence ours in times like these. You women . . . possess so much generosity and magnanimous unselfishness that you can and do assist in inspiring a high-souled, self-sacrificing patriotism, which diffuses an aroma of virtue through Society."[30]

While these assurances may have partially relieved women's sense of exclusion and irrelevance, they did not speak to the need for action and occupation; flattery did not provide women much to do. Unlike white women of the lesser orders, for whom husbands' departures meant dramatically increased burdens of physical toil in household and farm, women in more prosperous slaveholding families did not need immediately to devote themselves to achieving a subsistence. The greater financial resources and resiliency of their households as well as the presence of slaves to undertake most physical labor left many privileged white women without pressing responsibilities. Diffusing what John Minor called an aroma of virtue did not fill lonely days and anxious nights. Yet, as Virginian Sara Pryor remembered in her later *Reminiscences*, "To be idle in war is torture." Describing what she recognized in retrospect as almost ridiculous busywork—embroidering razor cases or decorating soldiers' sewing kits—she at the same time affirmed its larger purpose: "Nothing is ridiculous that helps anxious women to bear their lot—cheats them with the hope that they are doing good." In the spring and summer of 1861 many articulate middle- and upper-class southern women began to seek opportunities to participate in the mounting conflict, active means of expressing their commitment to the Cause. Women began to unite to define the female purpose they all so eagerly sought. For the most part they were careful to heed admonitions to remain within their appropriate sphere. But in the course of their actions they would also redefine themselves.[31]

## A Part to Perform

For most of these southern ladies, the very act of binding together as women marked a new departure. Women's associations and organizations had not blossomed in the antebellum South as they had in the northern states. In considerable measure this difference derived from factors of geography and demography: the southern population was far more scattered and far less urbanized than that of the North, so that women tended to see less of one another and to have fewer opportunities to come together simply because of the logistics of travel. In fact, such prewar women's societies as did exist were generally located within the South's cities, and in these situations antebellum organization provided a solid basis for wartime activity.[32]

The comparative paucity of women's organizations in the prewar South cannot simply be attributed to its overwhelmingly rural character, however. Social factors played a role in these regional differences as well. Slaveholding southern women thought of themselves primarily as part of a hierarchical family or household, with their most significant connections tying them in relationships of dominance and dependence to their husbands, children, and slaves rather than to other white women. With its disruption of southern households, war would alter these relationships profoundly, and with them the sense of female identity the arrangements had helped to produce. The thousands of women's voluntary organizations that appeared in the South for the first time in response to the demands of war represent a significant locus in the formation of female self-consciousness, for here women saw themselves in groups; here they explored the meanings of gender in a way they had not previously been impelled to do. Women's associations in the Confederacy were intended to be conservative forces, representing and affirming traditional delineations of female roles, dedicating themselves, in the words of the Charleston Soldiers Relief Association to "assist[ing] the great cause, in the way best suited to the sphere of woman." But by their very existence these organizations defined and empowered women as women, independent of men.[33]

Female voluntary associations undertook a variety of activities, adjusting their efforts to changing needs within the Confederacy. More than 1,000 groups appeared across the South; by the end of 1861 in Alabama, for example, the Governor's Office listed 91 ladies' aid associations in that state alone, to which the governor distributed raw goods to be sewn into tents, cartridges, and uniforms. Sewing was, in fact, one of the first activities to which women turned in the weeks after secession. Lucy Wood wrote to Waddy Butler in May 1861, describing herself as nearly "broken down" from having sewed so intensively for the past three weeks. The ladies of Char-lottesville had assembled each morning at town hall with cloth and sewing machines and had worked steadily through the day, except for interruptions for group prayer. Exhausted, Lucy was nevertheless proud to report that she, too, was making her contribution to the Cause. "Our needles are now our weapons," she wrote, "and we have a part to perform as well as the rest. . . . Yes, yes, we women have mighty work to perform for which we will be responsible." After months as "foreigners," Lucy was gratified to be joined with Waddy again in "common cause." Yet even as she boasted, Lucy was careful to contain her indelicate pride by belittling her achievement in comparison with that of the men. "We have no glory, no fame to gain on earth." Women were meant to serve, she confirmed, as the supports and helpmeets of men.[34]

Often the wives and mothers of a particular unit readying itself for depar-ture instigated these sewing efforts. As wife of the captain mustering the men of the neighborhood for service, Catherine Edmondston assumed the obli-gations of her elite status and organized the women to provide tents and uniforms. "Thousands of Ladies who never worked before," she observed in May 1861, "are hard at work on coarse sewing all over our whole country."

Assigning the heavy task of the tents to seven of her female slaves laboring on the piazza at home, Edmondston herself joined the white ladies of the area at a nearby plantation, where together they stitched uniforms. "Never was known such unanimity of action amongst all classes," Edmondston remarked.[35]

Many such gatherings soon evolved into formal organizations with constitutions, dues, and women officers. But the unanimity of classes Edmondston described was not always present, for the associations remained the preserve and social outlet of the elite. When Mary Ann Cobb of Georgia canvassed her neighborhood to secure support for the soldiers, she was greeted with many refusals, especially from the less-privileged Athens inhabitants. One woman told her bluntly, "The whole Southern Confederacy was not worth a thimble full of blood." Cobb herself later resigned because of what she identified as dissension and inefficiency in the Athens society.[36]

By midsummer many organizations had shifted from sewing to knitting, with socks a high priority for the coming winter months. Kate Stone had never knitted before and so began with crewel comforters but was confident she would soon "advance to socks and gloves." Women began as well to collect donations to provide not just flags and uniforms but a wide variety of soldiers' necessities—from Bibles to lint for bandages to scissors to underwear. By the beginning of 1862 the Greenville, South Carolina, Ladies' Aid Association had supplied twenty boxes and three bales of contributions for soldiers' welfare. In Floyd County, Georgia, 300 members enlisted through a door-to-door canvass in August paid a dollar each in dues and by the end of the year had shipped five train carloads of provisions to the front.[37]

Many needed supplies had to be purchased rather than made, and even sewing and knitting required cloth and yarn. As a result, ladies' societies turned to money-raising efforts, from concerts and fairs to dramatic performances. Lizzie Ozburn suspected these efforts were primarily designed to provide occasions for women's socializing and thought citizens should just donate directly to the Cause. "I dont enjoy any thing of the kind," she wrote her husband after taking her contributions—a cooked tongue and some homemade wine—to be sold at a ladies' association fair in Georgia. "I think if the people were just right they would not have to be worked so many ways to get what they ought to do out of them they ought to go or give to their last dollar and to the last day of the battle." But few shared Lizzie's clear-sighted perspective, and benefits proliferated across the South. On September 23, 1861, the Ladies Relief Association of Spartanburg presented an "Amateur Concert" of twenty-one pieces. In Charleston an afternoon of music and recitations culminated with an original poem, "The Soldier's Dream in His Blanket on the Ground," by a lady of the city. The subject, the *Mercury* assured its readers, "at this time, will interest our community at large." After mistakenly reporting it to be the composition of a man, the paper apologized for its error and printed the eleven stanzas of the poem in their entirety. The concluding lines offer a sense of how relief societies served not just to raise funds but to provide occasions for patriotic expression and national solidarity.

> Then God bless him, bless the soldier,
>    And God nerve him for the fight,
> May he lend his arm new prowess
>    To do battle for the right;
> Let him feel that while he's dreaming
>    In his fitful slumber bound,
> That we're praying—*God watch o'er him*
>    *In his blanket on the ground.*

In this afternoon's entertainment Charleston's women combined their accustomed spiritual influence with more material goals to benefit the soldiers. The occasion provided as well an unusual opportunity for a female author to gain a voice.[38]

The most popular benefit performances throughout the South, however, were not concerts or recitations but *tableaux vivants*, staged representations of familiar themes enacted by costumed women posing as in a still life during a musical interlude. "Very much in fashion," tableaux appealed for their inspiration to literature and history as well as current events. Ada Bacot especially enjoyed the death scene from *Romeo and Juliet* and the presentation of a "Turkish Slave Market" by the ladies' association to which she belonged. Mary Legg wrote to a friend of a performance with more immediate relevance. "There was one tableaux I think you would have liked it was the 'Southern Confederacy' each state was represented by one of the girls dressed in white with a scarf of the State Colors, and the States were all united by a wreath of flowers, while Kentucky stood with folded arms, face rather averted from the southern Confederacy and looking towards the US flag; poor Maryland was dressed in black kneeling as though supplicating and bound by chains." Mary had at first felt reluctant to appear before an audience, but her friends had prevailed upon her, insisting that in service of so noble a cause, participation could not be unseemly. "They could not get enough girls to form the one I have just mentioned so I consented to be

Florida. Clemie was Texas." Maria Hubard of Virginia was less troubled than triumphant at her new dramatic accomplishments. "This day," she wrote on December 16, 1861, "will long be remembered by me, as one of the most remarkable of my life, as I made my first appearance in *public*. . . . [T]o day for the *first* time in my life *I* appeared upon a stage." Clara MacLean of Columbia, South Carolina, was astonished at her sense of pride in her first theatrical effort. "I feel quite important," she confided to her diary. In the theater of war, Confederate women had quite literally found a part to perform.[39]

Participation in benefit dramas and tableaux marked a significant departure from woman's customary place. Delicacy and propriety enjoined ladies from speaking in public, from signing their names in print, and even from permitting their names to be mentioned in the public press. To appear on a stage—even though a performer in a tableau neither moved nor spoke—represented an important challenge to these expectations. In uneasily consenting to be Florida, Mary Legg acknowledged her sense of transgressing gender boundaries, and while Clara MacLean expressed no such reluctance about her participation in theatrical benefits, she noted a new sense of self emerging from her unaccustomed activities.

The novelty of such behavior did not escape wider notice; it was not simply in private diaries and letters of women like Legg and MacLean that the Confederacy negotiated this troublesome dilemma. An indignant correspondent to the *Charleston Mercury* objected to the use of ladies' names in the newspaper's account of recent tableaux at Pineville; he thought the actresses should be silent, immobile, and anonymous. In Milledgeville, Georgia, a soldier signing himself "Hope" wrote to the *Confederate Union* to ask the paper's readers, "Is it right for young ladies to appear in public on the stage?" The excuse that such actions were undertaken in a good cause was not sufficient justification, he believed, for public appearances threatened to destroy "true modesty, delicate sensibility in our women." In an editorial the same day and a rash of letters in the next issue, the citizens of Milledgeville took up the debate. A second soldier pointed out that the seeming departure from custom was in reality no departure at all, for ladies had long appeared on stage at the end of school term for debate and examination. An editorial asserted that the problem lay not with the women but, rather, with the men who jeered and whistled. What, the editor demanded, did Hope think about public appearances that were not on the stage—as, for example, singing in parlor benefits or presiding over booths at fundraising bazaars? The majority of correspondents agreed with one anonymous author who insisted, "There *certainly can be no immodesty in a young lady doing that which a whole community approves.*" Hope was dismissed as behind the times and told that he "must revolutionize society before his notions can prevail."[40]

Emma Crutcher had other objections to the tableaux she attended in Vicksburg, Mississippi, in December 1861. The performance, she found, made "a very poor entertainment for an intelligent audience through an evening. . . . Amateurs on the stage only show their inferiority." Perhaps as a nonparticipant she could not share Legg's and Hubard's enthusiasm—or the consequent dulling of their critical faculties.[41] Whatever their artistic merits, tableaux succeeded in attracting crowds. Hubard's two performances netted $1,700, and Lise Mitchell noted that in Tuscaloosa "hundreds were turned back at the door." Ladies of Notsulga, Alabama, sent the governor $68 as proceeds from an evening's theatricals, and a group in Eutaw requested that their $82 be dedicated to helping needy soldiers' families. The young ladies of Shelby, North Carolina, presented an evening of tableaux that raised $200, which they sent to Governor Vance for the "comfort of the soldiers either at the Hospitals or Regiments."[42]

Women were often very explicit about how they wished their contributions to be used, and in at least one instance their choice of a philanthropic goal represented a genuine political and military intervention. Ladies in coastal cities had by early 1862 become anxious about the weakness of the Confederate navy and the consequent vulnerability of the South's ports to Yankee attack. As more and more men were mustered for service in Virginia, this issue of "home defense" attracted increasing concern from the women left behind. In early March the dramatic encounter between the *Monitor* and the *Merrimac*, or *Virginia*, at Hampton Roads drew attention to the technological miracle of the ironclad warship. Recognizing a possible solution to the crisis of coastal defense, groups of women in Charleston, Mobile, Norfolk, Savannah, and several inland Mississippi River ports organized to raise funds for the purchase of ships to protect their cities. Gunboat societies, gunboat concerts, gunboat raffles, and gunboat fairs became, as the *Charleston Mercury* described it, "all the rage." Here women's benevolence became public policy as defense spending followed the dictates of female organizations; here, for almost the first time, women expressed implicit displeasure with the Confederacy's failure adequately to ensure their welfare; here women acted together in advancing the interests not just of sons, husbands, brothers, but their own. "I am glad," Mrs. C. Love wrote with satisfaction in the *Mercury*, "that our people and especially the ladies, have at last aroused themselves to some practical demonstration in the defence of our coast, other than brave soldiers and weak batteries. I trust that it is not too late to redeem what we have lost by our too sanguine expectations of success."[43]

By fall the *Georgia* was in the water, and the *Palmetto State*, built with more than $30,000 in contributions, was ready for its ceremonial baptism. In full uniform, the orator of the day, Col. Richard Yeadon, paid homage to the "matrons and Maidens" of South Carolina. "He alluded," the *Mercury* reported, "to the inaction of the Government in the construction of naval defenses, and showed how the suggestion and example of one patriotic lady had stirred in the bosoms of the daughters of South Carolina the project of building these very boats. . . . This spirited action of our women had raised the Governments, State and Confederate, from their torpor." Philanthropy had been transformed into politics and policy. And in at least some of the language justifying their actions, women included implicit rebuke of Confederate failures to provide adequate coastal defenses. Charlestonians suggested that prompter action might have saved Port Royal from falling to the Yankees, and the Carolina coast might have remained "free from invaders."[44]

Women of Columbus, Mississippi, speculated in a similar manner on Grant's victories at Forts Henry and Donelson early in 1862 and wondered if "untold miseries might have been avoided if the waters of the Cumberland and Tennessee had been sufficiently guarded during the last summer, by the building of a number of ironclad gunboats." In their effort to equip a vessel to patrol the Mississippi River, however, the ladies were careful to assure their fellow Confederates that they did not presume "to interfere with the legitimate actions of Congress or the heads of department, appointed to superintend works of defense."[45]

The ladies of the Confederacy had in the early months of national emergency confronted a crisis of their own. Committed to providing "real and substantial aid" to their new country and determined to play a part in the events of the day, they also desired to make their contributions "without moving from the feminine sphere." These pledges of conventionality were no doubt welcome and reassuring—to the women themselves no less than their men. But women would almost immediately find themselves behaving in unconventional ways—banding together in new women's organizations, performing in public, and even shaping government defense policy. War thus inaugurated a process of exploration and negotiation. "What Shall We Do?" women asked men, one another, and themselves. As the soldiers of the South set forth to prove themselves men, females undertook the far less clearcut task of defining what it meant to be women within the new world of war.

# CHAPTER TWO

# A World of Femininity

## CHANGED HOUSEHOLDS AND
## CHANGING LIVES

### Thinned Out of Men

In April 1862 the Confederacy passed the first conscription law in American history, designating all white men between the ages of eighteen and thirty-five eligible for military draft. By 1865, amended legislation included males from seventeen to fifty, and although a variety of exemption laws were passed in the course of the war years, Confederate conscription succeeded in producing an extraordinary level of mobilization. Because of slavery, almost all nonmilitary labor in the South could be assigned to blacks, leaving a very high percentage of whites available for army service. As a result, three of every four white men of military age ultimately served in the Confederate army.

With the departure of so many men to the battlefield, the Confederate homefront became a world of white women and of slaves. Louisa Walton reported to her friend Isabella Woodruff that Chester, South Carolina, had by 1862 been "thinned out of men"; Margaret Junkin Preston wrote that in Lexington, Virginia, there were by mid-1862 "no men left." Hers was, she described, "a world of femininity with a thin line of boys and octogenerians." When Nettie Fondren recounted a friend's wedding plans in December of the same year, she explained that there would be no ushers, "for there is not enough young men around . . . to answer the purpose." But it was not just the composition of wedding parties that was revolutionized. As Mary Greenhow Lee of Winchester watched Confederate and Yankee men alternate control of the town full of women, then abandon it altogether in June 1862, she commented wryly in her diary, "I propose that we shall declare ourselves a separate & independent sovereignty, & elect a Queen to reign over us."[1]

In several states the male exodus was sufficiently dramatic to prompt citizens to write in alarmed tones to the governor, reporting in circumstantial detail the transformations of their communities. A group of women living near New Bern, North Carolina, for example, informed Governor Zebulon Vance that only 20 of the 250 white people remaining in their town were men. Of these, 11 were old and 3 were likely to be conscripted in the near future, so the women regarded less than 5 percent of the population as male and able-bodied. In Alabama, citizens reported similar reductions in male numbers: 2,016 of 3,000 voters in Randolph County and 1,600 of 1,800 in Shelby County had gone to the army. A resident of Carrollton, Alabama, wrote Governor John Shorter that the spring 1862 militia call "almost literally depopulates the county of men."[2]

As these worried citizens recognized, the impact of this level of mobilization was profound and probably represented the most significant single factor shaping the wartime experience of white southern women. On a personal and emotional level, repeated hundreds of thousands of times across the region, departures of loved ones brought loneliness and anxiety. "There is a vacant chair in every house," wrote Lizzie Hardin. But the scale of these departures gave them wider political and economic significance as well.[3]

In the overwhelmingly agricultural South the individual household was the fundamental unit of what scholars have called "production and reproduction"—the place where the most important economic as well as social and cultural work of civilization took place. The farm or plantation was the central economic institution of the Old South, the locus of productive activity, whether dedicated primarily toward independence and self-sufficiency, as in the case of smaller nonslaveholding units, or toward commercial staple crop production of cotton, rice, sugar, and tobacco by large gangs of slaves. But the farm or plantation also served as the primary site of social and political organization. The plantation embodied the hierarchical structures of southern paternalism. It functioned as the most important instrument of race control, and it similarly worked to institutionalize the subordination of white women, for the master was the designated head of what he frequently characterized as his "family white and black." Within this social order men and women, boys and girls, slave and free learned the roles appropriate to their age, gender, and race. Nonslaveholding households embodied analogous arrangements of male dominance within exclusively white families. Male prerogative and male responsibility thus served as the organizing principle of southern households and southern society; white men stood at the apex of a domestic pyramid of power and obligation that represented a microcosm of the southern social order. As John C. Calhoun, the South's most powerful antebellum defender, explained, "The Southern States are an aggregate . . . of communities, not of individuals. Every plantation is a little community, with the master at its head. . . . These small communities aggregated make the State in all. . . . Hence the harmony, the Union and the stability of that section."[4]

The removal of white men from households across the region thus inflicted a devastating blow to the most fundamental structures of the South's society and economy. In nonslaveholding families, the departure of breadwinners caused immediate hardship, requiring many white women to turn for the first time to demanding physical labor in the fields. The Confederate Congress passed the first conscription legislation in April 1862, during spring planting, when manpower needs were at their height, and so many farm families felt its impact at once. A correspondent from a "*poor* County" in Alabama wrote Governor John Gill Shorter that within days, hundreds of "Feemales" would be seen for the first time "between the handles of the plow."[5]

For women of more prosperous and, particularly, of slaveholding families, however, the effects of mass mobilization were more delayed and less direct. Middle- and upper-class southern families possessed capital and investments—as well as slaves to work behind the plow—and were not tied so directly to the seasonal cycles of planting and harvesting. Unlike land, slave property was movable, prompting many masters to transport their slave forces to safer areas where they could be resettled or hired out for cash. Texas, remote from military action, was a favorite destination, and one Confederate general estimated that some 150,000 bondsmen were transported to the state during the war years. But whatever strategies they had chosen to preserve their assets, most families had by the last months of the war exhausted wealth and resources. Even many of the South's most privileged women would, with homes and property destroyed, find themselves in the direst of financial straits. This transformation tended to be gradual, though, a process of evolution toward changed status that often began with a transformation in the structures of the household itself.[6]

Endowed with financial resources, regionwide networks of family and kin, and access to information and transportation, elite women possessed an opportunity to experiment with new domestic forms denied their poorer sisters. Women of the South's master class found themselves in a variety of new family and household arrangements as they struggled to adjust to the departure of their men. Many moved—sometimes long distances—to live with their parents or in-laws or even friends and acquaintances. Others packed up themselves and perhaps their children and followed their officer husbands from camp to camp, seeking appropriate accommodations in nearby towns or living at times in tents on the field. Still others traveled to the city in search of rooms and remunerative employment. Confronted with the uncertainty of the times, some left home with wagons full of valued possessions but no clear idea of a destination, convinced that their children and their property, human and inanimate, would be safer anywhere else. In the course of the war these families might move three, four, even a half-dozen times, retreating like the Confederate army before the Union advance and the steadily diminishing supply of life's necessities behind Confederate lines. Other women decided to take their chances where they were and to make necessary changes in existing arrangements rather than seek solutions through relocation. Many hired overseers or importuned male neighbors to assist them in directing and maintaining newly female-headed plantations; some invited their nieces, sisters, or sisters-in-law to join them in housekeeping, to stave off loneliness and to pool resources. Ladies who had dispatched their sons and husbands to the front lines often sent their daughters in the opposite direction, to boarding schools or relatives in remote areas regarded as safe from military conflict. But whether they moved or stayed at home, kept their children together or dispersed them to schools or kin, most Confederate women confronted dramatic changes in their domestic environment.

*Women of Confederate North Carolina. Courtesy of the Eleanor S. Brockenbrough
Library, Museum of the Confederacy, Richmond, Virginia.*

Had the Confederacy ever taken the census required of it by its constitution, the results would have been startling, for the sorts of households it
would have described would have confounded those expecting to see the
patriarchally structured families associated with the Old South. Instead, such
a survey, taken any time after the very first months of war, would have
reflected the attributes of this new world of women, reporting high numbers
of households headed by white females in all classes across the South.
Among the slaveholders such a survey would have shown an extraordinary
diversity of domestic forms, of makeshift "families" that in their departure
from custom provided new environments in which women had necessarily to
redefine themselves—accepting new responsibility for basic economic survival, experiencing changed configurations of emotional attachments, and
finding themselves in dramatically altered relationship to the South's "domestic institution" of African slavery. But such a survey never did take place;
we will never know with statistical certainty the precise dimensions of change
in household structures in the Civil War South. We cannot say how many
white women lived alone on large plantations or how many moved to urban
areas or how many moved in with kin. And, of course, these arrangements

changed constantly during the war years as individuals responded to ever shifting military circumstances. But the widespread alterations in household form can certainly be described in a manner that illuminates the sorts of choices and dilemmas confronting the inhabitants of this new female world: altered families required new structures of domestic power and responsibility. Nearly every woman who kept a diary or corresponded with family and friends had necessarily to discuss such questions, for even if she herself did not face decisions about where and with whom to live, her neighbors and kin were confronting these difficulties. Adjusting to the demands of reconfigured households was a major issue for white women of the Confederate South, and these new domestic circumstances brought other transformations in Confederate women's lives. From early in the war the very foundations of the South's paternalistic social order were necessarily imperiled by the departure of the men who served as its organizing principle.

## The Best Way for Me to Do

Many women were uncertain where or how they wished to live after their husbands' entry into the army. Laetitia Lafon Ashmore Nutt refused to accept a separation when her husband departed at the head of a company of partisan rangers he had raised in Louisiana. With three daughters in tow, she followed him across the Deep South, searching out lodgings close to his changing areas of operation. By 1864 she was exhausted and wished she had "left the children with my Mother and devoted all my time and energies to our sick and wounded."[7]

Sarah Jane Estes did leave her children to follow her husband, but her presence with him reflected his desire rather than her own. He was, she reported, "ordering me to Mississippi" in the summer of 1862. "Knowing my husband's disposition, I determined to leave all and follow him. . . . I must leave husband or children and I felt that they could do better without me than he could." She tried to dismiss thoughts of how she would do without them but was brokenhearted, fearing her one-year-old would forget her altogether before they were reunited. "My own happiness I have never consulted since leaving home," she wrote with both pride and some anger, "for there was little choice." Her understanding of woman's obligations had always dictated her path. "As a mother and a wife I hope I do not consider my own comfort, but live and work for those whom God has given, receiving my reward by making them happy." But here her duties to children and to husband were at cross-purposes, and Estes could not reconcile herself to failing as either wife or mother. Despite her obvious pain at her dilemma, she received little sympathy from her husband. "Mr. E reproved me for my desperate sorrow and bid me look to God for comfort, that I was acting very wickedly. I knew that but I was too wretched to think. But I have prayed for strength and now feel more able to bear up under my trials, but I may be deceived. I will still pray to be able to say, 'Thy will be done.'" The need to choose between husband and children seemed almost too much to bear, and Sarah Estes turned for resolution and consolation to God. After months trailing after her husband through Mississippi and Tennessee, she antici- pated no end to her exile. But she could no longer torment herself with thoughts of her absent children; she would act as if they were dead. "I will try and give my children to the Lord as if he had taken them home to him, and try and pray to be resigned never to see them again." Sarah Estes felt she had lost not her husband but her infant children to the war.[8]

Unlike Laetitia Nutt and Sarah Estes, most women did not follow their men to the front but instead tried to carry on at home or adjust to wherever the fortunes of war might take them. A North Carolina woman wrote her sister soon after her husband left in May 1862, explaining, "we have been trying how to studyout how it is the best way for me to do." Her mother had urged her to come home, but she was reluctant to close her own house and leave her slaves to work the place without direct supervision. But she cer- tainly did not want to remain alone. Perhaps, she entreated, her sister could stay with her, at least for a few months. Lila Chunn of Georgia was pleased that, after her husband, Willie, left in the fall of 1861, her sisters took turns sleeping at her house, so "I do not often stay by myself at night." This proved only a temporary solution, though, and Lila spent many nights alone before the deteriorating military situation in Georgia in the fall of 1864 finally displaced her. Recognizing that she and her children must move from the path of Sherman's advancing troops, she still had to decide whether to join her own parents or her in-laws. Her uncertainty arose from her desire to remain as close as possible to her husband's regiment, and she worried as well about being forced to sell her "negro property" at low rates because of her decision to move.[9]

Emma Crutcher of Mississippi shared some of Chunn's concerns. She had moved in with her in-laws in Vicksburg soon after the departure of her husband, Will, but by March 1862 Emma's own parents were discussing "our *debut* on the political stage as refugees." They had rented a large house in a remote and safe area, and Emma was torn about whether to remain where she was or join her own family. Her major concern was to be near a post office or railroad in order to communicate with Will. Lizzie Ozburn's father urged her to abandon housekeeping and move in with him if Jimmie was not released from service in late 1861, but, grown and married, Lizzie was determined not "to ever be dependant on him" again. Ellen Moore of Virginia felt quite differently about independence and sought to persuade her husband, Sam, that her decision to move herself and their children to her parents' house was wise. At home without him, she explained, "my spirits would suffer in so many lonely hours night & day there." She hoped Sam would be "convinced that as you cannot take care of me that with Pa is the best place."[10]

Many young women found living in the households of relatives very stressful. Jorantha Semmes and her five children moved in with her husband's cousins in Canton, Mississippi, crowding the house with seventeen occupants who grated on each other's nerves. Semmes believed they regarded her as an unwelcome "nuisance" but was herself angry at her hostess's "hyper-criticisms" and her host's presumption in daring to whip her children along with his own.[11]

Even in an era in which family conflict became commonplace, the experience of Ann Marie Stewart Turner may have been especially difficult. During her husband's army service she and her children lived with his family in North Carolina, where her mother-in-law's "unruly tongue" and "unhappy temper" made Turner's life miserable. The older woman accused Ann not only of stealing her son but of luring her husband away. She "said I had fondled around her husband till he cared more for me than any man might for any woman but his wife—*that he had a passion for me & I encouraged by combing his hair &c,*" Ann reported in despair to her own mother, who was thousands of miles away in Texas. But Turner's trials were only to increase. When her husband was killed at the Battle of the Crater in 1864, she regarded the blow as just retribution for her vengeful anger against her mother-in-law as well as an appropriate punishment to Mrs. Turner for her own "unkindness." Under the pressure of her domestic arrangements, Ann's grief expressed itself as a combination of self-loathing and rage. Separated from home by enormous distance and wartime upheaval, Ann remained trapped in the unhappy household of her in-laws, even though her strongest tie to them was gone.[12]

Often women left by themselves simply joined together both to provide companionship and to save on household expenses. A Tennessee woman recalled, "as I was alone in my home and my sister in law and two small

*White members of the household of John Minor Botts, near Culpeper, Virginia, September 1863. Photograph by T. H. O'Sullivan. Prints and Photographs Division, Library of Congress.*

children were left alone in my brother's home, I went to live with them." Clusters of adolescent girls in families other than their own were especially common. Many parents were eager to provide the young women with some diversion, for life behind the lines was often very tedious. Away from the concentrations of men at the front, courtship, the compelling occupation of privileged young women in their late teens and early twenties, all but came to a halt. Though the fate of nations may have been hanging in the balance, one young Confederate woman regarded life as unbearably dull. "There is nothing to mark one day from another now . . . always the same. Sew, knit, read. . . Spinning, weaving. Oh, I get so sick and tired of it." Twenty-two-year-old Malvina Gist was either bold or foolish enough to complain, almost on the eve of the burning of her hometown of Columbia in 1865, "it is frightfully monotonous, just because you are a woman, to be always tucked away in the safe places."[13]

But the Preston sisters of South Carolina, who joined Mary Chesnut's household in Richmond, found the times more than exciting. Both girls soon fell in love with dashing Confederate officers, and when their beaux were occupied with military matters, they amused themselves in the company of the other young ladies and the crowds of male admirers thronging Chesnut's wartime salon. As wife of a prominent aide to Jefferson Davis, Chesnut moved in the innermost circles of Confederate power. Residence in her household thus placed the Preston girls in the comparative safety of well-garrisoned Richmond and provided them access to the highest echelons of Confederate society.[14]

The safety and purity of young white girls was a particular concern in the wartime South, for they were seen as especially vulnerable in case of enemy invasion or slave uprising. Many families exerted considerable effort to keep them away from areas of military action and upheaval. "It was thought safer for a young girl just grown up to be well out of the reach of Yankee soldiery," one South Carolina mother remarked. Boarding schools offered one solution to this difficulty. Male colleges and academies closed their doors as men left the classroom for the battlefield, but many women's schools thrived. Hollins College enrolled 83 students in 1861–62 but had grown to 160 by 1864–65. J. F. Dagg, president of the Baptist Female College of Southwest Georgia, faced continual wartime disruptions—a smallpox epidemic in 1863, the donation of the school's tin roof to the Confederate government, and finally the transformation of the school building into a soldiers' hospital. But the school expanded nonetheless, from 36 pupils in 1861 to 82 by 1863 to 103 who in 1864 met in Dagg's residence because of the therapeutic purposes to which the schoolhouse had been put.

Boarding school left Sarepta Gregory homesick for Camden, South Carolina, but she knew she should be grateful to be at the Chowan Female Institute. "I thank my God that he has given me a place to stay and not to get hurt," she wrote her aunt. Robert De Schweinitz, the principal of Old Salem Academy in North Carolina, found running a school in wartime fraught with difficulty, for supplies were elusive, tuitions never kept up with inflation, and pupils often faced extraordinary emotional strains because of extended separations from loved ones. Yet De Schweinitz felt he had to keep the institution open almost as a public service: "We have so many scholars who either have no other homes or whose homes are within the enemies' lines, that we are in a manner compelled to keep on with the school." Old Salem was known as one of several institutions especially welcoming to refugees from eastern Carolina, and many schools explicitly presented themselves as havens for displaced young women. Farmville Female College, which pointedly advertised itself as "easily accessible from all parts of the State, and at the same time so remote from the seat of war as to be both safe and quiet," attracted one young Virginia girl whose family was convinced by the Seven

Days battles that it was no longer "wise to let a young girl stay" at their plantation outside of Richmond.[15]

But many young women had of necessity to remain close to enemy lines. In Winchester, Mary Lee presided over an establishment of five females—two of her dead husband's teenaged sisters and two of his nieces—who found comfort and some protection together while opposing armies moved back and forth through the town. Lee preferred the risks of enemy troops to those of displacement from home and friends. She and her young kin left Winchester only when expelled into Confederate lines by a Union general in February 1865. Even then she "indignantly denied" the name of refugee, threatening to shoot the next person who applied it to her.[16]

## The Bitterness of Exile

Lee's hostility to this term suggests unexplored complexities in the movements of people that so changed households in the Civil War South. The word *refugee* began to appear frequently in private and public writings in the South early in the war, and it acquired a somewhat different connotation from the more general notion of displaced persons with which it has since frequently been confused. *Refugee* was probably first applied to the low-country magnates who evacuated families and slave property from the Carolina coast when Yankee invasion threatened in the fall of 1861. The arrival of these aristocrats with their enormous populations of slaves in the more egalitarian Piedmont aroused much resentment, for upcountry Carolinians deplored their flight as cowardice, feared the increased numbers of potentially rebellious slaves in their midst, and worried about providing food and shelter for so many new residents. The term *refugee* soon came to be used most often for wealthy individuals who had chosen to abandon their customary place of residence, frequently with an eye to keeping property, especially slave property, out of Union hands. Smaller slaveholders and poorer farmers often felt this choice unavailable to them, and many regarded "refugeeing" as evidence of lack of patriotism. Inevitably, too, the presence of refugees imposed a considerable burden on the areas expected to provide for the wanderers. As more and more men left for the battlefield, the refugee population became overwhelmingly female, thus assuming a characteristic gender as well as class identity. There were, especially in the later stages of the war, families and even whole communities forced from home by military action, as, for example, when Sherman compelled all civilians to leave Atlanta in the fall of 1864, but these individuals are more properly considered displaced persons, not refugees, at least in terms of the particular Civil War usage, with its frequently pejorative connotations of privilege and self-interest. The power of these connotations is evident, for example, in Mary Lee's aversion to the label. She had not chosen her course of action; she had not abandoned her home; she was not running away, expecting others to take responsibility for her. She had been sent against her will, and this, she believed, gave her a morally superior status to those who could rightfully be called refugees.[17]

As Nancy Mae Jett anticipated the arrival of the Yankees in Georgia, she described her options to her husband, Richard, who was in the army. "I haint got the money to take us of [f] so we will hafter stand the test." She and her seven children lacked the wherewithal to move out of harm's way. Sarah Espy, a widow and small slaveholder from Alabama, observed that many of her wealthy neighbors were preparing to take their slaves and leave as the Yankees approached in the summer of 1863. But Espy knew she would have "to stay at home and take whatever Providence may send," for she did not know "where I could go or how." On an evening's visit to her rich friend Mrs. Finley, she discovered that her neighbor was planning to depart to North Carolina. Espy could not contain her resentment. "They are well off and are going to wealthy friends whereas I, and many others, have no friends and our children, even beardless boys, are taken from us and put into the service." Even though as a slaveholder Espy ranked among the most affluent southern families, she was, under the pressures of war, growing newly aware of class differences in the South, differences here marked by access to the option to seek refuge elsewhere. Mrs. Finley's freedom to leave wartime Alabama provoked Sarah Espy's bitter complaint. "There is a great wrong somewhere, and if our Confederacy should fall, it will be no wonder to me for the brunt is thrown upon the working classes while the rich live in ease and pleasure."[18]

For those aristocratic women who prided themselves on their inherent social superiority, the refugee experience could similarly reinforce class perceptions and identity. When at the end of the war Mary Chesnut found herself fleeing Yankee invaders, she took advantage of the hospitality of a North Carolina woman. Yet scorn rather than gratitude marked her response to this generosity. "Mine hostess is young & handsome, very well educated, talks well, seems so ladylike & kind. . . . N.C. aristocracy as far as it will go— but does not brush her teeth—the first evidence of civilization—& lives amidst *dirt* in a way that would shame the poorest overseer's wife. . . . A

*Refugees.* Departure from Fredericksburg before the Bombardment, *oil painting,*
*1865, by David English Henderson, a mapmaker in the Confederate army. Courtesy*
*of Gettysburg National Military Park.*

Lady evidently she is in manners & taste! & surroundings worthy a barbar-
ian." Perhaps Chesnut's unaccustomed need prompted her scathing remarks. Without the usual accoutrements of superior status, she lost the
substance as well as the trappings of gentility. A young Louisiana woman
fleeing with her family abandoned some of her romantic notions about
poverty when war introduced her to the realities of life among the less-
privileged orders. Enduring omnipresent bedbugs and meager fare as she
lodged with a variety of nonslaveholding white families during the course of
her travels, Sidney Harding remarked, "I used to think I would like to be
poor but having never seen any poor people before did not know what it
was. Have no such wish now." A new and enforced familiarity with her
supposed social inferiors encouraged not sympathy but revulsion. War
brought whites of different social classes together in ways that often undermined rather than enhanced southern solidarity.[19]

The controversy surrounding refugees in the wartime South centered on
this very issue of class, on the perception that certain southerners had the
resources to escape the "brunt" of war. A woman with the option to become
a refugee was in some ways like a conscripted man able to hire a substitute.

Refugees themselves often felt the direct heat of this resentment. Kate Stone's family had removed to Texas, that favored destination for planters hoping to locate slaves out of reach of Union armies. But Stone found "strange the prejudice that exists all through the state against refugees. We think it is envy, just pure envy. The refugees," she explained, "are a nicer and more refined people than most of those they meet, and they see and resent the difference."[20]

Refugees' presumptions of superiority did little to diminish the hostility they encountered. The *Daily Southern Guardian* of Columbia, South Carolina, tried to excuse this arrogance in the spring of 1864. "They know not how to beg; for being accustomed, during all their previous lives, to abundance at their former homes, they have been in the habit of *giving* of their plenty, rather than receiving anything at the hand of charity. This terrible discipline many of them are now passing through. It is a hard lesson to learn, which many of them cannot comprehend." Without wealth most southerners, like Jett or Espy, felt they could not choose to become refugees, yet, paradoxically, the refugee experience itself usually consumed assets rather rapidly, leaving many of the most aristocratic southern women without the affluence that had defined their identities. Yet these were identities, as the *Guardian* pointed out, they could not easily abandon.[21] Confederate humorist Bill Arp summed up the wanderers' plight, observing that although Job suffered much and "stood the test of all the severe afflictions his Maker visited upon him," he was spared the ultimate challenge, for "from a careful examination of his sacred record, I do not find that he was ever a refugee."[22]

Women wrote despairingly of their experiences, and indeed, objective conditions of refugee life were often most unpleasant. Transportation facilities grew increasingly inadequate in the wartime South, and traveling women found themselves on crowded trains that broke down with growing frequency, in dilapidated wagons, or even astride intractable mules. Temporary accommodations were dirty and overtaxed—and often infested with fleas and bedbugs as well as those whom genteel ladies regarded as human undesirables, both black and white. Sarah Morgan was astonished to be "actually sleeping under the same bed clothes with our black, shiny negro nurse!" Camping out was a novelty, and Sarah Wadley found her corsets an uncomfortable nuisance when she tried sleeping on the ground. Permanent dwellings were difficult to locate, especially in cities, so families accustomed to spacious mansions crowded into one or two rooms. Some of the most desperate displaced southerners lived in boxcars outside Atlanta or in a tent city near Petersburg, not to mention the inhabitants of Vicksburg who during the siege took up residence in hillside caves, complete with rugs and elaborate furnishings. War forced many southerners in less urgent circumstances to turn to whatever shelter was available. All struggled to find food for the table, especially as inflation sent prices skyrocketing. Living with her parents in rural Georgia in the last months of the war, Lila Chunn succeeded in procuring adequate nourishment for her children but complained that it was all of the coarsest type—a tedium of "meat & bread and bread & meat." The children, she mused, "are gladder to get a biscuit now than they were cake in former days." In Richmond in March 1865, Malvina Gist was not so fortunate and proclaimed herself hungry enough to "eat a tallow candle if I had a good one."[23]

Yet conditions were increasingly hard for all southerners, not just for those who had left their homes. Whatever bodily discomforts they experienced, refugees would readily have agreed that their psychological deprivations and displacements were far greater. Sarah Morgan, searching with her mother and sisters for a place to settle after the Yankee invasion of Louisiana in 1862, complained that she felt like a "homeless beggar." Margaret Beckwith was ashamed when after three years of war she left Virginia for North Carolina. She assumed the language of a soldier, echoing one of General Grant's famous statements of determination when she reported her "disgust at leaving the front. I felt like a deserter. I had wished to fight it out along this line." Grant had firmly resolved "to fight it out on this line, if it takes all summer," but Beckwith had abandoned Virginia by late spring. Lise Mitchell moved from Louisiana across the Deep South with her grandfather and the family's slaves, stopping and erecting new slave quarters near Vicksburg, Mississippi, before relocating again in Alabama. "Home," she remarked bitterly, "what a mockery to call this home, we have no home, we are poor refugees, how suggestive that word, refugee to my poor heart, of sorrows past, present anxieties, and future misery." Her new dwellings brought with them dramatically changed responsibilities, which young Lise did not entirely welcome. "I think it a pity for me to have undertaken for the first time, the duties of a housekeeper in such hard times for I fear I will soon be discouraged."[24]

Complaining of "l'amertume de l'exil qui pèse si lourdement sur nous," the women of the Grima family of New Orleans regarded themselves less as refugees than as exiles. Augusta, Georgia, was cold both physically and metaphorically, and, of course, they found few who spoke their native French. Young Louise seemed, her mother reported, to have fallen into a severe depression, refusing to eat and manifesting little energy. "Elle est tellement attristée de l'exil qu'elle ne sort presque jamais et se laisse trop abbatre."[25]

When Sherman menaced Georgia in 1864, George West's sons had already departed with the army, so he sent his daughter Josephine to accompany the family slaves to Mississippi. To her father she wrote of her uncertainties about slave management—how to tell if complaining laborers were really sick, how to respond to the overseer's declaration that "the negroes dont work," and how to deal with the homesickness of the slaves themselves. But to her mother she opened her "sad and desponding heart." "I have felt utterly forlorn. I feel like I can never be satisfied until I get home again. . . . [T]here is no wray of light in the future visibl[e] to me. Dear good Mother pray for your absent daughter that I may have more fortitude and be more resigned to my fate."[26] Living as refugees may have begun as a choice, but it came to seem like a sentence, one that the wanderers shared in large measure with the other, less-mobile southern households buffeted by war. For ultimately, the itinerant nature of refugee families proved to be just one among the many disruptive forces transforming the customary patterns of southern domestic life.

## Home Manufacture

As the northern blockade and the requirements of full-scale military mobilization continued to exert unrelenting economic pressure on the Confederacy, southern households began to reflect the impact of changes that extended beyond war's manpower demands. The outbreak of conflict with the North had resulted in a dramatically diminished availability of manufactured goods in the South, both because of the blockade's restriction of external trade and because of the increasing concentration of the South's limited industrial capacities on the production of war materiel. In the face of these domestic shortages, Confederate leaders began to call for economically independent southern households as essential to the political independence of the nation.[27]

In the South, as in the United States more generally, household manufactures had declined steadily in importance during the early 1800s until, by mid-century, most southern white families purchased significant proportions of the items required for daily life. Wealthier households and particularly those, such as staple-producing plantations, that were embedded in the market economy were especially likely to have shifted to factory-made goods. With the outbreak of military conflict, however, such commodities suddenly became difficult, if not impossible, to procure, and Confederate discourse and public policy soon addressed this consumer crisis.[28]

Newspapers urged white women of the South to revive home production, particularly in textiles, depicting such action as both patriotic and moral. Elite women, however, demonstrated a tenacious aversion to wearing a fabric associated with the lower classes. "Not five out of five hundred ladies," the *Southern Illustrated News* proclaimed in 1862, "would be caught in the street in a homespun dress." Jefferson Davis spoke out about the desirability and attractiveness of homespun, and in summing up his remarks the *Milledgeville Confederate Union* endeavored at once to quiet lingering qualms of vanity and appeal to women's loftier motives. "It is not only honorable to our women to weave and wear their dresses, but really homespun is becoming to them." Yet the paper's next exhortation seemed to belie this enthusiasm about the appearance of home-produced goods. To "rig themselves in material made of the great Southern staple," the article continued, would "prove to the world that the Southern woman's principle and patriotism are not subordinate to the pride of the eye." The *Richmond Enquirer* appealed more exclusively to women's idealism. "Away," the paper cried, "with running the blockade for Yankee goods. Let it be a point of honor to provide and wear our own homespun." Another newspaper tried both to inspire and to shame those "who loll on a sofa or carriage cushions and complain," by relating the tale of an Arkansas woman who not only wove eight yards of cloth a day but had taken up ax, saw, chisel, and auger to build the loom that made her achievement possible. Popular poetry extolled the "noble work" of weaving and spinning and urged God "to speed the shuttle and bless the hands that ply it." War ballads translated such sentiments into song, emphasizing not the scarcity but the unfashionableness of northern fabrics:

> Three cheers for the homespun dress
> The Southern ladies wear.
> Now Northern goods are out of date,
> And since old Abe's blockade
> We Southern girls can be content
> With goods that's Southern made
>
> . . . . . . .
>
> We scorn to wear a bit of silk
> A bit of Northern lace,
> But make our homespun dresses up
> And wear them with a grace.[29]

Rhetoric combined with necessity to encourage domestic cloth production. As early as February 1862 Mary Speight observed that "there is not a yard of domestics to be bo't in G[eorgia]." "Thrown," as Sarah Espy put it, "on their own resourses," ladies began to bring wheels and looms down from their attics and to learn to spin and weave. "This ancient work," Kate Cumming noted, "is all the fashion now as we are blockaded and can get no other kind of goods." Martha Jane Crossley found herself in 1862 spinning for the first time "since my childhood." Mary Legg of South Carolina expressed her admiration for her friend Hattie Palmer's new abilities at weaving and spinning and regretted that "my knowledge does not extend beyond knitting." In Florida, Octavia Stephens searched for a loom and for a neighbor who might teach her to weave, less out of absolute need than from the widely shared desire to feel useful. "I want something to do of some consequence and see if I cant rouse myself to some energy," she explained to her absent husband. Sarah Wadley resisted cloth making until 1865 and then was ashamed at how inept she proved to be. "I have commenced to learn to card and spin, and I never tried anything so difficult to me, or so tiring."[30]

Even though Jefferson Davis celebrated homespun, many southern men were deeply disturbed when they learned that their wives had taken up textile production. Such spinning and weaving as had persisted in plantation households had been mostly the work of slave women and was thus not considered appropriate for privileged white females. Will Neblett was distressed by Lizzie's account of her new efforts at the loom. "I do not like the idea of your weaving. It is mortifying to me. I wish you not to do it," he wrote in June 1864. Lizzie herself was not very happy about this new responsibility but explained to Will that she was "forced" to it in order to clothe her children and eleven slaves. George Peddy worried about the hard physical labor involved in working a loom, labor to which his wife was entirely unaccustomed. "I do not want you to do anything," he wrote his wife, Kate. "I did not espouse you for no such purposes. I done so for my high esteem of your intrinsic worth; also that you might remain handsome; also for the love I had for you[r] soft and pliant hands and loving face. I do not wish the latter to be furrowed by physical labor. Honey you must not weave the cloth you have the thread spun for." Amanda Bullock shared these views of the dangers of textile labor, explaining to her husband, "I am sorry to know that I cannot work hard, but experience teaches me that I cannot, for if I spin all day, the next day I look as if I had just got up out of a spell of sickness." Weaving seemed to threaten not just white women's health but their status, for it blurred the all-important lines of differentiation between them and their female slaves. Privileged white women's traditional identities conflicted with the campaign for home textile production.[31]

The propaganda effort surrounding homespun was designed to combat this resistance, but succeeded only partially in overcoming the identification of weaving and spinning as degrading physical labor. Yet ideological issues were only one factor limiting the extent of the wartime revival in home textile manufacture. The difficulty in finding wheels and looms, the paucity of white women with necessary skill, and the absence of adequate instruction for aspiring spinners and weavers also played an important part. Perhaps even more significant, however, was the serious shortage of cotton cards in the South throughout the war, a situation that created a bottleneck in the textile production process. The first step in the process of transforming seed cotton or raw wool into cloth was carding, combing the fiber through wire teeth mounted on two wooden boards. Before the war all cotton cards were manufactured outside the South, and as they began to wear out, the Confederacy could not replenish the region's supply. Desperate women called on Confederate officials for assistance, and eight state governors did attempt to respond to the crisis by passing legislation to encourage card production. John Shorter of Alabama, for example, appropriated $60,000 to bring cotton cards through the blockade and designated state funds for a card manufacturing establishment in Selma that proved less than successful. Confederate women recognized both the scarcity and the importance of cotton cards and tried to make them last as long as possible. When Lizzie Neblett found that a slave woman had ruined the household's last pair of cards by using them to comb her children's hair, she was reduced to tears. Lizzie feared the incident might mean the end of her spinning efforts, and indeed, the difficulty in procuring cards led many households to abandon their efforts at cloth production.[32]

The homespun revolution so heralded in the postwar accounts of white southern women's wartime achievements seems to have been actually of very limited scope. A recent study and museum exhibition entitled *Mississippi Homespun: Nineteenth Century Textiles and the Women Who Made Them* came to a conclusion that might be generalized to the entire South: "the oft-reported surge in spinning and weaving by women on the homefront during the Civil War was not reflected" in the surviving evidence from Mississippi. Women who had actively engaged in textile production before the war continued to do so; households where slaves had produced cloth before the war maintained or even increased their output; some women who had never spun or woven made efforts to produce fabrics, but their contributions did not have a significant impact in meeting the demand for textiles in the Confederacy. The most privileged households coped by importing cloth

*Cotton cards, a scarce item in the Confederacy. Courtesy of the Museum of the Confederacy, Richmond, Virginia. Photography by Katherine Wetzel.*

through the blockade or purchasing it behind enemy lines in trips to occupied areas such as New Orleans. Less fortunate southerners made do by recycling bed or table linens, curtains, and discarded garments. Economic pressures on Confederate households did not result in profound or widespread alterations in white women's relationship to home textile production. Women's resistance combined with more pragmatic considerations to limit the scope of change.[33]

If there was no homespun revolution, however, there were other areas of household labor and production in which white women, with varying levels of reluctance or enthusiasm, skill or incompetence, undertook new sorts of domestic work. As Mary Lee wrote in 1863 of her changed household responsibilities, "I find myself, every day, doing something I never did before." Even if they did not weave or spin, women took up knitting and sewing—both for soldiers and for their own families. For the most privileged southern women, who had concentrated their prewar efforts on fancywork or embroidery, knitting and dressmaking often represented a new departure. "Many of us who had never learned to sew," Mary Gay remembered, "became expert handlers of the needle, and vied with each other in producing well-made garments; and I became a veritable knitting machine." A South Carolina woman remembered that her enthusiasm almost overrode her usefulness, for she had never knit socks before and produced a pair so enormous that an equally large soldier had to be located to wear them. Young women may have found learning these new skills easier than did their older

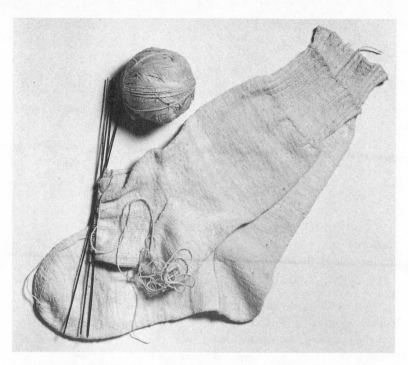

*Socks knitted by Mary Greenhow Lee out of the unraveled tents of the Union army. Courtesy of the Museum of the Confederacy, Richmond, Virginia.*

aunts and mothers. Emma LeConte reported she was almost driven to distraction by her mother's seeming incompetence and by her constant requests for aid. "I . . . can't at all understand," Emma complained, "how so simple an affair as knitting a sock should appear an insoluble problem." But some women, like Julia Davidson, were in fact skilled seamstresses and found themselves in constant demand as advisers and assistants to friends learning to cut patterns or alter dresses. Davidson even decided to put her abilities to remunerative purpose and take in sewing to augment family income. But her efforts as a skilled needlewoman did not involve her in the oppressive and seemingly endless toil that became the lot of the lower-class white women sewing to survive in Confederate military clothing bureaus in Richmond and other southern cities.[34]

Warborn shortages and economic pressures made it impossible for southern households to procure a variety of store-bought items that had become standard before the outbreak of military conflict. Southern families had to undertake unaccustomed sorts of economic production or do without.

White southern women took enormous pride, especially in retrospective memoirs and reminiscences, in their ingenuity and inventiveness in finding or making replacements for unavailable items—berry juices for inks and dyes, hats woven of straw, coffee made from okra seed or rye, shoes constructed of cloth or paper, twisted rags instead of wax candles that had been imported from New England, and of course, homespun. The pressure exerted by war to transform the southern household from a site of domestic consumption into what one Alabama woman recalled as a "miniature factory in itself" encouraged even the most elite southern women to undertake unfamiliar tasks and assume a new productive role.

We must recognize the limits of this change, however. Southern households did not become factories; women were more likely to sacrifice, to live with deprivation and shortage, and to hope for a swift end to the war or for the arrival of goods smuggled through the blockade than to become self-sufficient home manufacturers. The strains of war made most southern families poorer; it rarely made them significantly more productive. Shifts in the economic functions of southern households were far less dramatic than the alterations in their structures and composition introduced by conscription and the manpower demands of modern war. And white women's new responsibilities as slave managers would be of far greater social, political, and economic import than any war-induced changes in their relationship to domestic manufactures.[35]

The Civil War exerted a powerful impact on every southern household. Each family may have been unique in the particular way it experienced war's burdens, yet certain patterns of stress and change recurred, reshaping the structures and functions of southern domestic life. Perhaps most important, the departure of men presented a crisis and a challenge to which every white woman, rich or poor, had to respond. The internal realignment and often the geographical relocation of families changed the most fundamental aspects of domestic existence. The absence of men often combined with the arrival of female friends or kin to alter the character of women's emotional lives and interactions. Husbands and wives found themselves in changed relationships, as women came necessarily to rely more on themselves or other women than upon their mates.

But women on the homefront had to deal with more than physical and emotional dislocation. Shortages and economic pressures compelled them to undertake new sorts of labor in order to ensure both their own survival and that of the Confederacy. And, as we shall see, in households with sizable holdings of black slaves, managing human property became a central component of the wartime work that now devolved upon white southern females.

In mid-1864 Lila Chunn wrote her husband, Willie, describing the transformation of her domestic world and her new life as a refugee. "I will never," she concluded, "feel like myself again." Changed circumstances were creating a new self or, at least, undermining the old. Women's new surroundings confronted them with altered sets of expectations, with new obligations, and with new standards by which to measure themselves and their worth. In the middle of the war Susan Middleton, a young woman from the lowcountry aristocracy of South Carolina, wrote in some bewilderment and uncertainty to her friend Harriott Cheves: "The realities of my life and the situations in which I have been placed have been so strangely different from what my character and the early promise of my life would have led one to expect. Anxiety, responsibility, and independence of thought or action are what are peculiarly abhorrent to my nature, and what has been so often required of me." Susan Middleton would not be alone in discovering that war's requirements would not necessarily comport well with her character, her nature, or her expectations. The social order that had shaped her was not the one in which she now had to live.[36]

# CHAPTER THREE

# Enemies in Our Households

## CONFEDERATE WOMEN
## AND SLAVERY

When slaveholding men departed for battle, white women on farms and plantations across the South assumed direction of the region's "peculiar institution." In the antebellum years white men had borne overwhelming responsibility for slavery's daily management and perpetuation. But as war changed the shape of southern households, it necessarily transformed the structures of domestic authority, requiring white women to exercise unaccustomed—and unsought—power in defense of public as well as private order. Slavery was, as Confederate vice-president Alexander Stephens proclaimed, the "cornerstone" of the region's society, economy, and politics. Yet slavery's survival depended less on sweeping dictates of state policy than on tens of thousands of individual acts of personal domination exercised by particular masters over particular slaves. As wartime opportunity encouraged slaves openly to assert their desire for freedom, the daily struggle over coercion and control on hundreds of plantations and farms became just as crucial to defense of the southern way of life as any military encounter. Women called to manage increasingly restive and even rebellious slaves were in a significant sense garrisoning a second front in the South's war against Yankee domination.[1]

Nineteenth-century southerners often called slavery "the domestic institution." Such a designation is curious, however, for the term seems to imply a contrast with the public or the political. The very domesticity of slavery in the Old South, its embeddedness in the social relations of the master's household, made those households central to the most public aspects of regional life. The direct exercise of control over slaves was the most fundamental and essential political act in the Old South. With the departure of white men, this transcendent public duty fell to Confederate women.[2]

Although white southerners—both male and female—might insist that politics was not, even in the changed circumstances of wartime, an appropriate part of woman's sphere, the female slave manager necessarily served as a pillar of the South's political order. White women's actions as slave mistresses were crucial to Confederate destinies, for the viability of the southern agricultural economy and the stability of the social order as well as the continuing loyalty of the civilian population all depended on successful slave control.

Public discourse and government policy in the Confederacy explicitly recognized the gendered foundation of the Old South's system of mastery. Indeed the very meaning of mastery itself was rooted in the concepts of masculinity and male power. From the outset, Confederate leaders were uneasy about the transfer of such responsibility to women. After the passage of the first conscription act in April 1862, critics challenged the wisdom of drafting overseers and other white male supervisors, especially from areas with heavily concentrated black populations. In part this concern was economic, for agricultural productivity and efficiency seemed to depend on effective management. The "truth stares us in the face," declared one correspondent to a Georgia newspaper, "slave labor must support this war." There was, the writer continued, "but one way to do this, and that is, to place the negro under the immediate control and direction of the white man." An Alabama man warned Confederate authorities in March 1862 that there already existed "in the negro population . . . a disposition to misrule and insubordination occasioned no doubt from the withdrawal of our male population from their midst." The prospect of even fewer men at home generated profound fears of slave revolt, which combined with a sense of the particular vulnerability of white women. These issues went beyond questions of gender; they represented deep-seated worries about sex.[3]

As support grew in the fall of 1862 for some official draft exemption for slave managers, the *Macon Daily Telegraph* demanded, "Is it possible that Congress thinks . . . our women can control the slaves and oversee the farms? Do they suppose that our patriotic mothers, sisters and daughters can assume and discharge the active duties and drudgery of an overseer? Certainly not. They know better." In October Congress demonstrated that it did indeed know better, passing a law exempting from service one white man on each plantation of twenty or more slaves. But the soon infamous "Twenty-Nigger Law" triggered enormous popular resentment, both from nonslaveholders who regarded it as valuing the lives of the elite over their own and from smaller slaveholders who were not included in its scope.[4]

In an effort to silence this threatening outburst of class hostility and at the same time meet the South's ever increasing manpower needs, the Confederate Congress repeatedly amended conscription policy, both broadening the age of eligibility and limiting exemptions. Although a proposal offered by the House early in 1863 would have repealed the so-called Twenty-Nigger provision altogether, resistance from the Senate resulted instead in a compromise, a gradual restriction of the scope of the exemption through laws passed in May 1863 and February of the next year. This erosion of the statutory foundation for overseer exemptions greatly increased the difficulty of finding men not subject to military duty who could, as the original bill had phrased it, "secure the proper police of the country." Women across the Confederacy would find themselves unable to obtain the assistance of white men on their plantations and farms.

Conscription policy reveals fundamental Confederate assumptions, for it represents significant choices made by the Confederate leadership, choices that in important ways defined issues of class as more central to Confederate survival than those of gender. The initial acknowledgment by Congress that a white woman could not effectively "discharge the active duties" of an overseer was all but forgotten amidst the storm of protest over the exemption law. In order to promote at least an appearance of equitability in the draft, the Confederacy retreated from its concern about women left alone to manage slaves. White women in slaveowning households found their needs relegated to a position of secondary importance in comparison with the demands of nonslaveholding men. These men could vote, and the Confederacy required their service on the battlefield; retaining their loyalty was a priority. Minimizing class divisions within the Confederacy was imperative—even if ultimately unsuccessful. Addressing emerging gender divisions seemed less critical, because women—even the "privileged" ladies of the slaveowning elite—neither voted nor wrote editorials nor bore arms.[5]

With ever escalating military manpower demands, however, white women came to assume responsibility for directing the slave system that was so central a cause and purpose of the war. Yet they could not forget the promises of male protection and obligation that they believed their due. Women's troubling experiences as slave managers generated a growing fear and resentment of the burdens imposed by the disintegrating institution. Ultimately these tensions did much to undermine women's active support for both slavery and the Confederate cause. And throughout the South eroding slave control and diminishing plantation efficiency directly contributed to failures of morale and productivity on the homefront.


## Unprotected and Afraid

Women agreed with the Georgia newspaper that had proclaimed them unfit masters. "Where there are so many negroes upon places as upon ours," wrote an Alabama woman to the governor, "it is quite necessary that there should be men who can and will controle them, especially at this time." Faced with the prospect of being left with sixty slaves, a Mississippi planter's wife expressed similar sentiments. "Do you think," she demanded of Governor John Pettus, "that this woman's hand can keep them in check?" Women compelled to assume responsibility over slaves tended to regard their new role more as a duty than an opportunity. Like many southern soldiers, they were conscripts rather than volunteers. As Lizzie Neblett explained to her husband, Will, when he enlisted in the 20th Texas Infantry, her impending service as agricultural and slave manager was "a coercive one."[6]

Women's reluctance derived in no small part from a profound sense of their own incapacities. One Mississippi woman complained that she lacked sufficient "moral courage" to govern slaves; another believed "managing negroes . . . beyond my power." "Master's eye and voice," Catherine Edmondston remarked, "are much more potent than mistress'." An Alabama with two slaves pronounced herself "incompetent" to direct them; Martha Fort of Georgia sought a solution in renting out her slave property. "I shall not farm myself. I cant get along with negro men." Another Georgia lady sniffed that a woman was simply not "a fit and proper person" to supervise slaves. Even in anticipation the responsibility seemed daunting, and actual experience often bore out these anxieties. Slaves themselves frequently seemed to share their mistresses' views of their own incapacities. Ellen Moore of Virginia complained that her laborers "all think I am a kind of usurper & have no authority over them." As war and the promise of freedom encouraged increasing black assertiveness, white women discovered themselves in charge of an institution quite different from the one their husbands, brothers, fathers, and sons had managed before military conflict commenced.[7]

Female apprehensions about slave mastery arose from fears of this very rebelliousness and from a sense of the special threat slave violence might pose to white women. Keziah Brevard, a fifty-eight-year-old South Carolina widow, lived in almost constant fear of her sizable slave force. "It is dreadful to dwell on insurrections," she acknowledged. Yet "many an hour have I laid awake in my life thinking of our danger." Long accustomed to being alone with her slaves, Brevard grew more fearful as sectional conflict turned to Civil War. In the spring of 1861 she worried that "we know not what moment we may be hacked to death in the most cruel manner by our slaves." When her coffee tasted salty and her dinner rancid, she could not decide if her servants were attempting to poison her or just lodging a protest against their continued subjection.[8]

Early in the war, Mary Chesnut, who professed never to have had any fear of her slaves, felt compelled to reconsider her own safety when her cousin Betsey Witherspoon was smothered by her servants. An elderly widow who lived alone with her slaves, Witherspoon was well known as an ineffective and indulgent manager. Her murder underlined both the inadequacies and vulnerabilities of white women as slave masters; her fate was exactly what her South Carolina neighbor Keziah Brevard most feared. Another Carolina widow, Ada Bacot, contemplated Witherspoon's death and the prospects of her own slaves' loyalty with similar dismay. "I fear twould take very little to make them put me out of the way," she wrote.[9]

Rumors of slave insurrections abounded, and stories of individual outrages seized women's attention. On July 11, 1861, Sarah Espy of Alabama recorded news of "a most atrocious murder—that of an old lady . . . by her negro woman—the negro to be hung tomorrow." Just two days later she noted the report of "an insurrectionary movement among the negroes of Wills Valley, which was suppressed, however." At the Glenn Anna Female Seminary in North Carolina, the girls were in the weeks after secession "dreadfully frightened" by stories about "negroes rising and killing," especially "as there were no men at the Seminary." Even though it was all but impossible to separate rumor from reality, a slave conspiracy near Natchez in the spring of 1861 was particularly terrifying. The captured insurgents seemed to confirm women's profoundest fears, indicating, at least as white men recorded their rather elegantly phrased testimony, an intention to "ravish" "Miss Mary . . . Miss Sarah . . . and Miss Anna," wives and daughters of prominent slaveholders. Although secession and the outbreak of military conflict greatly aggravated both fears and rumors of such uprisings, reports of insurrections continued throughout the war, increasing in number when Lincoln issued his Emancipation Proclamation, when Union troops made significant advances, and ultimately when Confederate power was obviously disintegrating in late 1864 and 1865.[10]

Reports of individual acts of violence proliferated as well. Ada Bacot was certain the fire in her neighbors' house was set by their slave Abel; Laura Lee was horrified when occupying troops released a Winchester slave convicted of murdering her mistress. In September 1862 the *Mobile Advertiser and Register* noted that a slave had succeeded in poisoning his master; the same month the *Richmond Enquirer* recorded the conviction of one Lavinia for torching her mistress's house. Abbie Brooks of Georgia described the terrible scars on the face of a woman neighbor who had been shoved into the fire by a slave. "All that saved her life was the negro taking fire and had to let go of her mistress to extinguish herself."[11]

By the middle years of the war, women had begun publicly to voice their fears, writing hundreds of letters to state and Confederate officials imploring that men be detailed from military service to control the slaves. Hattie Motley of Alabama begged the secretary of war for the discharge of her husband, supporting her request with a description of how the previous week only a few miles away "in the night, a monster in the shape of a negro man" entered the house and then the bedroom of a young girl. "Such occurrences," Motley declared, "make woman's blood run cold, when they think of being left defenseless." Mrs. M. K. Smith was living as a lone white woman with an infant child on an Alabama plantation with forty-three slaves "in the enjoyment of their unrestrained freedom so far as they choose . . . to exorcise it by reason of their being no white male person on said plantation." Her situation, she believed, rendered her "liable to insult and being murdered by negroes at any time they may feel disposed to do so." Smith did not make clear which fate—death or dishonor—she regarded as worse, but other southern women were more direct. A group of women living near New

Bern petitioned North Carolina Governor Zebulon Vance for exemptions for the few men who still remained at home. "We pray your Excellency to consider that in the absence of all protection the female portion of this community may be subjected to a system of outrage that may be justly denominated the harrow of harrows more terrable to the contemplation of the virtuous maiden and matron than death." A petition to the Confederate secretary of war from a similar collection of "Ladies of the N.E. beat of Jas[ per] County, Miss." sought male protection against an anticipated slave insurrection. If that was impossible, they requested arms and ammunition to defend themselves from "the demonic invasion" so that "we die with honor & innocence sustained."[12]

These women chose different euphemisms to express their anxieties—insult, outrage, "harrow of harrows," dishonor, stain, and molestation—but the theme was undeniably sexual. The Old South had justified white woman's subordination in terms of her biological difference, emphasizing an essential female weakness that rested ultimately in sexual vulnerability. In a society based on the oppression of a potentially hostile population of 4 million black slaves, such vulnerability assumed special significance. On this foundation of race, the white South erected its particular—and particularly compelling—logic of female dependence. Only the white man's strength could provide adequate and necessary protection. The very word *protection* was invoked again and again by Confederate women petitioning for what they believed the fundamental right guaranteed them by the paternalistic social order of the South: "I feel unprotected and afraid," "unable to protect myself," "unable to stand up under her burden without the assistance of some white male to protect her." Denied such assurances of safety, many women would be impelled to question—even if implicitly—the logic of their willing acceptance of their own inferiority. In seeking, like the ladies of Jasper County, Mississippi, to protect themselves, Confederate women profoundly undermined the legitimacy of their subordination, demonstrating that they did not—indeed could not—depend on the supposed superior strength of white men.[13]

Significantly, the "demonic" invaders these Mississippi women most feared were not Yankees but rebellious slaves. In their terror of an insurgent black population, white southern women advanced their own definition of wartime priorities, one seemingly not shared by the Confederate leadership and government. "I fear the blacks more than I do the Yankees," confessed Mrs. A. Ingraham of besieged Vicksburg. In Virginia, Betty Maury agreed. "I am afraid of the lawless Yankee soldiers, but that is nothing to my fear of the negroes if they should rise against us." Confronted with news of a conspiracy in her own Mississippi county, Susan Sillers Darden found it "dreadful to think of it the danger we are in all the time by the Servants besides the Abolitionists." Living with slavery in wartime was, one Virginia woman observed, living with "enemies in our own households."[14]

The arrival of black soldiers in parts of the South represented the conjunction and culmination of these fears. Mary Lee of Winchester, Virginia, came "near fainting" when the troops appeared; she felt "more unnerved than by any sight I have seen since the war [began]." These soldiers were at once men, blacks, and national enemies—her gender, racial, and political opposites, the quintessential powerful and hostile Other. Their occupying presence in Winchester reminded her so forcefully of her weakness and vulnerability that she responded with a swoon, an unwanted and unwonted display of the feminine impotence and delicacy she had struggled to overcome during long years of her own as well as Confederate independence.[15]

Yet women often denied or repressed these profound fears of racial violence, confronting them only in the darkest hours of anxious, sleepless nights. Constance Cary Harrison remembered that in the daytime, apprehensions about slave violence seemed "preposterous," but at night, "there was the fear . . . dark, boding, oppressive and altogether hateful . . . the ghost that refused to be laid." Women sometimes questioned why they did not constantly feel overwhelmed by a terror that seemed all too appropriate and rational. Even as Keziah Brevard contemplated the hours she had lain awake wondering if she would be "hacked to death," she asked, "Why is it at times I feel safe as If no dangers were in the distance? I wish I could feel as free from it at all times." Catherine Edmondston marveled that with "eighty eight negroes immediately around me" and "not a white soul within five miles," she felt "not a sensation of fear."[16]

Some women in fact regarded their slaves as protectors, hoping for the loyalty that the many tales of "faithful servants" would enshrine in Confederate popular culture and, later, within the myth of the Lost Cause. Elizabeth Saxon, in a typically rose-colored remembrance of slavery during the war, recalled in 1905 that "not an outrage was perpetrated, no house was burned. . . . [O]n lonely farms women with little children slept at peace, guarded by a sable crowd, whom they perfectly trusted. . . . [I]n no land was ever a people so tender and helpful." The discrepancy between this portrait and the anxieties of everyday life on Confederate plantations underscores how white southerners, both during the war and afterward, struggled to retain a view of slavery as a benevolent institution, appreciated by blacks as well as whites.

During the war such "faithful servant" stories served to calm white fears. But examples of persisting white trust and confidence in slaves cannot be discounted entirely, nor can the stories themselves be uniformly dismissed as white inventions. There were in fact slaves who buried the master's silver to hide it from the enemy; there were slaves, like one Catherine Edmondston described, who drew knives to defend mistresses against Yankee troops. Such incidents reinforced white southerners' desire not to believe that men and women they thought they had known intimately—sometimes all their lives—had suddenly become murderers and revolutionaries.[17]

Much of the complexity of wartime relationships between white women and slaves arose because women increasingly relied on slaves' labor, competence, and even companionship at a time when slaves saw diminishing motivation for work or obedience. White women's dependence on their slaves grew simultaneously with slaves' independence of their owners, creating a troubling situation of confusion and ambivalence for mistresses compelled constantly to reassess, to interrogate, and to revise their assumptions as they struggled to reconcile need with fear. Although many agreed with Catherine Broun, who declared she was by 1863 "beginning to lose confidence *in the whole race*," other white women turned hopefully to their slaves as the only remaining allies in a dangerous wartime world. Some slave mistresses, especially in isolated plantation settings, found that in changed wartime households, their closest adult connections were with female slaves. When Rhoda died in April 1862, her owner Anna Green wrote in despair to her sister. "I feel like I have lost my only friend and I do believe she was the most faithful friend I had [even] if she was a servant." Leila Callaway described the death from smallpox of her slave Susanna in almost identical terms. "Next to my own dear family Susanna was my warmest best friend." "I have no one now in your absence," she informed her husband, "to look to for protection." In the disruptions of the South's hierarchies of gender and race, Leila Callaway had invested a black woman with some of the responsibilities—emotional and otherwise—of the absent white man.[18]

Kate McClure of South Carolina preferred her slave Jeff to the white men her husband had deputized to help manage plantation affairs during his military service. McClure believed Jeff to be more trustworthy and more knowledgeable, as well as more likely to accept her viewpoint and direction, than the two male neighbors. Maria Hawkins keenly felt the absence of her slave protector Moses and wrote to Governor Vance with a variation of the hundreds of letters to southern officials seeking discharge of husbands and sons. Hawkins requested Moses' release from impressment as a laborer on coastal fortifications. "He slept in the house, every night while at home, & protected everything in the house & yard & at these perilous times when deserters are committing depredations, on plantations every day, I am really so much frightened every night, that I am up nearly all night." In Hawkins's particular configuration of gender and racial anxieties, a black male protector was far preferable to no male at all.[19]

## The Fruits of the War

Within the context of everyday life in the Confederacy, most women slaveholders confronted neither murderous revolutionaries nor the unfailingly loyal retainers of "moonlight and magnolias" tradition. Instead they faced complex human beings whose desires for freedom expressed themselves in ways that varied with changing means and opportunities as slavery weakened steadily under unrelenting northern military pressure.

Often opportunity was greatest in areas close to Union lines, and slaveowners in these locations confronted the greatest challenges of discipline. "This must," wrote Catherine Edmondston of her increasingly unmanageable slaves, "be one of the fruits of the War, as we never had such a thing before." Ada Bacot, widowed South Carolina plantation owner, believed her "orders disregarded more & more every day. I can do nothing so must submit, which is anything but pleasant." When she left Carolina for a nursing post at the Monticello Hospital in Charlottesville, however, she soon discovered "Virginia Negroes are not near so servile as those of S.C." Even the chambermaid she had brought from home became insubordinate under the influence of her new environment. Slave intractability made Bacot's housekeeping duties "anything but pleasant." When an adolescent slave named William defied her order to clean up the dinner table in the house where she and the other nurses and doctors lodged, she called him to task. But the young slave was "so impertinent that I slaped him in the mouth before I knew what I did." His mother rushed from the kitchen to his defense, provoking Bacot to threaten both slaves with punishment. Unlike many Confederate slave managers, though, Bacot did not live in a world comprised exclusively of women. She turned for aid to the white male doctors who were also residents of the household, and they whipped both irate mother and insolent child.[20]

For many white women this physical dimension of slave control proved most troubling. In the prewar South the threat—and often the reality—of physical force had combined with the coercive manipulations of planter paternalism to serve as fundamental instruments of oppression and thus of race control. The white South had justified its "peculiar institution" as a beneficent system of reciprocal obligations between master and slave, defining slave labor as a legitimate return for masters' protection and support. But in the very notion of mutual duties, the ideology of paternalism conceded the essential humanity of the bondspeople, who turned paternalism to their own uses, manipulating it as an empowering doctrine of intrinsic rights.

Desiring to see themselves as decent Christian men, most southern slaveholders of the prewar years preferred the negotiated power of reciprocity to the almost unchecked exercise of force that was in fact permitted them by law. The paternalistic ideal regarded whipping as a last, not a first, resort, and as a breakdown in control that was more properly exerted over minds than bodies. Yet violence was implicit in the system, and both planters' records and slaves' reminiscences demonstrate how often it was explicit as well.

Just as "paternalism" and "mastery" were rooted in concepts of masculinity, so violence was similarly gendered as male within the ideology of the Old South. Recourse to physical force in support of male honor and white supremacy was regarded as the right, even the responsibility, of each white man—within his household, on his plantation, in his community, and with the outbreak of war, for his nation. Women slave managers inherited a social order that depended on the threat and often the use of violence. Throughout the history of the peculiar institution, slave mistresses had in fact slapped, hit, and even brutally whipped their slaves—particularly slave women or children. But their relationship to this exercise of physical power was significantly different from that of their men. No gendered code of honor celebrated women's physical power or dominance. A contrasting yet parallel ideology extolled female sensitivity, weakness, and vulnerability. In the prewar years, exercise of the violence fundamental to slavery was overwhelmingly the responsibility and prerogative of white men. A white woman disciplined and punished as the master's subordinate and surrogate. Rationalized, systematic, autonomous, and instrumental use of violence belonged to men.

Ada Bacot surprised herself when she lashed out and slapped young William, and it was in just such moments of rage that many Confederate women embraced physical force. But for the kind of rationalized punishment intended to function as the mainstay of slave discipline, Bacot turned to men. Women alone customarily sought overseers, male relatives, or neighbors to undertake physical coercion of slaves, especially slave men. As white men disappeared to war, however, finding such help became increasingly difficult. Sarah Espy had depended on her neighbor Finley to carry out necessary whippings, but when he departed to Carolina, she was without recourse. Yet Espy would have agreed with the woman who declared that "the idea of a lady doing such a thing" was "repugnant."[21]

In the exigency of war, however, many mistresses did inflict violence with their own hands, but more often than not rage had to override deep-seated feelings of conflict and ambivalence to make such actions possible. Susan Scott of Texas seemed close to the limits of sanity when she stood in the midst of a poorly cultivated cornfield shouting tearful curses at her slaves in language "equal to any man." Then she "whipped one . . . awfully, and said she would be damned if she dident have every d—— negro on the place whipped about the stand of corn." Emily Perkins of Tennessee was so infuriated at a slave woman who had announced she would never be whipped again that she hit her over the head with what she thought was a shovel. When it turned out to be just a broom, which broke instead of knocking the woman over, Perkins sent for a male slave to tie her down. Then Perkins "laid it on." Instead of an effective effort to exert dominance, white women's recourse to violence often represented a loss of control— over both themselves and their slaves.[22]

As slaves grew more assertive in anticipation of their freedom, their female managers regarded physical coercion as at once more essential and more impossible. Some white women began to bargain with violence, trying to make slavery seem benign in hopes of retaining their slaves' service, if not their loyalty. Avoiding physical punishment even in the face of insolence or poor work, they endeavored to keep their slaves from departing altogether. Leila Callaway wrote her husband, Morgan, of her efforts to appear a benevolent—and thus desirable—mistress: "I never was half as sweet tempered in my life as I have been this year." Catherine Broun, on the border of slavery and freedom in northern Virginia, confessed she was "afraid . . . to correct one of them least they should all leave." At the opposite end of the Confederacy, Texan Lizzie Neblett urged her part-time overseer not to beat a slave in response to his insubordination. "I told him not to whip Joe, as long as he done his work well . . . that he might run away & we might never get him & if he never done me any good he might my children." Lizzie worried as well that whipping might provoke violent retaliation against managers who possessed the obvious vulnerability of the Confederacy's white females. Many had, she noted, become "actually affraid to whip the negros."[23]

The Old South's social hierarchies had created a spectrum of legitimate access to violence, so that social empowerment was inextricably bound up with the right to employ physical force. Violence was all but required of white men of all classes, a cultural principle rendered explicit by the coming of war and conscription. Black slaves, by contrast, were forbidden the use of violence entirely, except within their own communities, where the dominant society chose to regard it as essentially invisible. White women stood upon an ill-defined middle ground, where behavior and ideology often diverged.

The Civil War exacerbated this very tension, compelling women in slave-owning households to become the reluctant agents of a power they could not embrace as rightfully their own. The centrality of violence in the Old South had reflected and reinforced white women's inferior status in that society. With Civil War, military conflict made organized violence the South's defining purpose and instrument of survival, marginalizing women once again. But even away from "the tented field," even on the homefront, women felt inadequate; their understanding of their gender undermined their effectiveness. Just as their inability to bear arms left Confederate women feeling "useless," so their inhibitions about violence made many females regard themselves as failures at slave management. As Lizzie Neblett wrote of her frustration in the effort to control eleven recalcitrant slaves, "I am so sick of trying to do a man's business when I am nothing but, a poor contemptible piece of multiplying human flesh tied to the house by a crying young one, looked upon as belonging to a race of inferior beings." The language she chose to describe her self-loathing is significant, for she borrowed it from the vocabulary of race as well as gender. Invoking the objective constraints of biology—"multiplying flesh"—as well as the socially constructed limitations of status—"looked upon as belonging to a race of inferior beings"—she identified herself not with the white elite, not with those in whose interest the war was being fought, but with the South's oppressed and disadvantaged. Increasingly, even though self-indulgently, she came to regard herself as the victim rather than the beneficiary of her region's slave society. Lizzie Neblett's uniquely documented experience with violence and slavery deserves exploration in some detail, for it illustrates not simply the contradictions inherent in female management, but the profound personal crisis of identity generated by her new and unaccustomed role.[24]


## Troubled in Mind

When her husband departed for war in the spring of 1863, Lizzie had set about the task of management committed to "doing my best" but was apprehensive both about her ignorance of agriculture and about the behavior she might expect from her eleven slaves. Their initial response to her direction, however, seemed promising. "The negros," she wrote Will in late April, "seem to be mightily stirred up about making a good crop."[25]

By harvest, however, the situation had already changed. "The negros are doing nothing," Lizzie wrote Will at the height of first cotton picking in mid-August. "But ours are not doing that job alone[.] [N]early all the negroes around here are at it, some of them are getting so high in anticipation of their glorious freedom by the Yankees I suppose, that they resist a whipping." Lizzie harbored few illusions about the long-term loyalty of her own black family. "I dont think we have one who will stay with us."[26]

After a harvest that fell well below the previous year's achievement, Lizzie saw the need for new managerial arrangements. Will had provided for a male neighbor to keep a general supervisory eye over the Neblett slave force, but Lizzie wrote Will in the fall of 1863 that she had contracted to pay a Mr. Meyers to spend three half-days a week with her slaves. "He will be right tight on the negroes I think, but they need it. Meyers will lay down the law and enforce it." But Lizzie emphasized that she would not permit cruelty or abuse.[27]

Controlling Meyers would prove in some ways more difficult than controlling the slaves. His second day on the plantation Meyers whipped three young male slaves for idleness, and on his next visit, as Lizzie put it, "he undertook old Sam." Gossip had spread among slaves in the neighborhood—and from them to their masters—that Sam intended to take a whipping from no man.[28] Will Neblett had, in fact, not been a harsh disciplinarian, tending more to threatening and grumbling than whipping. But Meyers regarded Sam's challenge as quite "enough." When Sam refused to come to Meyers to receive a whipping he felt he did not deserve, Meyers cornered and threatened to shoot him. Enraged, Meyers beat Sam so severely that Lizzie feared he might die. She anxiously called the doctor, who assured her that Sam had no internal injuries and that he had seen slaves beaten far worse.

Lizzie was torn over how to respond—to Meyers or to Sam. "Tho I pity the poor wretch," she confided to Will, "I don't want him to know it." To the other slaves she insisted that "Meyers would not have whipped him if he had not deserved it," and to Will she defensively maintained, "somebody must take them in hand[.] they grow worse all the time[.] I could not begin to write you . . . how little they mind me." She saw Meyers's actions as part of a plan to establish control at the outset: "he lets them know what he is . . .

& then has no more trouble." But Lizzie's very insistence and defensiveness suggest that this was not, even in her mind, slave management in its ideal form.[29]

Over the next few days, Lizzie's doubts about Meyers and his course of action grew. Instead of eliminating trouble at the outset, as he had intended, the incident seemed to have created an uproar. Sarah, a cook and house slave, reported to Lizzie that Sam suspected the whipping had been his mistress's idea, and that, when well enough, he would run away until Will came home.[30]

To resolve the volatile situation and to salvage her reputation as slave mistress, Lizzie now enlisted another white man, Coleman, to talk reasonably with Sam. Coleman had been her dead father's overseer and continued to manage her mother's property. In the absence of Will and Lizzie's brothers at the front, he was an obvious family deputy, and he had undoubtedly known Sam before Lizzie had inherited him from her father's estate. Coleman agreed to "try to show Sam the error he had been guilty of." At last Sam spoke the words Coleman sought, admitting he had done wrong and promising no further insubordination.[31]

Two weeks after the incident, Lizzie and Sam finally had a direct and, in Lizzie's view at least, comforting exchange. Meyers had ordered Sam back to work, but Lizzie had interceded in response to Sam's complaints of persisting weakness. Taking his cue from Lizzie's conciliatory gesture and acting as well in accordance with Coleman's advice, Sam apologized for disappointing Lizzie's expectations, acknowledging that as the oldest slave he had special responsibilities in Will's absence. Henceforth, he promised Lizzie, he was "going to do his work faithfully & be of as much service to me as he could. I could not help," Lizzie confessed to Will, "feeling sorry for the old fellow[.] . . . he talked so humbly & seemed so hurt that I should have had him whipped so."[32]

Sam's adroit transformation from rebel into Sambo helped resolve Lizzie's uncertainties about the appropriate course of slave management. Abandoning her defense of Meyers's severity, even interceding on Sam's behalf against her own manager, Lizzie assured Sam she had not been responsible for his punishment, had indeed been "astonished" by it. Meyers, she reported to Will with newfound assurance, "did wrong" and "knows nothing" about the management of slaves. He "don't," she noted revealingly, "treat them as moral beings but manages by brute force." Henceforth, Lizzie concluded, she would not feel impelled by her sense of helplessness to countenance extreme severity. Instead, she promised Sam, if he remained

*Lizzie Neblett. Courtesy of the Center for American History,*
*University of Texas, Austin.*

"humble and submissive," she would ensure "he would not get another lick."[33]

The incident of Sam's whipping served as the occasion for an extended negotiation between Lizzie and her slaves about the terms of her power. In calling upon Meyers and Coleman, she demonstrated that, despite appearances, she was not in fact a woman alone, dependent entirely on her own resources. Although the ultimate responsibility might be hers, slave management was a community concern. Pushed toward sanctioning Meyers's cruelty by fear of her own impotence, Lizzie then stepped back from the extreme position in which Meyers had placed her. But at the same time she dissociated herself from Meyers's action, she also reaped its benefit: Sam's abandonment of a posture of overt defiance for one of apparent submission. Sam and Lizzie were ultimately able to join forces in an agreement that Meyers must be at once deplored and tolerated as a necessary evil whom both mistress and slave would strive ceaselessly to manipulate. Abandoning their brief tryouts as Simon Legree and Nat Turner, Lizzie and Sam returned to the more accustomed and comfortable roles of concerned paternalist and loyal slave. Each recognized at last that his or her own performance depended in large measure on a complementary performance by the other.

Lizzie's behavior throughout the crisis demonstrated the essential part gender identities and assumptions played in master-slave relations. As a female manager, Lizzie exploited her apparently close ties to Sarah, a house slave, in order to secure information about the remainder of her force. "Sarah is worth a team of negro's with her tongue," Lizzie reported to Will. Yet Lizzie's gender more often represented a constraint than an opportunity. Just before the confrontation between Meyers and Sam, Lizzie had written revealingly to Will about the physical coercion of slaves. Acknowledging Will's reluctance to whip, she confessed to feeling the aversion even more forcefully than he. "It has got to be such a disagreeable matter with me to whip, that I haven't even dressed Kate but once since you left, & then only a few cuts—I am too troubled in mind to get stirred up enough to whip. I made Thornton whip Tom once."[34]

Accustomed to occasional strikes against female slaves, Lizzie called on a male slave to whip the adolescent Tom, then, later, she enlisted a male neighbor to dominate the venerable Sam. Yet even this structured hierarchy of violence was becoming increasingly "disagreeable" to her as she acted out her new wartime role as "chief of affairs." In part, Lizzie knew she was objectively physically weaker than both black and white men around her. But she confessed as well to a "troubled . . . mind," to uncertainties about her appropriate relationship to the ultimate exertion of force upon which slavery rested. As wartime pressures weakened the foundations for the "moral" management that Lizzie preferred, what she referred to as "brute force" became simultaneously more attractive and more dangerous as an instrument of coercion.

Forbidden the physical severity that served as the fundamental prop of his system of slave management, Meyers requested to be released from his contract with Lizzie at the end of the crop year. Early in the agreement, Meyers had told Lizzie that he could "conquer" her slaves, "but may have to kill some one of them." It remained with Lizzie, he explained, to make the decision. In her moments of greatest exasperation, Lizzie was willing to consent to such extreme measures. "I say do it." But with calm reflection, tempered by Will's measured advice, considerations of humanity reasserted their claim. Repeatedly she interceded between Meyers and the slaves, protecting them from whippings or condemning Meyers when he disobeyed her orders and punished them severely. Yet despite her difficulties in managing Meyers and despite her belief that he was "deficient in judgment," Lizzie recognized her dependence on him and on the threat of force he represented. She was determined to "hold him on as long as I can." If he quit and the slaves found that no one was coming to replace him, she wrote revealingly, "the jig will be up." The game, the trick, the sham of her slave management would be over. Without a man—or a man part time for three half-days a week—without the recourse to violence that Meyers embodied, slavery was unworkable. The velvet glove of paternalism required its iron hand.[35]

Violence was the ultimate foundation of power in the slave South, but gender prescriptions carefully barred white women—especially those elite women most likely to find themselves responsible for controlling slaves—from purposeful exercise of physical dominance. Even when circumstances had shifted to make female authority socially desirable, it remained for many plantation mistresses personally unachievable. Lizzie's struggle with her attraction to violence and her simultaneous abhorrence of it embodied the contradictions that the necessary wartime paradox of female slave management imposed. Lizzie begged Will to hire out his slaves or even to "give your negros away and, I'll . . . work with my hands, as hard as I can, but my mind will rest." Lizzie wished repeatedly to die, to be a man, or to give up the slaves altogether—except, tellingly, for "one good negro to wait upon me." White women had reaped slavery's benefits throughout its existence in the colonial and antebellum South. But they could not be its everyday managers without in some measure failing to be what they understood as female. The authority of their class and race could not overcome the dependence they had learned to identify as the essence of their womanhood.[36]

## More Expense Than Profit

Many women who feared experiences like Lizzie's hired out or sold their slaves rather than attempting to manage the troublesome property themselves. As food and clothing became scarcer in the ever more desperate South, simply finding someone else to assume responsibility for feeding slaves was often almost as important as securing cash income for their sale or rent. Lila Chunn's brother-in-law advised her to dispose of two slaves, Ann and Sandy. "He says," reported Lila's sister, "they ought to bring 4 or 5000 & you've been supporting her instead of her you." In areas of the South where large numbers of slaves had been taken by refugees, there emerged by the last years of the war a glut on the market. In Texas, for example, one estate executor complained that in 1864 he was unable to hire out slaves of a deceased owner for any price.[37]

For some white families, these changes in slave markets and availability represented an opportunity too great to ignore, for war's disruptions had made slave ownership possible for the first time. Women acting as heads of such households often welcomed new slaveholding duties as a warborn chance for upward mobility. Mary Bell of Franklin, North Carolina, took full advantage of the new fluidity of the South's labor force to acquire in 1864 a family of three slaves moved from the Carolina coast to her mountain community.[38]

After the departure of her husband, Alfred, for war in 1861, Mary had depended on two hired slaves nominally supervised by a white tenant to work her land. Tom and Liza were a constant aggravation, however, and by 1862 Tom had been discovered stealing meat as well as poisoning her brother-in-law's dog. Liza disappeared for days at a time, and Mary chafed with frustration at her inability to control her workers. Mary believed the situation resulted in part from the failure of the white men on whom she depended—her tenant and her father- and brother-in-law—to offer adequate assistance. "Your Pa does not control Tom as he ought to," she wrote Alf in May 1862. "He lets him have his own way too much. I wish I could be man and woman both until this war ends." As the white men upon whom she depended failed her, Mary wished for what she knew was impossible: the ability to exercise male power and male control herself. Mary was so exasperated, she was ready to give her hired slaves up altogether. "Tom never came back," she wrote to Alf a week later. "I am very well satisfied to do without him, he is too lazy to pay for his victuals and clothes and was always in some fuss."[39]

But Mary identified the source of her discontent as a slave manager as not so much her gender—though she saw that as part of the problem—or the wartime disruptions of master-slave relations, but the legal tenuousness of her hold on her workers. She was not their owner; her connection with them was defined as temporary rather than permanent. Perhaps in full ownership, she thought, lay the resolution of her difficulties.

With the assistance and advice of a brother-in-law, Mary therefore executed her "nigger trade" in March 1864, acquiring Trim, his wife, Patsy, and their daughter, Rosa. At first she was ebullient about her new property and pronounced herself "so well pleased with my darkies." But her enthusiasm soon waned. In November she wrote Alf that when he came home from the army and saw how bad everything was, he would want to return to camp. Patsy had proven to be in poor health, plagued by fits that would make her "a burden on our hands as long as she lives." Moreover, it turned out that Mary had been deceived in the sale and that Patsy was in fact a free woman. This meant that Mary had actually purchased one slave, not three, for Rosa's status would follow that of her mother. Trim's usefulness in the fields was proving limited as well. "Unless you could be at home I fear we will not make much farming," she wrote Alf in December.[40]

Mary began thinking of exchanging these slaves for others, but her expectations of what slavery might bring her had been scaled down considerably from her earlier hopes of upward mobility and increasing wealth. Burdened with a new baby of her own, Mary Bell, like Lizzie Neblett, came to regard slavery's greatest benefit as residing in the availability of someone to relieve her of household labor. Mary Bell's overwhelming desire by late 1864 was simply for a "woman that can get up and get breakfast. I am getting tired of having to rise these cold mornings."[41]

On balance, Mary Bell's experience as manager and fledgling slaveowner had been trying. In November 1864 she had written to Alf, "these negroes are going to be more expense than profit unless you were at home[.] I think then Trim would be of service to us." With an inadequate corn crop and potatoes rotting in the field, Mary proclaimed, "this year has put me completely out of heart." Beginning her duties as slave manager with optimism and enthusiasm, Mary Bell came ultimately to share with Lizzie Neblett a profound sense of failure and personal inadequacy. As she repeatedly told Alf, "unless you could be at home," "unless you were at home," the system would not work. "You say," Mary Bell wrote her husband in December 1864, "you think I am a good farmer if I only had confidence in myself. I confess I have very little confidence in my own judgment and management. wish I had more. perhaps if I had I would not get so out of heart. Sometimes I am almost ready to give up and think that surely my lot is harder than anyone else."[42]

A growing disillusionment with slavery among many elite white women arose from this very desire to "give up"—to be freed from burdens of management and fear of black reprisal that often outweighed any tangible benefits from the labor of increasingly recalcitrant slaves. Few slaveowning women had seriously questioned the moral or political legitimacy of the system, although many admitted to the profound evils associated with the institution. Gertrude Thomas noted its "terribly demoralising influence upon our men and boys," and Mary Chesnut's vehement criticisms similarly fixed on the almost unrestricted sexual access slavery gave white men to black women. Yet her concerns, like those of Gertrude Thomas, lay with the impact of these social arrangements on whites and their families rather than on exploited slaves. White southern women readily embraced the racism of their era. Blacks were, Chesnut remarked, "dirty—slatternly—idle—ill smelling by nature." Slaves were unquestionably inferior beings "blest," as one North Carolina woman wrote, "in having a home among Anglo Saxons." Jane Howison Beale of Virginia had no doubt that blacks "were ordained of High Heaven to serve the white man and it is only in that capacity they can be happy useful and respected."[43]

*[margin annotation: women's racism]*

Southern slave mistresses began to convince themselves, however, that an institution that they were certain worked in the interest of blacks did not necessarily advance their own. Confederate women could afford little contemplation of slavery's merits "in the abstract," as its prewar defenders had urged. Slavery's meaning did not rest in the detached and intellectualized realms of politics or moral philosophy. The growing emotional and physical cost of the system to slaveholding women made its own forceful appeal, and many slave mistresses began to persuade themselves that the institution had become a greater inconvenience than benefit.

In 1863, still anticipating Confederate victory, Lila Chunn urged her husband to consider a line of work after the war that did not involve slaves. "I sometimes think that the fewer a person owns the better off he is." Sarah Kennedy of Tennessee decided in 1863 that she "would rather do all the work than be worried with a house full of servants that do what, how and when they please. . . . [I]f we could be compensated for their value [we] are better off without them." Keziah Brevard agreed: "I am heartily tired of managing them—could I cast them off without scruples of conscience I would do so. . . . What is the use of so much property when I cant get one thing cooked fit to eat[?]" In 1862 Mrs. W. W. Boyce wrote her husband, a South Carolina congressman, "I tell you all this attention to farming is uphill work with me. I can give orders first-rate, but when I am not obeyed, I can't keep my temper. . . . I am ever ready to give you a helping hand, but I must say I am heartily tired of trying to manage *free* negroes." Gertrude Thomas noted in 1864 that she had "become convinced that the Negro as a race is better off with us . . . than if he were made free, but I am by no means so sure that we would not gain by having his freedom given him. . . . [I]f we had the same invested in something else as a means of support I would willingly, nay gladly, have the responsibility of them taken off my shoulders."[44]

Like Lizzie Neblett, many white women focused on slavery's trials and yearned for the peculiar institution—and all the troublesome blacks constrained within its bonds—magically to disappear. "I wish," wrote Keziah Brevard, "the Abolitionists & the negroes had a country to themselves & we who are desirous to practice *truth & love to God were to ourselves*—yes Lord Jesus—seperate us in the world to come, let us not be together." But like Neblett, many women who entertained such fantasies at the same time longed for just "one good negro to wait upon me." For white women, this would be emancipation's greatest cost.[45]

## An Entire Rupture of Our Domestic Relations

In the summer of 1862 a Confederate woman overheard two small girls "playing ladies." "Good morning, ma'am," said little Sallie to her friend. "How are you today?" "I don't feel very well this morning," four-year-old Nannie Belle replied. "*All my niggers have run away and left me.*"[46]

From the first months of the war, white women confronted yet another change in their households, one that a Virginia woman described as "an entire disruption of our domestic relations": the departure of their slaves. Sometimes, especially when Yankee troops swept through an area, the loss was total and immediate. Sarah Hughes of Alabama stood as a roadside spectator at the triumphant procession of hundreds of her slaves toward freedom. Her niece, Eliza Walker, en route to visit her aunt, described the scene that greeted her as she approached the Hughes plantation.

Down the road [the Bluecoats] . . . came, and with them all the slaves . . . , journeying, as they thought, to the promised land. I saw them as they trudged the main road, many of the women with babes in their arms . . . old and young, men, women and children. Some of them fared better than the others. A negro woman, Laura, my aunt's fancy seamstress, rode Mrs. Hughes' beautiful white pony, sitting [on] the red plush saddle of her mistress. The Hughes' family carriage, driven by Taliaferro, the old coachman, and filled with blue coated soldiers and negroes, passed in state, and this was followed by other vehicles.

*Sarah Hughes, Alabama plantation mistress. Courtesy of the Alabama Department of Archives and History, Montgomery.*

With the trusted domestics leading the way, Sarah Hughes's slaves had turned her world upside down.[47]

Usually the departure of slaves was less dramatic and more secretive, as blacks simply stole away one by one or in groups of two or three when they heard of opportunities to reach Union armies and freedom. In Middleburg, Virginia, Catherine Cochran reported, "Scarcely a morning dawned that some stampede was not announced—sometimes persons would awake to find every servant gone & we never went to bed without anticipating such an occurrence." In nearby Winchester, Mary Lee presided over a more extended dissolution of her slave force. Her male slaves were the first to leave in the spring of 1862. Emily and Betty threatened to follow, and Lee considered sending them off to a more secure location away from Federal lines in order to keep from losing them altogether. Having regular help in the house seemed imperative, though, even if it was risky. "I despise menial work," Lee confessed. But she had no confidence she would retain her property. "It is an uncomfortable thought, in waking in the morning, to be uncertain as to whether you will have any servants to bring in water and prepare breakfast. . . . I dread our house servants going and having to do their work." When Betty talked again of leaving in June 1863, Laura Lee, Mary's sister-in-law, locked up the clothes the black woman had packed in anticipation of departure. Laura was determined "not to lose them too, if I could help it." Temporarily thwarted, Betty left for good the next summer, and the Lees lost slave and clothing after all.[48]

By the time of her exile from Winchester in February 1865, Mary Lee was surprised that her household still enjoyed the services of a mother and daughter, Sarah and Emily, who, despite repeated threats and stormy confrontations, had not yet fled to freedom. Mary Lee entertained few illusions about the continuing loyalty of her slaves. Early in the war, she made it clear that "I have never had the least confidence in the fidelity of any negro." Her grief at their gradual disappearance was highly pragmatic; she mourned their lost labor but did not seem to cherish an ideal of master-slave harmony to be shaken by the slaves' choice of freedom over loyalty.[49]

A South Carolina woman, by contrast, became "miserably depressed" when her three most dependable house slaves fled. "If they felt as *I* do," she explained, "they could not possibly leave me." The Jones family of Georgia, devout Presbyterians, reflected the tenacity of their evangelical proslavery vision in their indignant feelings of betrayal at the departure of their human property. Eva Jones was distraught when three female slaves seized their freedom "without bidding any of us an affectionate adieu." Mary Jones felt deeply wounded by what she regarded as slaves' "ingratitude." Committed to a conception of slavery as a Christian institution founded in reciprocal rights and duties, she could understand blacks' desire for freedom only as an unjust failure to appreciate her dedicated performance of her obligations within the system. "My life long . . . I have been laboring and caring for them, and since the war have labored with all my might to supply their wants, and expended everything I had upon their support, directly or indirectly; and this is their return." Even the shock of the blacks' behavior did not help Mary Jones to understand that her construction of slavery as an institution of mutual benevolence was not shared by her slaves. With their sights set on freedom, the blacks felt no duty to abide by the terms of the system as the white South had defined them.[50]

Pressed by the exigencies of the war and by the unrelenting demands of household labor, most white women soon focused, like Mary Lee, on the practical rather than the ideological significance of the departure of their slaves. When Catherine Broun lost a servant of nineteen years in December 1861, she complained that her husband did not understand her distress. "He does not know how much a woman's happiness depends on having good servants." In truth, it was more than simply a woman's happiness. The elite southerner's fundamental sense of identity depended on having others to perform life's menial tasks. South Carolina aristocrat Charlotte Ravenel had been compelled to do her own cooking for almost ten days when she located a slave to assume the work. "Newport has taken the cooking," she wrote tellingly in March 1865, "and we are all ladies again." A Georgia woman succeeded in avoiding the fate Ravenel so narrowly escaped. "The first & only meal my Mother ever cooked," her daughter Emma Prescott remembered, was the "day after the negroes all left. Mother went into the kitchen to cook breakfast. She sifted some flour into the tray and stood, thinking what to do next—when an old negro man appeared at the window & said 'laws mistis is you cooking breakfast.' 'No I am not come in here and get it for me' which he did."[51]

In their reactions to slaves' departures, women revealed—to themselves as well as to posterity—the extent of their dependence on their servants. In our day of automated housework and prepared foods, it is easy to forget how much skill nineteenth-century housekeeping required. Many slave mistresses lacked this basic competence, having left to their slaves responsibility for execution of a wide range of essential domestic tasks. A generation ago historian Anne Firor Scott revolutionized prevailing wisdom about the southern lady. She was not, Scott insisted, the idle and pampered belle of myth and romance. Rather, Scott asserted, she was a worker, whose many contributions were essential to plantation efficiency and order. White women's reactions to the loss of their slaves offer a striking perspective on this argument. If plantation mistresses were indeed working hard, many of them, especially on larger farms and plantations, must have been devoting themselves overwhelmingly to organizational or managerial tasks—ordering food and clothing or planning and assigning work within the house—for war and emancipation revealed that many white women felt themselves entirely ignorant about how to perform basic functions of everyday life.[52]

A Louisiana lady who had "never even so much as washed out a pocket handkerchief with my own hands" suddenly had to learn to do laundry for her entire family. Kate Foster found that when her house servants left and she took on the washing, she "came near ruining myself for life as I was too delicately raised for such hard work." Mississippi planter Thomas Dabney was so horrified at the idea of ladies doing laundry that when his slaves departed, he insisted to his daughters that he himself would take on the washing. Lizzie Carter of Petersburg gained a new understanding of motherhood when she was left without a nurse. "I never knew before the trouble of children," she complained to her sister. Martha Horne of Missouri remembered after the war that "I had never cooked a meal when the negro women left, and had a hard time learning." Amanda Worthington reported her difficulties in learning to boil water and concluded she "never was cut out to be a cook." Malvina Gist wished in March 1865 that "I had been taught to cook instead of how to play on the piano. A practical knowledge of the preparation of food products would stand me in better stead at this juncture." When Henrietta Barr's cook departed, she assumed her place in the kitchen. "(Although a confession is humiliating)," she confided to her diary, "I must say I do not in the smallest particular fill the situation as creditably as she did. I certainly do not think my forte lies in cooking."[53]

The forte of the southern lady did not seem to lie in slave management either. These women were beginning to feel they could live neither with slaves nor without them. "To be without them is a misery & to have them is just as bad," confessed Amelia Barr of Galveston. Women already frustrated "trying to do a man's business" and direct slaves now discovered that they often felt equally incompetent executing the tasks that had belonged to their supposed racial inferiors. Like Henrietta Barr, many regarded the situation as "humiliating." "It is such a degradation," Matthella Page Harrison of Virginia wrote as she anticipated the imminent flight of her slaves, "to be so dependent upon the servants as we are."[54]

The concept of female dependence and weakness was not simply a prop of southern gender ideology; in the context of war, white ladies were finding it to be all too painful a reality. Socialized to believe in their own weakness and sheltered from the necessity of performing even life's basic tasks, many white women felt almost crippled by their unpreparedness for the new lives war had brought. Yet as they struggled to cope with change, their dedication to the old order faltered as well. Slavery, the "cornerstone" of the civilization for which their nation fought, increasingly seemed a burden rather than a benefit. White women regarded it as a threat as well. In failing to guarantee what white women believed to be their most fundamental right, in failing to protect women or to exert control over insolent and even rebellious slaves, Confederate men undermined not only the foundations of the South's peculiar institution but the legitimacy of their power as white males, as masters of families of white women and black slaves.

# CHAPTER FOUR

# *We Must Go to Work, Too*

On September 10, 1861, Maria Hubard of Virginia reported to her diary "a singular event in my life!" For the first time, she wrote with amazement, she had undertaken work "for which remuneration was to be received!!"[1] While many Confederate women struggled to manage slaves and fields and maintain their female-headed households, others confronted different, yet equally new, wartime responsibilities. Between 1861 and 1865 in the South, significant numbers of middle- and upper-class white women left their homes to undertake paid work for the first time.[2]

Because the South had remained overwhelmingly agricultural, the region had not developed the manufacturing and commerce that during the first half of the nineteenth century made thousands of Yankee women and men into wage laborers in the North's cities and factories. Financial necessity did drive some white women to seek employment in the fledgling industries of the prewar South, and women could be found in a wide variety of other occupations, serving, for example, as milliners, bakers, seamstresses, laundresses, and boardinghouse and tavern keepers. Overall, however, far fewer southern than northern white women were employed outside the domestic sphere of their own households, and fewer still of these were of the middling or upper orders. Those white southern women who worked did so out of necessity, and their labor carried with it a stigma of debased status and an aura of vague disreputability. In the South, even occupations, such as teaching or shopkeeping, that were regarded as appropriate and respectable endeavors for middle-class women in the North remained almost exclusively the province of men.[3]

Mass military mobilization and the demands of total war required a significant enhancement in the size of the southern workforce, one that could be met only by incorporating the labor of white females—including those middle- and upper-class women whose very understanding of themselves had been based on their distance from the public sphere of production. A war that had at the outset made so many women feel useless and irrelevant soon demanded significant labor and sacrifice from even the most privileged southern females. As the Reverend Robert Barnwell emphasized in an address to the ladies of Charleston, "WITHOUT YOU, THIS WAR COULD NOT HAVE BEEN CARRIED ON, FOR THE GOVERNMENT WAS NOT PREPARED TO MEET ALL THAT WAS THROWN UPON IT." Across the Confederacy, southerners remarked with curiosity upon the unexpected appearance of women in new roles and occupations. In 1862 Lila Chunn of Georgia reported such a phenomenon as part of the news from home to her husband, Willie, at the front: "Ladies keep the stores here now . . . their husbands having joined the army. It looks funny in Dixie to see a lady behind the counter, but it would be natural if we were in Yankeedom as it has always [been] the custom there, a custom however I do not like. The idea of a lady having to face and transact business with any and every body. It is alone suited to the North-[ern] women of brazen faces. But I say if it is necessary, our ladies ought to shopkeep and do everything else they can to aid in the great struggle for Liberty."[4]

Women were perhaps even more pushed by personal necessity than pulled by patriotic dedication to southern liberty. Ever more pressing financial circumstances made paid labor imperative for many Confederate women who had never before dreamed of earning a living. Gertrude Thomas, daughter of a planter worth $2.5 million, noted with wonder in September 1864 that "the idea has several times suggested itself to me that someday I would have to aid in earning my own support."[5]

However imperative for both individual and national survival, women's transition to paid public employment was not easy—either personally or ideologically—for it controverted deep-seated assumptions about female dependence and about the appropriateness of a separate and necessarily domestic women's sphere. The Confederacy's demand for female labor combined with many women's desperate need for remunerative work to pose a significant challenge to the South's understanding of female delicacy and respectability. Working women seemed "brazen," even to those like Lila Chunn who understood and encouraged necessary departures from tradition. Because of the unease with which southerners regarded these shifts, privileged women's movement from home to workplace generated widespread public discussion as well as private commentary about the proper components of both class and gender identity. At the same time, it created considerable personal turmoil, grounded in the complex responses of individual women to the opportunities and the difficulties inherent in their new lives.

## To Where Shall We Go for Teachers?

Not surprisingly, one of the first occupations to which women turned was teaching, an endeavor that seemed closely related to women's traditional maternal responsibilities as nurturers and instructors of their own young. In the North, a feminization of teaching had already occurred in the antebellum era, but the South had not encouraged women to assume classroom responsibilities. In North Carolina in 1860, for example, only 7 percent of teachers were women. During the war, however, this proportion rose significantly, until by the end of the conflict there were as many female as male teachers in the state.[6]

Public discourse in the Confederacy devoted considerable attention to this dramatic shift and to its larger implications about woman's intellect and character. The most common and direct argument for change insisted that women needed teaching and teaching needed women. As Calvin Wiley, superintendent of common schools for North Carolina, noted in his annual report for 1862, "Many ladies are compelled by the circumstances of the times, to labor for a living; and there is no employment better suited to the female nature, and none in which ladies can labor more usefully, than in the business of forming the hearts and minds of the young." The *Augusta Daily Constitutionalist* echoed Wiley's insistence that teaching was well suited to women's essential attributes. "Women," the paper sonorously declared, "are peculiarly fitted, naturally and morally, for teachers of the young." But the editor soon descended from the lofty heights of the classic argument from design to more practical considerations. The effect of the war had been to "swallow up" young men. "We are left no resource then but to have female teachers. . . . They must of necessity be our teachers, or we shall have to dispense with any."[7]

The *Central Presbyterian* similarly regarded the issue as "eminently a practical question." Announcing that the Female College of Statesville, North Carolina, had added a teachers' department, the paper urged that, like their brothers who had marched off to war, "the young ladies of our . . . country should volunteer in this service." J. K. Kirkpatrick, president of Davidson College, also perceived a parallel between male soldiers and female teachers—and anticipated some of the same parental resistance to sending daughters to the classroom as sons to battle. But he sought to enlist warborn patriotism in the cause of education. "It may not be just such a life as you may prefer for your daughter. . . . You have made your sons an offering on your country's altar. Would you withhold your daughters from a service, noble in itself and befitting their sex, without which their country must be subjected to a yoke more disgraceful and oppressive than that our ruthless enemies would lay upon our necks—the yoke of ignorance and its consequences, vice and degradation?" To a graduating class of North Carolina women, Kirkpatrick bluntly declared, "*Our females must engage in the work of teaching*. . . . [T]here is no other alternative."[8]

Wartime necessity and female nature combined to make this "enlargement of the sphere of employment for women" not just necessary but natural and desirable, at least in the ideological pronouncements of Confederate public discourse. The South, *De Bow's Review* counseled in 1861, must overcome its tendency to "rank teaching among the *menial* employments" or to regard it as "socially degrading" or "fit for Yankees only."[9]

As *De Bow's* noted, however, the difficulties to be surmounted extended well beyond these necessary shifts in attitude. The South lacked an adequate system of female instruction. Although the southern states had a "vast number" of institutions for educating women, which had certainly "effected a great amount of good," these schools had not for the most part "established that high grade of scholarship and literary attainment which ought to characterize Southern women"—particularly if these women were to be the educators of the new nation's men. The Confederacy's need for female teachers spawned a movement for the reform and upgrading of women's education and an examination of prevailing assumptions about the character of woman's intellect. *De Bow's* was explicit about the kind of curricular revisions it deemed necessary: the rigorous instruction of females in math, classics, and natural science, subjects that had often been slighted, if not omitted altogether, in girls' schooling. "Must she ever be cut off from the invigorating discipline of mathematics? Must the treasures which lie buried in the Grecian and Roman literature be always hidden from her eyes? Must the immense volume of nature be ever a sealed book?"[10]

The anonymous writer in *De Bow's* directly confronted the fundamental issue underlying the debate over female education. "There is a belief, unexpressed though it may be, that the female mind is . . . inferior to the male." Calling for governmental support for women's education, the author hedged about the question of gender equality, arguing that even if women were inferior intellectually, they deserved better schooling. "While then, we would not affirm that there are no original and congenital differences between man and woman, we do believe that the actual difference in the intellectual status of man and woman is mainly due to the different courses of training and development to which custom has subjected the two sexes. . . . But we do not go to the length of maintaining an absolute equality in the sexes." "Equivalence," yes; "equality," no, the author concluded. Yet even in stepping back from a radical claim for female intellectual parity, the author advocated dramatically changed policies that made abstract distinctions between "equality" and "equivalence" almost moot.[11]

The *Southern Field and Fireside* of Augusta picked up the discussion, adopting a similarly tactical approach to educational reform in an essay entitled "Educated Woman—In Peace and War." "It is not proposed here to insist upon her mental equality with man," the journal reassured its readers, "but that whether she is his equal or inferior in mind, she is none the less entitled to all the advantages which mental, moral and physical training can impart to her frail nature." This author—tantalizingly genderless in her or his anonymity—went beyond pragmatic justifications for female education to empower women with a fundamental entitlement to learning.[12]

Writers clearly identified as male argued in similar terms. Dr. James D. Ramsey addressed the "young ladies" of Concord Female College in North Carolina in 1863, dismissing the notion that any "mental advantage" remained with men and explaining any differences in achievement as the result of inadequate education for women. "No nation," he warned, "has grown great and strong, when women were not strong and great." Edward Joynes, a professor at Hollins College, argued forcefully for the education of women as teachers, declaring the current system of female instruction "a shallow pretension and a gross outrage." But Joynes was careful to maintain the notion of separate spheres, even as he advocated significant change. A reformed system of women's schooling "should be based upon the idea that *woman is woman*, and not *man*—nor a butterfly," neither man's "plaything nor his rival." A Confederate education should aim "to educate neither *belles* nor *bluestockings*, but *women*, for *women's sphere*." Neither existing southern nor northern models satisfied the professor. The new nation, born out of destructive war, had very special responsibilities to women. "They will occupy a larger space not only in relative numbers, but in relative influence." Woman's career must advance together with that of the Confederacy.[13]

Joynes had very practical ends in mind as he composed his essay, for he offered alongside his principles of female learning and national greatness a detailed plan for the founding of a normal school at Hollins, complete with government-supported scholarships for needy students. In 1864 Hollins launched this formal program for the training of women teachers, but with scholarships supported through donations rather than by public funds. The practical concerns of Confederate educational reformers about curriculum had their influence as well. The catalog of Tuscaloosa Female College in Alabama, for example, proudly advertised a "prominence in the course of instruction" for ancient languages equaled by "very few Female Colleges in the country" and listed algebra, geometry, trigonometry, and experimental natural science as central to its course of study.[14]

Despite the careful effort of educational reformers to deny and contain the radicalism inherent in their proposals, at least some public voices in the Confederacy recognized and decried the subversive implications of these wartime innovations. An essayist in the *Southern Illustrated News* noted in 1862 that it had "of late become extremely fashionable to advance woman, in the scale of intellect to an equal standard with man." The journal objected to this departure. When woman "aspires to ambitious situations, she steps out of the sphere allotted her by Nature, and assumes a character which is an outrage upon her feminine delicacy and loveliness." Some of these same reservations characterized individual southern women's responses to the opportunities and challenges of teaching.

In Huntsville, Alabama, Mary Jane Cook Chadick observed a "mania for teaching" among the "young ladies" of the town and regarded the enthusiasm as "certainly praiseworthy for if the young ladies do not volunteer their services in educating the present generation, to where shall we go for teachers?" *Mania* is a term that seems appropriately to describe the dozens of newspaper notices placed by young women seeking positions as teachers or governesses. Many of these advertisers were refugees, seeking new households in which to reside as eagerly as they sought employment. As one "Young Lady from Louisiana" explained in the *Richmond Enquirer*'s columns in 1863, she wished "to obtain a situation as a Teacher in a private family. . . . A pleasant home is more the object than salary."[15]

Virginia Daniel Woodruff, however, entered her new classroom in fulfillment of a lifelong search for purpose and achievement. Looking over the heads of a dozen "flaxen haired" girls, she celebrated her "place found at last, the vision that has been milling before me since childhood realised now in my position." Her original hopes had been more ambitious, she revealed, displaying some of the ambivalence that seemed to characterize so many of the Confederacy's new educators. As a young girl, "I never thought a teacher's life enviable." But she had revised her ambitions to meet available opportunities. "When planning for the future I could think of nothing else that would give me so wide a field of usefulness."[16]

Women found that teaching met their need not just for a place and purpose but served as well to distract them from the anxious idleness of wartime waiting and watching. Abbie Brooks's duty to nineteen pupils in Tennessee "entirely occupies my mind. I have no time to think of my troubles, or anything unpleasant, except my school troubles." As a refugee, Mary Stringfield had painfully felt "the lack of something *definite to do*," so she took on a school to ensure she would "not be idly dependent upon the bounty of my friends." Yet she was not entirely sanguine about what lay before her. "I *dread* the conflict of stupidity, ignorance and *ungoverned child* passions. But I anticipate the pleasure of interest and duty also." In spite of straitened circumstances, Jennie Pendleton of Mississippi was determined not to teach, for she feared "I would lose all my dignity." Emily Perkins expressed horror at a friend's decision to teach: "Do you know what you are undertaking? . . . A life of self denial and pain." Sarah Morgan, Louisiana refugee, was far from enthusiastic as she contemplated teaching as an alternative to poverty and homelessness. "I'll work for my living. How I wonder? I will teach. . . . I would rather die than teach. . . . My soul revolts from the drudgery." She, like many of the critics of the movement for female teachers, regarded it as largely menial work, certainly undesirable, and probably inappropriate for southern ladies.[17]

Relatives of young women caught up in the teaching "mania" often shared Morgan's perspective. Even though the family desperately needed the financial support, Elizabeth Grimball's mother was "terribly mortified" by her daughter's plan to teach, and Lizzie Smith had to argue strenuously to overcome her father's and brothers' opposition to her work in the village school. A New Orleans woman badly in need of funds informed her husband in the army that she had thought of opening a school but had given up the idea in anticipation of his objections. Jo Gillis of Alabama deferred when her husband, an army chaplain, "vetoed my going to Benton to teach" in spite of her deep "disappointment." But a year later she was established in a new school. "I have braved all opposition, and the displeasure of all who love me and come here to teach. . . . I thought I never could be contented without teaching. . . . Mr. Gillis is very much *hurt at my perversity*."[18]

On the job, women often found good reason for their doubts and ambivalence. Caroline Davis confronted a classroom of unruly boys who made her "wish I did know better how to teach—I feel my inability often enough." When she lost her temper, she felt guilty, then longed for escape. "I wish at times I could get entirely out of hearing of every child on earth." Clara MacLean of South Carolina, compelled by her lack of income to take in pupils, compared the schoolroom to a place of combat, but she supposed "my lot is no harder than that which falls to the lot of every teacher. Since I have entered the lists, the heart-burnings, the tears, the bitterness always attending that occupation have become 'household-words' to me." A refugee from the South Carolina lowcountry, Emma Holmes took up teaching out of boredom as well as financial need. Struck by the social differences between herself and her new pupils, she could "hardly recognize my own identity, surrounded as I often am by such democratic specimens" as filled her classroom. She at first embraced the experience as "refreshing to my aristocratic prejudices" and assured her diary that she never let her sense of superiority show. But despite her good intentions Holmes was soon complaining about the ignorant "clod pates" she was required to instruct and quarreling with the parents who employed her. When in a fit of temper she informed two of her pupils that they were "dunces," she lost her post. In Georgia, Emma Slade Prescott assumed the duties of a village teacher who left for the army. "Before I had time to think about it almost—I was teaching." After just two months, however, she quit because "the nervous strain was too much for me."[19]

By contrast Abbie Brooks exclaimed that she was "enjoying" herself in the classroom "as well as I ever expect to this side of Heaven." But even she admitted "it is very hard work." With students all placed together in a single class, she had to deal with every level of learning "from Natural Philosophy down to cat." In addition, she found the financial yield from her efforts highly discouraging. When she settled her year's board bill, she discovered she had made nothing beyond her subsistence. Competition for pupils was in many areas of the South very keen, and financially pressed parents proved unwilling—and often unable—to offer generous or sometimes even adequate salaries. Amelia Pinkind remarked in 1862 that everything in the Confederacy was rising in price except teaching: "That they want done for very little, next to nothing."[20]

## Us Poor Treasury Girls

By 1864 Elizabeth Richmond of Caswell County, North Carolina, was so "worn out" with teaching's "duties and privations" that she wrote to Governor Vance in hopes of finding "a place of employment that will not require as much energy of mind and body, and yet, will give me a comfortable support." She, like hundreds of other southern women who petitioned Confederate and state officials, sought a government clerkship.[21]

As the Confederacy struggled to place every able-bodied white man in the ranks, officials turned to women to fill many of the resulting civilian vacancies. Women were employed in the War Department, the Post Office, the Quartermaster Department, and the office of the Commissary General, but the Treasury Department held the largest proportion of these posts. Females signed each of the hundreds of thousands of Confederate banknotes by hand and helped as well to cut the sheets on which the bills were printed.

The allocation of this "department work" is curious, for it seems to have been a form of government welfare distributed on the basis of gender and class. Ladies of the South's privileged orders who had fallen on hard times constituted the overwhelming majority of the women who received these desirable situations, and the recommendation of well-connected friends exerted significant influence. Women petitioned Davis for the jobs, emphasizing their need for assistance, the sacrifices they had made for the Cause, and their dependence, in the absence of other male support, on the Confederate president. "My only apology for troubling you with this communication," wrote Diana Johnston, a young war widow of Mobile, "arises from the fact that I regard you as 'the Father of the people' over whom God has called you to preside, and believe therefore that even amid the engrossing and perplexing cares of public business, there is sympathy in your great and noble heart for individual suffering, and a just regard for private claims." Lizzie Yarrington was upset when she had to write a second time in search of government employment, for she had expected the state to acknowledge and provide for her needs. "I think I deserve this at the hands of a government for which I have been gratuitously laboring since the first year of the war. To my eyes it looks very inconsistent that now when I am in absolute distress that I am unable to obtain assistance." General Samuel Cooper testified to the requisite "standing and necessities" of a seventy-eight-year-old widow who sought the "patronage" of a job in the War Department, but then he went on to explain that not she but a young relative would actually do the work of copying reports. Miss M. H. Sydnor informed Davis of her sad decline from "a state of independence" and sought to strengthen her claims to office by promising recommendations "to prove me to be a lady of the first social position." Catherine Windle of Williamsburg referred to the posts as "Government gifts" in Davis's "bestowal" to meet her urgent circumstances.[22]

Other women felt they deserved jobs not so much because of their past contributions to the Confederacy or because of their pronounced distress, but because of their superior qualifications, attributes often indistinguishable from their social standing. Treasury posts required elegant handwriting, so the fashionably educated held a clear advantage. Jefferson Davis scribbled on the petition of a Yorktown refugee for a Treasury job, "Writing as shown by this note is quite good." Another applicant submitted a sample of her name signed twenty-five times.[23]

The salary scale for female clerks reveals their social location and influence as well. Privates in the Confederate army were paid $11 a month. In 1862 and 1863, by contrast, female clerks received $65. By 1864 the annual salary of women holding Treasury posts had risen to $3,000 in the South's depreciated currency. These women were seen to be worth more than the Confederacy's ordinary fighting men and to have needs and expectations for special treatment that the Confederacy did not wish to gainsay. Clearly, too, they were regarded differently from most other females in national service.[24]

Ordinary women performed a variety of government work across the South. Seamstresses for the Clothing Bureau—3,000 to 4,000 of whom took in piecework in Richmond by the last years of the war—made $1.00 for a shirt, $1.50 for a pair of pants, or $4.00 for a coat, which might take days to complete. In Augusta the 500 women employed by the Georgia Soldiers'

Clothing Bureau made $6.00 to $12.00 a week. Arsenal workers in the same city sewed cartridges for $1.00 a day. Richmond's female ordnance workers, nearly 50 of whom were killed in an explosion in March 1863, confronted danger as well as low wages, and they organized to express their grievances in a strike for better pay. One supporter of their action saw clearly the differentiation the Confederate government made between these female workers and their well-connected and well-born counterparts. "Why is it that . . . poor women engaged in a perilous and hazardous occupation . . . are denied a living compensation for their labour, when so many of the departments are filled with *young ladies* (not dependent on their pay) with nothing to do, at salaries equal to and in some cases better than the best male clerks in the different departments?"[25]

Meanwhile Mary Darby DeTreville, employed in the Treasury Department, felt embarrassed to receive any salary at all. She worked assiduously signing notes at an expected rate of 3,200 between 9:00 in the morning and 3:00 in the afternoon each day. But "when pay-day came, the first time I had ever worked for wages, how mean I felt when I went up and signed for my pay." Volunteer work could be incorporated within the image of woman as ministering angel, as moral force; uncompensated labor could be seen as simply an extension of the work women did for their families. It involved no entry into the public world of the marketplace, and it offered no fundamental threat to woman's ultimate dependence. Wage labor, however, posed serious challenges to existing assumptions about behavior appropriate to women of the South's ruling class. At the same time arsenal employees advanced their claim to specific rights as wage laborers, their elite sisters still maintained their commitment to the familial relationships of female dependence, relationships in which support was expected as the bounty—the "gift," as Catherine Windle put it—of the benevolent patriarch. That this benevolence now came in the form of office employment marked a significant departure, but that it was bestowed by the supreme earthly father, Jefferson Davis, in response to humbling petitions begging assistance represented strong continuity with the past. It is revealing that unlike white working-class women striking for a living wage, Mary DeTreville felt uneasy about the notion of wages and paid work altogether. With its implication of individual right and of autonomy and independence, the exchange of labor for wages controverted the tenets of the social order of paternalism within which privileged white women had established their place and constructed their identity.[26]

Criticism of "department girls" was fervent and widespread. Clara Mac-

Lean, who had herself grudgingly taken up teaching, disapproved of a friend who spent her days cutting Confederate bonds, then had to walk home "in the broiling sun. See what this dreadful war has brought delicate ladies to." Mary Chesnut was even more horrified by the notion of women working in public, outside the "rooftree" of the prescribed domestic sphere. She and her friend Mrs. John Preston vowed never to submit to such degradation. "Survive or perish—we will not go into one of the departments. We will not stand up all day and cut notes apart, ordered round by a department clerk. We will live at home with our families and starve in a body. Any homework we will do. Any menial service—under the shadow of our own rooftree. Department—never!"[27]

Perhaps a generational difference made Adelaide Stuart, just twenty, more enthusiastic about the Treasury post she assumed in 1864, for she proclaimed herself able to adapt "easily to all circumstances." Within six months she had developed "much greater facility than formerly in signing my name" and was able to finish early and help slower employees complete their daily quotas. In September 1864 she reported proudly "a compliment paid to me at the office—The 4500 bills are only given to a few favoured girls who have great beauty of signature." With her days filled with work and her evenings occupied by social outings, Stuart had "not a moment to myself." But she was thriving. "I am rarely ill now even with a headache—the fact is I have not the time to be giving up to such lady like ailments as nervousness—headaches etc." Stuart concluded that the "loss of property" that had pushed her into the workforce was "the best thing that could have taken place for me—It is bringing into active service, & strengthening all the best parts of my character & enabling me to root out all that was objectionable."[28]

Malvina Gist, who at age twenty lost her husband to war, seemed quickly to forget her grief amidst the excitement of her new Treasury job. As the speed of her signature increased, her employer assured her she was "a treasury girl worth having." But Gist seemed more interested in her activities outside the department. When Sherman threatened Columbia, Gist prayed the note bureau would not be returned to the comparative safety of Richmond. "It is high time," she asserted, "I was having some experiences out of the ordinary. . . . I want to stay. I want to have a taste of danger." In fact, the move to Richmond proved highly satisfactory. The secretary invited all "us poor Treasury girls" for a dinner and somehow managed to produce, even in the last weeks of the war, a "varied menu, elegantly prepared and daintily served." With her dead husband apparently forgotten, Gist was most thrilled by the Confederate capital's "surging, intoxicating stream" of men in uniform. Gist's and Stuart's independence was just what clucking matrons like Mary Chesnut regarded as most dangerous about women's new public roles.[29]

## The Florence Nightingale Business

When elite Confederate women began to offer their labor in the South's military hospitals, they undertook perhaps their most dramatic and frightening departure from traditional female roles. In the twentieth century, nursing has become so overwhelmingly female that the notion of women hospital workers as threatening is difficult to comprehend. In the mid-nineteenth century, however, hospital nursing was regarded as employment appropriate only for individuals of the lower classes and preferably of the male sex. In the immediate pre–Civil War years, convalescent patients of both sexes joined skilled workers who had often risen from the status of inmates to that of long-term hospital employees to serve as nurses. In almost all cases, these were, like early nineteenth-century hospital patients generally, individuals from humble backgrounds and circumstances. In professional armies, nurses were almost invariably detailed or disabled soldiers, males, of course, who fit neatly within the structures of military hierarchy and routine.

Manpower shortages, escalating casualty rates, and patriotic ambitions, however, overrode custom and pushed southern women toward work with the sick and wounded, a movement encouraged by the innovative and much admired role Florence Nightingale had played in Britain's Crimean War of 1853–56. A woman of unchallenged respectability and high social standing, Nightingale had through her selfless actions and her widely read *Notes on Nursing*, first published in the United States in 1860, established a conceptual legitimation for female nursing. The notion that woman's moral and emotional attributes uniquely fitted her for hospital work gained strength and currency, and women North and South found in Nightingale a model for female heroism.[30]

Yet resistance to nursing as indelicate—it did after all involve some level of intimacy with male bodies, often those of the "degraded" classes—persisted, and physicians and medical officials struggled against the logic of expanding female authority inherent in the Nightingale program. Within the Confederacy, nursing became the focus of public debate as well as the site of overt class and gender conflict, for inconsistent sets of assumptions warred against one another within hospital settings, within the families of prospective nurses, and even within individual women torn between imperatives of service and of propriety.

Like teaching, nursing seemed in one sense an almost natural undertaking for women, an obvious component, as one hospital matron described it, of "woman's true sphere." The *Mobile Advertiser and Register* found the "spectacle" of women attending to Richmond's wounded as "inexpressibly touching. All the poetical phrases which describe woman as a 'ministering angel,' fail to convey the idea of the wonderful new reality now enacting before our eyes." Women could serve as substitutes for soldiers' absent mothers and sisters, dressing "their wounds of mind," the *Milledgeville Southern Federal Union* explained, as well as their bodily injuries.[31]

From the outset, however, even those public voices encouraging female nursing expressed reservations. The *Confederate Baptist* offered its general approval but warned about women's assumption of undue power on the wards. "In their proper sphere," wrote the paper in an invocation of the standard language of female subordination, "they are most valuable auxiliaries; but when they presume to direct or control the physician, their services may well be dispensed with." Even more worrisome was the challenge of hospital work to women's "delicacy," "modesty," and "refinement." An essayist in the *Southern Monthly* of May 1862 at once praised Florence Nightingale and warned against regarding her as a model for women of the South. "Many of her eulogists," he wrote, "have forgotten to place due limitations on their recommendation of her example. Her unselfish and heroic spirit, we should all aspire to; her deeds were such as few are fitted to perform." Ladies, he urged, should satisfy themselves with making clothes for soldiers and providing "comforts and delicacies" for camp and hospital. "Such services can be performed without a doubt of their propriety."[32]

As in so many dimensions of Confederate women's experience, the unanticipated demands of an ever expanding war soon began to undermine abstract ideological commitments to notions of appropriate female roles. Eager to be useful, southern women greeted the appearance of unexpected numbers of sick and wounded soldiers in the summer of 1861 as an opportunity for action, an eagerly sought means of contributing to the Cause. Many of their efforts grew out of the existing sewing and soldiers' aid societies, as ladies simply shifted their attention from clothing to healing. By mid-August, for example, the Ladies Aiken Relief Association of South Carolina was gathering medicine for shipment to the front. The ladies of Portsmouth, Virginia, turned an abandoned hotel into a hospital. Georgia women formed the Atlanta Hospital Association and at the same time collected boxes of wine, syrup, jam, and linens to forward to field hospitals in Virginia. The Ladies Soldiers Aid Society of Natural Bridge, Virginia, invited invalid Confederate soldiers to recuperate in their homes and partake of the healthful mountain air.[33]

Women nearer battlefields and troop encampments subject to waves of epidemic disease soon felt compelled toward more direct intervention in behalf of soldiers' health. Mary Rutledge Fogg of Nashville presumed on her descent from Edmund Rutledge and Arthur Middleton, both signers of the Declaration of Independence, to request Jefferson Davis's assistance in establishing badly needed hospitals in Memphis and Knoxville as well as her own city. Having witnessed "*50* brave soldiers" die "for the *want* of proper nurses," she reported to Davis, she had, through the auspices of the Ladies Tennessee Hospital and Clothing Association, recruited "a corps" of women to send as nurses to Virginia. She intended, she informed the president, to dispatch them the very next day—whether anyone in Virginia was prepared to receive them or not.

Other women of equally illustrious background, empowered in no small part by the habit of command and the sense of *oblige* that accompanied their *noblesse*, undertook extemporaneous efforts to deal with the suffering that confronted them. Letitia Tyler Semple, relative of the tenth president, arrived in Williamsburg in the summer of 1861 with the intention of helping sick soldiers and discovered, she informed Davis, much to be done "in the domestic arrangement" of the hospital. She assumed full charge of all "details of kitchen, pantry and laundry" and asked the president, seemingly somewhat after the fact, to appoint her female superintendent of the Williamsburg and two other hospitals. In the days after First Manassas, Sallie Tompkins, of distinguished Virginia lineage, applied some of her substantial means to outfit a Richmond house as a hospital that ministered to soldiers throughout the remainder of the war. Juliet Opie Hopkins, who reportedly had managed her father's sizable slaveholding in western Virginia before her 1854 marriage to an Alabama judge, arrived in Richmond in the summer of 1861 and took charge of provisions and organization for the hospitals treating Alabama troops. She was referred to as both matron and superintendent and eventually had her picture placed on Alabama state currency, even though she seems never to have held any official position in the Confederate medical structure. "If you had been a man," one of her Alabama male admirers wrote her, "you would have been a commanding general." His wife, he reported, particularly admired Hopkins for "your talents for operating on a large sphere—as it is all . . . [my wife] can do to sew on shirts &c for the soldiers."

*Juliet Opie Hopkins, hospital matron and superintendent. Courtesy of the Alabama Department of Archives and History, Montgomery.*

The dearth of trained nurses in the South, the crying need for medical care, and the energy of women seeking a means to make a contribution to the Cause combined in the early months of war to encourage exceptional and privileged southern women to improvise solutions to the suffering they could not, as women, bear to ignore. While few thought or acted as daringly as Fogg, Semple, or Hopkins, women responded to the confusion and crisis of Confederate medical care by inventing new roles and new institutions. Always in the forefront of their minds, the compelling story of Florence Nightingale helped them imagine how they might serve and emboldened them to claim nursing as within their female sphere.[34]

By the middle of the first year of war, women's organizations across the

Confederacy had devised one of the war's most innovative and successful medical facilities, the wayside home or hospital, a combination infirmary and travelers' aid for wounded soldiers in transit home from the front. In October 1862 the *Milledgeville Confederate Union* enthusiastically pronounced judgment: "This is one of the best institutions which the war has developed in our country." Fourteen women of Union Point, Georgia, established such a hospital in the fall of 1862, and in the following two years they registered in excess of 20,000 soldiers who had benefited from more than a million meals and other services provided. In North Carolina, Louise Medway estimated that the Soldiers' Aid Society established by Wilmington's ladies fed and dressed the wounds of between 6,000 and 8,000 soldiers a month as they passed through that port city. Yet these efforts by women in their hometowns across the South could not begin to meet the need for battlefield care. By mid-1862 casualty rates would mount to unimagined heights—more than 20,000, for example, in a single day's fighting at Antietam.[35]

Brigadier General J. B. Magruder was only one of a number of Confederate commanders to believe volunteer soldiers ill suited to the care and nursing of the sick and wounded, and he petitioned the secretary of war to be permitted to hire black women as nurses. Magruder thought such laborers would be in "every way suitable to perform these duties," fitted by both race and gender to subservience and menial labor as well as to the particularly female work of caregiving. Whether in response to Magruder's suggestion or simply as a matter of prudent policy, large numbers of slaves, male and female, were in the course of the war hired to serve in hospital wards across the Confederacy. But deficiencies in patient care and management persisted.

Attacks on Confederate military medicine and especially hospital administration and staffing were so widespread during the summer of 1861 that legislators felt compelled to investigate. A committee appointed by the Confederate Congress in August to examine conditions in the Commissary, Quartermaster, and Medical Departments discovered significant inadequacies in nursing services and noted a severe shortage of personnel. The one bright spot in the report seemed to be its concluding testimonial to the "women of the country," who with "the tenderness and generosity of their sex," had offered provisions, funds, and service to the Confederacy's hospitals.[36]

But complaints about disorder, inadequate care, and patient neglect continued. Kate Cumming, daughter of a wealthy Mobile merchant, confronted chaos in the hospital where she worked after the battle of Shiloh in April

1862. "We have men for nurses, and the doctors complain very much at the manner in which they are appointed; they are detailed from the different regiments, like guards. We have a new set every few hours. I cannot see how it is possible for them to take proper care of the men, as nursing is a thing that has to be learned, and we should select our best men for it—the best, not physically, but morally." This widely shared sense of the healing strength of moral force, powerfully articulated by Florence Nightingale, reinforced pressure for the acceptance of women, regarded as terrestrial custodians of virtue, into nursing.[37]

A committee on hospitals chaired by Senator William Simms of Kentucky investigated continuing complaints about military medicine and encouraged a growing appreciation for women's contribution to improved care. There could be little doubt, the report proclaimed, about "the superiority of female nurses as compared with males. . . . When males have charge, the mortality averages ten per cent; where females manage, it is only five percent." Objections to female nursing could not prevail against such powerful statistics. As Senator Semmes of Louisiana explained, "I will not agree to limit the class of persons who can affect such a saving of life as this."[38]

In September 1862 Congress adopted legislation that specifically designated positions for women in military hospitals. Two matrons were charged with "superintendence over the entire domestic economy of the hospital, to take charge of such delicacies as may be provided for the sick, to apportion them out as required, to see that the food or diet is properly prepared and all such other duties as may be necessary" for a salary of $40 a month. Two assistant matrons bore responsibility for the laundry, the clothing and bedding of the sick, and other necessary duties, for a salary of $35 a month. Each ward would have two ward matrons, salaried at $30 a month to prepare beds and bedding, assure cleanliness, administer medicine, and supervise nursing. In addition surgeons were charged with procuring nurses at $25 a month, with "preference in all cases to females where their services may best subserve the purpose." The much celebrated and oft repeated statistics on the successes of female hospital supervision encouraged the Confederate government to enact a measure of labor force management that also served as one of its very few explicit efforts to deal with the role of women in the creation of the new nation. In the face of persisting reservations among the southern people at large about the appropriateness of female hospital work, the Confederate government invoked traditional notions of female nurturance to support a manpower policy that filled noncombatant jobs with individuals ineligible for military service. It seems not insignificant that the

Confederate Senate debated the new hospital bill and the proposed amendments to conscription and exemption policy, those that would result in the October enactment of the infamous "Twenty-Nigger Law," on the very same day. The legislation of September 1862 was a significant intervention—both ideological and practical—by the government into the family as both ideal and reality, one that called for the subordination of the domestic to the service of the state and the nation in the service of total mobilization and total war. Together with the conscription and exemption policies enacted in April and October of the same year, the Hospital Act represented an important statement of Confederate policy concerning the relationship of the state to its female citizens.[39]

Phoebe Yates Levy Pember, a thirty-nine-year-old widow from a prominent and prosperous South Carolina family, was living unhappily with refugee relatives in Marietta, Georgia, when in November 1862 her friend Mrs. George Randolph, wife of the Confederate secretary of war, urged her to apply for one of the newly created matron's posts. By the end of the year Pember had assumed her duties at Hospital #2 of the enormous Chimborazo complex in Richmond. She was not without reservations about this departure from her customary life and from prevailing standards of female gentility. "The natural idea that such a life would be injurious to the delicacy and refinement of a lady—that her nature would become deteriorated and her sensibilities blunted, was rather appalling." But it was less appalling, apparently, than remaining with those "who never cared for me."[40]

Pember was well aware of the revolution in hospital management and gender roles that her arrival marked, as were the surgeons and doctors who greeted her presence with "horror" as the advent of an unwanted "petticoat government" imposed by the recent legislation. A particularly blunt physician welcomed her to Chimborazo by noting in "a tone of ill-concealed disgust, that 'one of them had come.' "[41]

Prior to the law of September 1862, Pember observed, "there had been a great deal of desultory visiting and nursing, by the women" across the South, which, she judged, had resulted in "more harm than benefit to the patients." Pember had no doubt heard the tales cherished by those opposed to female hospital work—the story of the young girl who killed a dysentery patient by feeding him turnovers, or the woman who loosened an amputee's bandages and caused him to bleed to death, or the soldier who simply had to put up with a dozen eager but useless volunteers washing his face in a single morning. Even with the field "open" for a significant and regularized

*Phoebe Yates Levy Pember, matron at Chimborazo Hospital. Courtesy of the Eleanor S. Brockenbrough Library, Museum of the Confederacy, Richmond, Virginia.*

contribution from southern females as a result of the new legislation, Pember complained that only "a few, very few ladies, and a great many inefficient and uneducated women, hardly above the laboring classes, applied for and filled the offices."

A number of women of prominent background did take matron's posts during the war. Kate Cumming, Ella Newsom, Fannie Beers, and Emily Mason all recorded their experiences in memoirs widely read in the postwar years. For the most part, however, southern ladies regarded a matron's duties as too laborious, too indelicate for women of their social standing. When Ada Bacot of South Carolina was invited to assume the matronship of Midway Hospital in Charlottesville after a year of working as a volunteer, she declined upon the advice of a physician who had become her patron and friend during her months of hospital service. "He . . . was of the opinion I had better stay where I am[,] that I was not born in the same station of life that Mrs. Rion [the departing matron] was[,] that I had never been accustomed to labour, therefore I could not undergo what she did except at the expense of comfort, pleasure & health."[42]

Phoebe Pember did indeed find her new post just such a challenge to her peace of mind and her physical well-being. Housekeeping, cooking, and nursing for 700 men was now her responsibility, and, she confessed, she did not even understand the meaning of "requisition," much less how to place one. But when she tentatively asked for a pair of chickens from the steward, they seemed to appear miraculously, confronting Pember with yet another test of will and commitment. "For the first time I cut up with averted eyes a raw bird, and the Rubicon was passed."[43]

Far more troubling than these adjustments to new tasks was the continuing hostility Pember faced from doctors and staff. The hospital as she described it was a battleground of class and gender, exacerbated by the new legislation appointing and empowering women. For Pember, the focus of these conflicts became what she dubbed the "wars of the whiskey barrel," the fight over control of medicinal liquor. The law entrusted whiskey to the matron's government, a provision surgeons regarded with great resentment as an inappropriate embodiment of female authority. Pember, well aware of the propensity of some physicians to help themselves to cheering nips from the hospital barrel, saw matters of both principle and practicality in her retention of control.

In anticipation of the battles to come, Pember selected ward nurses with this issue in mind. Although she preferred males, for "good and strong reasons" that she unfortunately chose not to explain, she decided to hire women upon "the supposition that liquor would be no temptation to them." Ladies of Pember's own social class drank sparingly of wines and cordials and rarely touched hard liquor. But Pember erred in assuming this to be universal female behavior. She was mistaken, too, in her expectation that women of "the common class of respectable servants" would be "more amenable to authority" than "ladies of education and position." Pember received neither deference nor sobriety from her new employees. One woman took advantage of female control of the whiskey barrel to get drunk. Another appropriated hospital furniture and partitioned off ward space to set herself up in comfortable living quarters, where, to Pember's horror, the new nurses sat around a spittoon and dipped snuff. All resented that Pember did not invite them to call, for they " 'considered themselves quite as much ladies as I was.' " Only the intervention of the surgeon-in-chief in support of Pember's authority enabled her to dismiss the unsatisfactory employees. Challenges of both class and gender had undermined Pember's position.[44]

In the continuing wars of the whiskey barrel, the chief surgeon proved "an unfailing refuge," one of a number of men whose helpfulness permitted Pember to assure her readers that "antagonism was not always the rule" between the matron and male hospital staff. Neither was it the exception, however, and Pember's experience was far from unique. Kate Cumming, serving as matron in hospitals of the western theater, encountered similar hostility. From the outset she noted that there was "a good deal of trouble about the ladies in some of the hospitals of this department. Our friends here have advised us to go home, as they say it is not considered respectable." At first she, like Pember, wavered about the propriety of her new position, but the possibility of alleviating some of the terrible suffering she had witnessed and the legitimating model of Florence Nightingale reinforced her determination. "It seems strange," she wrote, "that the aristocratic women of Great Britain have done with honor what is a disgrace for their sisters on this side of the Atlantic to do." For Cumming the Christian and feminine imperative of service far outweighed superficial notions of female delicacy. Employing one dimension of feminine ideology to dismiss another, Cumming despaired of her southern sisters, inhibited by false claims of modesty and respectability from undertaking desperately needed hospital work.[45]

Empowered by her strong sense of mission, Cumming was undaunted by male opposition. "It is useless," she proclaimed, "to say the surgeons will not allow us; we have our rights, and if asserted properly will get them. This is our right and ours alone." In practice these rights would prove more difficult to secure. In the summer of 1863 Cumming left one Georgia hospital because the hostility of the chief surgeon so hindered her effectiveness. She recorded daily conflicts very like those Pember experienced in Richmond. Her story of a "triumph for us ladies" in the summer of 1864 is telling. A woman had concocted a lotion for use against inflammation, but the surgeons at first ignored it "as it had been made by a lady." When the substance seemed to have undeniably positive effects, however, one doctor requested more. Such a simple acknowledgment of female competence warranted not just notice but celebration in Cumming's eyes.[46]

Cumming's complaints were not restricted to men. Throughout her diary she railed against the failure of Confederate ladies to do the nursing work the nation so desperately required. "Are the women of the South going into the hospitals? I am afraid candor will compel me to say they are not! It is not respectable, and requires too constant attention, and a hospital has none of the comforts of home!" She had, she declared, "no patience with women whom I hear telling what wonders they would do if they were only men, when I see so much of their legitimate work left undone. . . . I could name many things they could do," she continued in a revealing concession to prevailing anxieties about respectability, "without ever going into a ward."[47]

As Kate Cumming's criticisms remind us, she and Phoebe Pember were exceptions within their class in their assumption of formal, full-time, remunerated hospital work. Yet "nursing" within the Confederate South extended well beyond such structured roles, defining a universe of activities quite different from what we would consider nursing today. In fact, we might well describe Pember and Cumming as hospital administrators rather than nurses, for they were not responsible for direct patient care. Cumming confessed that she never dressed a wound until May 1864, more than two years after her entry onto the wards. As she described her work, "It is as much as we can do to see that the nurses"—in her case overwhelmingly detailed soldiers and slaves—"do their duty."[48]

What southern women called "nursing," we might better designate as "hospital work," for it encompassed a wide variation in activities and levels of commitment that persisted in spite of legislative efforts to regularize hospital labor. Perhaps the most widespread and most casual of these undertakings was hospital visiting. Emma Crutcher, a young Mississippi wife, made this distinction explicit when she wrote to her husband in the army informing him that she had been appointed to Vicksburg's "visiting committee, for next week (not nursing, remember)." After her first day's experience, she announced she had "enlisted for the war." But in spite of the implication of free choice in the military language she employed, she defended her involvement by representing herself as conscript rather than volunteer, assuring Will, "the ladies have to do it, and I did not offer my services, but was called on and appointed." She knew how "uneasy" he would be at the idea, but she reminded him that this was "my way of serving my country." The "ladies," she reported soothingly, "have none of the drudgery of the nursing, there are convalescents detailed to do that, besides servants," and her father-in-law had insisted she never go to the hospital without a slave to accompany and wait on her. The visitors distributed meals and medicines, oversaw patient and ward cleanliness, and read the Bible to

*Kate Cumming, hospital matron, in a postwar photograph reproduced from the frontispiece of her* Gleanings from the Southland *(Birmingham, Ala.: Roberts and Son, 1895). Courtesy of the Eleanor S. Brockenbrough Library, Museum of the Confederacy, Richmond, Virginia.*

the men. Emma Crutcher had worked out in her mind a clear set of standards of behavior to guide her and to maintain her gender and class identity in this uncharted hospital world. "I shall never take on myself anything that a servant can do as well, and never do anything that a lady may not with perfect propriety do. I shall not talk familiarly with the patients. . . . [I]n fact, I shall maintain every particle of the dignity which belongs to my sex and position, and at the same time I think I can be kind and useful."[49]

After two weeks of actual work, Crutcher's enthusiasm had dimmed in the face of the sordid realities of disease and death. "To tell the truth," she admitted to Will, "there is not much romance" in hospital work. The soldiers in her ward were "uninteresting specimens of uneducated Arkansas," poorly dressed in rough baggy uniforms, "with so little attempt at the 'pomp and circumstance of war.'" Even though she did not touch the patients, she found herself infested with lice, a condition hardly consonant with what she had so revealingly called the "dignity which belongs to my sex and position."[50]

Many southern women recorded experiences very like Emma Crutcher's. They visited soldiers to bring delicacies—buttermilk, custards, and fruits— or to supervise the preparation of food on site, to write letters for incapacitated or illiterate men, and sometimes even to wash faces. Some of these efforts seemed almost frivolous, even to contemporaries, who remarked with irony upon Richmond ladies sending silver trays filled with fine china, linens, and vases of flowers to the grim and crowded wards. Other efforts were ill conceived, as patients made clear when, for example, they spurned soup delicately flavored with parsley, which, in the words of one invalid, appeared to be contaminating "weeds."

Moments of military crisis, however, often expanded visitors' responsibilities. The work of volunteers assumed the utmost purpose when necessity involved women in direct care of severely wounded soldiers. Sara Agnes Pryor chronicled her transformation into a nurse in the Virginia hospitals during the bloody Seven Days battles of 1862. Presenting herself to the matron as a volunteer, Pryor could see the doubt with which the experienced woman regarded her untested eagerness and her obviously upper-class background. "The work is very exacting," the matron warned, detailing to the lady standing before her the menial nature of the position she sought. "There are so few of us that our nurses must do anything and everything—make beds, wait upon anybody, and often half a dozen at a time." Pryor confirmed her willingness to do all that was asked of her and proceeded down a row of patients to subscribe her name. Beside one bed, a nurse knelt holding a pan beneath the stump of an amputated arm. Pryor immediately fainted, only to open her eyes and see the skeptical matron peering down at her. "It is as I thought. You are unfit for this work."[51]

Humiliated by her failure, Pryor recognized that her contribution had been only to interrupt "those who were really worth something. . . . I resolved I would conquer my culpable weakness." When she returned to the matron the next day, she was greeted with kindness and some practical advice. Promising to station her near the door, the more experienced woman

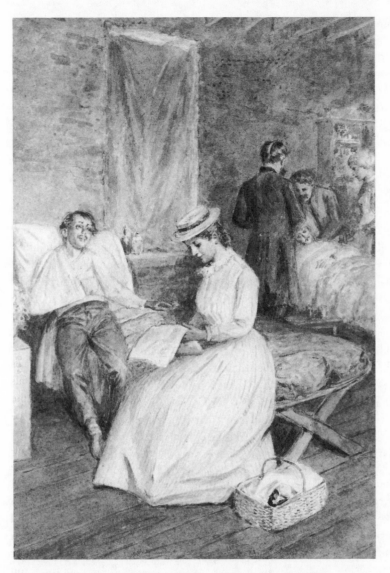

*A female hospital visitor.* In the Hospital, 1861, *watercolor by William Ludwell Sheppard. Courtesy of the Eleanor S. Brockenbrough Library, Museum of the Confederacy, Richmond, Virginia.*

counseled Pryor to run outside at the first sense of dizziness. Pryor was determined to overcome what some other of the nurses contemptuously called her "fine-lady faintness." She went far toward reinstating herself in the eyes of her colleagues when she arrived one morning with most of her household linens torn up into clean, well-rolled bandages. By the end of the week she had won a promotion. Instead of carving the fat bacon, swatting flies, fetching water, or making beds, she was given the care of a particular patient. Soon the matron assigned her to a standard seven-to-seven day shift, "and we went on duty with the regularity of trained nurses," always assisted by "efficient, kindly colored women."[52]

Other women shared Pryor's sensitivities but lacked her determination. Mary Chesnut resisted hospital work despite the example and entreaties of her friend Louisa McCord, who oversaw much of the patient care at the facility established on the grounds of South Carolina College in Columbia. McCord's strength and determination seemed to Chesnut almost unnatural—the characteristics of a man rather than a woman. After "fainting fits" in a Richmond hospital, Chesnut "deemed it wise to do my hospital work from the outside," by raising supplies. But shame made her return to a wayside hospital, where she worked half of each day in the "feeding department." Although she had few concerns about maintaining her own propriety, Chesnut did not like seeing younger ladies, particularly unmarried women, exposed to the scrutiny and the comments of common soldiers, who too often showed insufficient respect for female delicacy. "I cannot bear young girls to go to hospitals, wayside or otherwise," she wrote.[53]

Cornelia McDonald of Winchester endured extraordinary hardships with her children in that occupied city during the course of the war, but nursing proved almost more than she could stand. "I wanted to be useful," she explained, "and tried my best, but at the sight of one face that the surgeon uncovered, telling me that it must be washed, I thought I should faint. . . . The surgeon asked me if I would wash his wound. I tried to say yes, but the thought of it made me so faint that I could only stagger towards the door. As I passed, my dress brushed against a pile of amputated limbs heaped up near the door." It seemed always to be the amputations that were most upsetting, providing the severest challenge to women's dedication and composure. The pile of severed limbs, an image repeated again and again in the war's diaries, letters, and memoirs, graphically and powerfully represented the horror and irony fundamental to the American Civil War. Here was man's inhumanity to man now perversely extended into the realm of healing; here was a technology and a therapeutics that maimed and mutilated but rarely cured; here was humankind despiritualized and dismembered, rendered less than even a body, transformed from its uniqueness and individuality into a pile of unidentifiable parts.[54]

Mary Lee shared some of her neighbor Cornelia McDonald's aversion to hospital work, but as Winchester changed hands again and again in the course of the conflict, Lee and the other young women of her household undertook a variety of tasks to aid the wounded, both Yankee and Confederate. One of Lee's primary motivations arose from her concern that during times of Yankee occupation, southern soldiers in the town's hospitals would not be given adequate care, and she was energized as well by the sight of huge numbers of wounded pouring in from battles just to the north—several thousand after Antietam and as many as 5,000 after Gettysburg.[55]

Lee's predominant contribution to the hospitals was to procure and prepare food. Using her ties to farmers and families in the northern Shenandoah Valley, she struggled amidst growing shortages to ensure that patients received adequate and healthful diets. At times she supervised a "cooking room" and wryly remarked that she seemed to have found "my peculiar vocation (that of feeding people)." In addition she scurried around town and countryside in search of supplies and, to her considerable consternation, was at one point officially designated by Winchester's chief surgeon as responsible for providing whatever the doctors might need. "I hear of all sorts of queer people having supplies to sell & I hunt them up, as it is the only chance of getting anything, the stores being entirely bare." Lee was also directly involved with patients, going with her nieces to sing to one ward, reading prayers to suffering men, and dressing wounds, including those of an embarrassed colonel who had to be "considerably disrobed" to permit her ministrations.[56]

Lee's specific duties shifted at least as often as Winchester changed hands, however, and newly arrived Union officers frequently had to be cajoled into permitting her to aid in the care of the wounded. Her Christian principles compelled her to act kindly toward wounded Yankees, but even under close northern scrutiny, she endeavored to reserve her finest delicacies and tenderest ministrations for the Confederates.

Like many of the South's most committed female hospital workers, Lee found her labors both satisfying and exhausting. She expressed great relief in the spring of 1862 when Dorothea Dix arrived with a corps of Yankee nurses, ensuring that for a time at least, Lee would not be needed. She often complained about the demands the hospital made on her energies. "I sometimes am so selfish as to wish I had never begun to attend at the Hospitals."

Her sister-in-law Laura worried that Mary was overexerting herself and reported that one day she came home so debilitated that she fainted dead away for several worrisome hours. But Lee loved her work as well. When in November 1863 the men in her hospital were evacuated to Staunton, she felt bereft of her community and her purpose. "I could not have imagined that I would miss my Hospital duties so sadly; I did not know how interested I was, individually in each man. . . . I dawdled away the morning, not knowing how to get rid of the time which I spent at the Hospital." She would undoubtedly have understood Cordelia Scales's observation after a group of soldiers she had nursed in her house near Holly Springs, Mississippi, told her how much good she had done them. "I am afraid," she wrote, "I shall think myself of some importance after a while." For Ada Bacot of South Carolina the first months of nursing in Virginia represented the happiest days of her life. "I feel almost for the first time in my life that I am of some use." Even though she complained that she had grown sick of the very sight of men, she declared her work "more satisfying than I can express."[57]

However rewarding, hospital work posed intimidating demands and real dangers. Bacot contracted jaundice; numbers of other nurses were afflicted with typhoid. When Miss Wight from a Virginia hospital died from the disease, one of her fellow nurses justly observed that "she saved life at the sacrifice of her own." Juliet Opie Hopkins of Alabama herself became a casualty when she broke her leg while lifting a wounded officer on the battlefield at Seven Pines. She limped for the rest of her life. Curiously, public discussion of nursing's dangers ignored these physical threats to women's well-being, concentrating instead on the cultural and social perils inherent in its challenges to morality and propriety.[58]

Whether southern women feared losing their respectability, their lives, or simply the comforts of home, they did not volunteer for hospital work in the numbers needed in the face of mounting casualties. Advertisements seeking female nurses continued to appear in southern newspapers throughout most of the war, and the makeshift arrangement of much of Confederate hospital care persisted, despite efforts by the government to centralize and standardize military medicine.[59]

In some sense these continuing irregularities gave women more varied opportunities, perpetuating hospital roles outside the multitiered system of surgeons, matrons, assistant matrons, ward matrons, and nurses established by Confederate legislation. Even in the most carefully administered institutions, the neat bureaucratic prescriptions of the law poorly described day-to-day reality. Wives, mothers, and sisters arrived to nurse their own kin. On one of Phoebe Pember's wards such a visitor even appropriated her husband's cot to deliver a baby during the course of her lengthy stay. Volunteers wandered through the wards with Bibles, eatables, or words of cheer. Many facilities depended on contributions from women of the surrounding community to meet basic needs for food and supplies, and thus "feeding departments" attracted significant female energy. These official hospitals comprised only a part of the South's effort to care for its fallen soldiers. There were simply never enough government hospitals to deal with the thousands of wounded who appeared in the aftermath of bloody battles. Whole communities near the sites of costly encounters found themselves abruptly transformed, as almost every citizen, regardless of inclination, experience, or considerations of propriety would be called upon to aid in the crisis. In Winchester after Antietam, for example, Laura Lee described twenty-four hospitals set up in almost every available public space—schools, churches, banks, and town hall—in addition to the countless private homes that took in small numbers of injured Confederates. The town, she noted, had become a giant hospital, and all its remaining inhabitants—overwhelmingly female—hospital workers. Those unwilling to confront the carnage fled to become refugees.[60]

But in spite of the variety of opportunities for hospital work and the sometimes all but irresistible demands for their labor, most elite women served intermittently or not at all. The government's effort to enlist substantial numbers of Confederate women for the hospitals was doomed to fail. Unlike military conscription, the Confederacy's manpower and mobilization policies for women rested on persuasion rather than coercion. Confronted with a choice, most white southern women avoided the hospital's hardships and dangers. After her initial difficulties, Mary Chesnut ultimately volunteered in a wayside hospital, where patients were generally convalescent rather than critical or moribund, and other women, like her, took advantage of the continuing variety of options to temper their involvement and to avoid the most trying medical environments. For many women who worried about performing their Christian duty, it often seemed enough to send provisions, visit wards to read the Bible, or serve meals to soldiers passing through by train—to make occasional contributions rather than any commitment to full-time or long-term duties.

What were the salient factors shaping women's decisions? Why did so many women disappoint Kate Cumming, Phoebe Pember, and Susan Smith by not embracing this opportunity for female service and patriotism? Why, as Cumming asked, was woman's "sacred duty . . . left undone"? Why, in

Smith's words, did "more ladies not lend a helping hand . . . when there was such a wide field for every indispensable usefulness before them"? What were the special attributes or motivations that distinguished those who did defy convention to undertake these essential roles?[61]

Many young ladies were clearly unable to overcome the fears for what Emma Crutcher called "the dignity which belongs to my sex and position." The notion of ladyhood—with its dimensions of both class and gender identity—comported poorly with much of hospital work. But numbers of women struggled to balance such considerations against their compelling urge to be useful by performing services that, like Crutcher's, were carefully delimited by dictates of propriety. Emma Crutcher almost perfectly embodied the tension between the attractions of nursing as exciting, patriotic, and meaningful work and its repulsions as sordid and demeaning. At one juncture Emma sought to resolve her ambivalence by reminding her absent husband that he could exert his authority and forbid her further involvement at the hospital. Like Crutcher, other women seemingly escaped their own inner conflict by inviting or invoking male pressure as justification for avoiding hospital duties they acknowledged as both appealing and important. Even after she had gone to Virginia as a nurse, Ada Bacot was, as we saw, relieved to have a physician friend make the decision about whether she should take on a hospital matronship. Augusta Jane Evans, a best-selling author in her late twenties, explained that her plans to serve as a nurse had initially been vetoed by her brothers, and so she had dutifully submitted— "reluctantly and with great disappointment." Sarah Morgan cited the force of similar opposition. "If I was independent, if I could work my own will without causing others to suffer for my deeds, I would not be poring over this stupid page, I would not be idly reading or sewing. I would put aside woman's trash, and take up woman's duty, and I would stand by some forsaken man and bid him God speed as he closes his dying eyes. That is Woman's mission! and not Preaching and Politics. . . . If I could help these dying men! Yet it is as impossible as though I was a chained bear[,] . . . coward, helpless woman that I am! If I was free," she pondered. Yet as Morgan at once excused and berated herself, it seems almost as if she was relieved not to confront the responsibilities of freedom.[62]

Women who served in permanent, quasi-professional hospital positions did tend to be, as Morgan suggested, "independent." Pember and Bacot, for example, were widows, and Cumming was an unmarried lady of sufficient maturity to be considered a spinster. Many of the South's most active volunteers—Louisa McCord and Mary Lee, for example—were widows as well. It was women outside the structures of direct patriarchal control and domestic obligation who found it easiest to devote themselves to public responsibility. As one aspiring nurse explained in her letter of application to Juliet Opie Hopkins, she was "without any incumbrance."[63]

Serious, committed, long-term hospital work remained the domain of these exceptional women. It was not the experience of the overwhelming majority of the South's ladies, "only a few, a very few" of whom, in Pember's words, became matrons or nurses. Women's contributions as nurses in the Civil War have often been hailed as a landmark in their progress toward equality and toward an expanding sense of achievement and self-worth. Civil War nursing itself has been regarded as the beginning of women's entry into the health professions. For the South, neither of these celebratory characterizations is accurate. Although training schools for nurses were established in the North after the war and although leaders of wartime nursing such as Clara Barton exerted significant influence on health policy and women's roles in the postwar years, no such developments occurred in the southern states. The Cummings, Pembers, and Newsoms of the South wrote their memoirs and faded away.

Taken as a whole, the hospital work of white southern women was not calculated to foster new confidence about themselves and their abilities. As many of the South's most dedicated nurses made clear, women's overall record was one of failure, not success. They had not come forward in the numbers requested and, in the eyes of Kate Cumming, would bear much of the liability for the South's ultimate defeat. "I have said many a time that, if we did not succeed, the women of the South would be responsible. . . . Not for one moment," she continued, "would I say that there are no women in the South who have nobly done their duty, although there was an adverse current, strong enough to carry all with it."[64]

On an individual level even the most successful and dedicated of these women found the experience ambiguous—enormously gratifying on one level but frustrating and disheartening as well. Attributes traditionally regarded as female or ladylike—the very foundation of these women's prewar identities—had to be abandoned as disabilities. Delicacy and propriety had to be sacrificed, "fine-lady faintness" overcome, sensibility hardened, and compassion contained within bounds of pragmatism. The best nurses seemed often in the judgment of other women to have appeared surprisingly like men. How Louisa McCord's "strength contrasts with our weakness!" Mary Chesnut remarked. She had "the brains and energy of a man." Eliza McKee, at work in Virginia's hospitals, was in her friend Clara MacLean's eyes just the person to "undertake such a duty. She is decidedly the most strong-minded woman I ever saw—almost masculine. Indeed I used to tell her I never felt easy in her society if discussing *delicate* subjects: I could scarcely persuade myself she was not in disguise." The Civil War experience in the South would in significant ways reinforce the perception that womanhood and nursing were incompatible.[65]

Women of the southern elite for the most part shared the perspectives of Chesnut or MacLean: their contact with nursing rendered them newly and painfully aware of their own inadequacies, of the debilities that arose from their femininity and their privilege. They were shocked by their own weakness, by their incompetence and ignorance, by their revulsion at many of the common soldiers whom they were supposed to regard as heroes, and by their preference for the comforts of home. Mary Chesnut tried on the one hand airily to diminish the importance of the "Florence Nightingale business." But even after her failures, she kept coming back to hospital work, sending foods, offering her services in the feeding department, and looking for a way in which she might successfully contribute. Her embarrassed comparison of McCord's commitment to her own meager efforts suggests that Chesnut fully understood the urgency of the duty and knew as well that she was not good enough to do it.[66]

Elite women's failures as Florence Nightingales made at least some Confederate ladies recognize that, as Cumming put it, "even when a woman does her best, it is a mite compared with what our men have to endure." Cumming complained that she was "weary" of the "usual compliments to the ladies," who she knew "did not deserve all that was said in their praise." It is not clear, however, whether Cumming was able to see and acknowledge who really bore the burden of Confederate nursing. Staffing records of the South's military hospitals reveal the presence of various workers: physicians, stewards, matrons, detailed soldiers and convalescents, and even nuns. But overwhelming all others in number are black southerners, male and female, impressed or hired from their owners, or captured from the enemy, who served as cooks, laundresses, but above all nurses to the Confederacy's wounded. For all their undeniable and important contributions, it was not the Confederacy's ladies but its African Americans who cared for the South's fallen heroes. In the domain of nursing, as in the domestic world of cooking and washing, many Confederate ladies would prove themselves less able and less effective than their supposed inferiors.[67]

Entry into the world of work outside the home brought many white southern women face to face with their most basic assumptions about themselves. Doubts about their capacities and a new awareness of their limitations of both competence and commitment emerged from their gradual recognition of the difficulty and the drudgery of wartime labor in classrooms, offices, and hospitals. But elite women were perhaps even more impressed by their confrontations with new sorts of people, with individuals they had rarely seen during their years of confinement within the protective circles of home and family. In schools and on hospital wards, women encountered white southerners of other classes who behaved in ways that prompted ladies to reevaluate the very bases of their self-definition. Emma Holmes could "hardly recognize my own identity" as she interacted with the ignorant and ill-mannered children of South Carolina's lower orders. Phoebe Pember was compelled to revise her understanding of the essential attributes of womanhood when she discovered that white female hospital workers drank and swore and in general acted quite differently than she. Both work itself and an unaccustomed proximity to common whites threatened to blur the distinctions elite women increasingly recognized as essential to their identities, to what Emma Crutcher called "the dignity" of "my sex and position."[68]

Kate Cumming maintained that "respectability" transcended circumstance and that it could not be diminished by association with the socially undesirable or by the sordid and menial aspects of nursing. Indeed, she argued, ladyhood had a spiritual, an intrinsic character that could be only enhanced by Christian service to others. But few shared Cumming's confidence. A far greater number of women felt the need to define their status by clearly separating themselves from the masses, often avoiding any suspicion of what Lila Chunn called brazenness by entirely eschewing the contaminations of the public sphere—"Department—never!" as Mary Chesnut vowed. The entry of many Confederate women into the world of work outside the home had significant implications for elite women's understanding of the importance of class to their identities and self-conceptions. Thrown together with pupils, patients, or co-workers of lower status, elite females felt impelled to assert a superiority they had seldom before needed to defend. The Civil War made privileged women more insistent about their rank and position even as it drew the bases for such distinction increasingly into question.[69]

# CHAPTER FIVE

# We Little Knew

## HUSBANDS AND WIVES

### Separation Is Always Very Sad

In October 1863 Kate Peddy wrote her absent husband, George, confessing that she dreamed of him "nearly every night." Sometimes she had nightmares filled with distressing anxiety about his safety; other times she was so happy she woke believing he had returned. But his presence was so frequent and so vivid, it was almost as if their disrupted relationship had resumed to thrive in a nighttime world of vision and fantasy.[1]

Emma Crutcher's dreams restored her husband, Will, to his rightful place as her guardian and protector. "Last night," she wrote, "I dreamed of you, and you were watching over me and taking care of me through a long series of adventures and somehow it cheered me, for I knew that you really would care for me." Will continued to appear to her at night, and on one occasion Emma was dismayed and chagrined by the realism of her dreams of reunion. Her "powers of self control," she explained, were "somewhat benumbed" by sleep, and her vision was "something that I never should have allowed had I been fully roused." Her imagination had re-created in all too lifelike and sensual detail the relationship that war had interrupted.[2]

Some Confederate women regarded dreams as predictive of future events and tried to read them as prophecies. Cornelia Noble found particularly ominous a dream that her wedding ring had broken in two. But Emma Crutcher understood the meaning of dreams differently, believing them to reveal "our motives divested of all the self-deceptions and palliations which we all use, even to ourselves." In one dream she regarded as especially revealing, Will came home with a wounded leg. But rather than feeling grief at his suffering, Emma was overjoyed. Lame for life, Will could, Emma reasoned, neither return to battle nor attract another woman; he was forever hers. Emma concluded upon awakening that this dream displayed her "unmitigated selfishness." Her deepest fears were about his fidelity and his survival; her profoundest desires were not for victory or independence or even peace, but for her husband's permanent return.[3]

For Emma Crutcher, as for tens of thousands of other Confederate women, cherished marital ties became for a time, if not for eternity, the stuff of dreams and fantasies. Absent by day, husbands returned in the vividness of their wives' sleeping imagination to fill the emptiness that had replaced the intimacy of domestic life. The warborn transformation of the structures of southern households had altered their hearts and souls as well. Women of the Confederate South confronted a changed emotional landscape in which the most fundamental personal attachments became as elusive as dreams, only as tangible as the letters that served as the residual substance of these ruptured ties.

The emotional lives of Confederate couples separated by war did in fact depend heavily on the mundane inadequacies of the new national postal service. "Writing what I know your eye will rest on," Emma Crutcher explained, "cements me with you more closely than anything else." Communication, professions of love and support, and even the simplest exchanges of information occurred almost exclusively through the mail. For educated members of the South's privileged classes, the challenges of meaningful expression were by no means as great as those confronting the often marginally literate common soldiers who frequently relied on letters dictated to others as the sole means of marital intercourse. But for rich and poor alike, the inefficiencies and expense of the Confederate mail service worked as a significant impediment to maintaining emotional bonds. Confederate statesmen believed that any subsidization of the mail would represent an unwarranted support for the nation's commercial interests. Thus postal rates reflected actual costs, a policy that sent the price of stamps skyrocketing after secession. In the fall of 1861 Gertrude Thomas noted that the price of sending a letter must act as a "serious drawback" to ordinary southerners, and the next year postal rates doubled. When the cost of sending a letter rose to ten cents in May 1862, Emma Holmes expected to feel the impact "considerably as it will restrict my correspondence in these hard times." By the later phases of the war, even members of the upper strata of southern society found themselves unable to write as often as they wished. Caroline Davis of Virginia complained in February 1865 of the scanty news from family members in Richmond. "I wish we could afford to hear from each other every mail."[4]

Despite its high cost, mail delivery was far from reliable, and southerners reported instances where service was interrupted for months at a time. The impact of these failures was wide ranging. Perhaps the most distressing result was the perpetual inadequacy of information about military casualties. Women would sometimes not hear for weeks or even months whether their loved ones had survived particular battles. Waiting became so unbearable that the worst news arrived almost as a relief. Into the void of insupportable uncertainty, Dame Rumor entered to exert her cruel and arbitrary sway. Many women tried to settle near locations—towns and cities, telegraph offices, or junction post offices—that promised regular and reliable information in order to minimize the torture of anxiety. "I feel the impulse each hour stronger to go where I can hear constantly from Hal," wrote Mary Dulany of Virginia. "I cannot bear to wait." Lizzie Ozburn of Georgia had an even better idea. "I wish," she declared to her husband, Jimmie, "you & I had a Telegraph."[5]

But it was not just life and death matters that could not be effectively communicated. The mass of almost trivial details that comprise the emotional intimacy of married life were similarly impeded. As a Louisiana woman wrote after not having received any letters from the front in almost four months, "L'absence est toujours bien triste, même avec la consolation de pouvoir écrire librement, mais lorsque l'on est privé de recevoir des n[ouv]elles de ceux qui sont si chers, c'est horrible à supporter." The Post Office, one study of the Confederacy's mail service has justly observed, played a significant part "in demoralizing the homefront."[6]

*Unidentified Confederate couple. Courtesy of the Atlanta History Center, Atlanta, Georgia.*

Perhaps their cost and scarcity made letters all the more valuable. "I never knew," Emma Crutcher observed, "what precious things letters could be." When Fannie Gordon received an eagerly awaited note from her husband, General John Gordon, she transformed the sheet into a substitute for the man himself. Placing the letter under her veil, hidden from all eyes, "I pressed to my lips over and over the spot that yours had touched and tried to imagine I could feel your own precious lips & that dear moustache that I love so much." For many women, letters were the "highest pleasure" remaining in their lonely and pressured lives. Composing their responses could provide an emotional outlet nowhere else available. Confederate offi-cials and the public press worried about military morale and urged women, "DON'T WRITE GLOOMY LETTERS." But many wives did exactly that, preserv-ing bonds of intimacy by sharing the many troubles war had brought. Mary Bell of North Carolina explained to her husband, Alfred, in 1862, "I know you will think, I wish Mollie would not write such desponding letters but it has always been my notion to confide to my best friend my worst fears it is such a relief, especially if that friend will sympathize with you."[7]

Lizzie Neblett agreed. "I must have someone to tell my troubles too." Her letters to Will served, she told him, as her "safety valves." But they were also, she confessed, "mirrors of my heart." It worried her a bit that she found herself writing "so fully and openly of my feelings," especially since Will remained so self-contained. Emma Crutcher embraced a new openness toward her Will as well. She discovered she "could write more freely to you than I could talk." Separation paradoxically seemed to encourage a new frankness, a new emotional accessibility, and a new intensity of feeling between husbands and wives.[8]

Often men, in particular, struggled with this new language of personal revelation and implicit vulnerability; Will Neblett was not alone in his re-serve. George Peddy felt compelled to apologize to Kate for his shortcom-ings. "I wish I could tell or write to you how well I love you. When I undertake to do so I am at a loss for words & language strong enough to express it. In fact, my letters fall so far short of your[s] that I am ashamed to try to write anything." David McRaven of North Carolina was not ashamed to try but embarrassed at the result. "Amanda I am getting romantic you will laugh at an old fellow 48 years writing Love like a boy." Alfred Bell feared Mary would regard his "loveing letters" as "crazy and foolish," although she promptly assured him "them are just the kind I like to get."[9]

Rose Lewis could not decide if her husband had come to love her more or was simply using letters to say it more frequently. Wartime separations encouraged recognition, acknowledgment, and articulation of emotions that had in peacetime been ignored or taken for granted. Even her new patriotic sentiments, Emma Crutcher proclaimed to Will, paled in comparison to "the intensity of feeling which your absence awakens." But this new love was bittersweet. "I loved you enough before," she wrote, "to make me happy—now it remains to see, whether I don't love you enough to make me miser-able." Southerners marveled at the wonders of emotional discovery, at the sudden awareness of what had always been there yet had remained hidden until it was threatened. "Oh Johny," wrote Julia Davidson with both passion

*Confederate Brigadier General John Hunt Morgan and his wife, Martha Ready Morgan, at the time of their marriage in 1862. She was widowed less than two years later when he was killed in a surprise Union attack. Carte de Visite. Courtesy of the Eleanor S. Brockenbrough Library, Museum of the Confederacy, Richmond, Virginia.*

and regret, "we little knew how dear we were to each other until we were called on to make this great sacrafice."[10]

This new awareness of marital devotion made at least some Confederate wives confront unprecedented feelings of vulnerability as well. Women's letters are filled with confessions of anxiety about impending loss. Sarah Kennedy of Tennessee wrote her husband about how she was haunted by fears of his death. Her greatest terrors came as she lay down to sleep after the day's round of busy activity. "The idea that you may never return comes often into my mind and I am so distressed that I have to get up, and I spend hours at night in this way." Susan Caldwell of Warrenton, Virginia, explained how her apprehensions compounded the difficulties of being apart from her husband, Lycurgus. "Separation is painful, but with it an anxious heart is almost unbearable."[11]

The survival of their loved ones amidst the appalling carnage of Civil War battles rested uppermost on these women's lists of anxieties. Many wives, though, feared the loss of their husbands' affections almost as intensely as they worried about the loss of their lives. Women's concerns about their husbands' loyalties derived in considerable measure from their sense that southern men passed into a new and uncharted world as they departed for war. In part, wives feared the temptations of lewd women and the promiscuous behavior traditionally associated with army life. But their apprehensions also encompassed a broader sense that their men were traveling into an unknown realm, where past ties and allegiances might become meaningless. In the Confederate army, men often talked of "seeing the elephant," a term used to describe—or perhaps not describe—one's first encounter with combat. Women bore a similar sense of the ineffable mystery inherent in military initiation, and they feared that the experience of this rite of passage might permanently alter and estrange their men. "You ask me," John Davidson wrote in response to the concerns of his wife, Julia, "if my change of life or manor of living, will not wean me from my wife & children. I can answer it at once. never never can there be any change in me my Love for my Wife & children is unceasing." He was, he assured her, "the same man that I was when I went into the service."[12]

Women's frequently voiced feelings of uselessness in the face of men's all-important military contributions reinforced a more profound sense of inadequacy and self-doubt about their continuing attractiveness and significance to these new Confederate heroes. Whenever George Peddy even mentioned a woman in his letters, Kate worried that he was comparing his new acquaintance to "homely sensless me." She often wondered, she wrote, "why do you love me at all." Often her letters dwelt on the differences between them, a contrast that their wartime lives had only intensified. "You are self relient and independant, able and competent to battle with all the whims of fortune, while I am but a weight that retards and keeps you back from the position which nature designed [you] to occupy."[13]

Mary Bell of North Carolina worried explicitly and constantly about Alfred's entanglement with other women. A sudden formality in his letters combined with a spate of rumors about wanton behavior in his company impelled Mary to direct accusation. When Alfred replied with hurt and anger, denying any such transgressions, Mary apologized. But she continued to wonder "if you are satisfied to do without me, and think that some other woman will do you just as well."[14]

These sentiments of insecurity and vulnerability arose from a dependence that was more than simply emotional. Frustrations at the daily tribulations of Confederate life—at managing slaves or providing for families amidst inflation and scarcity—generated profound feelings of inadequacy. Women often felt crippled by what Lizzie Neblett called "my entire inability to help myself." Sarah Kennedy found that by 1864 she was "ready to despair of competency to perform the duties and responsibilities that necessarily devolve upon me." Warborn independence and autonomy were lamented rather than celebrated.[15]

Women mourned the loss of male protection—physical, emotional, and financial. Emma Crutcher wrote revealingly to Will after they had been apart for six months, "I wish I had you to rely on now for somehow . . . I feel wearied of acting for myself and deciding for myself. It is sometimes very pleasant to stand alone, but we women all get tired of it. I have been entirely independent since you went away, for the first time in my life, not even consulting anyone. . . . And your little wife is tired, and wants to give up the reins, and lay her head on your shoulder and *rest*." Throughout their separation Emma repeatedly invited Will to exert his authority over her—to prohibit her hospital work or to direct her how to dress. If, she once warned him, "you . . . tell me to 'do just as I please, that you would not presume to interfere' I shall never forgive you. . . . If you would only *tell me* to do something, I would like it so much—I should feel like I *was* your wife, and that you claimed your property." When Emily Harris's husband returned to the army after a furlough at home in South Carolina, she felt severely depressed and declared, "I shall never get used to being left as the head of affairs at home." Such responsibility was against her nature. "I am constituted," she wrote, "so as to crave a guide and protector. I am not an

*Confederate wives visiting their husbands in camp near Richmond, Virginia,*
*1862. Courtesy of Special Collections Department, Robert W. Woodruff Library,*
*Emory University, Atlanta, Georgia.*

independent woman nor ever shall be." Soon after R. L. Dabney's departure
for war, his wife, Lavinia, wrote inquiring about his adjustment to military
discipline and celebrating the bonds of female subordination. "How do you
like having a *Master?*" she asked in language especially resonant within
southern society. "I like it if you do not & I can't begin to say how much I
miss mine."[16]

Amidst the overwhelming uncertainties and changes brought by Civil
War, women clung ever more tenaciously to structures of authority and
belonging that had given them both identity and security. As cherished
relationships seemed ever more imperiled by the rising death toll, preserv-
ing their traditional forms may have appeared all the more important. In a
particularly bald affirmation of the continuing power of patriarchy, Susan

Caldwell throughout the war addressed her absent husband as "Dear Papa" and signed each of her letters, "Your affectionate daughter."[17]

Although some men, particularly during the initial months of separation, tried to exert control over routine decisions at home, most quickly abdicated their authority. Even letters full of agricultural advice often ended in much the same manner as one written by E. P. Petty to his wife in December 1862. "I approve anything you do. . . . I am not now the head of the family and dont pretend to dictate." Morgan Callaway carefully instructed his wife, Leila, about how to harvest the cotton, ensure a good potato crop, and cultivate turnips. But then he caught himself short. "Dear me," he wondered, "why should I advise an experienced farmer like yourself[?]"[18]

In many cases women seemed more uneasy about their unaccustomed power than did men. John Davidson sought to reassure and encourage his wife to meet the new demands before her. "Julia you must do the best you can. you have to act the Man & Woman both which I fear will go rather hard with you being so timid and reserved but I am happy to see that a great deal of your timidity is waring off. you have traveled alone & had to manage for yourself so long that you have become to be quite a soldier." Female independence, in John Davidson's construction, required the transformation of women into men, of ladies into soldiers. Despite his supportive tone, his very acknowledgment of differing gender capacities might well have alarmed as much as encouraged his reticent wife.[19]

## My Longing Wears a Curb

Painful separations, anxieties about loss and infidelity, and issues of marital power and authority converged in the vexed problem of wartime sexuality. The emotional openness of much Confederate correspondence included in at least some instances explicit discussions of the physical dimension of married love. When Mary Bell listed the many ways she missed her husband, she concluded, "I miss you sleeping with me as much or more than anything else." In a dream of his return home, she was distraught when he left before bedtime. "I know that dream will never come to pass," she wrote, "for if you was to come I would make you stay all night if I had to tie you."[20]

Bell was seemingly unconflicted in her enthusiastic lust, but other women found their desire inhibited—if not overwhelmed—by a profound fear of pregnancy. Childbirth, Octavia Stephens emphatically proclaimed, "is horrible, horrible, horrible." By the 1860s, American birth control advocates had published tracts describing a variety of contraceptive forms, including coitus interruptus, vaginal syringes, rubber condoms, and vaginal sponges. The reliability of these methods was far from absolute, and it is unclear if necessary information or technology was available to women of the Confederate South. Whether the problem was ignorance, access, or safety, southern women continued to regard abstinence as the only certain guarantee against conception. Amanda Bullock of Georgia wrote her husband, Robert, of her joy that she had not conceived during his recent furlough. "But aint I glad[,] . . . for none but myself can tell my dread of such suffering, but for all that I would not have you stay a way from me for any thing in the world[.] just to be with you a little while will compensate me for a great deal, and I will hope that the something will not happen."[21]

Lizzie Neblett, who delivered her fifth—and unwanted—child two months after Will's departure, called her fears of pregnancy her "crazy subject." "I had rather meet a woods full of bare," she declared to Will, "than meet you after a long absence, when I feared the love I bare you would . . . make me willing for your sake to risk a certain event happening. Even as it stands now I dread to see you, tho' I love you better far than I do my own life." Lizzie insisted that before Will come home, he must agree to her regulation of their sexual contact. With an authoritative tone she seemed unable to muster in her efforts to manage the slaves, she informed her spouse, "If you cant comply with my orders . . . about the preventives to come in your pocket home—you may come without, but must submit, to my laws after reaching home & you need not fear that they will not be made strict enough to ensure my safety." Will confessed to feeling flattered by Lizzie's fears of yielding to him against her rational judgment. But in the face of Will's apparent calm, Lizzie remained tormented by the conflict between her love and her terror. "This constant & never ceasing horror I have of childbearing constantly obtrudes itself between me & my desire . . . & thus my longing wears a curb."[22]

The Davidsons of Atlanta shared many of the Nebletts' anxieties, worrying about their frustrated sexual desires as well as unwanted pregnancy. "Julia," John wrote to his wife, "I have not slept with a woman so long I have almost forgot how warm they are. I suffer with cold during The cold nights and I have *suffered considerable* in some *other ways*."[23]

John spoke openly about the availability of "Fancy Women" on Saint Michael Street in Mobile, and he reported that a great many of the soldiers from his camp nearby were regular customers. "I never have seen so much

*Will and Lizzie Neblett after the war. Courtesy of the Center for American History, University of Texas, Austin.*

Ludeness in all my life." But, he assured Julia, "I dont patronize them myself." Commercial sex is an almost inevitable accompaniment to any army, and the Confederate military was no exception. It is almost impossible to gauge, however, the impact of easy and widespread access to prostitutes on Confederate marriages or to assess how many or which southern soldiers were likely to have indulged. Evidence is all but nonexistent, and even John Davidson's denials, articulated in letters to his wife, cannot be taken at face value.[24]

A medical problem Will Neblett developed during his army service suggests that his equanimity about Lizzie's restriction of their sexual intimacy may have had its roots in alternate sexual activity, perhaps with prostitutes in Galveston. Will was diagnosed with a hydrocele, essentially an edematous testicle, and Lizzie worried that others would assume "the worst kind of venereal disease" if news of his complaint became public. In fact, promiscuity may or may not have been the cause of his ailment, but Lizzie, for her own part, seemed unperturbed, all but dismissing the possibility of his infidelity. Her primary concern, like that of Julia Davidson and so many other Confederate women, focused on anxieties about unwanted pregnancy.[25]

Fears of pregnancy no doubt combined with dread of shame and ostracism to limit women's sexual license. A strict code of purity regulated white women's behavior in the Old South, particularly among members of the region's gentry class, where female chastity was closely tied not just to women's identities as ladies but to the honor and standing of their men. In wartime, however, some women found both need and opportunity for transgression. As in the case of men, it is difficult to separate rumor and surmise from actual behavior, for women, perhaps otherwise preoccupied, did not confide their own affairs to diaries or correspondence, although they willingly discussed the supposed transgressions of others. George Peddy informed Kate that "A Gentleman in Camp" had told him about the scandalous activities of the ladies of nearby Newnan, Georgia. "He has slep frequently with Mrs. Hanvey, Mrs Steve Smith & the Taylor's wife (I forget his name) & some others, & he is a man of truth." In 1864 Julia Davidson wrote John that her brother had decided to seek a divorce after he discovered that his wife, Fannie, was sleeping with at least one other man. Lizzie and Will Neblett corresponded about rumors abroad in Texas, and Will concluded, "the women at home got to acting as badly as the men." He had heard of a "young lady" recently delivered of a mixed-race child. The "people," he reported "have hung the negro up in front of the house." Lizzie embellished the tale, reporting that it was not one girl but several and that it was said they had tried to bury their babies alive.[26]

With husbands absent for as long as years at a time, it seems inevitable that at least some white women would have established sexual liaisons not only with white men but with male slaves. Testimony before the American Freedman's Inquiry Commission taken in areas liberated by Union troops contained sufficient numbers of examples of such behavior to warrant an entry in the index of the proceedings under "Intercourse between white women and colored men common—Instances of." Many of these examples, historian Martha Hodes notes, involved women of the planter class who used their power over slaves to initiate sexual contact. One former slave reported that his forty-year-old mistress had after a year of widowhood " 'ordered him to sleep with her, and he did regularly.' "[27]

The sense of new opportunity for such forbidden relationships no doubt fueled the widespread conjecture about interracial affairs. When Lizzie Neblett had her young slave Bill drive her to a party, she stimulated an outburst of speculation in Grimes County, Texas, about the nature of her connection to the black man. Gossip paradoxically served to make such behavior imaginable and possible and, at the same time, to control it by stigmatizing it as scandalous—even, as in the case of the Texas slaves reportedly hung for fathering mulatto babies, life threatening. If sexuality between white husbands and wives was fraught with terror and ambivalence because of fears of impregnation, extramarital relations must have produced far greater anxiety and reluctance. Few couples would have wanted to find themselves in the situation of a man in Will Neblett's company who, in seeming innocence, petitioned for a furlough, saying his wife would soon deliver a child and he had not been granted an opportunity to visit her for nearly eighteen months.[28]

In the Civil War South fear of pregnancy—its pain and danger, if not its shame—fundamentally structured women's emotional as well as sexual relationships with men. Lizzie Neblett's sister-in-law, begged by her husband to visit him in camp, declined to go because she dreaded returning home pregnant. If he had been sick, she noted, she would not have hesitated to go care for him, but his robust health represented too great a threat for her to bear. John and Julia Davidson were sufficiently apprehensive that they corresponded in detail about her menstrual periods, referring to them as "that lady friend" or "your old acquaintance" and greeting their arrival after John's visits with undisguised relief. When Julia's usually irregular menses temporarily assumed a new predictability, John found it "strange that she is so punctual. she has never been so kind before. perhaps she thinks it is war times and the Ladies kneed all the help they can get." Between two visits home in the spring of 1864, John wrote to inquire, "Has our old friend called on you again or has she concluded to wait untill I get home and *ask* in that *old* friend of mine and have a rejoicing together. I hope so." On this occasion, Julia could reassure him, "My friend has not forsaken me." But soon she would pay in "suffering and mental anxiety" for "the pleasure of your society." By fall she was pregnant with her fourth child, who was born in early 1865 after Sherman's advance had made Julia a refugee.[29]

Willie Chunn had been absent from home for about four months when Lila wrote to confirm their "fears about my condition." She revealed at last the anguish she had been experiencing almost since the day of his departure. "I have refrained from disclosing to you the deep grief of my heart because I knew that it would cause you pangs of sorrow. . . . I have tried to become reconciled and am to some extent more resigned. Would that I could at all times and under all circumstances say 'Thy will O Lord be done.'" George Peddy imagined Kate's emotional distress during the last phases of her pregnancy, but he anticipated that her misgivings would extend beyond childbirth to encompass marriage as well. "No doubt," he wrote in June 1864, "ere this you have thought you would have been better off if you had remianed in your single blessedness. . . . Women frequently regret marrying at such times."[30]

Women's aversion to childbearing in the Confederate South arose both from general medical realities and from conditions specific to wartime. Apprehensions about the dangers of childbirth, all too rational a fear until well into our own time, were intensified as women faced the likelihood of delivering without the presence and direct emotional support of their husbands. Recent scholarship on "lying-in" in nineteenth-century America has portrayed childbirth as a largely female ritual, an event from which men were excluded as all but irrelevant. Confederate women's letters suggest, however, that within the South's master class, at least, the presence of men at the time—even if perhaps not in the very room—of childbirth was of fundamental importance to expectant mothers. For their confinement these women clearly desired the emotional aid and encouragement of their husbands, even if they of necessity eventually settled for the comforts of a "female world of love and ritual." Lila Chunn begged Willie to do whatever was required to get a furlough in time for her confinement. If his colonel refused, she felt it would be "almost a death blow to me." Only weeks from her due date, Lizzie Ozburn threatened to write to "Yancy Cobb & even Davis" to make sure Jimmie could be home for the birth of their baby. "If ever a woman feels the need of an arm to lean upon it is when they are as I am now."[31]

Leila and Morgan Callaway argued continually about her confinement during the final six months of her pregnancy. She could not imagine that he would not be at her side; but he warned her repeatedly that his duties as chaplain in Virginia might keep him away, and he reminded her that the pain she anticipated could not compare with that he was witnessing at the front. "I know you suffer. But dearest, could you see, as I see daily hundreds of sick men, burning with fever . . . tortured with pain, . . . you would see that your suffering was light." Women's travails meant little in comparison with the sacrifices of Confederate men.

Undaunted, Leila continued to claim what she thought her wifely due and informed him that his "presence during Nov is absolutely indispensable." Each letter contained an entreaty and an expression of faith that he would indeed meet her request. "And will my precious disappoint my happy expectations? No I will never believe it!!!!" Morgan relented to the point of at least applying for a furlough in mid-October; but his request was refused, and Leila delivered without him. "You know not my dear one how sad I feel when I think of the ordeal through which I must so soon pass, and that my Morgan cannot be here to comfort me." Her slave Susanna shared her mistress's distress "that I must be alone," but Leila was confident she would "wait upon me just as well as she can." With the help of Susanna and "my Heavenly Father" Leila safely delivered a fat baby boy on November 4, 1862. She named him Morgan.[32]

## Little Animals

Overburdened women worried about the additional work of new babies in an environment where the possibility of slave childcare was increasingly uncertain. Additional mouths to feed in an economy of growing scarcity were equally unwelcome. One Louisiana woman sent rather pointed wedding felicitations to her cousin: "I wish you peace, security, and happiness, and few children in this time of war." Emma Crutcher, oldest of a large family, felt she knew as much about babies as any grandmother in the Confederacy. Still childless herself, Emma was delighted to remain so, at least for the time being. "I think any one who is free from the '*little animals*' can scarcely be thankful enough in these days of war. It is hard enough for a woman to take care of herself, without assistance."[33]

Some women, however, at least found with children the love and intimacy denied them in their disrupted marriages. "If the war continues," Gertrude Thomas declared, "I shall endeavor in my children to find my principal comfort." Wives wrote husbands of sweet baby kisses, of cute sayings, and of proud achievements—starting to walk, sprouting a tooth, or learning to read. Many women were struck—with amazement and sorrow—at how children incorporated the war into their lives. "Almost their entire set of plays have reference to a state of war," Margaret Junkin Preston observed. Boys and girls marched and drilled, built hospitals of blocks, made ambulances out of chairs, and imagined themselves with missing limbs. Two little girls "playing Sherman" became so caught up in their game that they smashed all the toys in their playhouse and bit the head off a doll. Even the youngest could not be entirely shielded from the violence and turmoil of war. "The children," Ellen Moore wrote her husband, Samuel, "all are soldiers here."

Older boys and girls turned from play to work, serving as helpmeets to their overburdened mothers. Sarah Kennedy warned her husband that he would find a "Yankee" family when he returned, for after the departure of the slaves, the children had taken up household labor. Sally now stayed home from school altogether to make her contribution. "Jimmy brings up the coal and kindling evening and is my man of all work. Sally minds the little children. Mary goes to school, but makes all the beds every morning before she leaves."[34]

Carrie Berry, a ten-year-old Atlantan, kept her own diary during the siege of her city in 1864. On her birthday in August she wished above all that by the time she turned eleven, "we will have peace in our land and I can have a nice dinner." But before peace there would be yet more terrible trials. Federal shells landing in the family's garden drove them into the cellar. When Sherman marched into the city in September and informed the residents that they must evacuate, Carrie remained unperturbed, even in the face of her parents' near-hysteria. "I think it would be so funny to move." The young girl displayed a resilience the rest of her family must have found heartening. Although she filled her diary with yearnings—for a nice dinner, for peace, and for church and Sunday school to open again—her daily life was one of solemn attention to family obligations, helping her mother with household tasks appropriate to one well beyond her young years.[35]

Not all Confederate children were as dutiful as Carrie Berry or the Kennedys. Many were less like miniature adults and closer to the "little animals" Emma Crutcher sought to avoid. Southern women confronted problems of authority in controlling children just as they had in managing slaves. In the middle of a letter to Alfred, Mary Bell abruptly announced she would have to stop writing as the children "are about to run me crazy." He would be amused, she thought, at how angry they could make her. Compelled to resort to whipping, she informed Alfred that her new role as disciplinarian "is no fun to me." Another Mary Bell, from Tennessee, had a daughter with the temperament of a "lioness." Hardly more than a toddler, the little girl constantly managed to win her way against her mother's wishes. "I have never been able to conquer yet she will strike back & kick me to the last. . . . I

*Carrie Berry, age ten. Courtesy of the Atlanta History Center, Atlanta, Georgia.*

think the spirit of the times must have had some influence on her disposition it is so decidedly beligerent." Cornelia Noble of Texas acknowledged her "deep solicitude about my children" but confessed a painful awareness of "how poorly and ineffectually I govern them." Ellen Moore of Virginia similarly concluded, "I am . . . a miserable manager of children."[36]

Susan Caldwell was exhausted by the demands of her three children, especially when the exodus of most of Warrenton's slaves left her without accustomed household help. Her children had, she realized, "known little else than indulgence from all. Now I find they need to be properly disciplined and it is to me a very great responsibility." Although Susan found the labor of childrearing debilitating in itself, the profounder challenge was that of control. Disciplining subordinates—be they children or slaves—had been the ultimate responsibility of white male heads of household in the prewar South, and much of day-to-day care and drudgery had rested with slave nursemaids. Controlling and caring for children was for many women as new an obligation as earning money or ruling slaves. "Only think," wrote Leila Callaway, "of my having to manage the children alone." "I believe you are equal to it," Morgan replied. "Be firm at the outset and continue so and you will have but little trouble." Boys, encouraged early to anticipate the social authority that would accompany their manhood, tended to offer mothers the greater challenge. Mary Bell of Tennessee in a sense confirmed this widely shared expectation when she declared that her "lioness" of a daughter "has too much spirit and courage for a girl." She was an exception proving the rule.[37]

Lizzie Neblett, so tortured about her duties managing slaves, seems to have found her ill-behaved children equally trying and perhaps even more out of control. Bob mistreated the horses; Walter used a cowhide to beat the cat; all the children's faces bore the permanent scars of Billy's fingernails; and infant Bettie cried ceaselessly. Afraid to use physical force against her slaves, Lizzie was not so intimidated by her children. She threatened to whip Billy every day if necessary, "& I do it well when I begin." "I can't get him to do anything unless I get the cowhide in hand." Bob, she complained, just "don't mind me as well as he once did." By the time baby Bettie had reached ten months, Lizzie confessed to Will, "I have whipped her several times." Reporting her aunt's stern disapproval of beating such a small child, Lizzie admitted she was surprised when Will did not scold her as well. As she restrained herself from abusing her slaves, Lizzie turned in anger, frustration, and self-loathing to beating an infant child—a child who happened to be not just speechless and helpless but named for Lizzie herself and "cursed like her mother with the female sex."[38]

Prewar childrearing practices within the South's gentry class had been characterized by an indulgence that historian Bertram Wyatt-Brown has argued was intended to encourage aggressiveness, especially in boys. Violent behavior in young males attracted admiration only slightly tinged with anxiety. Limits, when imposed, came almost inevitably from fathers and

*Unidentified woman and two Confederate children. Daguerreotype.*
*Courtesy of the Eleanor S. Brockenbrough Library, Museum of the Confederacy,*
*Richmond, Virginia.*

more often than not involved physical coercion or punishment. As Judge
William Sharkey explained the gendered nature of childrearing in a prewar
Mississippi custody case, "A system of training must be adopted which is
often repugnant to the wishes of the child. Which is best calculated to do
these things, the doting, partial mother with whom every fault is a virtue,
every wish a command, or the less partial father who looks to future welfare
rather than the gratification of childish folly?" When the departure of fathers
for war upset this patriarchal order, the tenuous balance between indulgence

and control was tipped in ways women often found difficult to redress. As in the management of slaves, women were called upon to maintain a system founded in an assertiveness and a violence they could not fully embrace as their own.[39]

## How Queer the Times

The conditions of Civil War exerted significant strains on family relations. Often disappointed in themselves and tormented by feelings of frustration and inadequacy, women began, as the war ground on, to question their men's infallibility as well. In February 1865 Grace Elmore of South Carolina commented, "How queer the times, the women can't count on the men at all to help them; they either laugh at us or when they speak seriously tis to say they know not what to advise, we must do the best of our ability."[40]

For Virginia French of Tennessee this transformation was more than simply queer or curious. In a diary kept throughout the war, French chronicled her rising exasperation with her husband, "the Colonel," who consistently disappointed her expectations about how a man ought to behave. At the beginning of her record, Johns Hopkins French was always "Darling"; but by 1865 the term of endearment had disappeared, and her wedding anniversary, previously noted with great joy, passed unobserved. "I have wished a thousand times," she wrote in September 1864, "that I had never married—that I had no family pressing upon me—no little children over whose present and future welfare to vex and worry."[41]

Lucy Virginia Smith French was a woman of considerable intellectual ambition. Daughter of a college president in Virginia, she had before the war served as associate editor of the *Southern Ladies' Book*, a periodical issued from New Orleans, and she herself had published a play and a collection of poems. Early in the war Union troops overran Tennessee, and French and her family sought safety in their summer house in the mountains near McMinnville. French labored to care for her young children—even worrying about basics such as bread and meat—and at the same time struggled to continue as a productive writer. It was an exhausting regimen. "My work," she wrote "is never done—I toil all the day with my hands and at night abridge my sleep to work with my brain." These unrelenting demands prompted her at last to ask, "Does any other member of my family work as I do? I should think not."[42]

Unlike so many southern wives, French did not have an absent husband.

"The Colonel," a wealthy stockman in the prewar years, did not serve in the military. Instead he remained at home, "knock[ing] around," as Virginia described his daily activities. His "principal employment," she reported in disgust in September 1864, seemed to be what he called "'going to town!' I often wonder what men were made for! To keep up the species, I suppose— which is the only thing they are 'always ready' and never slow about doing! For my part I am quite wearied and worn out with their general no-account-ability—and wish they were all put into the army where they could kill each other off—the less of them the better! . . . I suppose," she continued after this eloquent outburst, "I am beginning to become embittered by years of hardship, privation and sorrow."[43]

As the war's end drew near and its outcome unmistakable, French grew increasingly upset at her husband's failure to prepare for the future, and she complained of "the passiveness of one on whom I . . . have to depend. It is the inability of that one to make new conditions—who submits to circum-stances as Fate, and never lifts a hand to make his circumstances or conquer those which are adverse." Her husband seemed to her too much like Dick-ens's Micawber—waiting for something to turn up. Virginia wished the Colonel could instead emulate Russell Aubrey, the hero of Alabaman Au-gusta Jane Evans's 1864 novel *Macaria*, the southern best-seller of the war. "But do such strong men live in reality—no. I expect they only exist in books."[44]

When slaves disappeared to the enemy, it was Virginia who took on their work. When her old house servant Martha died, it was Virginia who read the burial service while another slave sang "When I Can Read My Title Clear." When no other schooling was available, it was Virginia who became her children's teacher. At the same time she was trying to write ten to twenty pages of prose each day. Yet she felt "powerless . . . insignificant . . . incapable," and angry that those for whom she was making her many sacri-fices neither recognized nor appreciated them. Virginia French confided to her diary that above all she sought justice for herself; she did not feel she was receiving what she deserved. But, she noted, justice "is the hardest thing for man to give to woman. They will be lenient, affectionate, generous—any-thing and everything but just." Affection, leniency, and generosity imply patronage, even condescension. The justice French desired presumed equality.[45]

In some ways Virginia French and her experience seem to contrast with the loving proclamations of devotion and loneliness exchanged by many couples separated by war. A closer look, however, shows them to be simply

*Unidentified couple from Texas. Courtesy of the Witte Museum,
San Antonio, Texas.*

different aspects of a shared phenomenon, different manifestations of a
common set of gender definitions displaced and disrupted by war. For
French as for many other southern wives, war meant a breakdown in expectations about men's and women's roles within marriage. Wives desperately
missed the emotional and material support they had taken for granted as
their husbands' obligation, duties previously all but unrecognized because
they seemed so natural a part of everyday life. When Julia Davidson wrote
John "we little knew," she acknowledged the way in which war's subversions

of marital and gender roles prompted unprecedented scrutiny and new awareness of men's and women's mutual devotion as well as responsibilities. One result of this reexamination was the intensification of feeling that arose from recognizing that marital bonds could be destroyed by death or separation and could not simply be taken for granted—absence making the heart grow fonder.

But as women assumed many of the burdens they had regarded as male and sacrificed the privileges of protection they believed their due as female, resentment and dissatisfaction appeared. Both love and anger arose from women's sense of loss—loss of individual men and loss of the world of marital and gender relations in which they had forged their female identities. Not to be able, as Grace Elmore put it, "to count on the men at all to help them" cast into question the whole logic of female subordination. Not to have your husband at your side for the birth of a baby you regarded as his responsibility if not indeed his fault, generated disbelief, then resentment and anger. Some of this rage was directed at the Yankees for causing the war in the first place, some at Confederate statesmen and officers for not winning it sooner or granting the desired furloughs, and some, inevitably, at husbands. Julia Davidson was furious when in obedience to military orders John left her almost ready to deliver in the midst of the siege of Atlanta. "The men of Atlanta," she wrote, including John among them, "have brought everlasting stain upon their name. [I]nstead of remaining to defend their homes they have run & left Atlanta. . . . Well Johny what have you done? . . . [E]very one who has talked to me say you did very wrong, transfer or no transfer, to leave until you saw your family at a safe distance. . . . There is not a man who would have done as you have." John had, in his wife's view, failed in his fundamental duties as a husband and a man by yielding to his orders as a soldier.[46]

The intensity of feeling so many women articulated when separated from their men was an intricate part of a larger recognition of the tenuousness, the insecurity of the ties of love and obligation southern women had assumed as the foundation of their world. War destabilized these presumptions. The absence of the loved one made him all the more desired and desirable; the absence of protection and of material and emotional support underlined the importance of these male responsibilities and generated resentment at their withdrawal. Thus the same dynamic that enhanced feelings of love and devotion in many instances later yielded sentiments of anger and doubt as women found what they suddenly so much needed was not available to them. As in the case of slavery, the obligations of family life began to outweigh its benefits. Catherine Edmondston, taking up new tasks in the face of the recalcitrance of her disobedient slaves, felt overburdened by "household cares." "What a drag it sometimes is on woman," she remarked in her diary, "to 'lug about' the ladder upon which man plants his foot and ascends . . . in ignorance of the machinery which feeds his daily life." But quickly she stifled her resentment, reiterating the ideology of separate spheres and female subordination. "Yet it is not always so," she consoled herself. "Rightly managed, prayerfully taken, women also may ascend, using each of their petty cares as an advance toward that 'heaven' which is governed by *self conquest*, self abnegation." Woman, she confirmed, should find not anger but fulfillment in martyrdom.[47]

Unlike Edmondston, Virginia French did not stifle her discontent. As the war ended, she still continued to do all that was expected of her as a mother and a wife, but she no longer understood why. "I work for other people's interest—labor for them—make sacrifices for them—deny myself good in order to do them good—yet it is not because I either love them, or wish them to love me. In truth I don't care at all if anybody loves me or not. I do it because somehow I think I ought to." Virginia expressed her anger at her husband and her disillusionment with her domestic role more forcefully and eloquently than most southern wives. She was after all a professional writer. But, perhaps more important, the distribution of wartime sacrifice in her marriage was particularly unbalanced. Her civilian husband went not to war but "to town"; he was not risking his life or, apparently, assuming significant responsibility on the homefront. Yet Virginia French was far from alone in her feeling that southern men were not carrying out their obligations to their wives and children because of a war that seemed as the years wore on less and less a noble and romantic Cause than a bloody and tragic slaughter. "How many lives," Martha Fort wrote bitterly to her husband, George, "are to be laid on the alter of ambition of men. I look on this war as nothing else but to gratify unholy ambition." Men went off to worship at the altar of ambition while women were relegated to the altars of sacrifice. As ambitions failed and sacrifices grew, it was an allocation of roles that became increasingly untenable.[48]

# CHAPTER SIX

# To Be an Old Maid

## SINGLE WOMEN, COURTSHIP, AND DESIRE

If war disrupted and transformed existing relationships between husbands and wives, it reshaped the lives and expectations of unmarried women perhaps even more profoundly. "The reflection has been brought to my mind with great force," a young woman wrote early in 1864, "that after this war is closed, how vast a difference there will be in the numbers of males and females. Having made up my mind not to be an old maid, and having only a moderate fortune and less beauty, I fear I shall find it rather difficult to accomplish my wishes."[1]

Women of the South's master class had always defined themselves in relationship to men—first as daughters and sisters, then as wives and mothers. When Texan Lizzie Scott contemplated her impending marriage to Will

Neblett in the early 1850s, she recognized that "my identity, my larger existence will be swallowed up in my husband." A woman's life, Kate Foster of Mississippi reflected, "is incomplete without a man's sustaining influence." Selecting a mate was the most important decision of a woman's life, and the activities and rituals surrounding that choice traditionally occupied a significant proportion of the time and attention of any unattached woman who could still be considered of marriageable age. But the carnage of civil war suddenly forced women across the South to contemplate spending not just the duration of the conflict but perhaps the whole of their lives outside the protections and intimacies of marriage—to be women without men.[2]

Such anticipations rendered some young ladies all the more determined to be counted among those who did succeed in finding mates. A young Georgia girl was unwilling to abandon her cherished hopes, and she urged a friend to join her and "hasten" to capture husbands before the limited supply was gone. Anna Kirtland of Memphis recognized that a determination to marry might require some compromise in the prewar definition of acceptable partners. "Just think Hattie," she wrote a South Carolina friend in May 1862, "we'll have to marry some poor one legged or one armed somebody, but never mind, we may get a whole soldier, but at any rate *half* a soldier is worth hundreds of whole men that did not go to the war." *Love's Ambuscade*, a popular and rare example of Confederate drama, took up just this theme, demonstrating the triumph of true love over a heroine's initial revulsion at the wounded and maimed form of a returning lover—"left knee in a wooden leg, right sleeve armless, black patch over left eye." In life as on the stage, women struggled to accept the notion that "the cause glorifies such wounds." But as one South Carolina belle exclaimed with both honesty and irony, "I fear it will be my fate to marry one who has lost his head."[3]

Other women submitted to the disappointing prospect of never marrying at all or adopted a critical view of wedlock designed to minimize the pain of lost opportunity. Emma Walton, in her mid-twenties, noted the rapid passage of time as she celebrated yet another birthday, and she pondered "the fate probably in store for your humble servant and many others similarly situated—but we shall be resigned to our destiny and endure for the good of the cause!" If Walton could regard the single state as a patriotic mission, it was because wartime circumstances had at least partially removed the stigma customarily attached to the failure to find a husband, for matrimony was judged the chief accomplishment of a woman's life. In the new world in which they found themselves, "it will be no disgrace to be an old maid," a Petersburg refugee declared with some relief. "We can always swear our going-to-be husband was killed in the war."[4]

A few young women embraced their anticipated spinsterhood with neither resignation nor resistance but an enthusiasm born of necessity. "I mean to be an old maid myself," Sarah Morgan boldly proclaimed in July 1862, "and show the world what such a life can be. It shocks me to hear a woman say she would hate to die unmarried." Ellen Roberts sought to protect herself from war's worst wounds by retaining the invulnerability of the unattached. "I think we have enough to grieve about without a husband. Some of the girls who have married say they have one consolation—if the war lasts ten years they will not be old maids, but I think happy is the girl who has no husband." For some, changed expectations about marriage yielded a newly critical stance toward the institution. With a cynicism one might expect to be the fruit of long and bitter experience, teenager Lucy Buck lamented the wedding of a Virginia friend. "I feel sad to hear these young brides indulge in such bright anticipations as these—I think of the contrast between married life as they imagine it to be and married life as they will find it to be ten years hence." Jo Gillis of Alabama professed to find the idea of wedlock highly unappealing. "I dont care to marry," she proclaimed in November 1861. "I see married women have to do and submit to things that my uncurbed I may say *high* temper, never could brook, and that would make the whole house unhappy, besides I see nothing repulsive in an 'old maid's' life, so ho fo[r] single blessedness for me. Tis true I would or do *now* pine for love, but husbands do not love as I have pictured *my* husband should love me, and the slights I see some wives submit to would quite crush out life and hope." Yet before many months had passed, Gillis was wed, caught within a union unhappier than even her bleak anticipations. Only death in childbirth would bring her final release.[5]

Wartime realities required young women of the Confederate South to reevaluate their futures as they acknowledged the altered place marriage seemed likely to play. Changed attitudes and often changed strategies proved necessary as women recognized that men were becoming ever scarcer resources. Because the lives of young women of the South's gentry class had been so exclusively focused on courtship and wedlock, because their identities had been so tied up with their visions of themselves as wives and mothers, and because their emotional expectations had been so fixed on the intimacies of heterosexual love, war and its mounting death toll would prove devastating not just to their life plans but to their fundamental self-definition. The wartime death of nearly a quarter of southern men of military—approximately the same as marriageable—age necessarily transformed both the emotional lives and the behavior of single women as it altered their social choices.

*Lucy Buck, age eighteen, and her younger sister Nellie, age sixteen, photographed in 1860. Courtesy of the Laura Virginia Hale Archives, Warren Heritage Society, Front Royal, Virginia.*

## Ever Lovingly and with a Great Desire

Young girls deprived of the distractions and excitements of heterosexual courtship and romance turned increasingly to one another for a surrogate interior life. Historians of nineteenth-century women have identified intense loving relationships between females as commonplace, but the circumstances of war may well have heightened these customary ties. Schools, especially the boarding schools that became an ever more popular refuge for gentry daughters, often provided the context for such personal connections to flourish. "As a band of sisters," one valedictorian at a Virginia female institute proclaimed, "many and joyous have been the hours we have spent together, and it may be," she continued with ominous reference to the costs of battle, "that the future has no gift in store to recompense us for their loss."[6]

Eighteen-year-old Nettie Fondren found the Lucy Cobb Institute in Athens, Georgia, almost filled to capacity by war. Engaged to a soldier at the front, Fondren nevertheless believed her education to be a necessity in uncertain times. Older than most of her schoolmates, she looked with some disdain at what she regarded as the childish occupations and attachments of the girls around her. A friend Rebecca, at another female seminary nearby, was at once envious of Nettie's betrothal—"Most of us here would give our head to look upon, much less captivate, a man in arms"—and jealous of Nettie's close friendship with another girl. "I *do love you and cannot help it*," Rebecca proclaimed. "I dreamed the other night, dear, and I actually thought myself kissing you—when I awoke to find it all an idle dream." Rebecca expressed her hope that such declarations did not cause offense, but she indicated her intention henceforth to abandon the intense and time-consuming infatuations that seemed to comprise the essence of student life. "I like all the girls in common, but," she vowed, "shall never permit myself to love another affectionately." Her statement indicates a clear recognition of the difference between friendship and the more impassioned attachments so common in her boarding school circle—the difference, as she put it, between "like" and "love."[7]

Clara Solomon of New Orleans recorded her crushes as well as those of her older sister, who was serving as a teacher in Clara's school. The "pleasantest" hour in Clara's day was when she could be close to her beloved Belle. "I gazed upon those cherry lips and with all the passion of my heart pressed mine to them. When I see her beautiful hair, I think 'how lovely,' and when I behold those orbs of 'blue serene' I think 'oh! nothing can be lovelier,' and when I see that mouth, as ripe and delicious as the fruit just plucked, I say 'oh!' for a lovelier sight do I care not. . . . I encircled her waist with my own arm, and thought 'Oh, if her heart could only reciprocate the love which mine could yield to her.' "[8]

For all her fond hopes, though, "the green eyed monster took possession" of Clara "when I saw her and M. walk home together." Clara referred to her sister "courting" a beautiful friend, admitted her own special attraction to blondes over brunettes, and described a "tantalizing" dream in which she "lavished . . . the fondest kisses and caresses" on an older female acquaintance. "But how I enjoyed them," she reported. "Had they been genuine, my joy could not have been more intense." In short, Clara under-stood her relationships with other young women within a framework of language and meaning customarily associated with heterosexual courtship. Her adolescent emotional extravagance, her fantasy life, and particularly, her attention to the physical expressions of love seem to us in the twentieth century suggestive of homosexuality. In her time, however, her words and emotions would have been regarded as far from unusual or deviant; such expressions represented a sensitivity and authenticity of feeling celebrated in this sentimental mid-Victorian era as appropriate to true friendship as much as true love.

Whether the eroticism Clara lived in her dreams ever found fulfillment in her daily life or in the lives of the many other young Confederate women who shared such romantic visions, we can never know. The extent of actual physical contact and sexual pleasure that accompanied such intense friend-ship remains undocumented. But to the women of the mid-nineteenth cen-tury such questions would have seemed irrelevant. In their pre-Freudian era, they would not have understood our rigid definitions of heterosexuality and homosexuality. Intense—even seemingly erotic—female friendships co-existed harmoniously with male-female courtship and even marriage. If nineteenth-century southerners had more restrictive and unchanging pre-scriptions of gender roles, it may be that we have more fixed and absolute notions of sexual identities. What we would label as sexual behavior be-tween women may well have been seen in the mid-nineteenth century as simply a natural extension of already powerful ties of emotional attraction and dependence. In the peculiar circumstances of wartime, adolescent emo-tional excess had almost necessarily to fix more frequently on members of the same sex. The already high value placed on intense female friendship and on expression of romantic sentiment made such developments both more likely and more acceptable. "The war," Mary Lee noted, "is prolific in developing feeling, in all its various forms; deep affliction, friendship, love, all grow with hothouse precocity."[9]

A striking example of the blurring of what we would consider eroticism with the excesses of adolescent infatuation appears in the schoolgirl diary of Louise Nichols, a seventeen-year-old Texan. The object of Nichols's affec-tions was her teacher, "Mrs. Rice," with whom she regularly shared a bed, apparently negotiating with Rice's husband, also a teacher, for access. "Mrs. Rice has slept with me every night this week except Monday," Nichols noted in May 1863. But the next day she reported, "I tried a little to get Mr. Rice to exchange tonight for Friday but he would not." Another week Nichols recorded her success with some satisfaction. "Mrs. Rice slept with me Tuesday, Thursday and Friday nights. I bought her of [f] Mr. Rice by writing in my Arithmetics." Nichols's feelings about her teacher were intense. "I do love her *so much* I do not know what I should do without her." The older woman evidently reciprocated her pupil's devotion. When Rice joined the Methodist Church, Nichols was sharply disapproving, and Rice worried about the loss of her young friend's admiration. Seizing Louise's diary, Mrs. Rice made an entry of her own. "I wish she would trust me. I love her truly and sincerely, and would do almost anything to make her happy. Louise *please* take back what you said that you did not care if I *never* slept with you again. Are you in earnest?"

It is almost impossible to imagine this triangle of relationships and to understand not just the nature of the interaction between Mrs. Rice and Louise Nichols, but the perspectives of the even more mysterious husband, who remains entirely silent in the historical record. "Sleep with" did not carry the same euphemistic significance in the nineteenth century that it does now, but both women's declarations of love, combined with their evident focus of powerful desire on the sharing of a bed, suggest that sleeping had important romantic, even if not necessarily sexual, implications.[10]

Across the wartorn South, women found themselves coming together for friendship and support, in newly created female households of relatives and friends and in women's hospital and aid societies. But females, particularly the young and unmarried, often turned to one another not just for companionship but for the passion and feeling more generally associated with heterosexual attachments. As Sarah Wadley explained, she thought of her absent friend Valeria "constantly . . . ever lovingly and with a great desire." Such relationships were not entirely a product of the war, but changed circumstances certainly encouraged and intensified these ties. "So often lately," Nannie Haskins of Tennessee observed rather disapprovingly in 1863, "I have noticed girls carrying on over each other kissing each other and so on. I think it looks right foolish sometimes."[11]

## *I Wish I Was a Soldier's Wife*

Despite frequent expressions of deep love for an absent female friend, Nannie Haskins, like many unmarried Confederate women, invested her most intense emotions in speculating about her future chances for matrimony. "I wonder if I will ever marry or if I will always be simple *Nannie Haskins*." The tuneful lament of a boarding school girl in Tennessee expressed what was probably the sentiment of the great majority of unattached young women of the South: "O my life! what a strife / I wish I was a soldier's wife."[12]

The boundaries where military encampments intersected with civilian settlements became frenetic scenes of courtship as young women strived to occupy their present and secure their future. "There seems to be," Judith McGuire observed, "a perfect mania on the subject of matrimony." Amanda Chappelear of Fauquier County, Virginia, confessed in September 1862 that she fell in love with nearly every man she encountered—a visiting minister or the dentist who extracted an aching tooth—but above all with the soldiers who passed en route to Maryland. Alice Ready was delighted by the arrival of a band of soldiers near her Tennessee home. "I think the girls here must appreciate their visits more than almost any others, because beaux are a *very* scarce article." Richmond was regarded as the site of greatest fascination and opportunity. Mary Chesnut, residing in the Confederate capital with her statesman husband, became a combination hostess/chaperone for a bevy of eligible South Carolina belles whose romantic adventures absorbed much of Chesnut's attention—and diary. Life in Richmond was, as one South Carolina maiden described it, a "surging intoxicating stream of brass buttons, epaulettes and swordbelted manhood. . . . [W]e exist in a tremor of ecstasy." There were almost too many men in Richmond to handle—an embarrassment of riches after the paucity of males in Columbia. "A delicate piece of business, is this managing of so many men in one lump!" It seemed to Phoebe Pember, matron at Chimborazo Hospital, that "every girl in Richmond is engaged or about to be."[13]

Amanda Worthington found that her life became much more interesting when Confederate troops moved into her Mississippi neighborhood. Early in 1862 the lack of escorts made her prefer staying home to attending concerts and tableaux. "We didn't have any beaux and knew we would have to go trailing in to supper by ourselves." Even the small supply of men still at home seemed to prefer her more sophisticated older sister. It was particularly galling, she found, to have to play companion and chaperone during her sister's flirtations. Dr. S. courted "Sister every time he comes up. I have to sit in there so I get the benefit of it all for he dont mind saying all he has to say before me. I dont listen though half the time but sit up and keep my mouth shut." By 1863 such silence was no longer necessary. The Vicksburg campaign and other military activity in the West had brought regiments

*Young Virginia woman, photographed in 1864. Prints and Photographs Division, Library of Congress.*

of troops to Mississippi, and Amanda Worthington took advantage of their proximity. "I do like to talk to soldiers & hear their adventures & anecdotes of camp life." Many of the men were quite unlike the suitors she would have encountered in peacetime, but their uniforms defined them as worthy objects of her romantic attention. "I like Mr. G. better than any of the scouts," she confessed, "but I can easily see he didn't associate with our class of society before the war. But I love all Confederate soldiers." Class lines seemed at least temporarily erased. "To be in our army is a passport," Kate Cumming observed. "The men are all gentlemen" and thus all appropriate objects of ladies' attention.[14]

The powerful feelings inspired by wartime danger combined with the desperation of many women for mates to yield unconventional alliances. As Emma Holmes observed, there were many "strange marriages & matches made by the war." Some of these at least, she suspected, resulted from sexual indiscretion. "The Blockade don't keep out babies." As Amanda Worthington's experiences suggest, however, middle- and upper-class women met and were courted by men of much humbler social origins, men they would not normally have encountered before the war. Conventional notions about age differences began to crumble as well. In 1862 Ada Bacot bemoaned a new "fashion" that she believed had "crept into society . . . that of a woman marrying a man younger than herself," and an Alabama observer commented on "little boys not over thirteen or fourteen . . . flying around grown young ladies in Montgomery." Both prescriptions for appropriate mates and regulations about acceptable courtship behavior relaxed under wartime pressure. Mary Chesnut was horrified by widows flirting shamelessly with strangers on trains and by public displays of affection between men and women, even among those of her own class. "I might . . . never have known," Chesnut wrote after traveling from Richmond to the Carolinas, "of girls who kissed the backs of horrid men's necks—faugh! Or widows who brushed with their eyelashes their cousin's cheeks in the public cars." Like many matrons, she deplored the speed of wartime courtship and the seemingly headlong rush into anticipated nuptial bliss. One woman's complaint about lovers lost to war seemed to a shocked observer less a lament than a mating call. "As soon as she began whining about her dead beaux I knew she was after another one. . . . She won't lose any time."[15]

Sixteen-year-old Esther Alden of South Carolina explained the sense of urgency and the lowering of expectations that influenced many young women's choices. "One looks at a man so differently when you think he may be killed to-morrow. Men whom up to this time I had thought dull and commonplace . . . seemed charming." An Alabama woman marrying in 1863 perhaps best expressed the very self-conscious abandonment of romantic ideals that accompanied her decision to settle on a mate. Her intended was "different in many respects to the hero of my old day dreams—yet I never have and never expected to meet one to come up to those dreams. *Life is real.*" Perhaps life is even more real in wartime. Clara MacLean bluntly noted that "numerous ladies . . . are reduced to marry men whom they do not love merely because they crave affection." She might have added that they sometimes sought financial as well as emotional security. Isabella Woodruff, a teacher perilously close to middle age, became engaged through the mail to a recent widower she had not seen in years. A woman friend had counseled her, at least partially in jest, that if she married "a nice rich gentleman" and grew "tired of your bargain," she could always hurry him off to the wars. Isabella Woodruff would find no such simple solution to what

*A young woman bereaved by the war. Ambrotype found beside a dead Confederate soldier at Chancellorsville, 1863. Courtesy of the Eleanor S. Brockenbrough Library, Museum of the Confederacy, Richmond, Virginia.*

turned out to be a miserably unhappy marriage. A clipping in Mary Early's Civil War scrapbook justly observed, "The war brought about a great many marriages, some of them entered upon hastily, to be repented at leisure."[16]

The preoccupation of unattached women with courtship extended beyond those seeking husbands for the first time. Sarah Kennedy wrote her husband that the widows in her Tennessee community were cutting quite a social figure. While wives gloomily awaited news of absent mates, "widows and widowers, are the only ones who are having a gay time. They are styled the rejuvenating club." Popular wisdom cast young widows as the most attractive of all women—"fascinating and irresistible." "How much more the heart is touched," Mary Bell of Tennessee observed, "by the tender beauty of a woman who has loved and suffered than by the gay shallow pink & white prettiness of a girl. I believe this is the secret of the attraction that widows seem to possess." One young woman charged widows with being even more eager for marriage than maidens, explaining that those who already knew the pleasures of married life were less willing to live outside it.[17]

But the shocked attention paid to courting widows only underlines their atypicality, their seeming transgression of accepted standards of behavior. The war created an unprecedented number of very young widows, women with decades of life remaining before them who did not wish to pass these long days alone. Confederate widows actively seeking romance and remarriage defied conventions about faithful grieving wives living only for their husbands' memories. Their actions suggested that they did indeed have identities apart from their departed mates and that their lives would not just continue, but perhaps begin again. Widows' courtship behavior, especially the rapidity with which many bereaved ladies took up the pursuit of new partners, seemed vaguely scandalous, challenging notions of a female fidelity that should stretch even beyond the grave and affirming the existence— and persistence—of female desire. To court and to remarry was to assert one's claims to happiness as prior to one's dedication to self-sacrifice and self-abnegation. The great majority of Confederate widows did not reappear on the marriage market, but enough did to attract attention and remark and to be regarded as representing a new departure for women past the first blush of youth seeking personal satisfaction and individual fulfillment.

The actual result of the intense absorption of unmarried southern women of all ages with courtship and matrimony is impossible to measure. Surviving statistical data on Confederate marriages is incomplete at best, and population shifts during the war were so pronounced that accurate rates of marriage (marriages per hundred adult population) are impossible to determine. The subject was, however, of considerable interest to Confederates themselves, for they recognized changes in courtship patterns and practices as one of the most significant social transformations brought about by war. From time to time the *Richmond Enquirer* offered data on the numbers of weddings within the capital city. At the end of 1862 the "matrimonial census" for the year totaled 286. "The war," the newspaper concluded, comparing this figure to past totals, "has had but slight material effect upon the progress of the tender passion." By 1864 the sum had dropped to 117. The "question of bread, (a very difficult one to solve in these times,) had had," the paper concluded, "considerable to do in lessening the number of devotees of Hymen." The *Enquirer* was evaluating totals of marriages, not rates, for it made no allowance for the dramatic increase in the size of the population in the swollen Virginia city during the war years. When these shifts are taken into account, the decrease in the number of weddings is even more significant.[18]

Marriage provided southern women with a social place and an identity; courtship offered them an occupation and a purpose. When war undermined their prospects for matrimony and their opportunities for courtship, women began to think critically about what they had long taken for granted —about the social and political order that was denying them their long-cherished dreams and about the substance of those dreams themselves. Once marriage was no longer all but inevitable, at least some women began to see it as problematic, as often less than wholly desirable. More common, however, were those single women who remained committed to increasingly impossible hopes, who continued to regard wedlock as an unfulfilled yet fond desire. Often such women were all but overcome by feelings of desperation and urgency; not infrequently they lapsed into a posture close to that of bereavement, manifesting a sense of deprivation not unlike that of their once-married sisters parted temporarily by military service or permanently by death from their men. A married woman feared the loss of a particular husband; a single woman worried about forfeiting the more abstract possibility of any husband at all.

In many ways the day-to-day lives of single and married women were more similar in war than they had been in peace. In the new "world of femininity" on the Confederate homefront, numbers of married as well as unmarried females were without the regular company and comfort of men. Women of different marital statuses joined together in these circumstances to find meaning and satisfaction in activities outside the disrupted domestic sphere—in service to country or community rather than to individual men or families. Both wives and single women increasingly sought emotional support from one another, from female friendships and interactions that assumed growing importance in this new warborn world. Harriette Cary expressed her delight at having two women friends staying with her in Williamsburg for an extended visit. "Were this pleasure denied us in what should we occupy our leisure hours? What relief and consolation it brings to be sympathized with in our troubles—to bear *together* with humble resignation the adversity with which God has seen fit to afflict us." In many instances these relationships were simple companionship, but their emotional significance was often considerably more intense. Particularly in the case of adolescent girls, female friendships became one of few remaining contexts for the expression of passion. It may be that older women felt similar ties and attractions to one another yet had outgrown the effusive romantic rhetoric that has guaranteed the survival of evidence of younger women's crushes in the historical record. Or perhaps older women had outgrown passion as well.[19]

Young and old alike, however, embraced a common need for a level of closeness and intimacy that implicitly affirmed their recognition of themselves as desiring human beings, as individuals to whom life should offer more than just the opportunity for sacrifice. Once again the deprivations of war worked to imbue Confederate women with a new sense of themselves and their interests.

CHAPTER SEVEN

# *An Imaginary Life*

## READING AND WRITING

Women of the southern elite found in the privilege of their education and their literacy a significant source of wartime consolation. Just as nighttime dreams reunited them with absent loved ones, so waking excursions into the realm of books and intellect offered them a world beyond suffering, war, and death, a world in which they found an order, a meaning, and a sense of control and purpose too often lacking in their disrupted, grief-filled lives. From their engagement with books, many Confederate women "gleaned," in the words of Alice Ready, the "comfort and courage" necessary to survive.[1]

Middle- and upper-class women of the nineteenth century have long been recognized as the chief consumers of the novels that became, as the *Southern*

*Literary Messenger* proclaimed in 1854, the "characteristic literary effort of the present age." From at least the time of Nathaniel Hawthorne's celebrated disparagement of the legions of "scribbling women" polluting the national literary scene, the popularity and productivity—if not the artistic distinction—of female writers has been grudgingly acknowledged as well.[2]

Beginning in the 1820s both a national publishing industry and a profession of literary authorship had begun to appear in America, the result, in no small part, of the emergence of middle-class women as readers and writers. The growing appeal and commercial success of female authors such as Caroline Gilman, Caroline Lee Hentz, E. D. E. N. Southworth, Marion Harland (a pseudonym for Mary Virginia Terhune), Susan Warner, Harriet Beecher Stowe, and Augusta Jane Evans depended in large measure on the thousands of women who comprised the great majority of consumers of "sentimental" or "domestic" fiction. By mid-century, America's female novelists had come, in the words of historian Mary Kelley, "to dominate a substantial literary marketplace." Marion Harland's *Alone*, published in 1854, sold more than 100,000 copies. Southworth was estimated to have made more than $6,000 a year in the heyday of her career. Abraham Lincoln hailed Harriet Beecher Stowe's *Uncle Tom's Cabin* as a factor triggering the outbreak of civil war.[3]

Middle- and upper-class women's engagement with this literature and with reading more generally is evident not just in the statistics of their book consumption but in diaries and letters that depict the centrality of reading in their lives. Books served as a focus for searching self-examination and definition. Generic narratives of female trials and triumphs enabled women to imagine challenges beyond their own, customarily limited experience. Fictional characters seem often to have become nearly as real and as influential as the actual friends and relatives inhabiting women's lives. Reading was far more than just recreation, for it offered an environment within which to explore the dilemmas of a rapidly changing American social world and the new complexities of female identity. The crisis of civil war, its transformations of southern life, and its challenge to traditional understandings of femininity made such issues all the more acutely felt at the same time that it introduced considerable pain and suffering into women's lives. As a result, both the pleasures and the instructions of reading came to assume even greater importance for Confederate women than they had in antebellum years.[4]

Books were one of very few sources of enjoyment remaining to women deprived of husbands and lovers, of adequate food and clothing, and even of news of the whereabouts and safety of kin. "Life to us," wrote Virginia

French on New Year's Day 1865, "is devoid of pleasures and made up of endurances. . . . I do not really enjoy anything now but a good fire and a pleasant book." If Virginia French could recall a time when other satisfactions abounded, Emma LeConte of South Carolina was too young to have many such memories. In the same month French wrote, LeConte reflected on all she had missed by passing into adulthood in the midst of war. "If it had not been for my books it would have indeed been hard to bear. But in them I have lived and found my chief source of pleasure. I would take refuge in them from the sadness all around." LeConte articulated a notion of reading as refuge that was widely shared by other Confederate women of her class; a book was not an object so much as a place to escape a reality that by 1865 had become all but insupportable. Reading served as both drug to soothe and fantasy to divert the troubled mind.[5]

Often books provided women with almost pure escape. "I strive to get away," Gertrude Thomas wrote in March 1865, "to forget in reading . . . the ever present, the one absorbing theme of war." Emma Crutcher ashamedly regarded her engagement with books as almost equivalent to a personal declaration of surrender, a separate peace. "I know, it is contemptible," she wrote her husband, Will, "but I feel like I have given all that I possibly can give, to my country, and have felt like withdrawing myself as far as possible from the horrors now enacting, and in books . . . as far as I can, avoid the hourly lacerations of heart." Caroline Davis of Virginia was bewildered by her reaction to the news of defeats at Gettysburg and Vicksburg in the summer of 1863, for she found herself all but overcome by what she regarded as an inappropriate desire for a good novel "to plunge into." "I wonder that I can feel like novel reading. What has come over me. My feelings are strange to me," she confessed to her diary. Yet they should hardly have seemed surprising, for hundreds of her countrywomen shared her need, especially in moments of extreme stress, to "get away from the horrid present by forgetting myself in a book."[6]

Reading served, however, as more than simply escape and avoidance. Books transported women toward new lives as well as away from existing ones. Lucy Buck of Virginia, almost the same age as Emma LeConte, described how in reading she entered a world of literary imagination in which she became an active participant. Delighted with a new novel, she explained the nature of this joy to her diary in March 1862.

There seems to be so little real happiness that I would like to make for myself an imaginary life in the mimic world created by the author's pen. I like to merge my individuality into that of the imaginary characters, enter into all their joys, share their trials and forget the ugly realities of real life around me. 'Tis wrong I know, enervating to the mind and unfitting one for the part which, however reluctant, we must play in the world and in the end creates for us a great deal of unhappiness, but, for the present, it diverts one from sad reflections, and I feel that anything is preferable to thinking and fretting over disappointments entirely unavoidable and irremediable.

This is an extraordinarily self-conscious statement of the purposes of reading and their relation to woman's place in the wartime South. Together the "ugly realities of real life" and Buck's powerlessness to change these conditions occasion her flight into imagination; "disappointments" are "entirely unavoidable and irremediable." Books offer a happy diversion from sentiments of both sorrow and frustrating uselessness shared widely by women of the wartime South. But Buck describes a process of reading that is more than just diversion and forgetting, more than anodyne or escape.

Like LeConte, Buck seeks to "live" in her books, to make reading active, not simply "enervating"—as was so often charged by the critics of nineteenth-century women's novel reading whom Buck defensively echoes. In a rhetorically forceful sentence, phrased in an almost staccato burst of active verb clauses, Buck tells us she would like to "merge," "enter," and "share"; she re-creates both herself and the book she is reading, making, as she explains it, a new life, a new identity for herself within the novel's fictional world. In stories Buck finds an escape not just from reality but from dread uselessness into active possibility and participation. She discovers the means to imagine and narrate a changed life course, to escape the constraints of her situation and her society, and to begin in imagination a transformation of self and consciousness.[7]

Like many Confederate women, Buck frequently read aloud, gathering together with her sisters in their Front Royal, Virginia, parlor. Oral presentation enhanced the vividness and saliency of literature and at the same time made it possible to share the books and newspapers that were all too scarce in the print-starved Confederacy. The five females resident in Mary Lee's Winchester household came together every evening to read aloud a wide variety of American and European fiction, embracing choices not unlike those of dozens of other women across the South: William Thackeray, Charles Dickens, Wilkie Collins, and Victor Hugo as well as southerners Beverly Tucker and Augusta Jane Evans. Lee found books a "great resource" in keeping up both her own morale and that of her domestic establishment more generally. If she was calm enough to listen to what was being read, she explained, the books "draw my thoughts from myself." Even when she was distracted and distressed, "they prevent the necessity for talking," discouraging the women of the household from fueling one another's fears through anxious conversation, yet at the same time eliminating the depressing alternative of dread and gloomy silence. Caroline Davis and her sisters became so engaged in Walter Scott's Waverly novels that they lost track of time and continued until their light burned out late in the night. "An interesting crisis of the fascinating narrative" in Marion Harland's best-selling novel *Alone* so captivated Lucy Buck and her sisters that when two Yankees burst into the room to search for Rebel soldiers, the women were taken almost entirely by surprise. Life's unpleasant realities could be all but forgotten when women moved together into the world of their books.[8]

By combining books with household obligations, some women managed to read almost all day. Louisa McCord Smythe remembered that after considerable practice many females were able to prop up thick tomes and read and knit or sew simultaneously. In the absence of such skill, women took turns as designated reader while others in the circle continued to work. Anne Martin of Mississippi, a reluctant seamstress, summed up one such day's activities: "interminable dress . . . interesting book."[9]

As a refugee in Camden, South Carolina, Emma Holmes had broader goals for a reading group she established in the fall of 1862. Separated from lowcountry friends and kin, Holmes hoped to "produce sociability" with a club modeled on one she had known in Charleston. The young women agreed to meet for two hours on Tuesdays and Saturdays. The first gathering proved a great success, due in no small part to the skills of the appointed reader. "Charlotte [Boykin] reads delightfully—her voice is so musical & so expressive in its intimations—her face equally interesting in its constant changes." Reading aloud transformed a customarily solitary act into an event approaching theater, into an occasion for companionship, social cohesion, and female solidarity. Just as books supplied an imaginary escape from the loneliness war had brought so many Confederate women, so the social setting of reading offered an antidote to isolation by bringing women together to share the "imaginary life" that helped sustain them all.[10]

## A Regular Course of Reading

What women read depended in no small measure on what was available in a literary market as disrupted by war as were southern society and economy more generally. Louisiana refugee Sidney Harding proclaimed herself "famished for something to read but there are no books in this miserable piney woods country." Emma Holmes was luckier in her flight to Camden, for she gained access to a resident's collection of contemporary fiction, "a perfect treasure to me." The prewar dependence of the South on northern publishing, however, greatly limited the availability of new works in the Confederacy. Mary Chesnut lamented the money she had thrown away on subscriptions to English and northern periodicals—"*Blackwood's*, &c &c—*Atlantic*, *Harper's*, *Cornhill* &c."—all stopped by the blockade. The *Richmond Enquirer* noted in 1863 that some books were being successfully smuggled into Charleston, "but for the most part, shippers who freight the steamers destined for Confederate ports load them with powder and ball—not with libraries." Kate Stone, a refugee in Tyler, Texas, struggled to fill tedious empty hours with sparse reading material. One local woman sought to make ends meet by renting books to the Stones for fifty cents a week, but Kate still found herself rereading old books for lack of new. She had "nearly memorized Tennyson," then returned to Shakespeare and her favorite, Sir Walter Scott. Perhaps her fondest desire, however, was to procure a copy of *Harper's*. "The literature of the North," she observed, "is to us what the 'flesh pots of Egypt' were to the wandering Israelites—we long for it." Harriette Cary of Williamsburg "regret[ted] sincerely" that the best books seemed to be "mostly in Yankee Land," although by 1864 Emily Andrews of Georgia had begun to look forward with eager anticipation to the "flood of new books there will be when peace is made."[11]

In spite of these limitations, Confederate women managed to find a great deal to read. Novels offered the most intense attraction, for women seemed to read with their emotions as much as their eyes or their intellects. Anna Maria Green of Georgia wondered if she ought not abandon fiction altogether, because even a "mere love story" would make her "tremble like an aspen leaf my whole frame quivers and sharp pain shoots up and down my back and I become so weak I can scarcely lift a hand." Amanda Worthington was grateful for a novel that made her feel "miserable," for, as she explained, "it suits me precisely," and Amanda Chappelear of Virginia enjoyed a cathartic cry over *The Curse of Clifton*, for it "suited my feelings to a great extent for the last few weeks." Emma Holmes confessed to "tears . . . in my eyes" when she finished a novel by Alfred de Vigny, for she felt she had lost personal friends when the tale came to an end. The characters were so compelling, "you feel as if you had lived and moved among them." Like many Confederate women, Holmes was particularly delighted by Miriam

*Kate Stone. John Q. Anderson Manuscript,* Brokenburn, *Louisiana and Lower Mississippi Valley Collections, Louisiana State University Libraries, Louisiana State University.*

Coles Harris's novel *Rutledge,* published in 1860, and like many women readers, she used the characters to explore her own expectations of men, courtship, and marriage. The figure of Arthur Rutledge represented for Holmes "my ideal of the man I would marry," a "master spirit," a man with "depths of tenderness." "Some one, I forget who," she wrote, "objects to the word *tender* as applied to a man—but I love it, for it conveys a world of meaning—far beyond *loving.*"[12]

If Rutledge represented young Emma Holmes's hopes, Augusta Evans's character Russell Aubrey crystallized matron Virginia French's mature disappointment with men and marriage, for her encounter with him in *Macaria* cast her husband's shortcomings into sharp relief. Confederate women projected themselves and much of their emotional life into the fiction that often filled their days and sometimes their nights as well. "How could I sleep?"

demanded Mary Chesnut after sitting up all night with a novel during the crisis of McClellan's move against Richmond in the spring of 1862. In fiction she could both live out and quell her insupportable anxiety.[13]

Mary Chesnut found consolation in nonfiction as well. Early in 1862 she borrowed Edward Creasy's *Fifteen Decisive Battles of the World* from a Columbia, South Carolina, library and noted on March 10 that she "Did Marathon today." Chesnut looked on the past as a kind of historical laboratory and sought parallels that would assist her in understanding her own time. She worried about the significance of Thermopylae and Waterloo, contemplated the character of Alexander's leadership, wondered at the small size of Greek armies, and compared the Roman imperial hordes to the massive Union forces. In John Motley's *Rise of the Dutch Republic*, Chesnut searched for insights into the struggle for independence and representative government. Ellen Moore was delighted with Elizabeth Ellet's *Women of the Revolution* and found it "so suited to the times." Reading that her fore-mothers had suffered yet triumphed "quite nerves me up to undergo anything," she wrote with exhilaration. Elizabeth Pringle of Charleston similarly turned to history for "*instructive reading*" to provide a balance to the novels she so enjoyed. Although she seemed to "get on very slow"—spending some seven months on Motley's *Dutch Republic*—she found in the trials and triumphs of the Netherlands "encouragement to hope" for the Confederacy's future.[14]

Like Pringle, numbers of Confederate women sought to apply themselves to what Alice Ready called "a regular course of reading"—"something more than novels and poetry." Lise Mitchell regarded her enforced idleness as one of Mississippi's refugees as an "excellent opportunity of improving my mind." She had been devouring fiction but determined she "ought to confine myself to reading history for the next few months." After the war Constance Cary Harrison remembered her own strict intellectual discipline. "I read constantly, and studied. We had almost no ephemeral publications, therefore no temptation to stray out of the straight and narrow path of standard literature. . . . [N]o day passed in which I did not write something." Catherine Edmondston read critically in history and philosophy, testing her own beliefs against those of the authors she encountered. She found such engagement at once uplifting and humbling to her intellectual ambition. After reading Francis Bacon's essays "regularly through, one every day," she reflected that "sometimes I come upon a thought or an idea that I fancied I had thought out of myself, which I had hugged to my heart as my own, when hey presto! I recognize it again stamped by the hand of a master in a form so terse, so complete so chisled . . . that . . . with a sigh I relinquish my proprietorship."[15]

While war subjected Confederate women of all classes to unaccustomed work, requiring even members of the elite to weave and sew, to procure and prepare food, to supervise slaves and care for their own children, and even to seek remunerative employment, it at the same time left numbers of females idle and underemployed. Refugees boarding with friends or relatives often had no fixed set of domestic obligations; in the absence of so many men, young ladies and adolescent girls lacked opportunities for the courtship activities that under normal circumstances would have occupied much of their time; and away from frontline areas, even matrons sometimes found that the demands of their domestic establishments failed to fill the hours they might have spent with now absent husbands or in the customary peacetime whirl of entertaining and hospitality. In the fall of 1861 *De Bow's Review* drew attention to the way slavery offered white women a special opportunity. "The circumstances are peculiarly favorable. The form of our society relieves her from that manual labor which falls to the lot of women in other nations, and thus ample time is left for literary employments." "Ample time"—inactivity and resulting boredom—combined with women's yearning for usefulness to impel numbers of elite females toward intellectual work. For some this commitment might involve little more than a "regular course of reading," an effort to use available time for self-improvement. But others harbored what they readily acknowledged as far more grandiose "ambition."[16]

## The Liberty of Writing

Inevitably, such expansive aspirations involved not just reading but writing, and in its most fully realized form encompassed a desire to join the nineteenth century's sorority of scribbling women—southern females adopted Hawthorne's epithet with pride. The Civil War made thousands of white women of all classes into authors—writers of letters and composers of journals recording the momentous and historic events as well as creators of published songs, poetry, and novels. Thus the war preserved the women's voices that serve as the most significant source for our understanding of them and their era.[17]

But writing not only reflected changed lives and eventful times; the very process of authorship itself nurtured new female self-consciousness. As one

Georgia woman observed when she began a journal she would continue for almost nine years of peace and war, "A journal rightly kept would be equivalent in its effects to a regular *Class Meeting*. It would lead us to examine our hearts and profit from past infirmities." Although she phrased her insight in the terms of her own Methodism, she recognized the much broader role of a journal as an agent of spiritual and emotional growth. Writing about one's experiences—even in letters, but more emphatically in a diary or journal—required self-reflection, the acknowledgment of self as individual and subject, as well as the imposition of some narrative structure of direction and purpose on the variegated events of particular lives. Writing is inescapably an act of discovery; autobiographical writing inevitably produces new exploration and understanding of the self. It is as much a process of self-creation as of self-description.[18]

As we have seen, correspondence between wives and absent husbands often prompted unprecedented intimacy, new frankness, heightened self-awareness, and self-revelation. Before the war, as Julia Davidson observed to her husband, John, "We little knew how dear we were to each other"; they discovered both themselves and each other in their wartime correspondence. Learning to write love letters, historian Karen Lystra has argued, required exploration and thus new awareness of one's interior being and one's subjectivity. For nineteenth-century men and women, she writes, "the self" was "brought into clearer focus through the communication process required by the conventions of romantic love. . . . Personal expression in various forms was perhaps the most important means by which this inner reality was developed and maintained. Given the power of language to shape reality, little wonder that the act of inscribing one's life to another—both outward events and inner feelings—should have cultural consequences in itself." The "intimate acts of self-examination and self-disclosure" embodied in love letters encouraged new personal awareness and, for women socialized in self-abnegation and denial, a new focus on themselves and on the value and importance of their own feelings.[19]

Women compelled by separation to turn to writing as the fundamental vehicle for their most cherished relationships also found themselves composing other sorts of letters for the first time. Reaching beyond the customary feminine sphere of domestic concerns, petitions and appeals to government officials demanded public attention for what had once been regarded as essentially private matters—personal subsistence and the safety and well-being of loved ones. Here women's writing represented not just an evolution toward a newly valued self, but a more explicit and bolder claim to a public voice and a political identity. Many of the women audacious enough to address Confederate officials understood the act of writing as a dramatic departure from conventional feminine behavior. Letters from women to Jefferson Davis or to state governors customarily opened with apologies and disclaimers for the unseemly assertiveness the composition of a letter represented. Adelia Etheridge began her appeal to the Confederate president by begging him to "excuse me for addressing you." Lucy White apologized for her letter to Davis by explaining that a male member of her family would have undertaken to write, but all had departed for the battlefield. Mrs. Thomas Womack begged North Carolina governor Vance's "pardon" for the "liberty" of writing, but her trials, she explained, left her no other avenue of appeal. Mahala Hundley was even more discomfited by the necessity of describing her desperate circumstances in an effort to procure Vance's aid. "I am forced to write to you," she explained, "though I assure you it is a very painful task." Women's uneasiness about these letters and the need they felt to apologize represent an implicit acknowledgment of the profound significance—of the dangerous novelty—attached to their decision to take pen to paper to petition state or national officials. Inherent in their act was a personal assertiveness that they felt compelled to balance with declarations of self-effacement. The claim to a public voice that these letters represented rested uneasily with their definitions of themselves as women. Necessity and desperation, however, pushed them toward a use of language and of writing that embodied a new female self Confederate women neither welcomed nor fully understood.[20]

If letters were vehicles of self-transformation with a significance women only partially comprehended, diaries evoked much more self-consciousness. Confederate females reflected openly about their motivations for keeping journals, perhaps because diaries seemed to lack the instrumental purposes often served by letter writing. Petitions to officials sought concrete ends—the discharge of a husband or son or the acquisition of necessary food or supplies—and letters to absent loved ones could be construed as acts of charity that fit easily with notions of female service and sacrifice. But a diary smacked of self-indulgence and self-absorption, and women often felt compelled to explain and justify their efforts. As with reading, emotional needs were often paramount. Sarah Morgan sought "some vent for my feelings," and Judith McGuire, "agitated and nervous," turned to her diary to soothe hers. By 1862 Morgan believed her journal had become "a necessity to me. . . . I get nervous and unhappy in thinking of the sad condition of the country . . . and just before I reach the lowest ebb, I seize my pen, dash off half a dozen lines . . . and Presto! Richard is himself again! O what a resource that and my books have been to me!" Morgan feared she would "die without some means of expressing my feelings." Clara Solomon regarded her diary as the equivalent of an intimate friend, addressing it with the proper name Philemon and seeking in its pages the "sweet society" of a "comforting angel."[21]

Mary Lee's journal also became her "silent friend," one to whom she could complain and one to whom she could show the weakness and despair she dared not reveal to the four young female housemates for whom she felt such maternal responsibility. But she professed to regard her diary more as an instrument for repressing than venting her emotions, designating her "scribbling" almost as a kind of busywork meant to divert her from unpleasant realities. Her paramount rule, she declared, was to "write of events, not feelings." Catherine Edmondston similarly intended her diary to deal more with public than private matters, more with the "stirring events through which we are now passing" than with her interior life. Personifying her "Journal," capitalizing it and addressing it in the second person, Edmondston nevertheless warned it not to "set yourself up by thinking you are my confidant. I do not tell you one half I feel." Emma Holmes had an equally historic sense of her purposes as diarist—"how valuable" her journal would be "in after years," she mused in June 1861, "as a record of the events which mark the formation and growth of our glorious Southern Confederacy."[22]

Many southern women diarists hoped to claim their part in the national struggle by becoming its chroniclers. Lise Mitchell of Louisiana had often heard the query, " 'Who will write the history of the present war?' but," she wryly observed in August 1862, "it is a more perplexing question to me 'who will not write it?' " Perhaps most self-conscious and most ambitious among these would-be historian-diarists was Mary Chesnut, whose seven surviving volumes of wartime records C. Vann Woodward has so insightfully analyzed and explained. During the war Chesnut kept what Woodward has called her Journal, an ongoing record of events that served as the basis for the greatly revised and artfully crafted postwar rendition of her experiences. From early in the conflict Chesnut regarded herself as a writer. "The scribbling mania is strong in me," she confessed in October 1861. "I have an insane idea in my brain to write a tale." In the postwar years she did just that, producing three manuscript novels as well as carefully reworking her wartime chronicle. Unlike the popular nineteenth-century women novelists she was certainly seeking to emulate, however, Chesnut in her lifetime never reaped the rewards of literary fortune. She sold but a single short sketch—for $10—to the *Charleston News and Courier* in 1883.[23]

Many other females shared Chesnut's literary aspirations. The success of women novelists in the prewar years had made them media heroines to their overwhelmingly female reading public and had defined the role of the woman writer as one warranting admiration and envy. A young girl at boarding school in Georgia, for example, could hardly contain her excitement when she discovered in 1863 that one of her teachers had contributed to a short-lived Confederate periodical and was thus "a real, true living authoress!!" Writing came to seem one of the most attractive and plausible callings for ambitious yet respectable females. It was work that could be done at home, and it had the potential to be highly remunerative—at least for the likes of Marion Harland, E. D. E. N. Southworth, or Harriet Beecher Stowe. It could also be imbued with transcendent moral and spiritual purpose. As a result, women often fixed on literary endeavors as they struggled to define useful contributions they might make to the world around them—and to a new Confederate nation in need of its own indigenous culture. "Perhaps the time has now arrived," wrote one Mississippi woman author to Jefferson Davis just weeks after his inauguration, "when the South will awaken from her lethargy and appreciate her own literature."[24]

If men were to find fame, honor, and purpose on the battlefield, women could look to the arena of letters for parallel satisfaction. Young Nannie Haskins of Tennessee understood the appeal of literary ambition even though she felt herself unequal to the challenge. "Yes," she admitted in September 1864, "I would like to do something worthy of a woman's name —But what could I do[?] I am not capable of writing a novel and yet if I could it would only be a continued repetition of what has already been given to the world a thousand times with a few variations—I cannot write 'Memoirs' for I have none, but what every girl of eighteen has had—I cannot write my 'travels' for I've never been beyond the lines of my own native state." She was, she concluded with both pride and regret, "not a Hannah More—nor a Charlotte Bronte—nor a Madame deStael but a Nannie Haskins."[25]

Abbie Brooks, a Georgia schoolteacher, was similarly eager for achievement yet equally realistic. "I long," she confessed, "to be a writer of merit to be classed among those who can compose and write sentences which will startle and electrify the reader." But she recognized, "There are such a vast amount of scribblers in the world now; they cannot all become celebrities or great writers, some must be content with small things." Some must be an Abbie Brooks or a Nannie Haskins.[26]

Or an Emma Holmes. She too admitted she had "so long yearned . . . to distinguish myself in some way . . . to feel that I had not lived utterly in vain, and that I should leave behind me a single stone to add to the grand fabric of human intellect." Yet she too doubted her abilities. "Original I know I could not be." Her "true vocations," she concluded, were translation and teaching—communicating the work of others rather than creating her own. Far better, she thought, to limit her goals than "aspire through conceit to what I feel is beyond my powers." Even Virginia French, who had published extensively before the war, had persistent doubts as she tried to write amidst a domestic environment that gave her little leisure. "I almost despair of being able to accomplish anything—my time is so occupied and my head so worried about things that are necessary to keep body and soul together." But her self-doubt arose from more than just a recognition of her challenging circumstances. "Perhaps if I even accomplished the book," she wrote in February 1864, "with great labor and pain to myself—it would not be successful—so where's the use? . . . I fear that in a few years I shall have passed away—leaving no mark behind which shall say I lived to any purpose. I who have from childhood yearned to be something, longed to do something good and great and memorable, shall have . . . died and made no sign."[27]

Catherine Edmondston attributed the constraints on her literary ambition not so much to self-doubt—although she possessed plenty of that—as to an acute sense of feminine propriety. She wrote sheaves of poetry but never submitted it to newspapers or journals. It was not so much her recognition that her verses were "mediocre" and "not . . . worthy of a place in the Poet's corner," but her wariness of "stepping out of your sphere" that served as inhibition. "Then indeed you would forget a woman's first ornament, modesty. Women have no business to rush into print; so wide an arena does not become them."[28]

Mary Lee would have agreed; she was horrified when a newspaper appended her name to what she had intended as an anonymous letter. Substantial numbers of respectable southern ladies, however, demonstrated their dissent from such traditional notions by articulating a literary ambition that sat uneasily with expected feminine virtues of self-abnegation and self-denial. Even women like Edmondston acknowledged such egotistical yearnings at the same time that they suppressed them out of deference to propriety. Women's growing acceptance of authorship as appropriate to their gender represented a significant new departure in the Civil War South. In the antebellum years respectable women had been far more like Edmondston or Lee than the thousands of Confederate females who eagerly printed their songs, poems, stories, and even novels. Few any longer felt the anguish that had gripped Caroline Gilman upon the unauthorized publication of some of her verses in 1810. "I wept bitterly, and was as alarmed as if I had been detected in a man's apparel." The mantle of authorship belonged increasingly to both sexes.[29]

With men so preoccupied with military matters, culture became to a considerable degree the domain of women in the Confederate South. Newspapers regularly included sentimental poetry—often on war-related subjects—attributed to female authors, and women were a major source of the articles that filled Confederate periodicals. Constance Cary Harrison, a Virginia aristocrat who married Jefferson Davis's secretary, contributed steadily to the *Southern Illustrated News*, the *Magnolia*, and the *Richmond Examiner* but retained the forms of gentility by adopting the pseudonym "Refugitta." By the end of the war she had completed a full-scale novel, but a fire that engulfed her Richmond publisher's office when the city fell to the Yankees in 1865 destroyed the manuscript. Clara Dargan MacLean worked as a governess in South Carolina during much of the war but won prizes for the stories she found time to write for the *Southern Field and Fireside*. Confederate poet laureate Henry Timrod proclaimed her a "sister of the quill."[30]

Amy Clarke had been a valued contributor to the *Southern Literary Messenger* but wrote the editor to explain a brief interruption in her submissions. Her husband was in the army and she had moved to North Carolina to be with her father and sister. Traveling by train en route to a military encampment where she intended to nurse wounded soldiers, Clarke composed a piece entitled "The Battle of Manassas." An officer seized it from her, read the poem to his troops, and requested permission to publish it in the *Richmond Enquirer*. Then the editor of the *Raleigh Standard* issued it as a broadside, with profits to go toward the care of sick soldiers. Since then, she reported, "I have had applications for it from all parts of the Confederate states, and shall get the Edt. of the N.O. Picayune to issue it in New Orleans in the same style." Now she was writing to request similar action by her Richmond publisher.[31]

Public discourse expressed fewer reservations about women writers than it did about nurses or teachers. The profession of letters seemed consistent with many of the ideals of domesticity. It did not require ladies to leave the home or to undertake demeaning physical labor that would threaten their class status; although it did expose their words and sometimes their names to public scrutiny, it left their actual persons sheltered within the domestic sphere. The cultural needs of the new nation combined with the psychological and financial necessities of its women to encourage female writing in the wartime South, and the public presses reflected this widespread enthusiasm. In the fall of 1861 the *Augusta Weekly Constitutionalist* hailed local women whose work had appeared in Confederate periodicals. Mary Bryan was "the unrivalled songstress of the South"; Annie Blunt's stories had won her "immortality." Writing contained the potential to create a new life not just in the escapist, imaginary world of the mind but in reality, for it offered women a tantalizing opportunity for the fame and fortune, the public notice and acclaim, that seemed all too exclusively the prerogative of men.[32]

## Writing and Reading the Confederate Novel

The wartime creation and reception of the Confederacy's best-selling novel forcefully illustrates the meaning of both writing and reading in southern women's lives. Augusta Jane Evans published *Macaria; or, Altars of Sacrifice* in 1864, dedicating it to the Confederate army as an "inadequate tribute" from a woman "debarred from the dangers and deathless glory of the 'tented field' " to the "patriotism and sublime self-abnegation of her dear and devoted countrymen." Born in 1835 to an old and prominent southern family, Evans was an avid Confederate patriot. She had rushed from her home in Mobile to participate in the celebration of Alabama's secession at the state capitol in Montgomery, and she greeted the outbreak of war with a flurry of public-spirited activity, organizing women to sew sandbags for the defense of Mobile, founding a hospital and later an orphan asylum, and serving as a nurse despite the objections of her brothers. But she, like so many other Confederate women, still chafed in frustration at her comparative uselessness in the national crisis. "It is not," she regretted, "my privilege to enter the ranks, wielding a sword, in my country's cause," and she felt compelled to "lament the limited circle of action, the insignificant role" available to women "in the mightiest drama that ever rivetted the gaze of the civilized world." To ensure that "the cause of our beloved, struggling Confederacy may yet be advanced through the agency of its daughters," Evans turned to what she disingenuously called her "feeble, womanly pen." Her posture of self-effacement could hardly obscure the reality of Evans's enormous success as the author of *Beulah*, published in 1859. At the outbreak of war she was already a best-selling novelist with a significant national reputation. Writing was thus all the more logical an outlet for her frustrated patriotic ambition.[33]

*Macaria*, as its dedication page made clear, was explicitly intended as a paean to the Confederacy, but at the same time it reflected Evans's own search for a wartime role, a quest for "Womanly Usefulness" that was emblematic of the lives and struggles of southern women more generally. Composing the book on scraps of paper as she sat at the bedside of wounded soldiers, Evans intended her narrative to provide white women with models for emulation in their search for what Evans called "agency" within the Confederate cause.

The title of the novel itself alludes both to Evans's design to make the work her own sacrificial offering and to the long tradition of women's war stories within which she intended to place her effort. In classical times Macaria had saved Athens from invasion by giving herself as a sacrifice on the altar of the gods. Like the mythological figure of the title, the book's main character, Irene Huntingdon, is herself "ambitious of martyrdom" (260). But she progresses toward that goal and discovers her "life-work" (255) as a laborer in "God's great vineyard" (414) only in the face of daunting obstacles. She must resist the insistent courtship of Hugh, the cousin her father has chosen to be her husband, as well as her father's threats to disinherit her if she does not bow to his will. Yet far more difficult than rejecting a loveless marriage, she must, because of an old family feud, hide her devotion from her true love, Russell Aubrey, until the moment he marches off to battle and to death. Ultimately she must sacrifice both Russell and her father to the Confederate cause.

Like many nineteenth-century women novelists, Evans employs paired heroines. Although somewhat less prominent and less arresting a character, Electra Grey follows much the same life trajectory as her friend Irene. Imbued with imagination and artistic creativity to parallel Irene's rational and intellectual powers, Electra too resists a loveless match and ultimately consecrates herself to the Confederate effort, even carrying dispatches through the northern blockade in what Evans intended as a thrilling depiction of female heroism.

Irene's and Electra's struggles correspond to the essential conflict within the structure of the book as a whole. In a recent study of women's writing, Carolyn G. Heilbrun has distinguished between plots traditionally found in men's and women's fiction, arguing that conventionally men's stories are "quest" narratives, in which activity in the world takes precedence over adventures of the heart. In contrast, women's stories trace the path of the heroine toward romantic fulfillment, which in nineteenth-century domestic fiction is translated into wedded bliss. In *Macaria*, however, war gives Irene the unprecedented choice of whether to live her life as a quest or a romance,

*Augusta Jane Evans, author of* Macaria. *Courtesy of the Alabama Department of Archives and History, Montgomery.*

just as Evans herself confronts the possibility of an alternative structure for her novel. The fundamental struggle within *Macaria* is between these two plot resolutions and definitions, these two ways of envisioning the female life. Will Irene and Electra hold to their insistence never to marry? Will Evans resist the romantic formula that the contradictions of her earlier novel *Beulah* seemed to show her struggling futilely to defy? Literary scholar Anne Goodwyn Jones has suggested that Evans achieved the conventional denouement in *Beulah* only by "wrenching her heroine out of character." Evans does no such disservice to Electra or Irene. When Russell begs at the moment of his departure for war that he at least be permitted to correspond with her, Irene rejects both romance and the romantic narrative out of hand. "I want neither your usefulness in life nor mine impaired by continual weak repining" (326). In a striking departure from usual male fictional roles, Russell has found that his "ambition dims . . . in comparison with . . . your love" (323). But Evans will not permit him to lapse into acceptance of romantic goals. In an inversion of the conventional identification of males with worldly achievement and women with love, Evans has Irene insist that both she and Russell dedicate themselves to their particular quests.[34]

Throughout the novel, which opens nearly a decade before the outbreak of the war, Irene and her alter ego, Electra, struggle for their independence. Motherless in the tradition of romantic heroines, both work to earn their financial as well as their emotional autonomy. Even as a young child Irene declines to permit a slave to carry her schoolbooks. "I don't choose," she declares, "to be petted like a baby or made a wax-doll of. . . . I am strong enough to carry my own books" (14). Electra, too, insists on her own strength, rejecting monetary support from her cousin Russell—"I must depend upon myself" (70)—as well as a newly discovered inheritance—"I am young and strong, and I expect to earn my living" (104). Both women speak of themselves in the language of bourgeois individualism, stressing their rights of self-ownership and self-determination. To her cousin Hugh, who insists, "You belong to me, and you know it," Irene responds, "NO! I belong to God and myself" (23). In the face of her father's explicit order that she marry, Irene weighs duty to him against duty to herself and her maker. "I am responsible for no acts but my own," she says; "I am a free-born American. . . . I, only, can give myself away" (200). Having declared her independence, Irene is overcome by a "thrill of joy; she had burst the fetters; she was free" (202).

At the same time that she celebrates personal autonomy, however, Evans denounces the "selfishness" (85) that arises from entirely unchecked individualism, and her reservations constitute a sharp critique of the philosophy of bourgeois liberalism as it was evolving in mid-nineteenth-century America. Evans's own notion of self-fulfillment remains closely tied to the organic connections of family and community so often seen as its opposite. Self-realization, Evans acknowledges, necessarily involves being true to oneself, just as Irene successfully "grew up what nature intended her to be" (40). Yet the self-fulfillment that is true freedom cannot be achieved apart from a social community to which one is connected by ties of duty and belonging. Irene deplores the "parasitic clinging" of dependence but recognizes as well the lessons of her friend and mentor, the minister Harvey Young, who counsels that "people are too isolated, too much wrapped up in their individual rights, interests or enjoyments. I, Me, Mine, is the God of the age. . . . [W]e ought to live more for others than we do" (85).

Irene's declaration of independence thus only begins her struggle for self-discovery. Despite her private scholarly pursuits and despite the abstruse astronomical researches she undertakes while her father and household sleep, she feels purposeless and finds the fashionable life of southern society empty of meaning: "Everybody ought to be of some use in this world, but I feel like a bunch of mistletoe, growing on somebody else, and doing nothing." All who seek true happiness, she recognizes, "should be employed in some way" (51). Electra voices almost identical sentiments, indicating her commitment to following a quest in her own life. "I want to accomplish some work," she declares, "looking upon which, my fellow-creatures will proclaim: 'That woman has not lived in vain; the world is better and happier because she came and labored in it.'" Electra is unreservedly ambitious, desiring her name carved on "the living, throbbing heart of my age" (213).

In the context of Irene's persistent cry, "I want to be useful" (316), a cry that echoes sentiments expressed in Evans's own life as well as in nearly every extant Confederate woman's diary, the war comes as a fortuitous solution. In Confederate independence Irene and Electra find both true personal independence and fulfillment; through war they discover the path to the ultimate spiritual peace represented by Irene's given name. Women, Evans suggests, thus need not simply endure the war but might justly celebrate its unprecedented opportunities for self-realization. Through Confederate nationalism these women thus may truly find themselves.

In 1864, with nearly half the white male population of the South wounded or killed, the single life was for many inevitable. Evans felt she could dare to make it seem desirable. Necessity became not so much the mother as the legitimator of fictional invention. *Macaria*, the word itself meaning "blessed" in Greek, ends with a celebration of single blessedness. A woman who "dares to live alone," Irene confirms, is certainly "braver, nobler, and better" than one who consents to a "loveless marriage" (413). More important, however, is the unmarried woman's potential for vocation, for service, and for achievement. Even though a married woman may be superficially happier, Evans concedes, the single woman is unquestionably more useful, "because she belongs exclusively to no one, her heart expands to all her suffering fellow-creatures" (413). Like Evans herself, Irene recognizes that "upon the purity, the devotion, and the patriotism of the women of our land, not less than upon the heroism of our armies, depends our national salvation" (414). Like Evans herself, Irene devotes her time to nursing wounded soldiers and establishing an orphan asylum.[35]

Electra, whose Greek name means "unwedded," similarly embraces spinsterhood and dedicates her life to creating artistic forms for southern national greatness. With Irene's financial backing, Electra will direct a school of design for aspiring women artists cast upon their own resources by the exigencies of war. Strikingly, Evans presents a version of the late twentieth-century notion of comparable worth to argue for an enlargement of woman's role. The "remuneration of the peculiar employments of women," she notes, "is always far below that of employments of equal skill carried on by men. . . . Hence, in improving the condition of women, it is advisable to give them the readiest access to independent industrial pursuits, and extend the circle of their appropriate occupations" (410). Evans has in *Macaria* significantly undermined the restrictiveness and transformed the meaning of the female sphere by releasing women from exclusive domesticity and providing them a critical role in the public life of the new nation.

Nevertheless, Electra has no illusions but that women's hands remain significantly "tied; and they walk but a short, narrow path, from hearthstone to threshold, and back again" (368). Evans's call to women in fact invokes the notion of a limited set of "appropriate occupations." *Macaria* makes no direct attack on these persisting constraints. Instead the novel reaffirms prevailing ideas of woman's proper sphere and explicitly decries northern feminism and woman suffrage. "Southern women," Irene assures the novel's readers, "have no desire to usurp legislative reins; their appropriate work consists in moulding the manners and morals of the nation" (368). Men are "at home with state papers, machine-shops, navies, armies, political economy, and agricultural chemistry," whereas women "have a knack" for "embroidery on the coarse grey serge of stern, practical every-day life" (184).

Despite her use of the language of liberal individualism, Evans remains committed, in her novel as in her private correspondence, to a hierarchical view of the social order in which race, class, and gender all play a part in assigning individuals to their designated places. She sees no apparent contradiction between Irene's proud claims to ownership of her person and the bondage of the slaves who serve as background characters throughout the book. Imperatives of duty, as Russell explains, mean "we are all in bondage, more or less" (221). At the same time that Irene professes to "despise . . . ridiculous nonsense about aristocracy of family" (14), she, like Evans herself, firmly opposes the "demagoguery" of universal suffrage. Irene's individualism and the principles of personal independence she and Electra insist on throughout the book rest uneasily with the assumptions of hierarchy *Macaria* simultaneously espouses. Evans's warborn subversion of the domestic novel and her adoption of a male quest plot for female fiction exacerbate the contradictions already inherent in her views about woman's place as well as embedded in the generic structures of the woman's novel.

*Macaria* does not leave these contradictions unattended; Evans struggles to contain her subversion within acceptable boundaries by turning to religion for resolution of the paradoxes she and her heroines confront, paradoxes of self-realization and self-denial essential to the experience of so many Confederate women. Evans redefines the work that is at the center of both Irene's and Electra's self-fulfillment as but a special form of divine worship. For the painter Electra, "Aesthetics is a heavenly ladder, where . . . pure thoughts and holy aspirations come from and go to God" (357). Irene's astronomical observations serve above all to remind her of the "immeasurable heights and depths, the infinitude, the grandeur, and the glory of the universe—and there, as nowhere else, I can bow myself down, and say, humbly and truly, 'Not my will, oh, God! but thine'" (378). The self-assertion implicit in the pursuit of artistic or intellectual goals is thus subsumed within the larger context of religious submission.

Although the recurrent language of individual realization in one sense undermines the theme of martyrdom central to the title and the book, the invocation of Christ at last valorizes the concept of sacrifice and resolves the contradictions of the plot. Irene, Electra, and even Russell on his deathbed are all converted to evangelical religion, finding in doing God's will at once the perfect fulfillment and abnegation of their own. In divine thrall each character discovers perfect freedom, while Evans identifies a means of having it both ways. Once, Electra explains, artistic "fame was all that I cared to attain" (413). Now, she continues, she hopes to spend her years as a painter in pursuit of spiritual as well as earthly immortality. Her worldly achievements are no longer directed toward crass ambition but divine service. Her quest, like Irene's, becomes a pilgrimage. "Thus," Evans writes, "by different, by devious thorny paths, two sorrowing women emerged upon the broad highway of Duty, and, clasping hands, pressed forward to the divinely-appointed goal—Womanly Usefulness" (380). God has in a very real sense taken the place of a man in these women's lives; single they might be, but their independence, asserted throughout most of the book, is by the conclusion once again safely contained. Evans in the end subverts her own subversion.

The nature of *Macaria*'s reception in the Confederacy makes clear the resonance of its themes—and the tenaciousness of its paradoxes—within southern culture. The popularity of the book is hardly surprising. Evans was an established—even beloved—author; *Macaria* was one of only a handful of original novels published and available in the wartime South, and its Confederate subject matter and its patriotism enhanced its timeliness and appeal. Even before *Macaria* went on sale, Mary Legg of South Carolina wrote enthusiastically to Hattie Palmer, "I see Miss Evans has written another. I would like very much to see it. I like Beulah so well." Women such as Cordelia Scales or Belle Edmondson, with pets named Beulah, had certainly exhibited the kind of involvement that would make them eager for a new Evans novel.[36]

Nearly every Confederate woman who discussed her reading in a diary or in her correspondence mentioned *Macaria*. Some expressed their frustration at not being able to procure a copy; the luckier ones recorded their reactions to the tale. "I have been reading 'Macaria' today. I like it very much," Nannie Haskins wrote in October 1864. "[I] think Miss Evans decidedly the best writer (female novelist) of this day." Mary Lee, older and more critical, complained about the "mass of pedantic nonsense" at the outset of the novel but proclaimed "the last part, about the war," to be "admirable." Gertrude Thomas similarly found the prewar portions of the novel unsatisfactory. "How tame and uninteresting ordinary life appears and reads when compared with the life we lead." When she reached the war years, though, Thomas succumbed to Evans's "spell of enchantment"—and to the power of her call for "Womanly Usefulness." *Macaria*, Thomas reported, made her "hear the groans of wounded men. . . . I felt my cheek burn as I reflected how indifferent and careless I had grown to the suffering of our men—*and the next evening I visited the hospital!* The best commentary upon the good Miss Evans book effected." Russell Aubrey emerged as so powerful a figure in the minds of *Macaria*'s many readers that his name became a commonplace in Confederate speech. "Few Russell Aubreys" one young nurse replied with a smile when asked if she had many interesting cases on her ward.[37]

The intensity of the South's involvement with *Macaria* was evident as well in the treatment of the book in the public press. Evans's revision of the structures of the domestic novel did not pass unnoticed, and her articulation of the conflicts confronting Confederate women evoked vehement responses from readers across the South. A lengthy essay in the *Richmond Age* complained that Evans had "done no inconsiderable violence to our just expectations." In fact, the reviewer asserted, *Macaria* was only a "quasi-novel—a new experiment in the art of book-making called forth by the times through which we, the citizens of the Southern Confederacy, are now passing," for "although love forms the great staple of the work, yet it is introduced with the special design of making it subservient to what is regarded as the higher dictates of patriotism." In *Macaria* woman had dared to privilege public over private matters. The reviewer objected to Irene's puzzling over the heavens when she should have been entertaining her father's guests; domiciling herself in a hospital filled with men, rather than in her own home; abandoning her opportunities for motherhood; and worst of all, adopting the "mistaken idea" that the single state is anything but one of "isolation and discomfort." Evans may be "skilful in sketching character," the reviewer concluded, "but not in casting a plot." The narrative of Irene's life, like the experience of thousands of Confederate women whose existence had been disrupted by war, deprivation, and death, was too much at odds with traditional models and expectations to make sense to this reviewer. Change in the form of the domestic novel, as in real life, was jarring and discomfiting. Belle Edmondson of Tennessee read the book in much the same way. "Delighted" with the novel at the outset, she declared herself "not entirely satisfied with the fate of some of the characters" at the end. The fate of Irene and Electra proved to be not unlike her own, however, for Edmondson, who served as Confederate spy and courier during the war years, died a spinster in 1873.[38]

A striking review of *Macaria* published in the *Mobile Evening News* originated as an essay for a local literary society in Oxford, Mississippi, composed by a woman calling herself "Fidelia." No southern maiden, she insisted, would have rejected "the dark and glorious Russell." Fidelia professed to love "the peerless Irene," but, she continued revealingly, "much as some . . . loved Fanny Kemble; we want but one Fanny Kemble." If many heroines like Irene should appear, "the world will need the new classification of men, women and Irenes." Fidelia explicitly associated Irene with an outspoken critic of the South, English actress Fanny Kemble, who in her divorce from Georgian Pierce Butler had become a notorious symbol of the dangers of women's independence. Perhaps most significantly, however, Fidelia noted the challenge *Macaria* offered to the prevailing system of gender categories. Irene seemed to fit nowhere—recognizable as neither woman nor man—and thus her character called the entire basis for fixed and certain gender identity into question. Her very existence made male and female attributes seem dangerously negotiable.[39]

Augusta Jane Evans regarded herself as anything but a feminist. Readers of *Macaria*, however, charged the author with so violating gender conventions as to have created an androgynous heroine, to have denaturalized and denatured their southern social world by introducing a new and anomalous gender category. If *Macaria* raised questions and destabilized certainties about the nature of female and male identity, it fell short of providing answers or resolving the conflicts it provoked. Both the plot and the characterization of *Macaria* demonstrate a writer taking advantage of warborn opportunity to extend the limits of the possible and of the imaginable—in her fiction as in her own life. But the response of at least some of her readers suggests that Evans may have tried to extend those boundaries too far. *Macaria* appeared to its public as a "new experiment," but one that seriously violated many "just expectations."

Evans's choices as an author, her movement to transform in significant ways the assumptions on which her fiction was based, might be seen as a literary act directly parallel to the social actions of Confederate women who, like herself as hospital nurse, moved into a variety of previously male roles. In her depiction of Irene, she was creating not just a new gender, as Fidelia charged, but a new genre as well. Yet Evans demonstrated the persistence of social conservatism, the power tradition wielded over privileged white southern women. Even in *Macaria* Evans ultimately offered a sharply conflicted message and stepped back from a celebration of genuine female autonomy.

In her own postwar life and writing, Evans might be said to have made the same retreat. Her immediate and highly ambitious project after Appomattox was to write another war story. This time Evans planned not to restrict herself to the woman's sphere but to try to escape altogether the confines of the domestic novel. Evans hoped to compose the definitive history of the South in the Civil War, to define the terms in which the Confederacy would live into posterity.

Evans never realized her goal, and in 1867 she explained why. Her extraordinary statement exemplifies the fate of female ambition in the South—its transformation into coexisting docility and assertiveness, compliance and repressed rage. Evans abandoned her intention to write a Confederate history in deference to former vice-president of the Confederacy Alexander Stephens, who planned one of his own. "I humbly put my fingers on the throat of my ambitious daring design of becoming the Confederate Xenophon and strangled it. . . . I confess it cost me a severe struggle to relinquish the fond dream[,] . . . but abler hands snatched it from my weak womanly fingers and waved me to humbler paths of labor."[40]

Evans's ambition was crushed—"strangled"—only indirectly by male prerogative; the actual murder took place at her own hand. Evans immolated herself on the very altars of sacrifice at which she had worshiped; she became the final victim of her own paradoxes. In 1867 she returned to the "humbler paths" of the domestic novel, publishing the enormously popular *St. Elmo*, with a heroine whose life and story culminate in conventional wedded bliss. In 1868 Evans herself, at age thirty-three, married a man twenty-seven years her senior. The war, *Macaria*, and single blessedness were over.

The reviewer for the *Richmond Age* who called *Macaria* an experiment offered an important insight into the meaning of women's reading and writing in the Civil War South. In books, particularly in fiction, women could invent new lives and could imagine new selves, new identities, and new meanings that seemed too frightening to contemplate outside the world of literary fantasy. Both reading and writing stimulated self-examination and discovery; both represented fundamentally "selfish" activities in which women at least temporarily freed themselves from the dictates of female abnegation and sacrifice for moments of self-indulgence and self-reflection. The consolations of reading and writing were considerable, but literary activity often proved disturbing as well, challenging, even if not overcoming, the tenacious traditionalism of the women of the master class. Religion played much the same double-edged role.

# CHAPTER EIGHT

# Though Thou Slay Us

## WOMEN AND RELIGION

On April 12, 1861, Emma Holmes awoke in her Charleston home to the boom of cannon firing on Fort Sumter. After weeks of anxiety about the future of the new Confederate nation, overt conflict seemed almost a relief. By the time she sat down to write in her diary late that afternoon, the Civil War was almost twelve hours old. Yet, Emma reported, nearly "every body seems calm & grave." Most Charlestonians were "so impressed with the justice of our cause that they place entire confidence in the God of Battles."[1]

From the opening day of the war, Confederates found both justification and consolation in religion. Government officials and church leaders alike nurtured belief in the divine purpose of the Confederate experiment. Episcopal Bishop Stephen Elliott affirmed that the Confederacy had been

*(did?) how change as war progressed?*

founded as "a nation to do [God's] . . . work upon earth," while the Confederate legislature pointedly selected "Deo Vindice"—"Defended by God"—as the motto for their new country. Ministers preached patriotism; politicians vaunted their religious purposes. Political nationalism and religious mission came to seem all but inseparable.[2]

The convergence of religion with politics, of the sacred with the terrestrial, had significant implications for white women of the wartime South, for it offered them a new legitimacy and a new language with which to approach public affairs. Religion, long regarded as a central component of the female sphere, opened an avenue into the male world of politics and public action. At the same time, it assumed profound personal import, serving as an essential intellectual and emotional resource and providing a framework for understanding and coping with the ordeals of war. Women used divine language and belief to explain the frightening new circumstances that confronted them, and to provide themselves as well with the strength and consolation that derives from faith.

## Affliction Sanctifies

Like Emma Holmes, many women regarded confidence in victory as a natural corollary to belief in God, and they met the outbreak of war with equanimity. "It matters not," Kate Carney of Tennessee asserted early in 1861, "how weak our cause, if but God and justice is on our side, we will at last triumph." Keziah Brevard explicitly founded her optimism in the Bible, copying a reassuring verse from the 118th Psalm into her journal: " 'The Lord is on my side; I will not fear; what can man do unto me.' " It seemed clear, she confirmed, that "the Lord is on our side in this national strife." As Henry Timrod, poet laureate of the Confederacy, proclaimed in his nationalist ode "Ethnogenesis," "To doubt the end were want of trust in God."[3]

Encouraged by bold pronouncements of divine favor from press and pulpit, southerners looked upon themselves as God's chosen and scoured the Bible for prefigurements and prophecies to support their sacred reading of national circumstance. The Confederacy, Richmond's *Christian Observer* proclaimed, "will be the Lord's peculiar people." The North, swept up in the corruptions of the modern age, in the lure of Mammon, represented an evil from which the South had been wise to secede. Emma Holmes carefully noted in her diary a consoling sermon by a Charleston minister who insisted on "an exact parallel" between the separation of the Confederacy from the North and the removal of the Israelites from "the Jewish Nation under Rehoboam's oppressive rule." Other preachers cited the withdrawal of the Israelites from Egypt or the departure of David from the House of Saul as the scriptural events that best foretold the South's independence. Many worshipers took heart from the uncanny language of the popular sermon text from First Jeremiah: "Then the Lord said unto me, out of the North an evil shall break forth upon the inhabitants of the land, and they shall fight against thee, but they shall not prevail against thee; for I am with thee." God had all but promised Confederate victory.[4]

The bloodless triumph at Sumter in April and the miraculous success against larger numbers at Manassas in August reinforced this belief in Divine Providence. Nancy Emerson of Augusta County, Virginia, for example, explained early Confederate victories and her own optimism in language of biblical prophecy. "This judgment from God has fallen upon the North because of their delusions from him. . . . [W]e shall achieve our independence, & if guided aright, shall fulfill a high destiny, & be far more prosperous than ever before. Never for one moment since the struggle commenced, has my mind wavered as to the final result."[5]

But mounting losses, personal as well as national, gradually forced a revision of war's typology to accompany eroding confidence. Death and battlefield defeat soon made clear that Confederates had perhaps been chosen not simply for God's favor but, like Job, for the suffering that tests and ultimately strengthens and purifies faith. A Charleston sermon in December 1861 reminded Emma Holmes of Job's words to his wife: " 'We have received good from the Lord & shall we not receive evil also?' " Sarah Estes of Tennessee struggled to remember that " 'The Lord loveth whom he chasteneth,' " and Laura Nisbet Boykin found deep comfort in a sermon that reminded her how "every wave of sorrow or affliction" casts up "pearls and gems to the shore. I believe it is true," she affirmed, "Affliction sanctifies."[6]

As the unimagined horrors of war began to reveal themselves, women turned to religion to make sense of their anguish and to find the courage to endure. "Oh that a righteous God may subdue the wicked spirits of man & cause them to cease this cruel war," wrote Annie Darden of North Carolina in the summer of 1861. "But he seeth best to afflict us more deeply. I say thy will be done, my Saviour & we will trust thee though thou slay us, for we know there is help in no other power but thine to quell the raging storm." Suffering, Christianity promised, was not useless. Rightly managed, it could prove the avenue to deeper faith and ultimate salvation. Wartime theology emphasized that chastisement demanded reformation; the Confederacy would have to repent of its sins to end the trial of war. God's punishment, expressed in interim defeats or failures, did not mean that ultimate success was impossible. Instead, setbacks had to be seen as warnings that called upon southerners to cleanse themselves of wickedness and impiety, to transform themselves and their world to find God's favor.[7]

Such a message, issued from pulpits across the South, consoled southerners by reassuring them that hardships and losses—Forts Henry and Donelson, and Antietam—were but way stations on the road to a grander victory, if only the Confederacy heeded God's warnings. Abby Slocomb reported a "splendid sermon" by Bishop Thomas Atkinson of North Carolina urging congregants to search their hearts for their own contributions to the "nation's iniquity" for which God was punishing them. Mattie Seward of Georgia was pleased by a sermon attacking "the specolators" and extortioners as the source of God's wrath, for she too believed that a preoccupation with gain threatened the fabric of her wartorn society. Julia Davidson would have agreed with Seward's diagnosis of social ills, and she herself expressed them in similar terms. "I tell you Johny dear we are not humble enough. There is too much extortion too much speculation too much grasping after wealth, fame & power, *riches—riches*, everybody is striving to get rich. I tell you we must humble ourselves before this war will close." Suffering and chastisement would ensure that southerners would be better fitted to carry out their purpose as God's chosen. "We will come out of the furnace doubly purified for the good work & fight that God has given us to do," Kate Foster explained, "For to the people of the Confederacy is given the sublime mission of maintaining the supremacy of our Father in Heaven."[8]

By casting the hardships of war into a narrative of punishment, reformation, and deliverance, clergy offered southerners a basis for strength and confidence even amidst disaster. Such a rendering of their experience made religion a fundamental source of consolation for Confederate women. "If we did not have a Bible," Lizzie Ozburn wrote to Jimmie, "what would we do—tis more comfort to me than anything else now." A young New Orleans mother was even more emphatic. "If it was not for . . . religion that keep[s] me up, I would kill myself," she informed her absent husband. Religion came to seem essential to survival itself. Huddled together in a Fredericksburg basement as shells fell around them, Jane Beale and her family recited psalms. "Tho' an host should encamp against me, my heart shall not fear." After three successive Confederate reverses in the West, Alice Ready of South Carolina banished her distress by designating the setbacks as "a

*Julia Davidson after the war. Atlanta History Center, Atlanta, Georgia.*

punishment . . . God has sent upon us for our boastfulness." Some defeats, she reassured herself, were to be expected. "It would be an unparalleled war were [we] to meet with none and so far am I from being discouraged, that my *faith* has only grown stronger—I feel that we must and will succeed finally with the help of God."[9]

Like the nation's trial, death itself was within Christian understanding simply another hardship on the route to a greater glory—of salvation and eternal life. The loss of loved ones, like military defeats, must be accepted as part of God's plan, even celebrated as the advent of immortality. Laura Haygood, daughter of a Methodist bishop, understood this well as she wrote from boarding school to a grieving friend. "I know how very difficult it is for the heart to learn the lesson which God would teach us by death, but when we do learn it the destroyers' dark path becomes a way of light to Heaven." When Sarah Espy's twenty-four-year-old son died in camp, she was able to stanch her sorrow with visions of the hereafter. "What a change from the sick, weary, harrassing camp life to the joys of Heaven! I feel that we should not grieve for him; for it is a happy release from these distressing times." Like many women who directly experienced war's dangers, Mary Hort of South Carolina found in religion a means to deal not just with the loss of friends or relatives but with the fear of her own death as well. When a Yankee soldier threatened her with a pistol and a knife, she calmly informed him, "If you kill me I shall go straight to heaven. I am a Christian."[10]

## The All Important Subject

Barred from "the tented field," women felt they could at least bear God's standard by strengthening the nation's Christian purpose. "We wanted to do so much more than we could," Mississippian Annie Harper remembered, "It was a satisfaction to invoke Almighty aid to do what we had left undone." As Alice Ready observed more directly, "ladies . . . can *pray*"—no small contribution given the framework of Christian meaning with which the war had been popularly endowed. "Pray, maiden, pray!" urged "a ballad for the times, respectfully dedicated to the patriotic women of the South" and published as sheet music in Richmond in 1864. If victory depended more on pure faith than on strong battalions, women had an important realm for action. "The great benefit of this war," Laura Comer remarked, is that "it allows *every one* the luxury and privilege of doing good."[11]

Traditional institutional religion, however, did not thrive on the Confederate homefront. Many churches closed their doors or sharply reduced the number of their services because of the departure of clergymen to the front. Countless southerners shared the experience of eleven-year-old Belle Strickland of Mississippi, who recorded in her diary in January 1865, "We went to church today but there was none." Sometimes several denominations were compelled to ignore their differences and meet together in order to share a single available minister. Even when services were held, however, lack of transportation often deterred worshipers whose horses, mules, and carriages had been impressed for war. Sarah Estes, a refugee, was unable to attend church because of her frequent relocations, and she feared "I will get to be almost a heathen." Near battlefields, churches became hospitals, making regular religious observances all but impossible. Many churches were severely damaged or destroyed. During the siege of Vicksburg one minister held services only at the insistence of two female parishioners, who had a difficult time finding places to sit amidst the bricks, mortar, and glass that filled the damaged structure. In areas held by the enemy, southerners frequently boycotted services at which they knew they would be required to mix with Yankee soldiers and endure prayers for the Union president. "We couldn't attend Church," Mary W. M. Bell wrote her husband from occupied Tennessee, "because the ministers are forced to pray for Lincoln. I haven't been to Church for 3 years on that account."[12]

Although religious revivals swept through the Confederate army from 1862 until the last months of the war, no comparable work of grace seemed to take place behind the lines. The *Biblical Recorder* found itself "constrained to believe that there is much more religion in the army now, than among the people at home." Charges of "coldness" or godlessness against Confederate civilians, however, must be examined within the framework of the particular style of religious expression that characterized the southern homefront. The falling off of formal worship and the scarcity of dramatic revivals comparable to those in army camps did not necessarily represent a failure of devotion or piety. Religious forms changed behind the lines, with emphasis shifting from church-centered liturgy and ritual led by ordained ministers to home-centered observances often both directed and largely attended by women. As the gender of civilian worshipers changed, so too religious practice moved from a more public and male to a more domestic and female sphere.[13]

Women organized regular prayer groups in towns and villages across the South and even tried to increase the power of their entreaties by coordinating the hour of their worship. Newly installed as heads of households, women often turned to formal group prayer for families black and white as a vehicle for strengthening solidarity and legitimating their new leadership. When the Holmes family fled from Charleston to the upcountry as refugees, Emma's mother inaugurated a system of family prayer morning and evening, something, the young woman noted, "we have never had before." During one of the first of many large religious meetings at her home in Winchester, Mary Lee felt awkward acting the part of minister for the several dozen assembled ladies, so even though she "conducted the services," she "confined myself to the prayer book prayers." Ready to serve as a conduit for God's words, she was not yet comfortable assuming the authority implied by uttering her own. At a hospital in Virginia, Kate Rowland and her mother served as nurse and matron but soon took on spiritual responsibilities as well. Not only did they read regular Sunday services to the convalescents; they offered a rite of Christian burial for patients who failed to respond to their therapeutic efforts. "We have had no Chaplain all winter," Kate explained, "so we had to make up the deficiency as far as possible ourselves."[14]

As army evangelists acknowledged, women had formed the foundation of the prewar church; it was largely men who at the outset of war remained unconverted and unobservant, "partial or entire strangers," the *Religious Herald* remarked, "to him who labors among them in word and doctrine." Gathered in the army, they offered an appealing target for revivalists, for they had heretofore proved "most inaccessible to pastoral influence." Women at home, already believers, provided no such field for the harvest. The focus of female wartime piety was therefore not conversion, as it became for Christian soldiers, but instead practice and even leadership, as civilian religion became in a sense domesticated—located and performed increasingly within the family and the home.[15]

At least some of the celebrated religious enthusiasm of Confederate army camps had its origin behind the lines among women fearing the loss of their husbands not just in this world but for all time. As women searched their own souls for shortcomings that might be contributing to God's displeasure, they urged their husbands to do the same. The organized churches exploited the power of this female message, institutionalizing it in the most popular of the many religious tracts supplied to soldiers during the war. By the end of 1862, interdenominational tract societies had distributed more than 150,000 copies of *A Mother's Parting Words* in the Confederate army, reminding soldiers that "of all men," they had "the greatest need for piety" and assuring them too that despite the female preponderance in prewar church membership, "Piety will not make you effeminate or cowardly."[16]

In peacetime, women had abided their husbands' lack of godly commitment, but the dangers of battle made disbelief intolerable. The death of an unconverted husband would mean eternal separation, the impossibility of a blessed reunion in the great hereafter. "Do you feel," Julia Davidson demanded of Johnny, "that you have made peace *with God*? tell me Johnny dear what are your *prospects* for *eternity*[?]" Julia was certain that spiritual things should "be the all important subject with us now [and] should swallow up everything else." Rachel Craighead felt sufficiently strongly about religious questions to risk an all-out confrontation with her husband by insisting that he attend services. He was furious at her presumption in trying "to rule," but she felt empowered in her assertiveness by the higher purpose that inspired her, even though his fury made her "miserable."

Margaret Houston wrote to her son in the army specifying Bible verses relevant to his situation as a Christian soldier. "It would be a good plan to commit the whole of these verses to memory." A schedule for reading the New Testament in daily excerpts seemed a wise idea as well, and Margaret reminded her son of the duty to sing hymns as enjoined in the fifth chapter of James. Piety was an important prerequisite for victory, and women felt encouraged to exercise considerable spiritual authority in its pursuit. "If our people were God fearing soldiers," Leila Callaway explained, "I should not fear defeat."[17]

## War Has Hardened Us

For all God's promises, though, it was hard to dispel doubt as months of war stretched into years and as the pain of individual bereavements mounted almost beyond endurance. In 1864 Mrs. C. A. Slocomb wrote from Columbia, where she was nursing her wounded son, to describe her alternating moods of discouragement and renewed faith. "I am very despondent at times, as the hope of a speedy peace seems so defered, and I almost fear our enemies are too strong for us—But then again I cannot think our Merciful Father will suffer us to sink under the weight of such a barbarous people as our foes have proved themselves. . . . I trust all these trials may be for our benefit and so purify us as a nation." Beginning with an expression of doubt, Slocomb invoked the narrative of chastisement and salvation to dissolve her fears. But she also revealed the anxiety and impatience that increasingly undermined women's confidence. Like so many Christians before them, Confederate women in war faced the vexed problem of theodicy—the difficulty of explaining why a just and all-powerful God permits the existence of evil. Sometimes it seemed hard to believe God intended the pain and adversity women found imposed upon them, and sometimes it was hard to believe that they could endure for much longer.[18]

The ever mounting death toll worked its terrible effects on women's sensibilities. By the middle years of the war almost no family remained exempt. On a round of visits to friends during a September day in 1863, Catherine Edmondston directly confronted the meaning of the bloody summer of Gettysburg and Vicksburg. Calling at eight houses, she found each one in mourning for a husband, a brother, or a son. As Kate Stone observed at the end of the year, "Nearly every household mourns some loved one lost."[19]

From the early months of war onward, mourning became overwhelmingly the concern of women. Men were in uniform, occupied with pressing military demands; it was women who remained to drape themselves in black and perform rituals of grief for the departed. To mourn slain soldiers was to impart to military deaths a broader Christian significance, to imbue political sacrifices with transcendent spiritual purpose. Women's tears consecrated the deaths of their men, assuring them spiritual and political immortality and ratifying each casualty as a contribution not only to Confederate victory but to a more sacred notion of Christian martyrdom with which the Cause had become confounded. Mourning fit neatly as well with prevailing assumptions about the particular attributes of women. Christian grief encompasses above all resignation and submission, an abnegation of self in the face of the power and will of the Almighty Father. Women, accustomed to assuming such postures within the terrestrial sphere, were especially suited for this religious work. In wartime mourning, Confederate women affirmed their acceptance of personal loss in deference to purposes both terrestrial and divine. A husband, a brother, a lover, or a son might be dead, but the will of the state and the will of God had been done. Women's mourning had the potential to serve as a comforting ratification of female subservience and compliance carrying political as well as religious implications.[20]

The possibility of such multifaceted reassurance may help to explain the enormous wartime popularity of *The Burial of Latané*. The painting, completed by William D. Washington in 1864, celebrated women's special responsibility for mourning as well as their new centrality in religious observance more generally. Originally hung in the artist's Richmond studio, the three-by-four-foot canvas attracted such "throngs of visitors" that it was moved to the capitol building. There a bucket was placed beneath the work for contributions to the Confederate cause; the painting took on the status of a national icon.

*The Burial of Latané* depicts the funeral of a young Confederate lieutenant killed during the Seven Days campaign of 1862. Left among strangers, southern civilians behind enemy lines, William Latané's body is consigned to the care of women, for neither minister nor family members can be summoned for last rites. Instead, a group of women and slaves gathers to inter the slain hero.

Firmly within the genre of narrative history painting, *Latané* recounts a story of Christian sacrifice and nationalist triumph at the same time it represents women as celebrants of what is at once a holy and a political communion. A matron, not a clergyman, leads the service, but she, like Winches-

The Burial of Latané, *oil painting, 1864, by William D. Washington. Courtesy of Judge John DeHardit.*

ter's Mary Lee, looks to God and prayer book for her words. Slaves, leaning on their shovels, join white women in symbolic rendering of homefront support for the Confederate cause. Ritualized grief, Washington suggested, unites and sanctifies. *The Burial of Latané* both depicted and enshrined women's cultural responsibility for mourning.[21]

In the early months of war, deaths were in fact marked with elaborate ceremony. When Charleston's slain were returned from First Manassas on July 26, 1861, business was suspended throughout the city, and three companies of cavalry escorted the bodies from the railroad depot to City Hall. There the dead heroes lay in state until more than a thousand soldiers accompanied them to St. Paul's Church and at last to Magnolia Cemetery. A little more than a year later Constance Cary described her distress at a very different burial scene in Richmond's Hollywood Cemetery: "six or seven coffins dropped into one yawning pit, and hurriedly covered in, all that a grateful country could render in return for precious lives." By late 1862, one observer noted, the wounded in Richmond were dying by the dozens and were buried four in a coffin, while the battlefield dead were simply thrown into ditches. At a military hospital in Oxford, Mississippi, a nurse remembered that soldiers had been interred "in bunches, just like dead chickens," with no minister available to mark their passage to eternity.[22]

This altered behavior marked significant shifts in attitude. Fannie Beers, a

*Mourning women. "Cemetery in New Orleans."* Frank Leslie's Illustrated
Newspaper, *April 15, 1863.*

hospital matron in Georgia, commented on the change in her own behavior
toward the dead. At first she had insisted on attending each dead soldier and
reading a part of the burial service at his grave. "But it had become impossible. The dead were past help; the living *always* needed succor." By the last
years of the war coffins were all but unavailable, and mourning clothes
impossible to secure. "People do not mourn their dead as they used to,"
Kate Stone observed in April 1864. "Everyone seems to live only in the
present—just from day to day—otherwise I fancy many would go crazy."
Not just mourning but death itself had taken on a new meaning. Carrie Fries
explained to her fiancé in 1863 that she viewed it "in an entirely different
light from what I did a year ago." "Death does not seem half so terrible as it
did long ago," Kate Stone agreed. "War has hardened us," confirmed young
Nannie Haskins in the summer of 1864. Numbness offered protection, a
defense against the unfathomable losses and pain. Kate Foster recognized
the origins of her own emotional transformation in her brother's death. After
his departure, "My heart became flint. I am almost afriad to love too dearly

anyone now." But such denial represented another kind of loss as well, an abandonment of feeling, a deadening of sensibility that was terrible in itself. "Bury me not in war times," Mary Lee remarked. "No one feels anything now."[23]

Christian doctrines of resignation seemed to support this psychological process of numbing and denial, but, however sanctified, submission to God's will remained a severe trial for those struggling to accept the pain of bereavement. Each new loss, each new horror threatened to break through the protective shell. Women invoked religious doctrines and texts almost as incantations in their effort to transcend suffering and grief, to wean themselves from the cares of this world. "Il faut se résigner à la volonte de Dieu et accepter les croix qu'il nous envoie. . . . Il faut me soumettre et prier et espérer," wrote A. Grima of New Orleans as she worried about her son at the front. Women reiterated Deuteronomy 33:25, a favorite verse for both sermons and meditation: "As thy days—so shall thy Strength be"—God's promise to balance trials with endurance and not to ask the impossible of his children.[24]

But resignation and denial had their limits. Julia Davidson characteristically blamed herself for her persisting distress. "I know if I was a good true Christian & had plenty of faith in the Almighty I would get along smoothly. I could say all will be well. Oh I wish I was. I then could be resigned to my fate whatever it may be but alas I know I come far short of my duty." Susan Caldwell complained repeatedly of her inability to "gain power over my own rebellious heart to say *God's Will be done*. Oh! how hard to be submissive." Even with the supports of religion, Caldwell believed "I cannot stand a great deal more." She longed to be a pious Christian, to live for heaven, and to be certain she would reach there and find rest. "But I find it hard. My heart is so *rebellious*." "I am trying to learn 'Thy will be done,'" wrote a Texas woman. "Give me the grace to learn oh Lord. 'Not my will but thine Oh God be done,'" pleaded a woman who had just heard of her husband's death at Gettysburg. As life's realities became ever less supportable, women sought in Christianity the conviction to "wear this world like a loose garment." An anonymous woman transformed her questioning and focused her "impious eye" in a poem for an Atlanta newspaper:

> I cannot weep, I dare not pray;
> Sad and rebellious thought
> Has swayed my lonely soul today,
> And night no calm has brought.

. . . . . . . .

> Why Might should trample on Right
> And Guilt on Innocence,
> And prayerful toil in sorrow's night
> Receive no recompense?

But after expressing her distress, the poet abandoned her challenge, impugning its very legitimacy in the face of God's omnipotence:

> Why? . . . but I turn my impious eye
> To yonder radiant heaven;
> I bow beneath the calm reply
> Its shining stars have given.

> Systems of worlds roll vast and grand,
> Each round its central sun,
> And *I* dare doubt their Maker's Hand
> Can wisely govern *one?*

> Humbled and awed, to earth I sink,
> How weak I seem, how vain
> When even this earth is but a link
> In great creation's chain.[25]

Doubt was resolved in female self-abasement, a belittling of the self, of the "I" that dares to question. Significantly, God's legitimacy here derived not from his benevolence but from his power; the evidence the poet cited for his wisdom was his strength, and she described her own worship as arising not from love but humility, awe, and weakness.

Some women, however, actively resisted humble acceptance of defeat and slaughter. Nannie Haskins, distraught at her brother's death as well as at a string of Confederate losses, was surprised when she read over a diary entry. "I write," she observed, "as if I was complaining against heaven." Quickly she moved to counter any hint of trespass against God's plan. "No after all it may have been for our good." Clara Solomon, bemoaning news of Confederate casualties, caught herself short. "But stop," she wrote. "We are quarrelling with Divine Providence. 'He doeth all things well.'" Contemplating the almost unmentionable possibility of ultimate Confederate failure, Alice Ready confessed, "I would not [wish to] rebel against His decree, but my faith has never been so weak as tonight." When Henry Timrod wrote in 1861 that to doubt the war's outcome was to lack faith in God, he had intended to invoke the South's unwavering piety to bolster Confederate nationalism. But he proved prophetic in a manner he did not anticipate. Weakening confidence in the Confederacy would instead begin to undermine religious certainty. Some women "plainly indicated," Mary Gay reported, "that if our cause failed they would lose all faith in a prayer-answering God."[26]

"Sometimes in my wickedness," Sarah Estes confessed in late 1862, "I feel as if God had forsaken us." Widowed, homeless, and destitute, Cornelia McDonald of Winchester described lying on a sofa through "dreadful hours of unbelief and hopelessness," feeling, like Estes, abandoned by God. But gradually memories of his goodness crept over her, and "with that remembrance came the resolve, 'Though he slay me, yet will I trust in Him.'" For Mary Gay a brother's death proved the test of her faith, but one that she failed. "I did not believe it was God's will that my brother should die, and I could not say to that Holy Being, 'Thy will be done.'"[27]

Significantly, some women no longer able passively to bear war's suffering were propelled to action in pursuit of their own interests in this world. Ida Wilkom of Louisiana abandoned resignation and calm acceptance of her lot for political expression when she wrote in 1862 to the Confederate secretary of war. Her words essentially turned the popular and consoling verse from Deuteronomy on its head. As thy days, God had promised, so shall thy strength be. But Ida Wilkom demanded her husband's release from the army, explaining, "I have tried everything to submit to the will of God in tranquil resignation; but I find, a human being can suffer only according to human strength." Wilkom here placed the limits of human suffering within a secular, terrestrial context. Her endurance was human, not divine, in capacity, and God had not provided his promised attentiveness in the meting out of pain; the demands of her days were exceeding the strength with which she had been endowed.[28]

The "rebelliousness" that for so many doubters remained theological and abstract had the potential to assume concrete form; activism like that of Ida Wilkom was a logical outcome of the merging of religion and politics in the Confederate South. If the war was but a metaphor or a type for larger religious questions, women could scrutinize current events for moral meanings and make legitimate judgments on the operations of the public sphere.

Terrestrial institutions of power were extensions of divine government. God had delegated his power to white men, his earthly surrogates, and had mandated the subordination of white women and black slaves. In the view of many southern women, this created a continuum of power with God the highest master, a patriarch one level of command above Jefferson Davis. Petitioning women of all classes often addressed Davis in language that bespoke this conception. Women's letters revealed the novelty of this new engagement with politics, as well as their comfortable familiarity with a more sacred realm of action and expression. A North Carolina woman requesting her husband's discharge explained, "I know not how to ask the favor that I have Attempted. Yet I have been taught to ask in faith beleive and I would receive and I now ask of you as Earthly Father one favor that is in your power to grant." A woman of Chesterfield County, Virginia, readily admitted that writing a public official represented a new departure. "I am unused to sue to any one save my Maker." Anna McConnell of Mobile appealed to Davis as "the redeemer of our country," and Henrietta McDonald entreated him just "as I would the God of heaven for the salvation of my soul," when she sought her son's discharge from the army. Political petitioning emerged directly from the traditions and habits and even the language of divine prayer.[29]

The governments of heaven and earth seemed of a piece. Elizabeth Collier, a young woman from Hillsborough, North Carolina, understood their relationship clearly: "the ultimate person on whom all depend is God—but it is also true that . . . women learn the necessity of dependence on Him by the necessary resting of their nature on men." Dependence and subordination were enjoined by both theology and politics. By the late years of the war, however, the protection that was their guaranteed accompaniment had seemingly disappeared, and dependence had proved dangerous. Neither God nor Jefferson Davis was attending to women's desperate needs. Women, now alone, struggled to take care of themselves, paying a high price for their new and enforced autonomy. Just as Davis's staff marked "File" on moving appeals from women seeking relief from intolerable circumstances, so God too seemed to be proving deaf to heartfelt prayers and pleas. Increasingly, suffering produced not resignation but anger—directed against both God and the state.[30]

Confederate surrender posed an all but insurmountable challenge to Confederate women's faith, to the system of belief that had explained their world and had justified the costly sacrifices demanded of them for four long years. Suffused with feelings of rage and betrayal, some women explicitly—even if temporarily—rejected God. "I know not how to bear it," Grace Elmore reflected in May 1865. "I cannot be resigned. Hard thoughts against my God arise; questions of his justice, of his mercy . . . refuse to be silenced." Women struggled to reconcile reality with the Christian narratives of suffering and redemption that had consoled them for so long, but they could find no reason, no understanding. "Day and night in every moment of quiet," Elmore explained, "I am trying to work out the meaning of this horrible fact." Virginia French wrote in much the same way of her search for some means to understand what within her existing system of belief was incomprehensible. "And this is what I am trying now to realize—I long to find out 'What golden fruit lies hidden in the husk?' . . . I believe we shall see it—if not now hereafter." Mary Lee confessed herself "utterly bewildered." She was, she wrote, "like a ship at sea without pilot or compass." The hierarchies of belief and social order within which they had located their souls and their identities had been overthrown. Neither God—as they had so long understood him—nor Jefferson Davis remained to pilot their vessel; neither Christianity nor Confederate nationalism seemed any longer adequate to serve as guiding compass.[31]

War had dealt a significant blow to the logic of Christian—and, by implication, female—submission. At the same time the warborn merging of religion and politics had brought to the South a justification for women's relevance within a more public realm. Antebellum northern reform had arisen out of just such a configuration of belief and action. But southern women had not shared the spiritual and social empowerment experienced by so many of their northern sisters during the prewar years. For southern women, necessity, not choice, would prove to be the source of change—what they would have called the "mother of invention." The realities of life in the Confederacy impressed on white southern women the dangers of dependence on God or man. A new sense of God's distance and disengagement combined with a distrust of the men on whom they had so long relied to impel Confederate women toward a new independence in the postwar world. Women themselves would feel required to act as both pilot and compass.

CHAPTER NINE

# To Relieve My Bottled Wrath

## CONFEDERATE WOMEN
## AND YANKEE MEN

Women's wartime rage expressed itself most unreservedly in what became their legendary hostility toward invading Yankee soldiers. Southern females, the northern press proclaimed, were hardly the genteel and gracious ladies of popular imagination, but "she-devils," vicious and vituperative in their verbal and even physical assaults on occupying troops. "Such . . . acerbity, vengeance and venom I have never seen exceeded," a correspondent for the *New York World* reported to his readers. "By all odds," another journalist observed, they were "far worse rebels than the men." With words, gestures, chamber pots, and even, on occasion, pistols, white women assaulted the enemy in ways that many southerners celebrated as heroic testimony to female courage and patriotism.[1]

Yet women's anger involved more than just a simple statement of political loyalties. The behavior of southern ladies toward northern troops represented simultaneous affirmations and transgressions of gender and class boundaries; women's actions reveal both the persistence and the subversion of traditional assumptions about their place and power. Women's own reflections about their unprecedented rage and aggression—which often surprised even themselves—demonstrate the displacement of other deeply felt resentments even more threatening to their long-cherished identities and attachments.[2]

## The Day of Woman's Power

Many Confederate females never came face to face with Union soldiers. As the North tightened its military grip, however, sending first conquering then occupying armies into the South, numbers of white women passed under the direct authority of enemy troops. On the borders of the Confederacy—in parts of Virginia, Tennessee, Louisiana, and Mississippi—southern ladies and northern soldiers confronted one another daily as civilian communities submitted to Union rule. Women found themselves living permanently "in captivity" in New Orleans or Nashville, or compelled in the Shenandoah Valley to negotiate alternating waves of Blue and Gray, as opposing forces struggled to hold contested positions. Perhaps most frightening, however, by 1864 women in Georgia and the Carolinas who had consoled themselves with their comforting distance from battle encountered a newly terrible face of war when Sherman explicitly identified the civilian population, or at least its property and its morale, as appropriate military targets.

Substantial numbers of southern women experienced war on rather than behind the lines, in a homefront that had been gradually transformed into a battlefront by modern warfare. As Catherine Cochran tellingly remarked after enemy forces arrived in her Virginia town, "we've seen the elephant at last." Understandably, women were perplexed about how to respond to these unprecedented circumstances. If they were by centuries-old custom barred from entering "the tented field," and if they were by socialization trained to repress anger and aggression and to eschew violence, what were they to do when the battlefield came to them? Astonished and all but overwhelmed by her belligerent feelings toward the Yankees who had taken control of Winchester early in 1862, Mary Lee begged an absent friend to

"Pray for me . . . that I may retain my Christianity & womanly attributes, as well as my patriotism." Her religion and the female role she had internalized seemed impossibly at odds with what she regarded as her new political responsibilities as a Confederate. Unwittingly compelled by war into a public sphere, Lee feared that the domestic virtues she had cultivated for more than four decades would be undermined.[3]

In March 1862 a Union officer arrived on Lee's doorstep to demand she relinquish a Confederate flag rumored to be hidden in her house. When he warned that he might not be able to restrain his men if they were compelled to search her property, Lee responded with fury. Instead of accustomed and expected male protection, she now confronted intimidating threats. "I never," she wrote, "had such feelings in my life. I was so mad I was trembling with passion." Like many elite southern women, Lee supposed that her status and gender should and would shield her—that before she was an enemy, she was a woman, and more than that, a lady. The officer's warning was infuriating in its direct challenge to these assumptions of prerogative. Mary Lee inaugurated her own three-year battle with the Yankees, endeavoring to establish her claims as a woman while she took advantage of gendered privileges to act in behalf of her Confederate sympathies. Early in the conflict, Lee sought an interview with the Union provost marshal, intending to educate him in the nature of woman's legitimate expectations. "I told Capt. Alexander . . . that we were all rebels but that we expected as citizens to be treated according to the usages of civilized warfare & as women, we demanded the courtesy that every lady has the right to expect from every gentleman." Whether out of deference to her person or to the power of her argument, Alexander "bowed and agreed with me." When two months later General Milroy threatened to billet soldiers in Lee's parlor and dining room, she appeared before him in a calculatedly "bland manner . . . simply to demand the protection that every woman had a right to demand from every man." Just as Captain Alexander had agreed, Milroy relented, implicitly affirming her claims.[4]

Like Lee, women across the South found comfort in the expectation that, whatever their differences, northerners and southerners shared fundamental cultural assumptions about the prerogatives of white womanhood. Confederate ladies consoled themselves with the faith that the armor of gender would protect them. Alice Ready, contemplating a northern advance in the early months of war, was "really surprised at myself how little fear I feel at their approach. Col. Hale said, 'true woman could disarm . . . their evil intentions'. . . . I am relying upon that." Yet fleetingly she wondered if a

*Confederate women and Yankee men in Savannah. "The Wives, Daughters, and Servants of the Chivalry of Savannah Accepting Aid from the U.S. Commissary."* Frank Leslie's Illustrated Newspaper, *February 25, 1865.*

pistol might not provide a more comforting basis for confidence. Like Colonel Hale, George Peddy encouraged his wife, Kate, to rely on the moral force of her sex and her position to serve as a defensive weapon. "Honey," he wrote, "should ten thousand come to your home, maintain your unsul[l]ied dignity as a lady and the cowards will crouch before your steady gaze." In Tennessee, Virginia French enhanced the force of her own steely eye with a blunt verbal reminder. As a Yankee marauder pushed to enter her house, "I laid my hand on his shoulder and looked him right in the eyes . . . and asked 'Are you a man?' he hesitated a moment—seemed surprised that I should dare interfere, and said, 'Yes' 'Are you a gentleman?' he did not reply. . . . Well, [I] said 'if he is a gentleman he will show it by going out of this house.'" Confident that the Yankees would not violate the innermost realms of feminine privacy, French had hidden her jewelry in pockets under her hoops. Like Emma LeConte and countless other besieged southern women, she assumed "they will hardly search our persons."[5]

The privileges of gender did in fact provide considerable protection for Confederate females and served also as the foundation for their much vaunted belligerence. Most Yankee soldiers were reluctant to harm white southern women, particularly those who seemed to be ladies of the middle or upper class. Union officers frequently restrained or reprimanded enlisted men who failed to show sufficient respect. Even when the scorched earth policies of the later years of the war threatened women's property—the basis, of course, for their ultimate survival—very few reports appeared of assaults on their persons. White females, particularly those of the elite, were rarely victims of rape by invading soldiers. In all likelihood black women served as the unfortunate sexual spoils when Union soldiers asserted their traditional right of military conquest.[6]

There were, of course, exceptions to this general pattern. In areas where bushwhacking and guerrilla warfare prevailed, undisciplined men were far more likely to challenge the usages of "civilized warfare" Mary Lee had invoked. The endemic violence in Missouri, for example, did not entirely spare white women, although historian Michael Fellman has argued that, in the abstract at least, even Missouri's guerrillas embraced a code that enjoined "harming women and children." Irregular forces, he has written, "had an even more desperate need than Union soldiers to believe that they were gentlemen to the ladies." In areas such as western North Carolina or eastern Tennessee, where civilian loyalties were divided and contested throughout the war, white women were seen as actors and therefore potential targets in the unconventional warfare. Reports exist of wives hung by their thumbs or crushed under fence rails in an effort to force them to reveal their husbands' whereabouts. The women victimized in these situations, however, were almost never from the privileged classes of slaveowning families. Elite southerners had never been numerous in these mountainous regions and would in any case have possessed both the means and the motivation to flee as refugees from impending social anarchy.[7]

Inhibitions about violence against white women provided Confederate females with opportunities and freedoms denied southern men. "This is surely," Mary Lee remarked in April 1862, "the day of woman's power; the men are afraid to do or say, anything, & leave all to us." Women, Amanda Chappelear confirmed, "do not fear to express their sentiments as the men do." "Being a lady," one Missouri slaveholder explained, she was "unaccustomed to being held responsible for anything she might say." Cornelia McDonald of Winchester was so outspoken in her verbal attacks on the Yankees who ruined her property and occupied her house that Mary Lee described her neighbor as "daring in her audacity," "one of the talking heroines." In spite of McDonald's belligerence, the soldiers never touched her. But they did seize an opportunity to beat and kick her teenaged son Harry when in response to their questions he proudly declared himself a "secesh." Kate Carney's mother was similarly spared. When she boldly resisted Yankee efforts to seize her horses, an exasperated soldier declared, "If she was a man I would whip her." Protections of class often reinforced those of gender. Mary Lee believed Winchester's invaders enthralled by the appeal of aristocratic southern women. "They are completely overwhelmed by a very stately & grand air; they have the most profound respect for the F.F.V.'s, & would do anything to get a civil word from us."[8]

Women readily seized on their immunity. Largely freed from fear of northern reprisals, many women seemed liberated as well from the inhibitions that had defined their positions as ladies. In their eyes Yankees seemed to exist outside all constraints of propriety or compassion. "I have such a thorough contempt of them," Mary Lee explained, "that I do not realize they are human beings." Alice Ready, who retained some compunctions about female propriety, hoped to avoid speaking to enemy soldiers directly for she did not think "I could control my tongue. . . . I feel as if I could spit upon them and never call them anything but dogs." Ready admitted she was "shocked at myself at times, when I think of the wishes which my heart frames and lips utter for them." Loss of control became the essence of the response of many women to the invaders; the presence of Yankees seemed to represent a license to vent emotions southern ladies were customarily expected to keep in tight rein. "I said many grotesque things," Catherine Broun admitted. Sallie Munford was "astonished at the force of my feelings against the Yankees." Catherine Cochran of Virginia was similarly surprised at the insolent remarks that issued from her mouth. "I couldnt help quarrelling with them[;] it seemed a relief to my rage." Emma Holmes of South Carolina confessed her great satisfaction in taunting Sherman's troops. "Oh how I enjoyed being able to relieve my bottled wrath." Holmes's frustrations after four long years of war at last found expression in an all but risk-free verbal assault on the enemy.[9]

Women proudly reported the cleverness of their responses to Yankee provocations, sometimes recording lengthy dialogues demonstrating their verbal triumphs. When a group of young women in Williamsburg, Virginia, gathered together for the first time during McClellan's occupation in the Peninsula campaign of 1862, Harriette Cary noted that "of course there was much to be told by each—instances of *courageous retort*, for which frequent opportunities have been given by these provoking villains." Kate Carney was delighted when she seemed to win over the Yankee enlisted men during a verbal contest with their officer. In a "cutting speech," she was berating Union troops for cowardly retreats at Shiloh, Bull Run, and Richmond, when a private broke in and urged her not to forget to question his captain about Yankees fleeing before the enemy at Pittsburg Landing.[10]

For women who had felt useless in the battle against invading northerners, such confrontations offered the satisfaction of direct participation in attacks on the enemy troops. What had for many Confederate women been "impotent rage" could in the face of Union soldiers achieve expression and find a target; southern females embraced the opportunity to employ what Sarah Morgan of Louisiana called "their woman weapon, the tongue." As Harriette Cary and her friends reassured one another, women too had a chance to be "courageous," to rival the boldness of their men, at least within their protected sphere of verbal warfare. "Ambition whispered now perhaps is the time to make a heroine of yourself," Alice Ready explained as Federal troops approached her Tennessee home. Imbued with the same romantic notions of war's glories that inspired their men, southern women seemed in the eyes of one Yankee officer to possess "a theatrical desire to figure as heroines."[11]

At times women progressed beyond words. In Rome, Georgia, students at a ladies' seminary emptied their chamber pots on troops below their windows. Elizabeth McKamy of Tennessee frightened herself when she responded with violence to a Yankee who snatched a crust of bread from her nephew. "Before I realized what I was doing, I began beating that Yankee over the shoulders with a stick of stove wood." One Arkansas woman pushed a soldier down the stairs when he tried to wrestle her dead brother's suit out of her hands, and another Arkansan filled a shovel with ashes from the hearth and emptied it on the table when six Federal soldiers walked in and sat down to dinner. The Yankees grinned and departed. Even when seventeen-year-old Belle Boyd drew a pistol from her skirts and shot a Yankee threatening to search her mother's Virginia house, Belle escaped punishment.[12]

## The Right to Bear Arms

A few Confederate women expressed their ambition for female heroism and their rage at the Yankees by attempting to become soldiers. From the outset, women had looked with envy as their brothers and husbands departed to reap war's glories, and many indulged fantasies about being men and taking part in the gallant fight. For some, this fantasy became reality. As many as 400 women North and South disguised themselves and served in the army. In January 1863 the *Charleston Mercury* recounted the tale of one of the best-known female soldiers, Amy Clarke, who volunteered as a private, the paper explained, in order not to be parted from her husband. After his death at Shiloh, she continued to fight, was twice wounded, and then was taken prisoner by the Yankees, who discovered her sex. "But they did not permit her to return" to the South, the *Mercury* explained, "until she had donned female apparel," the equivalent in this situation, apparently, of the customary parole of noncombatancy from returned prisoners. Actions like Clarke's were so exceptional they hardly proved threatening to prevailing assumptions about women's roles; the occasional Joan of Arc was unlikely to turn the world upside down, especially if, as in Clarke's case, her motivation for enlistment could be construed as wifely devotion. Nevertheless, in reporting the adventures of a woman with a story much like Amy Clarke's, the *Milledgeville Southern Federal Union* felt compelled to assure its readers it had "heard nothing in any degree to implicate the good character and standing of this gallant heroine." Her motivations had to be sharply distinguished from those of the camp follower.[13]

More common than instances of individual women passing as soldiers were reports of local companies organized for home defense. In the first months of war these efforts often represented women's desire to join in the unfolding drama of war, to find a purpose for lives that seemed all too useless in comparison with their men's. Students at Wesleyan Female College in Macon, Georgia, for example, organized themselves into military companies and held drills and parades. By the later years of the conflict, however, when so few men remained at home to provide protection, women often felt compelled to make some effort to defend themselves. In LaGrange, Georgia, women banded together to form a military company that they proudly named for Nancy Hart, a local heroine who had boldly trapped a group of British officers during the Revolution. Enlisting an experienced but disabled soldier as teacher, "nearly all the young ladies" of LaGrange took up marching and marksmanship, practicing in a farm field where they managed to kill a few innocent cows. When a force of Yankees approached the town, a fleeing Confederate ordered the assembled Nancy Harts to their houses, but not one "heeded such an unmilitary request." When the Federal cavalry arrived, they found the women soldiers armed to greet them. "Believing it to be good policy to conciliate the enemy," an officer of the company explained, she invited the Yankees to tea. LaGrange was spared the torch, and the Union commander later married one of the Nancy Harts.[14]

Reporting on her military experience years after the war, Leila Morris characterized it as a frolic. No intimation of fear or anger darkens her tale of female ingenuity and courage; hostility toward the invaders and the women's seriousness of purpose have alike all but disappeared in the romantic haze of postwar reconciliation. Twenty-eight women of Harrisonburg, Virginia, however, began to organize a regiment in quite a different frame of mind. In a December 1864 letter to the Confederate secretary of war, Annie Samuels, Irene Bell, and their associates requested that "the right to bear arms in defense of our homes be delegated to certain of the *fairer* portion of the ill starred Confederacy." The latest conscription bill, they explained, would take "every 'lord of creation' from sixteen to sixty." Having already been subjected to "every conceivable outrage and suffering" because of the "incompetency of the Confederate Army upon which we depend for defense," these women sought to take matters into their own hands. Angry at their "lords," both for abandoning and for failing to protect them, Harrisonburg's ladies prepared to defend themselves against Federal troops. "We are not quite ready," the secretary of war responded sardonically, "to call the Ladies to our help in the Field." But neither was he prepared to provide the women with the protection they sought.[15]

Women's anger was here simultaneously directed against Confederate and Yankee men—Confederates for their incompetence and Yankees for the tangible military threat they posed. Although the secretary of war mocked the ladies' military ambitions, he, like Confederate discourse generally, celebrated southern women's outspokenness against the Yankee foe. Far better, he might recognize, to have Harrisonburg's females focus their discontent on the invaders than on the "incompetency" of their own men. Whatever transgressive potential rested within ladies' unaccustomed and unseemly rage, there could be no more socially acceptable target or release than the Yankee, who served as a safety valve for emotions frustrated women might otherwise have directed within their own families, households, or social order. Women's anger and women's loss of control were in their confrontations with Yankees restrained within safe channels, actually posing little danger to the females themselves or to the broader conventions of southern womanhood.

## Discretion Is the Better Part

At least some women, dissenting from their sisters' aggressive and belligerent posture, worried that antagonistic behavior threatened both women's safety and prevailing standards of feminine propriety. In part these disagreements seem to have paralleled divisions of age, with older women more wary of the possibly dangerous consequences of unmitigated hostility and more practiced in the maintenance of decorum and self-control. Mary Lee was apprehensive lest the Yankees later choose to burn the dwellings of the Winchester women who had been most outspoken, and she was concerned as well about the ultimate impact of indelicate behavior on woman's character and virtue. "Will we ever," she wondered, "be gentle, refined ladies again, using mild terms & walking the streets with pleasant, friendly countenances[?] Scorn & contempt are such habitual expressions, that I fear they will not readily give place to more ladylike ones." Belligerent actions by women, she believed, were in "bad taste; cold contemptuous silence is more galling." She had quickly grown tired, she confided to her diary, of the contest "as to which [woman] shall make the most cutting rejoinders."[16]

Lee advocated manipulation rather than confrontation and prided herself at all she secretly accomplished—even under constant Federal scrutiny. Collecting clothing, boots, and supplies for Confederate soldiers from the countryside around Winchester, convincing Union doctors to permit Winchester's ladies to nurse and feed the Confederate wounded, and parrying repeated threats of Yankee seizure of her house and property, Mary Lee exulted in her "faculty for managing men." Just as southern women used their feminine hoops to hide their valuables, so Lee took advantage of the prerogatives of her gender to shield her treasonous activities. Mary Lee employed Yankees' chivalry and restraint against them. Violent confrontation might offer emotional release and satisfaction, Lee noted, but usually accomplished little for the Cause at the high price of degrading southern womanhood.[17]

Sarah Morgan of Louisiana reconsidered the purposes of the war in light of her revulsion at the "rude, illmannered behavior" of some of her female compatriots. "I insist, that if the valor and chivalry of our men cannot save our country, I would rather have it conquered by a brave race, than owe its liberty to the Billingsgate oratory and demonstrations of some of these 'ladies'. . . . Do I consider the female who could spit on a gentleman's face merely because he wore United States buttons, as a fit associate for me?" For Morgan, dictates of class and gender identity overrode those of nation. Kate Cumming agreed that silence was more eloquent and more seemly than outspoken insult. " 'Discretion,' " she affirmed, " 'is the better part of valor.' "[18]

Unmitigated hatred and hostility struck many pious southern women not just as unladylike but as unchristian. Alice Ready was "shocked" at the intensity of her hatred and confessed, "I sometimes fear I am loosing all the charity which I ever possessed." Nineteen-year-old Amanda Worthington of Mississippi worried that her inability to repress a "deep underlying thirst for vengeance" against the Yankees who had killed her brother would prevent her reunion with him in heaven. Both Mary Lee and Ada Bacot struggled to overcome their aversion to nursing wounded Federals hospitalized beside their heroic Confederates. "It will be hard," Bacot confessed, "to treat them as I do the other men but I know it is my duty." As Mary Lee had feared, her patriotism threatened to undermine her sense of Christian obligation. Sarah Morgan was appalled at the "wicked, malignant feelings that I did not believe could dwell in woman's heart." Devout females, filled with "all Christian meekness" would burst into "mad tirade[s] of abuse," wishing plague, fever, and famine upon the Yankees. "Oh woman!" she exclaimed, "into what loathsome violence you have abased your holy mission."[19]

Noting the hypocrisy of so many of her Christian friends, Phoebe Levy Pember congratulated herself that she had been born a Jew, adherent of a religion that advocated not forgiveness but, as she put it, an "eye for an eye." During an evening with a particularly "pious sett" of Christian women, she had encountered extraordinarily vengeful attitudes. One kept Yankee bones on view in her yard; another sought a Yankee skull to use as a jewelry box. "I proposed," Pember remarked, "that till the war was over they should join the Jewish Church, let forgiveness and peace and good will alone, and put their trust in the sword of the Lord."[20]

Considerations of both femininity and Christianity influenced some women to act with civility toward their captors. Particularly in occupied areas where extended contact brought the humanity of the foe into evidence, numbers of women turned to Union soldiers for assistance or companionship, as self-interest and traditional propriety combined to prescribe conciliatory behavior. Even in Winchester, noted for the outspoken hostility of its women, Mary Lee despaired that only one or two households were by late 1863 still refusing to entertain Yankees. Needy Virginia matrons were taking in Federal boarders to make ends meet. "Nearly all our friends," Lee wrote, "profit by having them in their houses." Not only did Union officers pay rent, they brought supplies of firewood and edibles, scarce commodities in the wartorn town. Cornelia McDonald, Lee's "talking heroine," had resorted to accepting—under cover of darkness—packets of food from charitable Yankee soldiers sympathetic to McDonald's difficulties in providing for her nine children.[21]

Southern ladies often found they had more in common than in conflict with Union men from similar class backgrounds. "When I come in contact with a *gentleman*," Mary Brown of North Carolina explained to her stepson, "I respect him as a gentleman, no matter if he does not agree in sentiment with me. I think some of the people of Asheville make themselves appear very ridiculous in their scornful manners towards the Federals." In occupied Natchez, this pattern of fraternization may have reached its apogee. The Mississippi town had been home to perhaps the wealthiest cotton aristocracy of the Old South, and in 1861 many citizens had felt they had too much to lose to embrace the secessionist revolution with enthusiasm. These political sympathies undoubtedly encouraged the residents of Natchez in their tempered response to the conquering Federals in the summer of 1863. "For some time," Annie Harper remembered, the women of the town "discussed whether we sh'd receive them into our homes, whether it wd be treason to our absent soldiers but many decided that we could not be less generous than our foe, and having accepted so many sorely needed favors and so many kindnesses that the best return we could make was to treat them hospitably." Harper recognized the peculiarity of such social intercourse between supposed enemies but invoked Natchez's almost uniquely aristocratic character as both explanation and justification. "Only people of the highest culture and dignity can sustain themselves honorably in such an anomalous position, and Natchez was the place to find such people."[22]

Kate Foster was torn when she saw many of her young Natchez friends "receiving attention" from the Yankees. It seemed disloyal to relatives and friends in the army, yet she recognized much that was admirable in the Union soldiers. "When the federals first came I was disposed to think there was not a gentleman among them. I have had kindness shown me and politeness most assuredly." Union general Crocker seemed more friend than foe, and the behavior of the troops made it evident to Harper, at least, that "none but gentlemen had been sent to Natchez." A shift in command and the replacement of "gentleman" soldiers by a "class of men of less polish" brought an end to the pattern of warm civilian-military relations. Faced with northern troops from social origins very unlike their own, Natchez ladies learned "what it was to fall into the hands of an enemy" at last.[23]

## Women (Calling Themselves Ladies)

If the early months of Natchez's occupation symbolized the possibilities for fraternization between Confederate civilians and their conquerors, New Orleans under Union major general Benjamin Butler represented its polar

*Confederate women and Yankee men in Mississippi. "The War on the Mississippi—Secesh Ladies Coming to the United States Commissaries for Provisions.* Frank Leslie's Illustrated Newspaper, *October 10, 1863.*

opposite. When the South's largest city fell to Federal forces in April 1862, Butler faced the daunting task of governing a bitterly hostile civilian population. Exhibiting little of the submission expected of the defeated, the residents of New Orleans refused to comply with orders from the newly arrived Federals and gathered in unruly mobs to threaten the safety of Butler and his troops. Compelled to rule by force and threat, Butler gradually abandoned any pretense of conciliation. Crowds unwilling to disperse were greeted by Union artillery. Shopkeepers who refused Yankee business found their stores seized and sold. A man destroying a Union flag was sentenced to be hung. Ministers resisting prayers for the United States president were banished to the North. "Very soon," Butler wrote, "there was no uncivil treatment received by our soldiers except from the upper class of women."[24]

Assuming themselves exempt from the harsh measures meted out to men, the ladies of New Orleans continued to treat the Yankees with contempt. Flouncing out of churches or streetcars if Union soldiers entered and spitting or emptying chamber pots on Butler's men, southern women sought to humiliate their conquerors. Butler was perplexed about how to respond to these outrages. He recognized that the perpetrators were generally young, often "pretty and interesting," and frequently socially prominent, the kind of individuals who would attract both attention and sympathy if harsh measures turned them into martyrs. At the same time, however, Butler knew he had to control their actions, for "a city could hardly be said to be under good government where such things were permitted."[25]

On May 15 Butler issued his infamous General Order No. 28, an astute invocation of prevailing assumptions about class and gender designed to compel the women of New Orleans themselves to restrain their hostile outbursts.

General Order No. 28.

As the officers and soldiers of the United States have been subject to repeated insults from the women (calling themselves ladies) of New Orleans . . . it is ordered that hereafter when any female shall, by word, gesture, or movement, insult or show contempt for any officer or soldier of the United States, she shall be regarded and held liable to be treated as a woman of the town plying her avocation.[26]

Butler's order drove to the heart of the ambiguities in white southern women's identities. By their behavior shall ye know them, he insisted, not by their categorical claims to the status and privileges of ladyhood. Women who acted with the vulgarity of harlots would be treated like harlots; if they abandoned appropriate feminine delicacy and restraint, they would be denied the protection accorded ladies. Unlike so many other Yankee commanders, Butler was not going to be manipulated by women's simultaneous use and abuse of their femininity. "I did not carry on war with rose-water," he explained. Yet Butler rightly anticipated that the desire of almost all southern females to be included within the rubric of "lady" would induce the conduct he desired without the necessity of day-to-day enforcement. The fear of being perceived as a "woman of the town" was so great, the threatened loss of honor so unthinkable, that no Yankee officer was ever faced with actually carrying out the order's threat. The measure, as Butler had sagely anticipated, "executed itself." Horrified at the prospect of being identified as women of the lowest moral and social order, the females of New Orleans policed their own behavior.[27]

On the most obvious level, Butler was manipulating deeply internalized class and gender identities to control southern women—or, more precisely, to coerce them into controlling themselves. "All the ladies in New Orleans," Butler explained, "forebore to insult our troops because they didn't want to be deemed common women, and all the common women forebore to insult our troops because they wanted to be deemed ladies, and of those two classes were all the women secessionists of the city." More profoundly, he was making a statement about wartime transformations in women's roles and status. General Order No. 28 held women accountable for their actions in the public sphere; Butler would not permit them to stand outside political responsibility or retribution. In taking such a position Butler acknowledged women as politically powerful. Their symbolic gestures—waving flags, spitting, and talking back—had substantive meaning. When, later in the summer of 1862, he demanded that all citizens of New Orleans take an oath of allegiance to the United States, he again produced surprise and outrage by including women within the scope of his edict. Attacked, like the "Woman Order," as "opposed to the chivalrous spirit that should actuate a refined people," General Order No. 76 was entirely consistent with the earlier measure, for it granted women both political agency and accountability.[28]

New Orleans females responded with fury to Butler's "war upon the women of the land." Like the Missourian who declared herself "a lady . . . unaccustomed to being held responsible for anything she might say," they resisted the liabilities of this new empowerment. Assailing General Order No. 28 as an assault on sacred female purity, New Orleans women, joined by defenders of traditional notions of womanhood from around the world, used the confrontation as an occasion to resist threatening wartime changes and to reaffirm the most traditional constructions of woman's place. In South Carolina, Mary Chesnut read the proclamation as simply "turning over the women of New Orleans to his soldiers"; New Orleans's erstwhile mayor characterized the measure as ordering soldiers "to perpetrate unexampled outrages upon virtuous women." As the *Mobile Advertiser and Register* saw it, General Order No. 28 "purports to be a warning addressed to the ladies, but is really a license, expressly given to the soldiers," an "instigation to the violation of the women of New Orleans." The *New York Times* protested the measure, and the London press and Parliament agreed on Butler's "intolerable brutality." The General was a Beast.[29]

Although the measure successfully eliminated the direct confrontations between individual Louisiana women and Yankee soldiers that Butler had feared would create martyrs, General Order No. 28 generated a wave of indignation and of sympathy for southern women. The discrepancy between the language and intention of the order and the interpretation placed on it by an international public offers significant insight into wartime conflict over gender issues. By construing the measure as a threat to female sexual purity, Confederate discourse invoked and reaffirmed the ideology of feminine weakness and dependence, the rationale for women's subordination that we have seen so deeply rooted in assumptions of women's vulnerability to sexual violation. Whether the women of New Orleans initiated or simply cooperated with men of government and the press in this invocation of female frailty, the immediate and widespread transformation of what Butler intended as a question of public order into an issue of sexual vulnerability is significant. General Order No. 28 in itself contains no explicit or implicit encouragement of sexual aggression by soldiers; women of the town, after all, negotiate to sell sex in transactions that involve more complex issues of female agency than overt rape. Butler's measure imputed responsibility and power to New Orleans women, recognizing them as political actors; the hostile response to the order cast women as passive victims of their biological attributes. Butler's order was about what scholars today would call gender, emphasizing the social constructedness of male-female divisions, the ideological bases for the assignment of men's and women's roles within any culture. General Order No. 28 represented a significant affirmation of the mutability inherent in a social understanding of female identities and behaviors, a mutability wartime circumstance had made increasingly clear. Yet the cries of his critics all but drowned out his pathbreaking and transgressive politicization of women by reasserting the "natural" and thus seemingly unchangeable basis for social dependence that derived from women's innate difference—and physical inferiority. Attacks on Butler, then, derived not from assumptions about gender but about sex, about biologically rather than ideologically rooted contrasts between women and men. In the terms they and the world chose to employ to protest Butler's edict, the women of New Orleans affirmed a traditional doctrine of fixed sexual divisions and of an enduring and necessary female subordination. Here, as in so many other instances, Confederate women fled from the responsibility of empowerment into the reassuring safety of tradition's protective shelter.[30]

Yet perhaps Butler's particular representation of empowered woman made such a response overdetermined if not inevitable. General Order No.

THE LADIES OF NEW ORLEANS before GENERAL BUTLER'S Proclamation.

*The effects of General Order No. 28.* Harper's Weekly, *July 12, 1862.*

28 recognized the wartime transformation of etiquette into politics. Woman had been unavoidably thrust into the public sphere; symbolic politics is politics nonetheless. Butler acknowledged these shifts, yet his language dismissed women's public actions with disdain. General Order No. 28 at once ratified the new public presence of women and derogated it by invoking an equivalence between a woman acting in public and a prostitute. The choice Butler offered women was thus, in the terms he presented it, no real choice at all. By recognizing their hostile acts he admitted them into a domain of responsibility and power, yet with the same words he used their lingering gentility to propel them back into the private sphere.

Butler's difficulties in pacifying the civilian population combined with crises about the rights of foreign nationals to lead to his replacement in December 1862 by Nathaniel Banks. Committed to a more conciliatory administration of the turbulent city, Banks was immediately challenged by residents who chose to regard his generosity as weakness. Women began

After GENERAL BUTLER'S Proclamation.

once again to insult Yankee soldiers and to make public profession of Confederate loyalties. Late in February 1863 women's continued outspokenness produced an incident enshrined in popular legend as the "Battle of the Handkerchiefs." When a group of captured Confederate officers was being shipped to Baton Rouge for a prisoner exchange, New Orleans ladies offered a bold expression of their continuing southern sympathies, gathering at the levee to cheer the departing heroes. Union troops endeavored to control the crowd and its treasonous enthusiasm but were confronted by a mob of women waving parasols and handkerchiefs and refusing to disband. Several women incurred slight injuries in the confusion. A southern newspaper poem celebrated the courage of the ladies and mocked the foolishness of the soldiers. More significant, however, was Banks's obvious reversion to a pre-Butler understanding of women as existing essentially outside political responsibility or retribution. The women's triumphant "victory" in the Battle of the Handkerchiefs depended on Yankee men's refusal to engage the enemy.[31]

The reluctance of so many Union officers to acknowledge war's politicization of women provided a few clear-sighted Confederate females with an unprecedented opportunity to contribute to the southern Cause. Like guerrillas in later wars, these women self-consciously used assumptions about their innocence and immunity from political reprisal to shield themselves and their partisan actions, frustrating the Yankees who feared abandoning the velvet glove in their dealings with the South's master class. Mary Lee, playing the accepted role of charitable female nurse and nurturer, repeatedly performed treasonous acts in occupied Winchester, smuggling letters, information, and supplies to Confederate forces. Her ability to "manage men," however, protected her until the very last months of war, when the new harshness that accompanied Sheridan's Valley campaign led to her expulsion from her home and her transportation beyond Confederate lines. But even amidst the new scorched earth policies of 1865, Lee was not shot, imprisoned, or in any way physically harmed. She continued to be surprised and outraged when Union actions acknowledged her as the powerful and effective southern partisan she in fact was. At the end of the war, news that an oath of allegiance would be required of southern women infuriated her. "Is it not absurd," she wrote, "that we should be made of so much importance, treating us as if we were men." The transgressive implications of her own actions for traditional gender roles was more than Mary Lee could—or wanted to—understand.[32]

## All Was Fair in Love and War

Countless numbers of southern women in occupied areas probably practiced the kind of day-to-day resistance exemplified by Lee in the effort to aid husbands, sons, and brothers in the Confederate military, and it has been estimated that Yankees expelled hundreds of women of doubtful loyalties into southern lines. Relatively few women, however, made treason a vocation in the manner of Belle Boyd, the Confederacy's legendary female spy. Boyd's exploits, known chiefly through her 1865 autobiography and her postwar theatrical tours, have often been discounted as fabulous inventions. But research undertaken by Louis Sigaud in the 1940s suggests that military and other records confirm the authenticity of most details she recounts about her life. For our purposes, however, the verifiability of every exploit is less important than Boyd's explanation of her strategies and her description of how much she got away with before at last being forced into European exile in 1864.[33]

Boyd is in every sense an exceptional rather than a representative Confederate woman. Yet the tactics she used against the Yankees simply represent the end of a spectrum; she is but the most extreme—and therefore perhaps the most striking and suggestive—example of the way some southern women invoked prevailing notions about femininity to achieve quite untraditional female goals. Boyd's career as a spy depended on the manipulation of gender conventions to make her espionage activities possible. Her female identity served as a disguise for her actions in the male sphere of partisan political and military struggle. With the element of surprise as her weapon, Belle succeeded in securing and transmitting information so valuable to Confederate troops that Stonewall Jackson commissioned her a captain and made her an honorary aide-de-camp. Even after her notoriety should long since have voided any claims to innocent womanhood, however, Boyd continued to receive from the Yankees special protections and dispensations that shielded her from full accountability for her efforts as a spy.

In comparison with Boyd, Mary Lee was a rank amateur at managing men. Born in 1844 in Martinsburg, just north of Winchester in Virginia's Shenandoah Valley, Belle Boyd was the daughter of a locally prominent slaveowning family. Belle was educated at a respectable female seminary outside Baltimore, but from an early age she cultivated a reputation as headstrong and unpredictable, once riding her horse into the family living room to protest her exclusion from an adult gathering.

Boyd first attracted public notice when in 1861, at age seventeen, she shot and killed a Yankee soldier for cursing her mother "in language as offensive as it is possible to conceive." Although his fellow enlisted men threatened to burn the Boyds' house, a group of officers investigating the matter concluded Belle had "done perfectly right." She was, they presumed, a lady exercising her right of defense against insult. For his failure to act the gentleman, the soldier had, it seemed, deserved to die.[34]

Less than a week after this incident the Yankees discovered Boyd gathering information in the course of flirtatious conversations with Federal soldiers and passing it on to Confederate officials. Once again Boyd was spared, as the commanding colonel chose only to read her the article of war indicating such actions to be punishable by death. Boyd's successful espionage career was launched.

As she described her exploits over the next three years, nearly every triumph derived from her use of Yankee assumptions about womanhood to entrap her unsuspecting foes. When her horse ran away into Federal lines near Martinsburg, she abjectly requested permission to return home from

*Belle Boyd. Carte de Visite. Courtesy of the Eleanor S. Brockenbrough Library, Museum of the Confederacy, Richmond, Virginia.*

her Union captors. Gallant Yankee cavalrymen offered to escort the lady back across the lines, and she gratefully accepted. But when they reached the Confederate pickets, Boyd delivered the Union soldiers as prisoners. Having extracted the courtesy of safe passage from the Yankees, she declined to offer them the same. "I consoled myself that, 'all was fair in love and war,'" she explained.[35]

As a confrontation between Union and Confederate forces at Front Royal, Virginia, began to seem inevitable in May 1862, Boyd sought to transport information down the valley into Jackson's hands. But she needed a pass to enter Union-occupied Front Royal. "Knowing Colonel Fillebrowne was never displeased by a little flattery and a few delicate attentions," she explained, "I went to the florist and chose a very handsome bouquet which I sent to him with my compliments, and with a request that he would be so kind as to permit me to return to Front Royal," where she had an uncle and aunt she frequently visited. The next day proved probably the best known of her career, as Belle rushed from town to deliver information that enabled Jackson's troops to capture Front Royal and move on toward Winchester. Legend casts the young woman standing amidst the oncoming Confederates waving her sunbonnet and shouting details of Yankee movements. Questioned about the Union disaster, Colonel Fillebrowne pointed to Belle's gift and explained, "That bouquet did all the mischief: the donor of that . . . is responsible *for all* this misfortune."[36]

Clearly the Federals had begun to recognize that they were paying a high price for exempting Belle Boyd from political responsibility. As one exasperated Union major told her outright, "You will do more harm to our cause than half the men could do." Yet Boyd herself continued to exploit her advantage and to press her womanly claims. When, in the aftermath of the battle of Front Royal, the northern press cried out for her punishment, Belle complained of the unwarranted "abuse" she was suffering from the press. "They seemed to think that to insult an innocent young girl was to prove their manhood and evince their patriotism."[37]

Belle's disingenuous assertions of innocence—after committing murder, treachery, and espionage—only make sense if connected with the words that follow her claim to blamelessness. She was, she insisted, an innocent young girl because her youth and her gender defined her outside the realm of responsibility. As we today might designate someone innocent by reason of insanity, Boyd claimed innocence by reason of age and femininity.

But Boyd had proved herself too dangerous to ignore. In July 1862 Union officials incarcerated her in Washington's Old Capitol prison. Well fed and comfortably housed, Belle was accorded special treatment even in captivity. During her two-month stay she managed both to become engaged to a fellow prisoner and to so charm the Old Capitol's superintendent that after her release he acquired a trousseau for her and shipped it by flag of truce to Richmond. After her return to the South Boyd made no further mention of her impending marriage. But at least she, presumably almost unique among Confederate women, enjoyed the benefits of a new wardrobe.

The flamboyant cynicism of Boyd's manipulations of men suggests itself in her next romantic adventure. Imprisoned and released once again, Boyd decided in the spring of 1864 to apply her talents to smuggling dispatches to Europe. But a Union naval vessel seized the blockade-runner *Greyhound* on which she sailed from Wilmington, North Carolina, soon after its departure from port. By the time her ship reached New York City for refueling, Belle herself had captured the Yankee officer in command of the *Greyhound*. She and Captain Samuel Hardinge were seen shopping and attending the theater before the vessel departed for its final destination in Boston. En route to Massachusetts, however, the Confederate commander of the ship, now a prisoner of war, mysteriously escaped, and suspicion fell on Hardinge, who was ultimately court-martialed and imprisoned on charges of complicity in the incident. Before his fate was determined, though, Hardinge had followed Belle, exiled from the United States, to London, where they were married.

Hardinge's ultimate destiny is shrouded in mystery. He returned to America to take responsibility for his actions on the *Greyhound*, but it is unclear if he ever rejoined Belle in London after his release from Fort Delaware in February 1865. Some accounts say he died after an illness contracted in prison; others insist he was drowned at sea. Even today rumors persist that Belle may have played some role in his disappearance and death. He had served his purpose in aiding both Belle and the captain of the *Greyhound* after their capture; Belle had little further need for his services. When the war ended in 1865, Belle was just twenty-one years old, a widow and the mother of Hardinge's young child. Compelled to earn a living, she turned to acting. It was a field in which she was already an expert.

Belle Boyd remains an enigmatic and curiously neglected figure. Few serious students of history have accorded her much attention. Her extraordinary exploits, however, represent the most extreme manifestations of ambitions and strategies embraced by hundreds of Confederate females who used women's weapons but did not play by women's rules. Long expert in managing men, Confederate women in wartime simply turned these skills to new purposes. Belle Boyd was perhaps the most exuberantly manipulative in the use of her femininity; few women so self-consciously plotted and planned their assaults on the northern foe, and few were as untroubled by doubt or remorse. Yet Boyd's exploitations of gender assumptions illuminate many of the fundamental principles governing interactions between men and women in the Civil War era, forcing northerners and southerners alike to recognize that females could be both powerful and, as one Union officer said of Belle, "dangerous." Feminine "weakness" served as the foundation of female strength. Perhaps most significantly, however, Boyd's story marks a destabilization of fixed assumptions that permitted her in some sense to live in two genders and two worlds of gender relations simultaneously. Belle Boyd maintained the dress and demeanor of a lady, but her actions and purposes were those of a man. Boyd and the hundreds of other Confederate women who, like Mary Lee, in one way or another thwarted the Yankees had in their own way seen the elephant and made a definitive entrance on the tented field.

Yet they neither welcomed nor even fully acknowledged this dramatic development. "I do not sit myself up as an advocate of the woman's rights doctrine," Belle Boyd proclaimed, "but would rather appear in the character of a quiet lady expressing her sentiments, not so much to the public as to her immediate friends." Belle insisted on maintaining the woman's sphere, for from it she derived her power.[38]

Spies succeed because they are not who they appear to be. In this sense the extraordinary Belle Boyd can both substantively and metaphorically represent southern women more generally. Like Boyd, they, in wartime, found themselves in disguise, in figurative costumes and roles ill suited to the identities they had nurtured in their prewar lives. Belle Boyd succeeded in turning these inconsistencies to her advantage; other women regarded the conflict as more a burden than an opportunity. But almost all looked upon themselves and their femininity with new eyes. Womanhood gradually came to seem less like a physical part of one's body and more like a dress one could alter or even change.

# CHAPTER TEN

# *If I Were Once Released*

## THE GARB OF GENDER

In the summer of 1862 Sarah Morgan of Louisiana confided to her diary that she had been considering trying on her absent brother's clothes. Jimmy's suit had been hanging in her armoire for six weeks when at last she was emboldened to remove it. "I advanced so far," she reported, "as to lay it on the bed." But then she turned aside to take her pet bird from the room. "I was ashamed to let even my canary see me." When she returned to contemplate the suit, "my courage deserted me, and there ended my first and last attempt at disguise. I have heard so many girls boast of having worn men's clothes; I wonder where they get the courage."[1]

Clothing became fraught with meaning for Confederate women. On the most obvious level, shortages of cloth and resulting privations marked loss of wealth and status for ladies of the slaveowning class. Perhaps even more significantly, however, choices of dress and evolutions in fashion expressed shifting perceptions of woman's identity and woman's place, representing a new awareness of the fluidity, the instability, and even the arbitrariness of gender categories. Dress became a language southerners used to explore and to communicate their relationship to the personal, social, and cultural transformations of war.[2]

For many women like Sarah Morgan, clothing at once expressed desire and dread, possibility and impossibility. "If I was only a man!" she exclaimed. "I dont know a woman here who does not groan over her misfortune in being clothed in petticoats; why cant we fight as well as the men[?]" Metaphorically equating clothing and gender, Morgan made garb the emblem of woman's constraints; petticoats at once embodied and symbolized female subordination. Yet such a representation contains powerful implications about the meaning of gender and the potential for transformation in female lives. Woman need only change her petticoats in order to overcome the "misfortune" of her sex, in order, presumably, to find herself able to fight alongside a man. If changing clothes entailed the acceptance of such responsibility, no wonder Morgan lacked the courage to try on Jimmy's suit. In the theater of war, gender—with its protections, privileges, opportunities, and responsibilities—had become only a costume.[3]


## Anything I Can Get


The Confederacy's economic weakness had a direct impact on the availability and style of women's clothing in the wartime South. As we have seen, all southerners, black and white, rich and poor, suffered from the region's prewar reliance on northern textiles. Revived household production met only a portion of this deficiency, and fabrics made at home tended to be rough in quality, too much like what white southerners called "negro-cloth." Her "underclothing," Emma LeConte complained in 1865, "is of coarse unbleached homespun, such as we gave the negroes formerly only much coarser." For reasons of both status and comfort, elite women sought—often unsuccessfully—to avoid homespun by turning to a variety of other expedients to keep themselves appropriately and adequately clothed. The most privileged sometimes procured fashionable northern or European attire from blockade-runners, but such fortunate individuals were few. More often, women of the slaveowning classes struggled to make do, often resorting to ingenious makeshifts like those of the fictional Scarlett O'Hara, who created a gown out of the living-room draperies. Not just curtains but household linens, tablecloths, and sheets, as well as worn out or discarded dresses, reappeared as underwear, petticoats, and even ball gowns.[4]

"As to my dress," Virginia's Mary Lee remarked, "I wear anything I can get, regardless of propriety." Even though she considered herself in deep mourning, she was compelled to go out in a flounced organdy skirt, and she had so few winter dresses that she continued in summer frocks till almost November, despite October's chill. The lure of fashion had not entirely disappeared, however. Occupying Yankee troops brought news of northern styles, and Lee recorded her valiant effort to keep up. "Altered the sleeves of a dress by the last New York fashion this morning," she noted in her diary. Parthenia Hague of Alabama dyed unbleached sheeting with barks and twigs to make a dress fabric in a rich brown and decorated plain homespun with scraps of worn-out old dresses—"part of an old black silk, and some red scraps of merino, and a remnant of an old blue scarf." A refugee, Kate Stone purchased used dresses from impecunious locals because "it is all we can get," but she felt "funny to be wearing other people's half-worn clothing." Margaret Preston met shortages not so much with ingenuity as with sacrifice. After the first year of the war she reported with pride that she had "rigidly abstained from getting a single article of dress." With similar self-denial Jo Gillis of Alabama pretended she did not care about clothes or finery so that all her family's resources could be directed toward attiring her preacher husband. Leather was so scarce that women sewed shoes out of cloth and paper and left their children barefoot. Eleven-year-old Mary Neblett, her mother Lizzie reported in May 1864, had not worn shoes in months. In Rutherford County, North Carolina, a group of women complained to Governor Zebulon Vance that "half the ladys" had to stay home from church because of the lack of shoes.[5]

Lizzie Neblett regretted that she had not dressed better before the war, when clothing was available and affordable. By 1864 her wardrobe was so threadbare that she found herself compelled to buy back a dress she had given one of her slaves several years before. The dress was a "pretty calico . . . as good as new," and for three and a half dollars Lizzie was delighted with her acquisition. In her enthusiasm she seemed oblivious both to the irony and to the loss of status implicit in purchasing her own cast-off dress from a slave. Mary Chesnut was more perceptive and analytical about shifting foundations of privilege. Like many of her friends in Richmond, the "ci-devant rich, the white ladies," she wrote acerbically, Chesnut regularly sold dresses to a mulatto woman who ran a shop catering to the capital city's free blacks. In areas of Union military advance, white southern females rarely missed the significance of emancipated slave women who sported their mistresses' captured finery as symbols of their new situation. Kate Stone was horrified by stories of the slaves abandoned on her family's Louisiana plantation "capering around" in her mother's clothes and "taking her place as mistress." African American women arrayed in brocades and silks violated the South's unwritten sumptuary laws. In a rendition of "the world turned upside down," an enactment of the eroding power of the South's master class, they used the language of clothing to assault the hierarchies of race with far greater assertiveness than Sarah Morgan had dared to challenge the structures of gender.[6]

## Hoops Are Subsiding

Wartime shortages may have been the origin of one of the most striking developments in Confederate fashion. The hoopskirt had come into style in the early 1850s and continued to define the female silhouette at the time of the outbreak of war in 1861. The hoop itself was an elaborately constructed frame of cloth-covered steel secured by ties at the waist. Worn under a dress, it served to make a skirt bouffant—"truly prodigious" in size, in the words of one historian of costume—sometimes more than five feet in diameter. We can only speculate about the cultural meaning and attraction of such a style, but it seems that the advent of hoops generally coincided with the emergence of Victorian ideals of domesticity and with the triumph of the ideology of a separate woman's sphere, a notion the hoop physically embodied. A lady in hoops transported her enclosed, private space with her; a wide skirt represented the circle within which a female was to be protected. Moreover, in a Victorian culture that denied and repressed the sexuality of middle- and upper-class women, hoops hid and reformed woman's anatomy. Enlarged skirts, requiring perhaps as much as twenty yards of fabric, made statements about class as well as gender position, for hoops necessitated a conspicuous consumption of cloth and could not easily be worn by those compelled to perform active physical labor. Efficient movement in such garments was all but impossible. The fashion was thus best suited to mark the privileged, protected, and largely passive woman of the middle or upper class whose duties in life focused on tasteful and lavish consumption.[7]

A decline of hoops in the wartime South attracted the attention of men

*A Confederate woman caught using her hoops to smuggle quinine into the South.*
*"Crinoline and Quinine."* Frank Leslie's Illustrated Newspaper, *November 22, 1862.*

and women alike. As Morgan Callaway reported from Richmond to his wife, Leila, in 1862, "Hoops are subsiding, some of the ladies wear none at all." Emma Crutcher of Mississippi informed her husband, Will, that she had "fallen into the fashion and discarded hoops," but only indoors. For formal attire, she confessed, she felt obliged to return to accustomed style. Kate Stone announced that she had abandoned hoops altogether in the summer of 1863 because they seemed extravagant—inconsistent with wartime short- ages and privations. "Nothing looks funnier," she remarked, "than a woman walking around with an immense hoop—barefooted." Many women gave up hoops to economize on the amount of cloth required for a skirt and on the materials necessary for the hoop itself. With most fabrics unavailable and simple calico not just scarce but by 1864 more than ten times as expensive as it had been at the outset of the war, such considerations gained increasing significance even for the wealthiest families.[8]

Like dresses, hoops, with their steel ribs and ties, did wear out, sometimes producing embarrassing incidents like one endured by young Amanda Worthington of Mississippi. On a spring morning in 1862 she set off to church delighted with her appearance in a yellow dress, but as she left the service, her hoop began to fall. "I rushed to the buggy hardly speaking to a soul and barely had time to get in before the hateful thing fell smack on the floor. I felt *dreadful.*"⁹

Some women, like Parthenia Hague, constructed new sets of hoops out of salvaged remnants. Others paid high prices—Anne Martin of Mississippi offered $50 for a set—for replacements. Still others, like Lizzie Hardin, persisted in a "desperate" but futile "hunt for hoops." Anticipating military movement north into Pennsylvania early in 1863, Ellen Moore forwarded a shopping list to her husband, Samuel, and specified new hoops as her most cherished desire. Attachment to the style was strong and lingering. Having willingly abandoned them at home, Emma Crutcher just did not feel right appearing in public without them. Catherine Cochran of Virginia admitted her continued use of hoops evidence of feminine "weakness," but she clung to them nevertheless. "I was not strong minded enough," she wrote, "to appear before my old friends without hoops." Cochran's recognition of hoops as an emblem of status, still coveted by women of the lower orders, may have reinforced her devotion to the style. Traveling in western Virginia, Cochran sought shelter with a mountain family. After her guest had dressed for bed, the woman of the house longingly requested permission to try on Cochran's hoops. In her hostess's yearning for fashion Cochran saw telling evidence of female "vanity." "Destitute of so many of the absolute comforts of life," possessing but a single teaspoon that she passed around the table for all to share, "what she wanted most in the world was a set of hoops." A sign of weakness and vanity perhaps, the hoops also served as a persisting line of social demarcation between Cochran and her mountain hostess, even after Cochran's wealth and position had been seriously eroded by war.¹⁰

Economy and practicality, however, gradually weakened the tenacious grip of the hoop. Clara Solomon, a teenager in New Orleans with a careful eye to fashion, worked on "the renovation of my hoops" in June 1862, but she determined to make them "as diminutive as possible." Others, by choice or necessity, preference or unavailability, abandoned them altogether. With the decline of hoops, female silhouettes became less artificial. The distinctions separating upper-class women from women of the lower orders became less sharp, and ladies gained a freedom of movement often required by their new wartime responsibilities. In a sartorial sense that paralleled broader wartime social realities, women experienced a decline in the separateness of their female sphere and in the size of the protected space that surrounded their persons.[11]

## *À la Soldier*

War inaugurated marked changes in women's hair as well as clothing styles. Young ladies began to prefer short hair, which disturbed and shocked many of their elders. As with dress, this new fashion bore a certain practical logic. Elaborate longer styles required considerable attention and extensive brushing and pinning, tasks often undertaken by slaves, whose labor proved decreasingly available as emancipation neared. After Yankee occupation of New Orleans, Clara Solomon must have wondered how much longer her slave Lucy would continue to arrange her hair. One morning in June 1862 as she awaited her daily coiffure, Clara worried, "How dependent I am, unable to look nice if L. does not 'have a hand' in my toilette." In fact Clara and her sisters did cut their hair, with Rosa's so short as to be almost shaved "à la Soldier; the height of the dear's ambition." A style called "shingling" became the rage across the South, and one South Carolina woman looking back at the war years explained that it had more than simple practical significance. "It was the fashion among some young ladies to wear short hair," she remembered. "If they could not go with their brothers to the war, they would, at least, look as military as possible." Eighteen-year-old Nannie Haskins of Tennessee joined two friends in July 1864, and "We all three had our hair shingled. I truly look like a scarred rabbit, with my hair all bobbed off. Ma is angry with me for it—she would not hardly speak to me til this morning." When refugee Sidney Harding had her hair cut short, she met with similarly hostile comment. "They all will never cease talking about it," she informed her diary. But the remarks of an elderly retired military officer seemed to Harding worth recording in detail. Her short hair, he remarked, gave her such a "commanding appearance . . . I ought to get up a brigade of bloomers and go to the war." As with clothing styles, differences between men's and women's hair fashions grew less pronounced.[12]

When women's lives and duties began to change, so too did their clothing needs and preferences. Amanda Worthington, who had been so annoyed at her falling hoops, undertook in the summer of 1863 to supplement dwindling household food supplies by regular fishing. But she found her dresses a severe impediment to her success. "I commenced making me a bloomer costume," she informed her diary, "so I can fish without getting so muddy." Cordelia Scales, carrying a pistol whenever she left the house, parted her hair on the side like a man and dressed as a guerrilla in order to enhance her safety. Significantly, one of only a handful of original novels published in the Confederacy made cross-dressing the central theme of its romanticized and fabulous plot. With both men and women donning garments belonging to the opposite sex, *Castine: A Charming Romance* transformed Civil War battlefields into sites of gender experimentation and confusion. But the highly melodramatic tale's exaggerated strokes did represent actual social behaviors and anxieties. As we have seen, as many as several hundred exceptional women in fact disguised themselves as men in order to assume the identities of soldiers, and thousands more representative Confederate females adopted aspects of male costume and fashion as part of their effort to share men's privileges, protections, and responsibilities.[13]

Other women tested new clothing choices in less purposeful, more playful and tentative ways. Wartime theatricals, in particular the widely popular tableaux, encouraged respectable women to don costumes and for the first time venture onto the stage, a place where roles and identities could be invented and changed. Costume became a sign of performance, opening the possibility of self-construction and redefinition in life as well as theater. Emma Crutcher, not a participant in an evening of Vicksburg tableaux herself, nonetheless became caught up in the adventure of gender and identity shifts. Finding a collection of costumes gathered to be returned the morning after the performance, she could not resist trying on the trousers of a page. The sensations generated by wearing men's clothing were unexpectedly powerful, prompting her to reflect to her husband, Will, about the ways in which dress shaped not just female bodies but female lives. "A woman," she wrote, "does feel so light and ethereal when she slips out from the long, tangling, encumbering skirts that wrap around her feet, that I expect I should find great difficulty in keeping my toes from flying up like a ballet dancer's if I were once released." Suddenly embarrassed at her childishness in playing dress-up, however, Emma quickly changed back to her customary garb. Yet she would not forget the sense of choice and possibility inherent in her experiment or the poles of release and encumbrance she had identified, at least within the realm of dress.[14]

In Petersburg, Virginia, in 1864 a group of young women took play-acting and cross-dressing well beyond the confines of the theater. Determined to test a widow's vow never to remarry, they encouraged one of their number to disguise herself as a "gay Lothario." The masquerader dressed in "all the paraphernalia that make up a gentleman's wardrobe," even including a moustache, and succeeded in winning the widow's heart. Plans for a wedding were under way before the tricksters revealed their secret. Assuring its readers that "both ladies are well known in the city and enjoy good standing in society," the *Richmond Enquirer* noted that this "courtship extraordinary" "almost made a 'married man' of a lady." In the strange new world of the Confederate South, women could seemingly turn themselves into men. Gender identity attained both an uncertainty and a fluidity warranting journalistic remark from an astounded and bemused Richmond editor. The South had long understood the notion of "passing" through racial categories, but now the fixed binaries of gender seemed subject to transgression as well.[15]

## In Female Attire

For all women's experimentation with clothing in the Civil War South, it was in fact a man who became the Confederacy's most famous—even if mythical—cross-dresser. When Jefferson Davis was seized at war's end in May 1865, his captors reported that he was dressed as a woman. In all likelihood Davis hid in a cloak—possibly his wife's—that gave the appearance of flowing robes. The public press and popular imagination, however, quickly elaborated a quite different tale. Cartoons and engravings depicted the deposed president in full female regalia—hoopskirt, petticoats, and bonnet. Historian Nina Silber regards the images as representing "a widespread desire among northern men to make a mockery of southern manhood." But southerners bore a different relation to these portrayals. Although the hostile depictions of "Jeff in Petticoats" were certainly not southern creations, in the months after Appomattox, defeated Confederates were inevitably exposed to them, in popular national magazines such as *Leslie's* and in broadsides, sheet music, and newspapers. Undoubtedly southerners would have regarded these representations as part of the North's spoils of victory, a painful humiliation of the defeated enemy. At the same time, however, southerners would necessarily have understood the images within the context of the meaning cross-dressing had assumed during the war years themselves. Jefferson Davis was hardly the first Confederate man to be seen wearing woman's robes.[16]

Rowena Webster, living in a contested area of Alabama, reported that women regularly outfitted Confederates "in female attire" when it was nec-

Jeff Petticoats, *handbill, 1865. One hundred thousand copies were printed for sale at ten cents each by the American News Company of New York. Courtesy of the Library Company of Philadelphia.*

essary to help them escape unexpected arrivals of Yankee forces, and men disguised themselves as women in order to serve as Rebel spies. Confederates donned female garb for purposes of play as well as for those of politics. Helen Garner remembered that a Louisiana regiment encamped near her Mississippi home presented theatrical entertainments to the townspeople of Columbus. Borrowing dresses from local ladies, the soldiers delighted the residents with their energetic performance. The "leading lady," Garner recalled, "had a perceptible moustache." As with women, the theater of war offered men an opportunity for experimentation with different gender roles, for play within a play and for seemingly frivolous behavior that had deeper significance. Just as a Petersburg belle could all but become a married man, so a leading lady could sport facial hair.[17]

Soldiers' theatricals partook of the carnivalesque, evident as well in other performances by cross-dressed Confederates. On New Year's Day 1863 young men from a college in Spartanburg, South Carolina, galloped around town dressed in women's garb. This celebration encompassed some of the characteristics of inversion, an acknowledgment of a world turned upside down that is typical of New Year's festivities across history and was certainly appropriate to the disintegrating social order of the slave South. Such behavior took on additional significance in the Confederacy, however, where the incursions of modern warfare and the blurring of homefront and battlefield had already mounted a severe challenge to the ideology of rigidly separate male and female spheres. The young men must on some level have been commenting as well on their rather anomalous position as students in a society where almost all young men had gone off to war. In Texas in 1861 women had sent hoopskirts to men who failed to volunteer for service; these Carolina boys may have been in parallel language expressing their own unconscious ambivalence and guilt about their protected status.[18]

Confederate women spoke openly of the desire and dread produced by war's challenge both to traditional clothing and traditional roles. Men were less explicit, but it is impossible to imagine that the same mixture of attraction and abhorrence was not at work. The image of Jeff Davis, associating femininity and defeat, certainly embodied the element of aversion to the humiliation and the potential loss of status involved in the destabilization of traditional gender roles. But Confederate men may have felt a longing to share certain attributes and shelters of womanhood as well. Most obviously, southern females were protected from military service—neither required nor expected to sacrifice their lives on the field of battle. What was initially seen as a male privilege became an increasing burden and liability as death tolls escalated.

An oft-repeated Confederate anecdote offers a window into soldiers' changing attitude toward women's exclusion from the tented field. Awaiting battle, an infantryman joined in a chorus of the popular "Rock Me to Sleep, Mother," a song that pleads for an escape from war back into childhood and a mother's protecting arms:

> Backward turn backward, oh! time in your flight
> Make me a child again, just for tonight:
> Mother, come back from the echoless shore
> Take me again to your heart, as of yore.

At the conclusion of the chorus the soldier abruptly stopped singing and feelingly interjected that as long as he was to be made a child again, it be a girl baby this time. Jefferson Davis's alleged resort to women's clothes expressed much the same desire for escape from masculine obligations and vulnerabilities. Women were not unique in their new recognition of the constraints and liabilities of traditional gender identities, nor were they alone in employing the language of clothing to express the at once thrilling and terrifying possibilities of changed garments and altered roles.[19]

## A Man's Heart and a Female Form

Occasionally women went beyond the discourse of apparel to articulate more deeply felt incongruities of identity and appearance. Chafing at feelings deemed inappropriate within prevailing standards of feminine behavior and sentiment, these women felt themselves imprisoned not just in the wrong clothes but the wrong bodies. "Lord," Lizzie Neblett implored, "if I was made a woman why were such rebelious such wicked feelings given to me[?] why cant I feel & think like a poor weak inferior slave should. God gave me life, but in my case he did not temper the wind to the shorn lamb." Sarah Morgan wrote in nearly identical terms, noting in addition an inversion of gender traits emerging in the face of war, as she displayed a courage the men around her lacked. "Only ask Heaven why you were made with a man's heart, and a female form, and the creatures with beards were made so bewitchingly nervous?"[20]

Nearly every female Confederate diarist at some point expressed the desire to be a man. "O if I was only a man,!" exclaimed Sarah Morgan. "Then I could don the breeches and slay them with a will!" "Only this morning," Belle Edmondson remarked in March 1864, "I did wish I was a man." "Would God I were a man," cried Elizabeth Collier. "How I wish I was a man!" seconded Emma Walton. "I do long sometimes to be a man," confessed Sallie Munford. Such sentiments were at once revolutionary and conservative, transgressive yet ultimately conventional. On one level these expressions represented the emergence of a newly self-conscious discontent, a dissatisfaction with the confines of the female sphere. By the later years of the war, women's frustration was often accompanied by an angry conviction that they would do a better job of executing men's duties than the men seemed to be doing themselves. Hearing of Butler's outrages in New Orleans, Abby Slocomb declared her "intense disappointment & disgust at the cowardice of the men" who remained in the city yet failed to protect Louisiana's ladies. Elsie Bragg was similarly dismayed. "If our soldiers continue to behave so disgracefully," she wrote after a series of Confederate reverses in the West, "we *women* had better take the field and send them home to raise chickens." Women greeted a force of soldiers retreating from Vicksburg with cries of "We are disappointed in you!" Winchester's females tried to seize the bridles of Confederate cavalrymen to prevent what they deemed an ignominious abandonment of the town to enemy forces. Appomattox was in one sense simply a final failure on the part of white men who had already lost control of the region's slave population and had proven themselves unable to feed, clothe, or protect their families.[21]

Yet both the wish to be men and the effort to make men act their assigned part translated women's dissatisfaction into gestures highly supportive of the status quo. In the war years, white southern women recognized a profound incompatibility between expectations placed on them and their own desires and needs. But they were unwilling and perhaps unable to articulate their frustrations in a manner designed to bring about significant change. Sarah Morgan chafed at the inability to express her discontent. "Am I to die with these nameless longings unfulfilled? I cannot define them, but . . . I am not satisfied! I am *not* content!" She, like so many others, turned to the fantasy of wishing herself a man. To resolve dissatisfaction by becoming—or desiring to become—a man is not to accomplish real change, however; it is to endeavor to flee from a system of subordination rather than to challenge the system directly. It is not to seek an expansion in women's roles; it is to reconfirm the appropriateness of existing constraints on women even as it articulates their individual dissatisfaction.[22]

Throughout the war Confederate men and women used the notion of cross-gendered behavior to contain the revolutionary potential of women's new roles and responsibilities. When women acted in newly assertive, powerful, or independent ways, their behavior would be cited as beyond the boundaries of feminine behavior and thus as no threat to prevailing understandings of female attributes. A Savannah judge made this strategy clear in his response to a trial of female bread rioters. "When women become rioters," he proclaimed in an attempt to deny the pathbreaking significance of their resort to violence, "they cease to be women." At the same time he sought to deny that women could or would act in such an unseemly manner, however, he also unwittingly acknowledged that women's appearance, their apparent female identity, no longer provided certain knowledge of their behavior. Dressed in the clothes and even the bodies of women, they were nevertheless acting like men.[23]

Brilliant women were often said to have a male intelligence. Maria Hubard's sister Lucy was so "singularly gifted," her mind was "almost masculine," and Mary Chesnut similarly regarded her accomplished friend Louisa McCord as possessing "the intellect of a man." Clara MacLean rationalized the strength of her neighbor Eliza McKee, recently departed for the battlefront as a nurse, in the same manner. She had always manifested such courage and self-assurance as to seem "almost masculine—Indeed I used to tell her I never felt easy in her society if discussing delicate subjects; I could scarcely persuade myself she was not in disguise."[24]

MacLean invoked the pervasive metaphor of costume, of theater, underlining once again the elements of surprise, of uncertainty in wartime gender roles. Yet she, like Mary Chesnut or the Savannah judge, at the same time affirmed traditional notions of essential womanhood. Females are not strong, brilliant, or courageous, and those who appear so must not be truly women but somehow men in drag. Amidst the new fluidity and negotiability of maleness and femaleness, most elite southern women in fact clung all the more forcefully to familiar notions and identities. In the case of Mary Chesnut one suspects that a reluctance to assume new responsibilities accompanied her resistance to change. Lacking the strength and courage to make an effective nurse herself, she felt threatened by McCord's achievements and therefore designated them not just extraordinary but unnatural.

Other females were more self-consciously critical of what Gertrude Thomas called the "conventionalism which characterises most Southern women." The ideas in ladies' heads, Catherine Edmondston confirmed, "are like old nails in a beam—break them off, drive them in, you can; but pull them out, never! When you think you have disposed of them, there they are as obstinate & rusty as ever." Yet both Thomas and Edmondston meant to include themselves within the scope of their strictures. Increasingly self-aware, women responded to the wartime threat to their identities more often than not by resisting the frightening prospect of self-transformation. "If I were once released" from the confines of feminine garb and roles, Emma Crutcher had speculated, "I expect I should find great difficulty in keeping my toes from flying up." A change in costume, an abandonment of traditional femininity, would literally as well as metaphorically destabilize her person. Her grounded identity and her control over her self and her behavior would disappear as if gravity itself had been eliminated. No wonder the possibilities for changing lives as if they were costumes seemed so terrifying. No wonder Sarah Morgan lacked the courage to try on her brother's clothes. No wonder white southern ladies approached yet ultimately avoided and even resisted changes that threatened to erode a self-definition and a separateness founded in the cherished prerogatives of race and class, of whiteness and elitism, as well as in the more ambiguous privileges and penalties of gender.[25]

CHAPTER ELEVEN

# *Sick and Tired of This Horrid War*

## PATRIOTISM, SACRIFICE, AND SELF-INTEREST

For all their efforts to cling to accustomed privileges and familiar identities, women of the South's master class found themselves buffeted by change and tried by adversity. As years passed with no end to war in sight, emotional and material deprivation took their inescapable psychological toll. A rising sense of personal desperation, an eroding confidence in those on whom they had relied for protection, and an emerging doubt about their own ability to endure prompted women to reconsider the most fundamental assumptions about their world. As females they had long been socialized to think first of others. But faced with the unrelenting hardships of war and the escalating difficulty of simple self-preservation, they had begun inevitably to think about themselves. The ideology and practice of self-sacrifice and the persistence of self-denial demanded by the dictates of patriotism seemed increasingly to threaten individual survival. By the end of the war, suffering and loss had produced a profound transformation in women's understanding of the relationship between self and society; pain brought forth a new conception of themselves as individuals with needs, interests, and even rights, not just duties and obligations. Beginning as personal and psychological, this change ultimately involved significant implications for society and politics in the late Civil War South.[1]

## So Much Rests upon the Mind

In the aftermath of Vietnam we have seen with new clarity and force the psychological impact of war on its participants. But our heightened awareness of these deep and lingering scars has focused almost exclusively on combatants, perhaps because American casualties and victims were overwhelmingly military personnel. For an invaded rather than an invading nation, however, suffering is more widely distributed, with civilians sometimes enduring even greater depredations and brutalities than uniformed troops. The people of Vietnam, like those of the Confederate South, understood this dimension of war all too well. The traumatic stress reactions that have been identified among so many Vietnam veterans would have had their Civil War counterpart, not just among soldiers but among southern civilians and, in particular, southern women, who faced significant terror, destruction, and loss.[2]

Women themselves recognized the challenge long years of war posed to their emotional stability. Mary Jane Cook Chadick of Alabama began her diary entries for 1865 with anticipations of difficult months ahead. Listing the "trying circumstances" she confronted—a seemingly endless separation from her husband, responsibility for the "care of a large family," and the gloomiest economic and political prospects—she noted that she was "just recovering from another one of my nervous attacks, which are becoming more frequent of late." In Tennessee, Virginia French seemed to suffer a similar fate: increasingly severe and frequent "nervous attacks." "I fear," she confessed, "that I am giving way at last under this long, long pressure of anxiety and tension upon the nerves." Emma Dobson of Virginia admitted she was "out of my mind at times[.] I candidly confess that from distress I sometimes have violent attacks of histeria." Complaining of her destitution and despair, Annie Upshur of Lynchburg declared herself "almost upon the borders of crazziness."[3]

The intrepid Mary Lee, who had passed most of the war on the front lines in the contested town of Winchester, felt that by 1865 she was coming "completely unhinged." She noted the admission to Virginia's Insane Asylum at Staunton of a number of new patients "made insane by the War—all women." But, she reflected, "I do not wonder at it." By June 1865, with the Confederate experiment in ruins, Mary Lee declared herself "completely broken down mentally." Catherine Cooper of Tennessee feared a similar loss of balance, which her circumstances made hardly surprising. Living in an area ravaged by both Union and Confederate forces, Cooper had given ten sons and five grandsons to the army. Five of her sons died and four returned wounded. News of the illness of a tenth, she reported, "almost derainged me. I think sometimes my trials are greater than I can bear." In the last months of the war Emily Harris of North Carolina repeatedly worried that she was going insane. From early in the conflict she had seen it her duty to "shut up my griefs in my own breast" in order to protect her young children. "Truly," she remarked, "I have no time to grieve." But this denial took its toll. By 1864 she had begun to question the purpose of her efforts. "Life is not desirable for life's sake," she remarked, "but for the sake of those who need my services." She began to fear the loss of her reason as well. "I have felt crazy," she wrote. "I could almost feel the wrinkles coming on my face and the hair turn gray on my head."[4]

Many women understood the relationship between their physical condition and their mental state. For some, material deprivation wielded a significant psychological impact. Cornelia McDonald of Winchester struggled to provide for her nine children; she herself often went without food in order to relieve their hunger. "Growing thin and emaciated," she found herself becoming "faint hearted" as well. "My feelings were beyond control. . . . I had lost the power of resistance and all my self command." Her depression was so intense she felt she "could willingly say 'good night' to the world and all in it." But physical debilitation was as often the result as the cause of mental strain. Women described worry so consuming that it rendered them unable to eat or sleep. "Every one is kept in such anxiety of mind by this dreadful war," Mary Legg wrote her friend Hattie Palmer in South Carolina, "that it is not strange when we see the body sometimes give way when so much rests upon the mind."[5]

Unremitting stress drove some women into the protection of an emotional numbness. Abbie Brooks of Georgia wrote just a few days before Appomattox that her "sufferings and trials" had "petrified" her, turned her

*Mary Greenhow Lee. Courtesy of the Winchester–Frederick County Historical Society, Winchester, Virginia.*

to stone and deadened her feelings. "I care very little for anybody or anything. I enjoy nothing, am neither sorry nor glad." Grief had, one Virginia woman remarked, "stunned and stupefied" many of her acquaintances, and Sara Pryor of Virginia observed that "everyone who has suffered a overwhelming misfortune must be conscious of a strange deadening of feeling." *Callous* was a word that many women chose to describe their changed outlook. "I have sometimes felt," Lizzie Neblett wrote her husband, Will, "like my heart was *seared*, incapable of feeling as it once did."[6]

Repression of feeling often encompassed depression of spirits and a sense of futility that arose both from the burden of suffering and its apparent uselessness in the face of mounting Confederate military losses. "For what am I living?" Belle Edmondson demanded. "Why is it that I am spared, from day to day with no happiness myself[?]" "Why have I lived to see this?" another woman angrily demanded. Under war's pressures, "I am wearing a way." The sense of threatened health and sanity gradually redirected women's attention away from nation and community, even sometimes from husbands and families, toward themselves and their own survival. "In my present frame of mind and state of health," Virginia French wrote after Union troops consolidated their hold over most of Tennessee, "I must confess I feel *unpatriotic* enough not to care a continental about it any way if I could only be well." She was, she admitted, "so low" that she persuaded herself she did not "care one jot for the Confederacy or anybody in it." "The Confederacy!" wrote Emily Harris, "I almost hate the word."[7]

## *You* Must *Come Home*

The patriotism women had so enthusiastically embraced in 1861 began to erode before seemingly endless—and increasingly purposeless—demands for sacrifice. After the defeats of the summer of 1863 Julia Davidson exclaimed to her husband, John, "Oh how I do pray this war was at an end. If the Yankees are going to whip us I wish they would hurry about it." Gertrude Thomas expressed a similar "impatience to have it over." As a New Orleans woman wrote her soldier son, "je ne vois que des sacrifices, des victimes, la ruine, la misère, rien de gagné." By 1864 the war's battles seemed no longer glorious but "massacres sans résultat." Women's willingness to be selfless, to embrace the needs of the nation as prior to their own, had begun to disappear. Their initial dedication to the Cause proved to be conditional, dependent on their own capacities to endure war's hardships and on a hope for the Confederacy's future that was rapidly evaporating. On a tour of the battlefield at Seven Pines in search of her wounded cousin, Constance Cary reported seeing men "in every stage of mutilation" and proclaimed herself "permanently convinced that nothing is worth war!" Margaret Junkin Preston greeted news of the death of her stepson and several of his friends by protesting, "Who thinks or cares for victory now!"

Sarah Jane Sams proclaimed herself "sick and tired of trying to endure these privations to which we are all subjected," and as early as 1862 Julia Le Grand had come to believe that "nothing is worth such sacrifice."[8]

A practical pacifism born of exhaustion and despair was replacing the mood of romantic militarism that had earlier gripped elite women. One of the most striking and curious expressions of this new outlook appeared in Marinda Branson Moore's *Dixie Speller*, published in Raleigh in 1864. During the war Moore produced a series of primers, readers, and spellers for Confederate youth. The 1864 speller was the last of these, and its lesson 22 contained sentiments very unlike the exuberant patriotic exercises that had filled the earlier volumes. In words of one syllable, Moore offered Confederate children a sharply dissenting voice, protesting not so much the South's political values but the cost of these commitments in human suffering.

> This sad war is a bad thing.
>
> My pa-pa went, and died in the army.
>
> My big broth-er went too and got shot. A bomb shell took off his head.
>
> My aunt had three sons, and all have died in the army. Now she and the girls have to work for bread.
>
> I will work for my ma and my sis-ters.
>
> I hope we will have peace by the time [I] am old enough to go to war.
>
> If I were a man, and had to make laws, I would not have any war, if I could help it.
>
> If little boys fight old folks whip them for it; but when men fight, they say "how brave!"

Moore's textbook offered the sentiments of a Confederate woman in the language of a small southern boy. To twentieth-century ears, though, it echoes the irony, the distance, and the detachment we have come to associate with writing from the Great War and the world that followed in its aftermath.[9]

As Confederate women discussed the war, they increasingly employed words such as *worth* and *gain*, scrutinizing their circumstances with a new attention to costs and benefits and with a new sense of self-interest born of what was for most elite southerners the novelty of privation and loss. Commitment to the Cause was not unbounded but had to be calculated in a balance sheet on which the burden of further hardship and the growing likelihood of ultimate defeat figured large. An elderly Virginia lady confessed her growing doubt about the whole Confederate experiment as she experienced the escalating trials of war. "I cannot help being unpatriotic—to

*Confederate women confront the enemy. "Arrival of a Federal Column at a Planter's House in Dixie."* Harper's Weekly, *April 4, 1863.*

feel a little selfish sometimes—and," she continued significantly, "regret our peace and comfort in the old Union." In October 1864 Sal Mabry of North Carolina asked her husband Robert, "what do you think of going back into the Union[?] dont you think it would be better than to have all our men killed[?] . . . I often think if I could make peace how soon I would have you and all my loved ones with me."[10]

By the last years of the conflict, war with its hardships and shortages had begun to nurture not nobility and sacrifice so much as a new selfishness, a novel awareness of individual needs and desires, of requirements for minimal personal survival, even if not happiness. In the Confederacy at large an emerging venality was evident in widespread speculation and extortion, problems that consumed considerable public attention, prompted state and national legislation, and won religious notice as the besetting sin of the South. Women were most often victims rather than perpetrators of these economic and moral crimes, however, for they participated in the market chiefly as consumers.[11]

Women instead displayed their new self-absorption and self-interest in a growing reluctance to continue to yield their loved ones to the Confederate army. At the outset of the war, women had urged husbands and brothers into service, but by the later years of conflict quite a different attitude became evident. Even at the expiration of men's first terms of enlistment, as early as

chicken or egg? (243!)

1862 or 1863, many wives insisted that their husbands had already given enough to the Cause. As Mary Bell of North Carolina bluntly proclaimed to Alfred in July 1862, "I think you have done your share in this war." An initial romantic fascination with military heroism had quickly given way to a sobering recognition of war's dangers. Louisa Rice of Georgia wrote her husband, Zachariah, at the end of 1862 urging him to leave the army for a post that would shield him from conscription. "You have served long enough," she declared, "to rest awhile." Mary Williams Pugh, a refugee in Texas in the fall of 1862, warned her husband that both she and her slaves required his return. Not only had he "done enough now to satisfy yourself & everyone else," but she had borne his absence so "patiently and cheerfully," she calculated, "that surely now I deserve some reward." Pugh urged him either to hire a substitute or to take advantage of the October 1862 law exempting slave supervisors. "My good behavior now is all put on & will soon disappear unless I see something brighter ahead." The expectation of his imminent return, moreover, was the only cause of his slaves' "good behavior," she warned. "The truth is . . . you *must* come home." In Florida during the same year, Octavia Stephens urged her husband, Winston, to "give up now while you have life." In her view it was foolish to "talk of the defense of your home & country for you can not defend them, they are too far gone now so give up before it is too late." Losing the war and keeping her husband seemed to Tivie Stephens a far better bargain than losing both, but Winston would fight for another two years before fulfilling Octavia's worst fears.[12]

Mounting draft calls prompted first reluctance then resistance from mothers, wives, and sisters. "We felt like clinging to Walter and holding him back," a Virginia woman explained. "I for one had lost my nerve. I was sick of war, sick of the butchery, the anguish . . . the fear." Emily Harris declared that she felt as much like fighting the men who kept her husband in uniform as she did the Yankees. In South Carolina, Margaret Easterling balanced the dictates of patriotism against her own desires and decided firmly in favor of the latter. With two sons in the army, she wrote Jefferson Davis, "I need not tell you of my devotion to my country, of the sacrifices I have made, and of the many more I am willing to make. . . . But I want my oldest boy at home." Facing the conscription of her last son, Mary Scales wrote movingly and revealingly to the Confederate secretary of war. "I know my country needs all her children and I had thought I could submit to her requisitions. I have given her cause my prayers, my time, my means and my children but now the last lamb of the fold is to be taken, the mother and helpless woman triumph over the patriot."[13]

Mary Scales sought to retreat from the public sphere of patriotic duty and to reassert the primacy of the domestic, the private, and the dependent in female lives. Scales hoped to reinstate the moral economy of gender in which women traded "helplessness" and subservience for care and protection; she sought a return to a world in which the needs of her heart, her family, and her household could take precedence over necessities of state. Writing to her son in a northern military prison, Mary Chichester expressed a similar desire. "I hope," she confessed, "when you do get exchanged, you will think, the time past has sufficed for *public* service, & that your own family require yr protection & help—as others are deciding." Gertrude Thomas saw the conflict of loyalties and its resolution clearly. "Am I willing to give my husband to gain Atlanta for the Confederacy? No, No, No, a thousand times No!"[14]

In one sense the erosion of women's patriotism simply represented a reversion to conventional female concerns, an almost reactionary reassertion of the private and domestic and a rejection of the more public and political burdens women had been urged to assume. But at the same time, women's new perspectives involved an articulation of individual right and identity, of self-interest, that was strikingly modern in its implications. Their retreat from the public realm was fueled in considerable part by their recognition that in the Confederacy the public interest did not encompass their own, for it threatened to kill their loved ones, deprive them of life's basic necessities, and require them to manage recalcitrant, rebellious, and often frightening slaves. A nation that had acknowledged no legitimate female political voice had in crisis failed adequately to consider women's needs.

Before the war, women of the southern elite had regarded themselves as dependents within an organic social order in which female subordination was accepted in return for protection and support. Yet white men's wartime failure to provide women with either physical safety or basic subsistence cast this world and its social assumptions into question. Relationships of unchallenged status, of assumed superiority and inferiority, were transformed into what political theorists would call social relations of contract. Women came to regard their sacrifice and subordination as no longer inevitable but contingent on men's fulfillment of certain expectations. The notions of "virtual" political representation—which argued that women's interests would be protected by their men—had proved hollow indeed. Women began to acknowledge and defend their own interests apart from those of their families and their nation and to regard themselves as individuals possessing rights and legitimate desires, not just duties and obligations.[15]

This warborn evolution in female self-perception parallels a much broader transformation in American political life, one that many scholars have designated as a shift during the early and middle years of the nineteenth century from republican to liberal political forms and values, as a replacement of virtue and community by faction and self-interest. The changing outlook of southern women in the course of the Civil War helps remind us of the psychological foundations of such a transformation, for women's shifting understanding of their larger social place arose from a newfound ability to perceive themselves as more than simply appendages to other, more important social actors.[16]

In their recognition of individual needs and desires amidst all but unbearable emotional and even material deprivation, Confederate women discovered both new self-interest and new selves. It was not, however, as so many discussions of women and war would have it, that new achievements and new accomplishments—as nurses or teachers or plantation managers—yielded the basis for enhanced self-esteem; this new sense of self was based not in the experience of success but in desperation, in the fundamental need simply to survive. "Necessity," as Confederate women so often intoned, was in this sense truly "the mother of invention"; only "necessity," as Julia Davidson wrote her husband, John, could "make a different woman of me."[17]

By the last months of the war many women, especially those of the middling and lower orders, were not just holding husbands and brothers back from service but were actively urging them to desert. The risk of execution and the shame of flight now seemed acceptable in the face of almost certain and almost certainly useless injury or death at the front. Confederate leaders recognized the power that women exerted in persuading soldiers to abandon their posts. One military officer even went so far as to urge the secretary of war to begin to censor the mails, for, he insisted, "the source of all the present evils of Toryism & desertion in our country is letter writing to . . . the army." As a Confederate official in North Carolina bluntly proclaimed, "Desertion takes place because desertion is encouraged. . . . And though the ladies may not be willing to concede the fact, they are nevertheless responsible . . . for the desertion in the army and the dissipation in the country." At every level of the social order women were making their particular contributions to Confederate military failure.[18]

Public lamentations about women's shortcomings as patriots became standard fare in the Confederate press. An 1864 correspondent to the *Montgomery Daily Advertiser* deplored eroding female commitment to the Cause. At first, wrote the pseudonymous Micare, "women were rivalling the other sex in patriotic devotion. . . . But a change, and such a change, has come over the spirit of their dream. The Aid societies have died away; they are a name and nothing more. The self-sacrifice has vanished; wives and maidens now labor only to exempt husbands and lovers from the perils of service." Beginning with a discussion of women's interference with military recruitment and retention, Micare moved to a second, widely articulated indictment of women's wartime failures. "Never," Micare continued, "were parties more numerous. . . . Never were the theatres and places of public amusement so resorted to. . . . The love of dress, the display of jewelry and costly attire, the extravagance and folly are all the greater for the brief abstinence which has been observed."[19]

## Mirth and Reckless Revelry

Late in 1864 Augusta Jane Evans published in the *Mobile Register* a similarly scathing attack on her countrywomen. "Can mirth and reckless revelry hold high carnival in social circles," she demanded, "while every passing breeze chants the requiem of dying heroes? . . . Are Southern women so completely oblivious of the claims of patriotism and humanity, that in this season of direst extremity, they tread the airy mazes of the dance, while the matchless champions of freedom are shivering in bloody trenches or lying stark on frozen fields of glory?" Evans invoked "spectral bands" of Confederate dead to join her in lamenting women's betrayal, in crying, "Shame! Shame upon your degeneracy."[20]

Evans was hardly unique in criticizing the frivolity that seized elite Confederate society in 1864 and 1865. Women's growing sense of self-interest shaded into self-indulgence; sacrifice was replaced by its polar opposite, excess. Even a council of Presbyterian elders in Alabama felt compelled in 1865 to reprimand their usually sober congregants and to "deplore the presence, and we fear, the growing prevalence, of a spirit of gaity, especially among the female members of some of our congregations." Sara Pryor of Virginia found this "disposition to revel in times of danger and suffering" to be "passing strange," but Grace Elmore of South Carolina understood that "utter abandonment to the pleasure of the present" offered the possibility of "shutting out for the moment the horrors that surround us." As hardships mounted, escape seemed all the more desirable. Gertrude Thomas tried to explain the gaiety in her Georgia town by suggesting that long years of war had to some degree hardened southerners' feelings and had left them insensitive to others' sufferings. James Chesnut certainly feared such a lack of sympathy in his wife, Mary, and declared her "dissipated" for her refusal to abandon constant parties and frivolity. Yet Chesnut was but one of dozens of Richmond hostesses contributing to the "whirl" of sociability that gripped the capital city in the last months of war. Preeminent was Mrs. Robert Stannard, who was reputed to have spent more than $30,000 on entertainment during a winter that saw Confederate troops camped in nearby counties suffering for bare subsistence.[21]

In February 1864 the *Richmond Enquirer* expressed its hope that the arrival of Lent would bring an end to the "season of reckless frivolity that has made Richmond during this winter, a carnival of unhallowed pleasure." Incessant parties and balls in the capital represented, in the paper's judgment, "shameful displays of indifference to national calamity . . . a mockery of the misery and desolation that covers the land." At the opposite end of the Confederacy, in Texas, "ladies of Galveston" planned a midwinter ball for the officer corps stationed in the port city. But the anticipated "revelry and carousal" so offended underpaid and underfed enlisted men that they plotted a raid against the tables of delicacies. When word of the soldiers' intentions reached Confederate officers, they ordered cavalry to stand ready to act against rebellious privates. The cavalry indicated its unwillingness to serve in such a capacity, however, and called for the cancellation of the ladies' entertainment.[22]

The frivolity that attracted such widespread attention and remark in the last months of the Confederacy represented an assertion of class privilege in the face—and in defiance—of its rapid erosion. The women indulging in much-criticized revelry were not those of the lower orders who lacked the means for such excess. Poorer women were more likely to express their dissent from the ideology of sacrifice and the reality of deprivation in the bread riots that swept across the South in the late years of the war. In Savannah, Mobile, High Point, Petersburg, Milledgeville, Columbia, and even in the capital city of Richmond itself, crowds of desperate females joined together to claim provisions they believed their due, and in more rural locations bands of female marauders swept into plantation areas to seize food crops ready for harvest in the fields. These seemingly unrelated phenomena—upper-class women's frivolity and lower-class women's violence—both represented responses to the Confederacy's violation of white women's expectations within the South's paternalistic social order. Bread riots and reckless revelry both embodied a new level of female self-assertiveness. Both represented forceful statements of women's desires, and both explicitly rejected the ideology of sacrifice.[23]

Differing economic and class realities and differing understandings of life's possibilities shaped emerging dissent to produce quite different behavior among women of the elite and women of the lower orders. Despite a common sense of deprivation and anger, these groups of females harbored little mutual sympathy; each regarded the actions of the other as depraved. Poor women accused elite families of abandoning their responsibilities to the less fortunate, even while "the rich livs as well as ever tha did"; respectable middle- and upper-class females were both frightened and appalled by rioters' abandonment of deference and propriety, even when they felt pity for their desperate plight. "The time appears rapidly approaching," Gertrude Thomas worried, "when we have almost as much to dread from our own demoralized mob as from the public enemy." Self-interest had undermined noblesse oblige just as it had eroded patriotism. As a poor woman complaining of starvation in Spotsylvania County, Virginia, wrote to the president, "it is folly for a poor mother to call on the rich people about here[.] there hearts are of steel[.] they would sooner th[r]ow what they have to spare to their dogs than give it to a starving child."[24]

War had called white women across the South to make many similar sacrifices. The gendering of the army as male and of the homefront as overwhelmingly female and the high rates of military enrollment—and military casualties—among men of all classes constituted important commonalities in white southern women's wartime experience. Yet class differences separated even as gender united Confederate females. At the end of the conflict Cornelia McDonald reflected on the comparative impact of the war on rich and poor. "I have often thought," she mused,

> that no greater despotism could be than that government was in the last months of its existence. To those whose education and habits of life made them enthusiastic, or whose pride acted as an incentive for them to endure and suffer, as was the case with the higher classes, it wore no such aspect, but to those who had but their poor homes and little pieces of ground by which they managed to provide little more than bread for their families, who knew that they would be as well off under one government as another, it was oppression to be forced into the army, and not ever to be free from the apprehension that their families were suffering.[25]

Put simply, upper-class southerners had a greater investment than their poorer countrywomen and -men in the system that had given them their superior status. For all their disillusionment with slavery, with Confederate leadership, and with their individual men, elite southern women clung to—

even reasserted—lingering elements of privilege. Even when patriotism had been exhausted by war and even when the Confederacy had died, elite white women of the South held fast to the traditional hierarchical social and racial order that had defined their importance. Indeed, their disillusionment with the Confederacy arose chiefly from its failure to protect and preserve that privilege, to serve white female self-interest.

In ladyhood southern women accepted gender subordination in exchange for continuing class and racial superiority. Yet their understanding of that bargain had changed profoundly in the course of the war. Their expectations for male protection had all but disappeared; their new sense of themselves, born in necessity rather than opportunity, made them sharply aware of both the dangers of dependence and the daunting demands of autonomy. Filled with doubts about both themselves and their men, elite southern women faced the postwar world with a new realism, a deep-seated bitterness, and a frightening sense of isolation. The social order they were determined to preserve offered them only the best of a bad bargain; the ideal of male strength and competence that had justified the paternalistic southern world had been proven mythical, and women had discovered little foundation in their own competence or effectiveness for trying to replace male power and authority with their own. In the face of the frightening reality of black emancipation, however, white women came to regard the rehabilitation of patriarchy as a bargain they were compelled to accept. The postwar commemoration of male courage and wartime achievement by the Daughters of the Confederacy, the Confederate Memorial Society, and other female celebrants of the Lost Cause represented women's effort to make what they regarded as necessary seem once again legitimate. If white men were once again to run the world, southern ladies would struggle to demonstrate the confidence in male superiority that would convince both themselves and others that such a social order was both natural and desirable.[26]

# We Shall Never . . . Be the Same

Mary Greenhow Lee never returned to Winchester after her expulsion by the Union army. She resettled in Baltimore, where she passed the remainder of a long life, taking in boarders and dedicating herself to church work and to the activities of the United Daughters of the Confederacy. "Political reconstruction," she observed late in 1865, "might be unavoidable now, but social reconstruction we hold in our hands & might prevent."[1]

Lizzie Neblett described "seven years of struggle" shared with her husband, Will, after the war as they tried to adapt to free labor on their Texas cotton land. The value of the Nebletts' real estate had fallen 60 percent by 1870, and their personal property, with the emancipation of the slaves, was 5½ percent of its former value. In the spring of 1871 Will died of pneumonia, leaving his wife five months pregnant with a third daughter. Widowed at thirty-eight, Lizzie had more than half her life to live. She survived until 1917, emerging briefly in the public eye as a temperance columnist in the 1880s. Ironically, she would pass the last decades of her life in the Austin household of her second daughter, Bettie, the unwelcome war baby.[2]

Jo Gillis of Alabama turned to teaching to support her family at the end of the war, for her husband's income as an itinerant minister did not even cover his board. Yet it was her household responsibilities that she found most demanding. "Sometimes I have a cook," she wrote in 1866, "and sometimes I don't and everything I do is done by guesswork. My ignorance and inexperience is a great trial." Often she cried all night contemplating her hardships and her husband's lack of support and understanding. In November 1868 Jo Gillis died from complications following the delivery of her second child.[3]

After Confederate defeat, Emma and Will Crutcher returned to Vicksburg from San Antonio, where they had gone to live as refugees in 1863 after Will's health had prompted him to withdraw from the army. Mother of two young sons, Emma contributed to her family's income by teaching at a girls' high school in Vicksburg.

In 1869 Kate Stone of Louisiana married a Confederate officer she had met during the war. He first worked as a plantation manager, then eventually acquired land of his own. They produced four children, only two of whom lived to adulthood. Kate became active in the United Daughters of the Confederacy and in local book and literary clubs, reflecting, no doubt, her unsatisfied hunger for reading material all through the war.

Impatient as she had been to see the war's end, Gertrude Thomas found life even more trying in its aftermath. Her husband, Jeff, proved financially incompetent and irresponsible, wasting what little remained of her inherited fortune in a series of disastrous business ventures. Gertrude took up teaching to support her children. By the end of the century she had emerged as a leader in the new southern temperance crusade and had been selected president of the Georgia Woman's Suffrage Association and national treasurer of the United Daughters of the Confederacy.[4]

Lucy Buck had been prescient indeed when she had observed as early as 1862, "We shall never any of us be the same as we have been." For each of these women, as for the thousands of others who, like them, had been part of the Old South's master class, Appomattox brought a new world, inaugurating lives unlike those they had anticipated or desired. Perhaps most conspic-

*The aftermath of battle.* The Return to Fredericksburg, *oil painting, 1865, by David English Henderson. Courtesy of Gettysburg National Military Park.*

uously, this was a world without slaves. Loss of the property that had provided the foundation for privilege undermined the wealth and position of formerly slaveowning families. For the white women within these households, however, emancipation had a more personal significance. The daily work of domestic life and the routines of white women's lives were revolutionized by the coming of free labor. "All the talk, everywhere now," Emma Mordecai noted just after the cessation of military hostilities, "is servants." More than a generation later, the "servant problem" continued to preoccupy southern ladies. Asked by a Vanderbilt social scientist in the early 1890s to specify the most significant impact of the war on the lives of white southern women of her class, a Carolina matron old enough to have memories of "better days" before emancipation did not hesitate. "From being queens in social life," she replied, ladies had become "after the war, in many instances, mere domestic drudges."[5]

But the increased labors of white women were not exclusively domestic. The disappearance of slave-based wealth left many formerly prosperous families struggling to make ends meet and dependent on women's work outside the home. Like Emma Crutcher, Jo Gillis, and Gertrude Thomas, many of these women turned to teaching. By 1880 the majority of southern schoolteachers had for the first time become female. The necessity for growing numbers of respectable women to find employment prompted southerners to direct more serious attention to women's education. In the 1890s the president of a southern women's college observed that nearly a quarter of his graduates now supported themselves. This expectation, he explained, led students to prosecute their studies with far greater earnestness and diligence than had their antebellum counterparts. Several southern state universities introduced coeducation in the 1880s, and women's colleges, such as Sophie Newcomb at Tulane in 1886, were established to offer women opportunities paralleling those of men. By the 1890s the Vanderbilt researcher noted the "growing respectability of self support" emerging from conditions of economic necessity, and one of his interviewees applauded the abandonment of prewar beliefs in "the nobility of dependence and helplessness in woman."[6]

After their experiences of war, southern women found it difficult any longer to celebrate helplessness. When male protection had disappeared, female dependence had proved far too costly and too painful. Women had not been prepared to manage slaves and farms, control children, and even work to provide their own basic support. The desperate plight in which the war had placed so many females proved an unforgettable lesson, one only reinforced by the postbellum lives of many women of the formerly slaveowning classes. The absolute necessities of widowhood imposed independence on many, but the erosion of slave-based wealth and political power often left even those whose husbands returned from war unable to rely on male support. The actions of white women in a wide range of postwar arenas and their frequent appearances in the public spheres of work and reform can perhaps best be understood as a determination never to be entirely helpless or dependent again. The enhancement of opportunities for female education, women's advocacy of reforms in married property law, and the movement for female suffrage emerging by the 1890s all represented women's efforts to define and defend their own interests. A mistrust of men fueled many of these women's zeal.[7]

In large measure, female dependence seemed dangerous because of the desperate condition of so many white southern men. Economic instability in the postwar environment enhanced the logic of the movement for married women's property laws. In a time of enormous financial uncertainty white men could protect the larger interests of their families by separating their wives' property from their own. Both Gertrude and Jeff Thomas would have fared far better had her wealth been immune from his indebtedness. New postbellum women's property laws, securing support from conservative men as well as most female suffragists, thus served both traditional and seemingly progressive interests. The implications of these new measures for domestic power and marital relationships were profound, however, for the laws embodied, as historian Suzanne Lebsock has written, a new "vision of masculine irresponsibility." Instead of playing its customary role in support of men's right and duty to serve as the protectors of women, the law here represented the intervention of the state to protect women from men.[8]

For many white southern males, difficulties were far more than simply financial. From Vietnam we have gained an appreciation of the depth and persistence of war's wounds that may help us to understand other postwar generations. It is not unrealistic to think that many former Confederate soldiers must have suffered from posttraumatic stress disorders in the years after Appomattox. Certainly family papers hint at such distress among white southern men. Nearly two years after the end of the war, Amanda Sims of South Carolina described her father as "shattered mentally and physically." Kate Stone remarked that her brother "rarely talks at all" and her grand-father was "much depressed." Jeff Thomas described himself as a "fit sub-ject for the Lunatic Asylum," and his wife, Gertrude, hinted at the alcohol-ism and the outbursts of rage that compounded his depression. Women were confronted not just with the delicate task of defending their own interests in the face of the failures and incompetence of their traditional "protectors"; they had to deal as well with these injured and broken men. For all the pain women had suffered in war, they had not so directly con-fronted the horrors of four years on the battlefield, nor did they bear the same accountability for failure and defeat. The rehabilitation of southern white men became a central postwar responsibility for Confederate women.[9]

The United Daughters of the Confederacy, the Ladies Memorial Associa-tions, and celebrations of the Lost Cause were designed in considerable measure to accomplish this restoration. Beginning in the years immediately after Appomattox, women began to organize to honor the dead with ceme-teries, monuments, and annual memorial day observances. By the 1880s the United Daughters of the Confederacy had broadened women's concerns to a more general celebration of the Confederate struggle as well as its martyrs. On a personal and psychological level these efforts were meant to reassure defeated Confederates about their honor, courage, and manhood and to bury the pain of failure by redefining it as noble sacrifice and ultimate moral victory. But the Lost Cause operated on a broader social and political level as well, for it was intended to rehabilitate the larger system of patriarchy as well as the egos of individual southern men.[10]

Doubting the competence of their men and recognizing the necessity of defending their own interests, women were at the same time reluctant, especially in the face of postwar racial upheaval, to abandon the possibility of white male power and protection entirely and forever. As Emily Harris had written in 1863 when her husband returned from furlough to the front, "I shall never get used to being left as the head of affairs at home. I am constituted so as to crave a guide and protector." Daunted by the experience of wartime responsibility, many women hoped to shift some of those burdens back to their husbands, brothers, and sons. They knew they could no longer entirely trust these men, but they wanted at least to avoid assuming all of their obligations. "Trying to do a man's business," as Lizzie Neblett put it, had proved for many Confederate women an almost overwhelming task. Thus, in what seems to our late twentieth-century eyes an almost inexplicable paradox of progressivism and reaction, Gertrude Thomas—and many southern women like her—could logically work for both female suffrage and the Lost Cause.[11]

Through the experiences of war, white southern women had come to a new understanding of themselves and their interests as women. Their new postwar environment would yield a continued enhancement of female consciousness through the women's organizations that now flourished in the South as they never had in antebellum years. Not just associations to support suffrage or the Lost Cause, but temperance societies, educational and civic reform groups, church and missionary organizations, literary leagues, and women's clubs involved ladies in a variety of efforts aimed at personal and social uplift. The power of association, Anne Scott has written, "had its own inner dynamic," propelling women into public life as well as into closer bonds with one another.[12]

These gendered identities, however, could not be separated from the prerogatives of class and race on which "ladyhood" rested. Inevitably the omnipresent issue of race tied white men and women together and undermined white southern females' willingness to challenge patriarchy. Black freedom seemed to pose an immediate and dangerous threat to the lady's status and to her long cherished privileges. In a tellingly symbolic civic gathering in turn-of-the-century North Carolina, for example, young white girls appeared on a float inscribed with the words *Protect Us* as part of a parade in support of a candidate committed to black disfranchisement. Even during the war itself, elite women had recognized the urgency of retaining "at least one good negro to wait upon" them. The much discussed late nineteenth-century "servant problem" was essentially the postemancipation expression of southern ladies' commitment to reestablishing the authority and benefits of whiteness. The men of their race would naturally serve as important allies in this struggle. Prerogatives of race thus undermined the imperatives and commonalities of gender in the postwar South, separating black and white women, weakening and retarding the development of southern feminism, and subordinating its agenda to the seemingly more pressing concerns of reestablishing class and racial privilege.

When some southern women began actively to advocate female suffrage in the 1890s, their movement displayed a regionally distinctive and racist cast. Their arguments for women's votes emphasized not female empowerment but the potential for privileged white women's suffrage to serve as an instrument to blunt the impact of black enfranchisement. The women seemed not to seek validation of their equality with white men so much as their superiority to black men. The letterhead of the Southern States Woman Suffrage Conference represented its adherents' sense of their rightful preeminence of both race and class, declaring "A government is not yet complete that withholds from its most enlightened women what it freely gives to its most benighted men." "Never before," proclaimed a speaker at a southern suffrage convention, "in the history of the world have men made former slaves the political masters of their former mistresses." In a calculated effort to create an alliance that would at once serve the interests of white women and white men, southern suffragists attempted to forge white unity through the definition of common class and racial goals and the adoption of a shared white supremacist rhetoric. In their elitism, in their emphasis on white superiority, and in their complementary concerns with protecting women and rehabilitating men, the suffrage movement and the celebration of the Lost Cause embodied the paradoxical interplay of old and new in the postwar South.[13]

White women of the postwar South were new people living in a new world. Yet for those who remembered the rewards of class and racial power in the Old South, the desire to cling to eroding status remained strong. The ladies of the late nineteenth-century South understood all too well what Mary Lee had perceived as early as 1865: "social reconstruction we hold in our hands & might prevent." The necessities of changed economic and social circumstances and the self-knowledge gained from four years of crisis gave white southern women the bases for inventing new selves erected firmly upon the elitist assumptions of the old.

# The Burden of Southern History Reconsidered

Within an American nation shaped by prosperity and success, the South has been distinctive in its experience of poverty and failure. "The burden of southern history," historian C. Vann Woodward has taught us, derives from the knowledge of evil and the tragedy of bloody defeat in Civil War. This legacy has persisted into our own time, leaving southerners little basis for the American delusion "that there is nothing whatever that is beyond their power to accomplish."[1]

The burden of the South's history has been culturally powerful, serving as the foundation for a regional literature in which the presence of the past has provided a central theme. For southerners, as William Faulkner has perhaps most eloquently reminded us, the past is never dead or even truly past; for every white southern boy, it is always two o'clock on July 3, 1863, just a moment before Pickett's Charge dealt a fatal blow to the cherished myth of southern invincibility.[2]

The very circumstantiality, power, and tenacity of Faulkner's oft-cited image should in the late twentieth century prompt us to ask new questions about this much discussed burden of southern history. Woodward himself revised his original speculations to encompass the challenges the Vietnam War posed to the American legend of success. But those reconsiderations only serve to underline the centrality of military achievement to the conception of national and southern identity at issue here. Southerners burdened with the past Woodward describes, like the southerners forever poised at two o'clock on July 3, are white southerners and they are male southerners.

The weight of southern history is just as heavy for women and for African Americans, but it is constructed rather differently. Those who lived in bondage for 200 years carry a legacy of oppression and resistance that has been extensively and powerfully explored in the rich traditions of both African American history and literature. The preceding pages remind us that the southern past embodies a distinctive burden for many white southern women as well, a burden that encompassed significant and lasting implications for women's roles and identities and for the fortunes of women's rights and of feminism in the region.[3]

The Civil War experience of the women I have treated in this book left them with profound doubts about what lay within their power to accomplish and thus with serious questions about the desirability of female independence or emancipation. Yet warborn reservations about the competence of their men imbued many white southern females with a simultaneous desire to protect themselves from reliance on men for survival. Assertions of female power in the late nineteenth and twentieth centuries often reflected this conflicted legacy, the burden of women's wartime failures and doubts. The optimism and ebullience that characterized the movement for women's rights elsewhere in the nation was not central to the effort in the South. The many elite females active as leaders in the southern wing of the woman suffrage movement, for example, articulated a disdain for men and a consequent need themselves to defend the interests of women and children. Invented from necessity and born of disappointment and desperation, southern female assertiveness grew from different roots than that of their northern sisters. The appeal, the character, and the extent of southern feminism has been shaped by women's sense of their own limitations. Southern women, like their men, had learned to think of success as elusive; their own experience made it difficult for them to identify with the confidence of Susan B. Anthony's much quoted rallying cry, "Failure is impossible."[4]

The detailed research necessary for deep and nuanced understanding of southern women of the late nineteenth and the twentieth centuries is only just beginning; the history of women in the American South is still in its youth—if we can perhaps congratulate ourselves that it has now at least passed beyond infancy. The patterns I am identifying and the legacy I describe can only be suggestive. Yet it seems to me consistent both with feminism's very restricted appeal in the South, even into our own time, and with a popular wisdom that embraces an ambiguous tradition of seemingly contradictory strength and frailty in white southern women. The road from Altars of Sacrifice to Steel Magnolias remains to be fully mapped, but we can hardly doubt that devastating wartime experience had a profound and lasting impact on women, an impact in significant ways different from its influence on southern men. White women of the postwar South have borne their own peculiar burden of southern history.

# NOTES

## ABBREVIATIONS USED IN THE NOTES

ADAH      Alabama Department of Archives and History, Montgomery, Ala.

AHC      Atlanta History Center, Atlanta, Ga.

BU      John Hay Library, Brown University, Providence, R.I.

CU      Department of Manuscripts, J. M. Olin Library, Cornell University, Ithaca, N.Y.

DU      Manuscript Department, William R. Perkins Library, Duke University, Durham, N.C.

EU      Special Collections Department, Robert W. Woodruff Library, Emory University, Atlanta, Ga.

GDAH      Georgia Department of Archives and History, Atlanta, Ga.

HC      Fishburn Library, Hollins College, Va.

HFPC      Historical Foundation of the Presbyterian and Reformed Churches, Montreat, N.C.

HL      Winchester–Frederick County Historical Society, Handley Library, Winchester, Va.

LC      Library of Congress, Washington, D.C.

LRCSW      Letters Received, Confederate Secretary of War

LSU      Department of Archives and Manuscripts, Hill Memorial Library, Louisiana State University, Baton Rouge, La.

MDAH      Mississippi Department of Archives and History, Jackson, Miss.

MOC      Museum of the Confederacy, Richmond, Va.

MUO      Special Collections, King Library, Miami University of Ohio, Oxford, Ohio

NA      National Archives, Washington, D.C.

NCDAH      North Carolina Division of Archives and History, Raleigh, N.C.

RU      Woodson Research Center, Fondren Library, Rice University, Houston, Tex.

SCHS      South Carolina Historical Society, Charleston, S.C.

SCL      South Caroliniana Library, University of South Carolina, Columbia, S.C.

SHC      Southern Historical Collection, University of North Carolina, Chapel Hill, N.C.

THNOC      The Historic New Orleans Collection, New Orleans, La.

TSL      Tennessee State Library and Archives, Nashville, Tenn.

TU      Special Collections, Howard-Tilton Memorial Library, Tulane University, New Orleans, La.

UFL      P. K. Yonge Library of Florida History, University of Florida, Gainesville, Fla.

US      Jessie Ball DuPont Library, University of the South, Sewanee, Tenn.

| UTA | Center for American History, University of Texas, Austin, Tex. |
| UVA | Manuscripts Department, Alderman Library, University of Virginia, Charlottesville, Va. |
| VHS | Virginia Historical Society, Richmond, Va. |
| VSL | Library of Virginia, Richmond, Va. |
| WC | Archives and Special Collections, Dacus Library, Winthrop College, Rock Hill, S.C. |
| WM | Manuscripts and Rare Books, Earl Gregg Swem Memorial Library, College of William and Mary, Williamsburg, Va. |
| YU | Manuscripts and Archives, Sterling Memorial Library, Yale University, New Haven, Conn. |

## INTRODUCTION

1. Lucy Rebecca Buck, *Sad Earth, Sweet Heaven: The Diary of Lucy Rebecca Buck*, ed. William Pettus Buck (Birmingham, Ala.: Cornerstone, 1973), 50.

2. "Stampede," quoted in Benjamin Quarles, *The Negro in the Civil War* (Boston: Little, Brown, 1953), 58; *Montgomery Daily Advertiser*, July 1, 1864. In the past decade, historians' use of the analytic categories of race, class, and gender has moved from being regarded, first, as innovative, then as fashionable, to, recently, as verging on the banal. At the same time, conservative critics of contemporary historical practice have fixed upon the mantra of race, class, and gender as a target for their attacks on alleged "political correctness." Yet I suggest that these categories were far from new or innovative in the 1980s and that they do not derive from present-day political perspectives. Their persistent acceptance and articulation argues for their fundamental importance. As the nineteenth-century women's voices that fill this book amply demonstrate, these were the categories by which women of the South's slaveholding classes consciously identified themselves. The intertwined features of race, class, and gender were the defining characteristics of ladyhood; these were also assumptions directly assaulted by the social and cultural forces unleashed by the Civil War.

3. For a significant early consideration of the role of slaves in freeing themselves, see Armstead Robinson, "Day of Jubilo: Civil War and the Demise of Slavery in the Mississippi Valley, 1861–1865" (Ph.D. dissertation, University of Rochester, 1976); see also Ira Berlin, Barbara J. Fields, Thavolia Glymph, Joseph P. Reidy, and Leslie S. Rowland, eds., *Freedom: A Documentary History of Emancipation, 1861–1867*, ser. 1, vol. 1, *The Destruction of Slavery* (New York: Cambridge University Press, 1985); Vincent Harding, *There Is a River: The Black Struggle for Freedom in America* (New York: Harcourt Brace Jovanovich, 1981); Leon F. Litwack, *Been in the Storm So Long: The Aftermath of Slavery* (New York: Knopf, 1979); and the debate between James McPherson and Ira Berlin in McPherson, "Who Freed the Slaves?," *Reconstruction* 2, no. 3 (1994): 35–40, and Berlin, "Emancipation and Its Meaning in American Life," *Reconstruction* 2, no. 3 (1994): 41–44. On women in the Civil War, see Mary Elizabeth Massey, *Bonnet Brigades: American Women and the Civil War* (New York: Knopf, 1966;

reprinted as *Women in the Civil War* [Lincoln: University of Nebraska Press, 1994]), and Francis Butler Simkins and James Welch Patton, *The Women of the Confederacy* (Richmond: Garrett and Massie, 1936), for early scholarly treatments; for examples of what is fast becoming an outpouring of contemporary interest, see George C. Rable, *Civil Wars: Women and the Crisis of Southern Nationalism* (Urbana: University of Illinois Press, 1989), and Catherine Clinton and Nina Silber, eds., *Divided Houses: Gender and the Civil War* (New York: Oxford University Press, 1992).

4. George Fitzhugh, *Sociology for the South: Or the Failure of Free Society* (Richmond: Morris, 1854), 217, 216, 214. On women in the Old South, see Anne Firor Scott, *The Southern Lady: From Pedestal to Politics, 1830–1930* (Chicago: University of Chicago Press, 1970); Elizabeth Fox-Genovese, *Within the Plantation Household: Black and White Women of the Old South* (Chapel Hill: University of North Carolina Press, 1988); Jean E. Friedman, *The Enclosed Garden: Women and Community in the Evangelical South, 1830–1900* (Chapel Hill: University of North Carolina Press, 1985); Catherine Clinton, *The Plantation Mistress: Woman's World in the Old South* (New York: Pantheon, 1982); and Suzanne Lebsock, *The Free Women of Petersburg: Status and Culture in a Southern Town, 1784–1860* (New York: Norton, 1984).

5. *Milledgeville Confederate Union*, January 17, 1865; Lizzie Neblett quoted in Drew Gilpin Faust, "'Trying to Do a Man's Business': Slavery, Violence, and Gender in the American Civil War," *Gender and History* 4 (Summer 1992): 197; *Montgomery Daily Advertiser*, July 1, 1864.

6. I am discussing here what feminist theorists have called multiple and shifting subject positions and the creation of subjectivities. See, for example, Catherine Belsey, "Constructing the Subject: Deconstructing the Text," in *Feminist Criticism and Social Change*, ed. J. Newton and D. Rosenfelt (London: Methuen, 1985). See also Evelyn Brooks Higginbotham, "African-American Women's History and the Metalanguage of Race," *Signs* 17 (Winter 1992): 251–74. On the "co-constructedness" of race and gender, see Ruth Frankenberg, *White Women, Race Matters: The Social Construction of Whiteness* (Minneapolis: University of Minnesota Press, 1993).

7. For comparative examples of women's conservative reactions to two other wars, see Mary Louise Roberts, *Civilization without Sexes: Reconstructing Gender in Postwar France, 1917–1927* (Chicago: University of Chicago Press, 1994), and Susan Kingsley Kent, *Making Peace: The Reconstruction of Gender in Interwar Britain* (Princeton: Princeton University Press, 1993).

8. On necessity as the mother of invention, see, for example, Clara Solomon Diary, May 18, 1862, LSU; Amelia Pinkind to Isabella Woodruff, August 4, 1862, Isabella Ann Woodruff Papers, DU; and Julia Davidson to John Davidson, September 8, 1863, Davidson Family Papers, AHC.


CHAPTER ONE

1. Title from *New Orleans Daily Picayune*, June 9, 1861; Lucy Wood to Waddy Butler, January 21, 1861, Lucy Wood Butler Papers, UVA. Because the subject of this

book is elite, white, southern women, I will not endlessly repeat the adjectives *elite*, *white*, and *southern* when discussing this group. I will assume that, like a pronoun with a clear referent, my meaning will usually be evident. I will repeat the adjectives in order to make distinctions clear when I am also discussing other groups of women and from time to time to emphasize an awareness of the dangerous tendency in some early women's history to conflate women of all classes and races and to ignore their differences. The construction and reconstruction of class and racial difference is central to my project in this book, as it was to the identity work that characterized the wartime experience of women of the South's master class. See Elizabeth Spelman, *Inessential Woman: Problems of Exclusion in Feminist Thought* (Boston: Beacon, 1988); Bonnie Thornton Dill, "Race, Class, and Gender: Prospects for an All-Inclusive Sisterhood," *Feminist Studies* 9 (Spring 1983): 131–50; and Nancy A. Hewitt, "Beyond the Search for Sisterhood: American Women's History in the 1980s," in *Unequal Sisters: A Multicultural Reader in U.S. Women's History*, ed. Vicki L. Ruiz and Ellen Carol DuBois, 2d ed. (New York: Routledge, 1994), 1–19.

2. Lucy Wood to Waddy Butler, January 21, 1861, Butler Papers, UVA; Kate Cumming, *Kate: The Journal of a Confederate Nurse*, ed. Richard Barksdale Harwell (Baton Rouge: Louisiana State University Press, 1959), 39.

3. Lucy Wood to Waddy Butler, January 21, 1861, Butler Papers, UVA. Wood's opposition to the African slave trade was shared by many Virginians, and the Confederate constitution prohibited the trade partly as a gesture to win over the wavering border states, especially Virginia.

4. Ada Bacot Diary, December 12, 1860, SCL; Amanda Sims to Harriet Palmer, December 9, 1861, Palmer Family Papers, SCL; Catherine Ann Devereux Edmondston, April 16, 1861, in *Journal of a Secesh Lady: The Diary of Catherine Ann Devereux Edmondston, 1860–1866*, ed. Beth G. Crabtree and James W. Patton (Raleigh: Division of Archives and History, 1979), 50; "Reminiscences of Lucy Bagby," Bagby Family Papers, VHS; Keziah Brevard Diary, January 6, 1861, SCL. See also Amy E. Murrell, "Two Armies: Women's Activism in Civil War Richmond" (senior honors thesis, Duke University, 1993). Elizabeth Varon's recent dissertation argues that these prescriptions were often honored in the breach rather than the observance in the prewar South as well. She documents much wider political activism by Virginia women than scholars have hitherto recognized, but she also shows the persistence of a conflicting ideology. See Varon, " 'We Mean to Be Counted': White Women and Politics in Antebellum Virginia" (Ph.D. dissertation, Yale University, 1993). On women and politics generally, see Paula Baker, "The Domestication of Politics: Women and American Political Society, 1780–1920," *American Historical Review* 89 (June 1984): 620–47, and Michael McGerr, "Political Style and Women's Power, 1830–1930," *Journal of American History* 77 (December 1990): 864–85.

5. Sarah Morgan, *The Civil War Diary of Sarah Morgan*, ed. Charles East (Athens: University of Georgia Press, 1991), 121, 73–74; Bacot Diary, January 19, 1861, SCL; Samuel Proctor, ed., "The Call to Arms: Secession from a Feminine Point of View," *Florida Historical Quarterly* 35 (January 1957): 267.

6. Edmondston, *Journal of a Secesh Lady*, 54, 34.

7. Susan Cornwall Diary, February 4, 1861, SHC; Edmondston, *Journal of a Secesh Lady*, 35. Slaveowning women of the Confederate South adopted the language of separate male and female spheres, of distinct public and private realms, to express their uneasiness with war's transformations and to understand and negotiate the changes in their lives. We must be careful to recognize that these are their analytic or conceptual characterizations and to distinguish their rendering of their experience from our own assessments of the shape of their world. In the course of the war, Confederate women used the language of "spheres" to legitimate resistance to change, to ease the shock of change by denying it altogether, and, on occasion, to make change more palatable by describing it in familiar terms. Their characterizations often represent ideals or prescriptions that seem to the historian strikingly at odds with their own behavior or circumstances. Their contradictory comments and actions in regard to secession politics make this clear at the outset. I have been more interested in the ideological and social strategies that their use of this language reveals than I have been in the accuracy of these terms as descriptions of their behavior and lives. Although I state in the Preface that private lives essentially ended in the South with the outbreak of war, Confederate women came to this realization slowly, haltingly, painfully, and incompletely. It is this evolution that is at the heart of their war story. For a discussion of how women's historians have often failed to separate their own analytic uses of "separate spheres" from those of their nineteenth-century subjects, see Linda K. Kerber, "Separate Spheres, Female Worlds, Woman's Place: The Rhetoric of Women's History," *Journal of American History* 75 (June 1988): 39.

8. N. Van Beel to Jefferson Davis, August 14, 1861, LRCSW, RG 109, reel 10, p. 5521, NA; Mary Early Scrapbook, 17, VHS; Edmondston, *Journal of a Secesh Lady*, 44; Fannie Page Hume Diary, April 17, 1861, UVA; Julia Davidson to John Davidson, January 8, 1861, Davidson Family Papers, AHC; Brevard Diary, April 13, 1861, SCL.

9. Margaret Crawford Adams, "Tales of a Grandmother," in *South Carolina Women in the Confederacy*, ed. Mrs. Thomas Taylor, Mrs. A. T. Smythe, Mrs. August Kohn, Miss M. B. Poppenheim, and Miss Martha Washington, 2 vols. (Columbia, S.C.: State Co., 1903), 1:210; Kate Rowland Diary, December 12, 29, 1863, EU.

10. Cumming, *Kate*, 49; letter from Ann Catron, *Winchester Virginian*, May 8, 1861; Sarah Lawton to General Henry Rootes Jackson, September 9, 1861, Sarah Lawton Papers, GDAH; Mother to William Vaught, March 18, 1862, William Vaught Papers, RU; J. M. Fain to Huldah Fain Briant, May 19, 1862, Huldah Annie Briant Papers, DU.

11. Sarah Espy Diary, April 19, 1861, ADAH; Lizzie Ozburn to Jimmie Ozburn, October 14, 1861, Katherine Elizabeth Ozburn Papers, GDAH.

12. William Vaught to Mary Vaught, August 9, 1862, Vaught Papers, RU.

13. Ella Gertrude Clanton Thomas, *The Secret Eye: The Journal of Ella Gertrude Clanton Thomas, 1848–1889*, ed. Virginia Ingraham Burr (Chapel Hill: University of North Carolina Press, 1990), 192; *The Journals of David Golightly Harris*, ed. Philip N. Racine (Knoxville: University of Tennessee Press, 1990), 268; Betty Herndon Maury, *The Confederate Diary of Betty Herndon Maury, 1861–1863*, ed. Alice Maury Parmalee (Washington, D.C.: privately printed, 1938), 3–4.

14. Richard B. Harwell, "Louisiana Burge: The Diary of a Confederate College Girl," *Georgia Historical Quarterly* 36 (June 1952): 153.

15. Myrta Lockett Avary, ed., *A Virginia Girl in the Civil War, 1861–1865* (New York: Appleton, 1903), 27; Edmondston, *Journal of a Secesh Lady*, 69.

16. Leila W., "Woman A Patriot," *Southern Monthly* 1 (October 1861): 115.

17. Public discourse and popular culture in the Confederacy might appropriately be considered what Michel Foucault has called "technologies of power," designed to rework human identities in accordance with shifting cultural and social needs. See Foucault, *The Discourse on Language* (New York: Random House, 1971) and *Power/ Knowledge: Selected Interviews and Other Writings, 1972–1977*, ed. Colin Gordon (New York: Pantheon, 1980).

18. Theodore von La Hache, *I Would Like to Change My Name: A Favorite Encore Song* (Augusta: Blackmar & Bro., 1863); *Charleston Daily Courier*, August 15, 1861; Davis quoted in unidentified newspaper clipping in George Bagby Scrapbook, 2:128, George Bagby Papers, VHS.

19. "Heart Victories," in *Songs of the South* (Richmond: J. W. Randolph, 1862), 68–69.

20. "Our Mothers Did So before Us," in ibid., 70–71; *Richmond Record of News, History and Literature*, September 3, 1863, 105; *Charleston Daily Courier*, August 19, 1861; "I've Kissed Him and Let Him Go," clipping in Bagby Scrapbook, 5:99, George Bagby Papers, VHS.

21. Priscilla Munnikhuysen Bond Diary, June 29, 1862, LSU.

22. Subheading from *New Orleans Daily Picayune*, June 9, 1861.

23. Julia Le Grand, *The Journal of Julia Le Grand, New Orleans, 1862–1863*, ed. Kate Mason Rowland and Mrs. Morris L. Croxall (Richmond: Everett Waddey, 1911), 52; Clara to Jessie Kittredge, May 4, 1863, Warren Ogden, Collector, Miscellaneous Civil War Letters, TU.

24. Sarah Morgan, *Civil War Diary*, 166.

25. Ibid., 411; Alice Ready Diary, April 13, 19, 1862, SHC. For other comments by women wishing to be men, see Emma Walton to J. B. Walton, May 12, July 15, 1863, Walton-Glenny Papers, THNOC; Caroline Kean Hill Davis Diary, February 13, 1865, VHS; Sarah Lois Wadley Diary, April 21, 1861, SHC; Emma Holmes, *The Diary of Miss Emma Holmes, 1861–1866*, ed. John Marszalek (Baton Rouge: Louisiana State University Press, 1979), 323; Amelia Barr to Jennie, February 15, 1861, Amelia Barr Papers, UTA; Mary Greenhow Lee Diary, June 3, 1862, HL; and Sarah Anne Grover Strickler Diary, May 11, 1865, UVA.

26. Sarah Morgan, *Civil War Diary*, 77.

27. Davis Diary, February 13, 1865, VHS; Kate Stone, *Brokenburn: The Journal of Kate Stone, 1861–1868*, ed. John Q. Anderson (Baton Rouge: Louisiana State University Press, 1955), 24, 17; Edmondston, *Journal of a Secesh Lady*, 611; A. Grima to Alfred Grima, July 23, 1864, Grima Family Papers, THNOC. For other examples of the widespread invocation of uselessness by women, see Wadley Diary, August 20, 1863, SHC; Amanda Chappelear Diary, April 19, 1862, VHS; Holmes, *Diary*, 251, 323. "Activity is a great remedy." French translated by the author.

28. Ready Diary, February 16, 1862, SHC; Bacot Diary, December 12, 1860, SCL.

29. Le Grand, *Journal*, 53; Davis Diary, February 4, 1865, VHS; Stone, *Brokenburn*, 87; *New Orleans Daily Picayune*, June 9, 1861.

30. "Educated Woman—In Peace and War," *Southern Field and Fireside*, April 11, 1863; *Augusta Weekly Constitutionalist*, July 17, 1861; Launcelot Minor Blackford, *Mine Eyes Have Seen the Glory* (Cambridge: Harvard University Press, 1954), 160–61.

31. Sara Agnes (Mrs. Roger) Pryor, *Reminiscences of Peace and War* (New York: Macmillan, 1904), 131, 133. See also Emma Crutcher to Will Crutcher, December 18, 1861, Crutcher-Shannon Papers, UTA; she undertook work for a benefit fair because "I had nothing else to do."

32. Subheading is quoted from Lucy Wood Butler to Waddy Butler, May 2, 1861, Butler Papers, UVA. On the rurality of the South and its impact on women, see Elizabeth Fox-Genovese, *Within the Plantation Household: Black and White Women of the Old South* (Chapel Hill: University of North Carolina Press, 1988), chap. 1; for an argument for women's culture and community in an urban setting, see Suzanne Lebsock, *The Free Women of Petersburg: Status and Culture in a Southern Town, 1784–1860* (New York: Norton, 1984). On women's organizations in the South, see LeeAnn Whites, "The Charitable and the Poor: The Emergence of Domestic Politics in Augusta, Georgia, 1860–1880," *Journal of Social History* 17 (1984): 606–16, and Varon, "'We Mean to Be Counted.'" Anne Scott argues for the extensiveness of women's organizations throughout the nation in *Natural Allies: Women's Associations in American History* (Urbana: University of Illinois Press, 1991), but she makes a far more convincing case for North than South, where her examples seem exceptional rather than typical. On the limitations of female organizations and bonding in the South, see also Jean E. Friedman, *The Enclosed Garden: Women and Community in the Evangelical South, 1830–1900* (Chapel Hill: University of North Carolina Press, 1985).

33. *Charleston Mercury*, January 1, 1863.

34. List of ladies' aid societies, January 1, 1862, Governor's Files, ADAH; Lucy Wood to Waddy Butler, May 2, 1861, Butler Papers, UVA. For a similar comment, see Ellen Moore to Samuel Moore, Samuel J. C. Moore Papers, SHC; on ladies' societies, see Francis Butler Simkins and James Welch Patton, *The Women of the Confederacy* (Richmond: Garrett and Massie, 1936), 22, and George C. Rable, *Civil Wars: Women and the Crisis of Southern Nationalism* (Urbana: University of Illinois Press, 1989), 139–40.

35. Edmondston, *Journal of a Secesh Lady*, 60, 30.

36. Mary Ann Huff, "The Role of Women in Confederate Georgia" (M.A. thesis, Emory University, 1967), 22.

37. Stone, *Brokenburn*, 47; Huff, "Role of Women in Confederate Georgia," 18–19; H. E. Sterkx, *Partners in Rebellion: Alabama Women in the Civil War* (Rutherford, N.J.: Fairleigh Dickinson University Press, 1970), 105. See also minutes of relief associations in Taylor et al., *South Carolina Women*, 1:11–12, 36–53; Ladies Defense Association Papers, MOC; Ladies Relief Association, Spartanburg, SCL; Greenville [S.C.] Ladies' Aid Association Minutes, 1861–65, DU; and E. Merton Coulter, *The Confederate States of America, 1861–1865* (Baton Rouge: Louisiana State University Press, 1950), 405–39.

38. Lizzie Ozburn to Jimmie, August 24, 1861, Ozburn Papers, GDAH; *Charleston Mercury*, April 29 (poem), March 18, 19, 1862. On dramatic performances encouraging

patriotism, see Nettie Fondren to Robert Mitchell, September 18, 1862, Mitchell-Fondren Papers, GDAH.

39. *Mobile Advertiser and Register*, September 25, 1862; Mary Legg to Hattie Palmer, January 15, 1862, September 26, 1861, Palmer Family Papers, SCL; Maria M. Hubard Diary, December 15, 16, 1861, VHS; Clara D. MacLean Diary, August 9, 1861, DU. See Mary Megan Chapman, " 'Living Pictures': Women and Tableaux Vivants in Nineteenth Century American Fiction and Culture" (Ph.D. dissertation, Cornell University, 1992).

40. *Charleston Mercury*, September 15, 1862; *Milledgeville Confederate Union*, October 18, 25, 1864.

41. Emma Crutcher to Will Crutcher, December 18, 1861, Crutcher-Shannon Papers, UTA.

42. Hubard Diary, December 16, 1861, VHS; Lise Mitchell Diary, April 3, 1864, TU; Sterkx, *Partners in Rebellion*, 157; R. Frombeign to Zebulon Vance, March 16, 1863, Zebulon Vance Papers, NCDAH.

43. *Charleston Mercury*, March 12, 14, 1862. See the letter of Martha Boddie to Mississippi governor John J. Pettus asking him to forward $1,200 worth of her diamonds to a ladies' gunboat society. Boddie to Pettus, February 1862, John J. Pettus Papers, MDAH.

44. *Charleston Mercury*, October 12, March 14, 1862.

45. *Mobile Advertiser and Register*, September 10, 1862.


CHAPTER TWO

1. Slave men, of course, remained in considerable numbers. It is clear from these white women's remarks, however, that they regarded black men as comprising a separate category from "men," who are assumed to be white. See Chapter 3 for more extensive discussion of white women's wartime perceptions of slave men. Subheading and first quotation from Louisa Walton to Isabella Woodruff, January 3, 1862, Isabella Ann Woodruff Papers, DU; Elizabeth Randolph Allan, ed., *The Life and Letters of Margaret Junkin Preston* (Boston: Houghton Mifflin, 1903), 137, 133; Nettie Fondren to Robert Mitchell, December 16, 1862, Mitchell-Fondren Papers, GDAH; Mary Greenhow Lee Diary, June 2, 1862, HL. For examples of similar comments, see Emma Crutcher to Mother, February 19, 1863, Crutcher-Shannon Papers, UTA; Sarah White to Judah P. Benjamin, March 9, 1862, LRCSW, RG 109, reel 76, W104, NA; Amanda Worthington Diary, February 13, 1862, MDAH; and Annie Harper Reminiscences, 14, 15, MDAH. On the draft, see Albert Burton Moore, *Conscription and Conflict in the Confederacy* (New York: Macmillan, 1924), and Memory Mitchell, *Legal Aspects of Conscription and Exemption in North Carolina, 1861–1865* (Chapel Hill: University of North Carolina Press, 1965).

2. Nancy Hall et al. to Governor Zebulon Vance, August 11, 1863, Zebulon Vance Papers, NCDAH; Citizens of Randolph County to the Governor, November 28, 1862, Governor's Files, ADAH; Jonathan Pitts to Governor John Gill Shorter, April 4, 1862,

Governor's Files, ADAH; M. L. Stansel to Governor John Gill Shorter, March 27, 1862, Governor's Files, ADAH.

3. Elizabeth P. Hardin, *The Private War of Lizzie Hardin: A Kentucky Confederate Girl's Diary of the Civil War in Kentucky, Virginia, Tennessee, Alabama, and Georgia*, ed. G. Glenn Clift (Frankfort: Kentucky Historical Society, 1963), 226. Her phrase alludes to a popular war ballad, *The Vacant Chair: or, We Shall Meet, but We Shall Miss Him* (Richmond: Davies & Sons, 186-).

4. John C. Calhoun, *The Papers of John C. Calhoun*, ed. Clyde N. Wilson, 22 vols. (Columbia: University of South Carolina Press, 1981), 14:84. See also Stephanie Mc-Curry, *Masters of Small Worlds: Yeoman Households, Gender Relations, and Political Culture in the Antebellum South Carolina Low Country* (New York: Oxford University Press, 1995).

5. Lawrence Jones to John Gill Shorter, March 17, 1862, Governor's Files, ADAH.

6. See Randolph B. Campbell, *An Empire for Slavery: The Peculiar Institution in Texas, 1821–1865* (Baton Rouge: Louisiana State University Press, 1989), 231-51.

7. Laetitia LaFon Ashmore Nutt, *Courageous Journey: The Civil War Journal of Laetitia LaFon Ashmore Nutt*, ed. Florence Ashmore Cowles Hamlett Martin (Miami: Seemann, 1975), 82. Subheading from Sallie to My Dear Sister, May 14, 1862, Mary A. Gash Papers, NCDAH.

8. Sarah Estes Diary, July 15, June 11, November 15, June 19, October 6, 1862, TSL.

9. Sallie to My Dear Sister, May 14, 1862, Gash Papers, NCDAH; Lila Chunn to Willie Chunn, October 25, 1861, November 14, 1864, Chunn-Land Papers, GDAH; Lila to Willie Chunn, December 14, 1863, Willie Chunn Papers, DU.

10. Emma Crutcher to Will Crutcher, March 1, 1862, Crutcher-Shannon Papers, UTA; Lizzie Ozburn to Jimmie Ozburn, Katherine Elizabeth Ozburn Papers, GDAH; Ellen Moore to Samuel Moore, October 8, 1861, n.d. [1861], March 23, 1862, Samuel J. C. Moore Papers, SHC. See also Minerva Bone to Robert Bone, December 19, 1861, Robert Bone Papers, EU.

11. Mary Elizabeth Massey, *Refugee Life in the Confederacy* (Baton Rouge: Louisiana State University Press, 1964), 116-18.

12. Ann Marie Stewart Turner to My Dear Mother, September 29, October 17, December 12, 1864, Ann Marie Stewart Turner Collection, RU. See also James Turner to Ann Marie Stewart Turner, August 18, 1863, ibid.

13. Elizabeth McKamy Recollections, TSL; Sidney Harding quoted in Massey, *Refugee Life*, 12; Malvina Gist, February 14, 1865, in *Heroines of Dixie: Winter of Desperation*, ed. Katharine M. Jones, 2 vols. (1955; rpt., Saint Simons Island, Ga.: Mockingbird Books, 1975), 2:173; see also Kate Rowland Diary, June 22, 1861, MOC.

14. C. Vann Woodward, ed., *Mary Chesnut's Civil War* (New Haven: Yale University Press, 1981).

15. Massey, *Refugee Life*, 15; Margaret Phelan Scott and Rachel Wilson, "Hollins and the Civil War," *Hollins Alumnae Bulletin*, Spring 1961, 16-18; Hollins Institute, *The Education of Teachers in the South . . . To which is Attached A Catalogue of the Institute* (Lynchburg: Virginia Power Press, 1864); *Minutes of the Bethel Baptist Association* (Macon, Ga.: Burke, Boykin, 1862-64); Sarepta Gregory to Dear Aunt, Febru-

ary 28, 1865, Sawyer Papers, NCDAH; Robert De Schweinitz to Zebulon Vance, July 7, 1863, Vance Papers, NCDAH; Lucy Worth London Anderson, ed., *North Carolina Women of the Confederacy* (Fayetteville, N.C.: Cumberland Printing, 1926): 61; Farmville Female College, broadside, August 10, 1863; see the many newspaper advertisements for girls' boarding schools, e.g., *Richmond Enquirer*, September 5, December 30, 1862, June 26, July 3, 1863; Mrs. Wellington Stevenson, Recollections, UDC Collections, 9:84–85, GDAH.

16. Mary Greenhow Lee Diary, March 14, 1865, HL.

17. Subheading is quotation translated by the author from the French, A. Grima to Alfred Grima, February 14, 1865, Grima Family Papers, THNOC. The classic work on refugees is Massey, *Refugee Life*; see treatments also in George C. Rable, *Civil Wars: Women and the Crisis of Southern Nationalism* (Urbana: University of Illinois Press, 1989), 181–220; Francis Butler Simkins and James Welch Patton, *The Women of the Confederacy* (Richmond: Garrett and Massie, 1936), 100–110; Jean E. Friedman, *The Enclosed Garden: Women and Community in the Evangelical South, 1830–1900* (Chapel Hill: University of North Carolina Press, 1985), 95–98; and Daniel Sutherland, "Looking for a Home: Louisiana Emigrants during the Civil War and Reconstruction," *Louisiana History* 21 (Fall 1980): 341–59. Massey comments on both the class and gender identities of refugees, in *Refugee Life*, 28, 29. For a discussion of class resentment against refugees, see "Claiborne," "A Dialogue Between a Wounded Soldier and Mr. S. Who Was Running his Negroes to Texas," [October 1863], clipping in M. L. Lawton Scrapbook, 36, AHC. See also Mrs. Thomas Taylor, Mrs. A. T. Smythe, Mrs. August Kohn, Miss M. B. Poppenheim, and Miss Martha Washington, eds., *South Carolina Women in the Confederacy*, 2 vols. (Columbia, S.C.: State Co., 1903), 1:174–75, and Margaret McCalla, "The Wartime Experiences of Margaret McCalla: Confederate Refugee from East Tennessee," ed. Robert Partin, *Tennessee Historical Quarterly* 24 (Spring 1965): 39–53. For a discussion of Sherman's unusual mass removal of working women from factories in Roswell, Georgia, to the North, see Hartwell T. Bynum, "Sherman's Expulsion of the Roswell Women in 1864," *Georgia Historical Quarterly* 54 (1970): 169–82.

18. Nancy to Richard Jett, June 12, 1864, Nancy Jett Papers, EU; Sarah Espy Diary, August 7, December 18, 1863, ADAH.

19. *The Private Mary Chesnut: The Unpublished Civil War Diaries*, ed. C. Vann Woodward and Elisabeth Muhlenfeld (New York: Oxford University Press, 1984), 230–31. These quotations are from the unpublished diaries, written during the war itself and thus do not bear the revised and considered position represented by much of the material Chesnut reworked in the 1880s. Sidney Harding Diary, January 9, August 8, 1863, LSU.

20. Kate Stone, *Brokenburn: The Journal of Kate Stone, 1861–1868*, ed. John Q. Anderson (Baton Rouge: Louisiana State University Press, 1955), 238. See also Anne Shannon Martin Diary, MDAH.

21. *Daily Southern Guardian*, April 22, 1864.

22. Bill Arp [Charles H. Smith], *Bill Arp, So Called: A Sideshow of the Southern Side of the War* (New York: Metropolitan Record Office, 1866), 103.

23. Sarah Morgan, *The Civil War Diary of Sarah Morgan*, ed. Charles East (Athens: University of Georgia Press, 1991), 481; Sarah Lois Wadley Diary, September 25, 1863, SHC; Lila Chunn to Mrs. Chunn, February 19, 1865, William Augustus Chunn Papers, EU; Malvina Gist, March 17, 1865, in Katharine M. Jones, *Heroines of Dixie*, 2:200.

24. Sarah Morgan, *Civil War Diary*, 211; Margaret Beckwith Reminiscences, 2:28, VHS; Lise Mitchell Diary, April 19, 1864, February 19, 1862, TU.

25. "The bitterness of the exile that weighs so heavily upon us"; "She is so saddened by the exile that she almost never goes out and has let herself get emaciated." French translated by the author. A. Grima to Alfred Grima, February 14, 1865, and to Felix Grima, January 7, 1865, Grima Family Papers, THNOC.

26. Josephine West to her father, October 6, 1864, and to her mother, October 3, 1864, George W. West Papers, DU.

27. Subheading quoted from title of an article in the *Richmond Enquirer*, January 13, 1863.

28. Lacy Ford has found that in the South Carolina upcountry, household manufactures fell in per capita value by one-third between 1810 and 1840. This decline held true for both slaveless and slaveholding families, and by 1850 in Spartanburg one-fourth of all slaveless families did no home manufacturing at all. Homespun, he concludes, was still one source of clothing for yeoman families, but hardly the sole source. See Ford, *Origins of Southern Radicalism: The South Carolina Upcountry, 1800–1860* (New York: Oxford University Press, 1988), 82–83. In lowcountry South Carolina, Stephanie McCurry finds continued household production of cloth among yeomen but emphasizes the "continuum of self-sufficiency, interdependency and market engagement" of these families. See McCurry, *Masters of Small Worlds*, chap. 2, n. 76. I am grateful to McCurry for sharing her insights and research notes with me. Steven Hahn's statistics from the Georgia upcountry show dramatic decline in home manufacturing on agricultural units of all sizes between 1850 and 1860. See Steven Hahn, *The Roots of Southern Populism: Yeoman Farmers and the Transformation of the Georgia Upcountry, 1850–1890* (New York: Oxford University Press, 1983), 299, 300, 302. For a more general discussion of the decline in home manufactures in this era, see Rolla Milton Tryon, *Household Manufactures in the United States, 1640–1860: A Study in Industrial History* (Chicago: University of Chicago Press, 1917), 242–376. Most plantations listed sizable purchases of "negro cloth" in their account books. For a contrasting example, however, see the diary of Minerva Marie Louise Hynes Cook, MDAH, who presided over a domestic cloth-producing operation with a workforce made up chiefly of slave women in the years leading up to the Civil War. Her diary unfortunately ends at that point. See also "Cloth Making during the Civil War" and "Patterns for Weaving Counterpanes," Lena Dancy Ledbetter Collection, UTA.

29. *Southern Illustrated News*, December 20, 1862; *Milledgeville Confederate Union*, January 13, 1863; *Richmond Enquirer*, January 13, 1863; clippings, n.d., M. L. Lawton Scrapbook, 26, 60, AHC; "The Homespun Dress," in *Folksongs of Mississippi and their Background*, by Arthur Palmer Hudson (Chapel Hill: University of North Carolina Press, 1936), 265–66. See also Carrie Bell Sinclair, *The Southern Girl with the Home-spun Dress*, broadside, n.p., 186-. The association of political independence

with economic independence had its origins in the revolutionary period, with its calls for domestic production, and was reinforced in later appearances of southern nationalism. Calls for homespun accompanied the nullification crusade in South Carolina in the 1820s and 1830s, for example. See McCurry, *Masters of Small Worlds*, chap. 2.

30. Mary Speight to Mary W. Bryan, February 19, 1862, John Heritage Bryan Collection, NCDAH; Espy Diary, April 9, 1862, ADAH; Kate Cumming, *Kate: The Journal of a Confederate Nurse*, ed. Richard Barksdale Harwell (Baton Rouge: Louisiana State University Press, 1959), 64; Martha Jane Crossley, "A Patriotic Confederate Woman's War Diary, 1862-3," ed. H. E. Sterkx, *Alabama Historical Quarterly* 20 (Winter 1958): 613; Mary Legg to Hattie Palmer, December 10, 1863, Palmer Family Papers, SCL; Octavia Stephens to Winston Stephens, Bryant-Stephens Papers, UFL; Wadley Diary, March 7, 1865, SHC. See also Stone, *Brokenburn*, 146, and Kate Rowland Diary, November 15, 1864, EU.

31. Will Neblett to Lizzie Neblett, June 17, 1864, and Lizzie Neblett to Will Neblett, April 5, February 12, 1864, Lizzie Neblett Papers, UTA; George Peddy to Kate Peddy, February 22, 1864, in *Saddle Bag and Spinning Wheel: Being the Civil War Letters of George W. Peddy and Kate Featherston Peddy*, ed. George Peddy Cuttino (Macon, Ga.: Mercer University Press, 1981), 216; Amanda Bullock to Robert Bullock, January 30, 1861, Robert Bullock Papers, GDAH. On slave women as textile producers before the war, see Elizabeth Fox-Genovese, *Within the Plantation Household: Black and White Women of the Old South* (Chapel Hill: University of North Carolina Press, 1988), 120–29, 178-85; on textile production by slaves during the war, see Mary Curry to Duncan Curry, November 17, 1862, Curry Hill Plantation Papers, GDAH, and Harper Reminiscences, 16, MDAH. See remarks on how odd it was to see white women spin, Sue Richardson Diary, August 2, 1864, EU.

32. See Mrs. E. Walters to Governor Zebulon Vance, April 17, 1863, and Nancy Key to Governor Zebulon Vance, August 25, 1864, Vance Papers, NCDAH; "Cotton Cards. How Secured for the People of Alabama During the War Between the States," compiled by Clyde E. Wilson, WPA, Governor's Files of Thomas H. Watts, ADAH; Octavia Stephens to Winston Stephens, October 23, 1862, Bryant-Stephens Papers, UFL, and Lizzie Neblett to Will Neblett, April 5, 1864, Neblett Papers, UTA.

33. It is very striking how many extant references to large-scale involvement in textile production come from memoirs written *after* the war. Sources from the war period itself are more likely to document the difficulty and struggle in acquiring skills, raw materials, and motivation for such efforts. See Mary Edna Lohrenz and Anita Miller Stamper, *Mississippi Homespun: Nineteenth Century Textiles and the Women Who Made Them* (Jackson: Mississippi Department of Archives and History, 1989), and Anita Miller Stamper and Mary Edna Lohrenz, "Manuscript Sources for *Mississippi Homespun: Nineteenth Century Textiles and the Women Who Made Them*," *Journal of Mississippi History* 53 (August 1991): 185-218. Stamper and Lohrenz include a description of a fascinating but seemingly highly atypical team of textile workers—a Tennessee woman and her slave who continued their partnership after the war. See the Narcissa L. Black Diaries, MDAH. See also Mary Lohrenz, "Two Lives Intertwined on a Tennessee Plantation: Textile Production as Recorded in the Diary of Narcissa L. Erwin Black,"

*Southern Quarterly* 27 (Fall 1988): 73–93. I am grateful for the opportunity to discuss wartime textile production in a telephone conversation with Mary Lohrenz, June 9, 1994.

34. Mary Greenhow Lee Diary, May 28, 1863, HL; Mary Ann Harris Gay, *Life in Dixie during the War* (Atlanta: Constitution Job Office, 1892), 42; Taylor et al., *South Carolina Women*, 1:190; Julia Davidson to John Davidson, February 25, 1864, and John Davidson to Julia Davidson, January 28, 1863, Davidson Family Papers, AHC. See also Simkins and Patton, *Women of the Confederacy*, 148–52. On the desperate condition of many lower-class women who sewed to live, see "Oppression," *Children's Friend*, December 1862, and *Montgomery Daily Advertiser*, June 23, 1864. Emma LeConte Diary, January 6, 1865, SHC.

35. See Mary Elizabeth Massey, *Ersatz in the Confederacy* (Columbia: University of South Carolina Press, 1952), and Parthenia Antoinette Hague, *A Blockaded Family: Life in Southern Alabama during the Civil War* (1888; rpt., Lincoln: University of Nebraska Press, 1991), for use of substitutes for unavailable items.

36. Lila Chunn to Willie Chunn, May 23, 1864, Chunn Papers, EU; Susan Middleton to Harriott Cheves, February 22, 1862, Cheves Family Papers, SCHS, quoted in Friedman, *Enclosed Garden*, 98.

CHAPTER THREE

1. Alexander Stephens, *Southern Confederacy* [Atlanta], March 13, 1861.

2. See Elizabeth Fox-Genovese, *Within the Plantation Household: Black and White Women of the Old South* (Chapel Hill: University of North Carolina Press, 1988), who calls slave management "a political question of the highest order" (206). In general, see also James L. Roark, *Masters without Slaves: Southern Planters in the Civil War and Reconstruction* (New York: Norton, 1977), and Marli Frances Weiner, "Plantation Mistress and Female Slaves: Gender, Race, and South Carolina Women, 1830–1880" (Ph.D. dissertation, University of Rochester, 1985). See also Jonathan M. Wiener, "Female Planters and Planters' Wives in Civil War and Reconstruction Alabama, 1850–1870," *Alabama Review* 30 (April 1977): 135–49.

3. *Macon Daily Telegraph*, December 17, 19, 1863, quoted in Clarence Mohr, *On the Threshold of Freedom: Masters and Slaves in Civil War Georgia* (Athens: University of Georgia Press, 1986), 221; James F. Bailey to General H. P. Watson, March 31, 1862, Governor's Files, ADAH. On Confederate conscription, see Albert Burton Moore, *Conscription and Conflict in the Confederacy* (New York: Macmillan, 1924), and Paul D. Escott, " 'The Cry of the Sufferers': The Problem of Welfare in the Confederacy," *Civil War History* 23 (September 1977): 228–40.

4. *Macon Daily Telegraph*, September 1, 1862, quoted in Mohr, *On the Threshold of Freedom*, 221.

5. See *The Statutes at Large of the Confederate States of America, passed at the Third Session of the First Congress* (Richmond: R. M. Smith, 1863), 158, 213–14; James M. Mathews, ed., *The Statutes at Large of the Confederate States of America* (Richmond:

R. M. Smith, 1862), 30; *Acts of Congress in Relation to the Conscription and Exemption Laws* (Houston: Texas Book and Job Printing House, 1862), 8 (quotation); *Southern Historical Society Papers* 48 (1941): 104; Moore, *Conscription and Conflict in the Confederacy*, 83–113.

6. Mrs. B. A. Smith to Governor Shorter, July 18, 1862, Governor's Files, ADAH; A Planter's Wife to Governor John J. Pettus, May 1, 1862, John J. Pettus Papers, MDAH; see also Letitia Andrews to Governor John J. Pettus, March 28, 1863, Pettus Papers, MDAH, and Lizzie Neblett to Will Neblett, April 26, 1863, Lizzie Neblett Papers, UTA.

7. Lucy A. Sharp to Hon. John C. Randolph, October 1, 1862, LRCSW, S1000, RG 109, reel 72, M437, NA; Sarah Whitesides to Hon. James Seddon, February 13, 1863, LRCSW, RG 109, reel 115, W136, NA; Catherine Edmondston, *Journal of a Secesh Lady: The Diary of Catherine Ann Devereux Edmondston, 1860–1866*, ed. Beth G. Crabtree and James W. Patton (Raleigh: North Carolina Department of Archives and History, 1979), 240; Frances Mitten to editors of the *Christian Index*, July 6, 1864, Thomas Watts, Governor's Papers, ADAH; Martha Fort to George Fort, October 7, 1861, Tomlinson Fort Papers, EU; Amanda Walker to Secretary of War, October 31, 1862, LRCSW, RG 109, reel 79, W1106, NA.

8. Keziah Brevard Diary, November 28, 1860, April 4, 1861, December 29, 1860, SCL.

9. C. Vann Woodward, ed., *Mary Chesnut's Civil War* (New Haven: Yale University Press, 1981), 198–99; Ada Bacot Diary, September 21, 1861, SCL.

10. Sarah Espy Diary, July 11, 13, 1861; see also June 3, 1861, ADAH; Reminiscences of Mrs. Ferrie Pegram, Lowry Shuford Collection, NCDAH; Winthrop D. Jordan, *Tumult and Silence at Second Creek: An Inquiry into a Civil War Slave Conspiracy* (Baton Rouge: Louisiana State University Press, 1992), 271, 288. See also Susan Bagby Diary, January 9, 1861, HC. On poisoning, see, for example, Annie Clark Jacobs Memoir, 59, MDAH; on arson, see Robert May, "Southern Elite Women, Sectional Extremism, and the Male Political Sphere," *Journal of Mississippi History* 50 (November 1988): 266; on murder, see Laura Comer Diary, June 5, 1862, SHC.

11. Laura Lee Diary, March 12, 1862, WM; Bacot Diary, February 27, 1861, SCL; *Mobile Advertiser and Register*, September 11, 1862; *Richmond Enquirer*, September 9, 1862; Abbie Brooks Diary, July 8, 1865, AHC.

12. Hattie Motley to James Seddon, May 25, 1863, LRCSW, RG 109, reel 103, M437, M430, NA; Mrs. M. K. Smith to Secretary of War, September 23, 1862, LRCSW, S997, RG 109, reel 72, NA; Nancy Hall et al. to Governor Zebulon Vance, August 11, 1863, Zebulon Vance Papers, NCDAH; Miss Lettie Kennedy in behalf of the Ladies of the N.E. beat of Jas. County, Miss., September 15, 1862, LRCSW, RG 109, reel 56, K148, NA. See also Lida Sessums to Governor John J. Pettus, October 8, 1862, Pettus Papers, MDAH.

13. Lucy Watkins to Secretary of War Randolph, October 13, 1862, LRCSW, RG 109, reel 79, M1091, NA; Harriet Pipkin to S. Cooper, Adj Gen. and Insp Gen, series 12 (LR), box 18, H2636, NA; Mary Watts to Hon. James Seddon, May 15, 1863, LRCSW, RG 109, reel 116, W315, NA. I obviously disagree with Martha Hodes, who states, "No great tide of sexual alarm engulfed white southerners as white men left white women at

home with slave men," in "Wartime Dialogues on Illicit Sex: White Women and Black Men," in *Divided Houses: Gender and the Civil War*, ed. Catherine Clinton and Nina Silber (New York: Oxford University Press, 1992), 239.

14. W. Maury Darst, "The Vicksburg Diary of Mrs. Alfred Ingraham," May 27, 1863, *Journal of Mississippi History* 44 (May 1982): 171; Betty Herndon Maury Diary, April 25, 1862, LC; Darden quoted in Jordan, *Tumult and Silence*, 304; Catherine Broun Diary, May 11, 1862, Broun Family Papers, RU. See also Clara Solomon Diary, May 8, 1862, LSU. On black troops, see also Ellen Moore to Samuel Moore, April 2, 1864, Moore Papers, SHC, and on black Confederate soldiers, Kate Rowland Diary, March 30, 1865, MOC.

15. Mary Greenhow Lee Diary, April 3, 1864, HL.

16. Constance Cary Harrison, "A Virginia Girl in the First Year of the War," *Century* 30 (August 1885): 606; Brevard Diary, November 28, 1860, SCL; Edmondston, *Journal of a Secesh Lady*, 301.

17. Elizabeth Saxon, *A Southern Woman's War Time Reminiscences* (Memphis: Pilcher, 1905), 33; Eugene D. Genovese, *Roll, Jordan, Roll: The World the Slaves Made* (New York: Pantheon, 1974), 99.

18. Broun Diary, May 1, 1864, RU; Anna Green to Martha Jones, April 16, 1862, Prescott-Jones Papers, GDAH; Leila Callaway to Morgan Callaway, January 22, 19, 1863, Morgan Callaway Papers, EU.

19. Joan Cashin, "'Since the War Broke Out': The Marriage of Kate and William McLure," in Clinton and Silber, *Divided Houses*, 200–212; Maria Hawkins to Governor Zebulon Vance, December 11, 1863, Vance Papers, NCDAH.

20. Edmondston, *Journal of a Secesh Lady*, 220; see also Octavia Stephens to Winston Stephens, July 15, 1862, Bryant-Stephens Papers, UFL; May, "Southern Elite Women," 255; and Bacot Diary, May 3, December 25, 1861, March 17, September 8, 1862, SCL.

21. Espy Diary, March 12, 1862, ADAH; see also arrangements made by Susan Blackford, described in Steve Tripp, "Restive Days: Race and Class Relations in Lynchburg, Virginia, 1858–1872" (Ph.D. dissertation, Carnegie-Mellon University, 1990), 151; Alice Palmer to Hattie Palmer, July 20, 1865, Palmer Family Papers, SCL; and Comer Diary, January 2, 1862, SHC. On this issue, see Fox-Genovese, *Within the Plantation Household*, 63. Catherine Clinton cites an unpublished study by Elizabeth Craven that finds, based on slave narratives and WPA interviews, that only 10 percent of slaves claimed to have been whipped by mistresses and 30 percent to have been ordered whipped by mistresses. Eight percent reported that mistresses had little or no authority. See Clinton, *The Plantation Mistress: Woman's World in the Old South* (New York: Pantheon, 1982), 187. See also, on plantation mistresses and war, Mohr, *On the Threshold of Freedom*, 221–22.

22. Lizzie Neblett to Will Neblett, March 12, 1864, Neblett Papers, UTA; Emily Dashiell Perkins to Belle Edmondson, February 22, 1864, in *A Lost Heroine of the Confederacy: The Diaries and Letters of Belle Edmondson*, ed. William Galbraith and Loretta Galbraith (Jackson: University Press of Mississippi, 1990), 192–93.

23. Leila Callaway to Morgan Callaway, November 7, 1862, Callaway Papers, EU;

Broun Diary, May 24, 1862, RU; Lizzie Neblett to Will Neblett, April 15, 1864, August 18, 1863, Neblett Papers, UTA.

24. Lizzie Neblett to Will Neblett, August 28, 1863, Neblett Papers, UTA. For a strikingly similar statement of female incapacity, see Carolina Pettigrew to Charles Pettigrew, June 19, 1862, Pettigrew Family Papers, SHC.

25. Lizzie Neblett to Will Neblett, April 26, 1863, Neblett Papers, UTA.

26. Ibid., August 18, 1863.

27. Ibid., November 17, 1863.

28. Ibid., November 23, 17, 1863.

29. Ibid., November 23, 1863.

30. Ibid., November 29, 1863.

31. Ibid.

32. Ibid., December 6, 1863.

33. Ibid.

34. Ibid., April 26, 1863. On Sarah's eavesdropping on other slaves, see also ibid., November 4, 25, 1863. Lizzie's comments on whipping appear in ibid., undated letter fragment [1864].

35. Ibid., February 12, July 3, June 5, 1864.

36. Ibid., March 20, 1864, letter fragment [1864].

37. Mollie to Dear Sister, September 23, 1864, William Augustus Chunn Papers, EU; Abigail Curlee, "A Study of Texas Slave Plantations, 1822–1865" (Ph.D. dissertation, University of Texas, Austin, 1932), 71. See also, on difficulties of hiring out, Martha Fort to George Fort, December 22, 1861, Tomlinson Fort Papers, EU; Sue Richardson Diary, January 2, 1865, EU; and Leila Callaway to Morgan Callaway, Callaway Papers, EU.

38. I am grateful to John Inscoe for drawing my attention to Mary Bell and the Alfred W. Bell Papers at Duke in a paper he delivered at the OAH in April 1992. My reading of her experience is quite different from his, however. See John Inscoe, "Coping in Confederate Appalachia: A Portrait of a Mountain Woman and Her Community at War," *North Carolina Historical Review* 69 (October 1992): 388–413, and "Mary Bell and Her Slave Purchases: Opportunity and Optimism in Confederate Appalachia" (unpublished paper kindly lent by the author). See also Gordon B. McKinney, "Women's Role in Civil War Western North Carolina," *North Carolina Historical Review* 69 (January 1992): 37–56.

39. Mary Bell to Alfred Bell, January 30, September 21, May 22, 29, 1862, Bell Papers, DU.

40. Ibid., March 11, 19, November 17, December 8, 1864.

41. Ibid., November 24, 1864.

42. Ibid., November 24, December 16, 1864. See Fox-Genovese, *Within the Plantation Household*, 142, on women's desire for household slaves.

43. Ella Gertrude Clanton Thomas, *The Secret Eye: The Journal of Ella Gertrude Clanton Thomas, 1848–1889*, ed. Virginia Ingraham Burr (Chapel Hill: University of North Carolina Press, 1990), 236; Mary Chesnut quoted in Elisabeth Muhlenfeld, *Mary Boykin Chesnut: A Biography* (Baton Rouge: Louisiana State University Press, 1981), 109; Mary Brown to John B. Brown, June 20, 1865, W. Vance Brown Papers, NCDAH;

Jane Howison Beale, *The Journal of Jane Howison Beale of Fredericksburg, Virginia, 1850–1862* (Fredericksburg: Historic Fredericksburg Foundation, 1979), 43.

44. Lila Chunn to Willie Chunn, March 18, 1863, Chunn Papers, EU; Sarah Kennedy Diary, August 19, 1863, TSL; Brevard Diary, January 26, 1861, SCL; Mrs. W. W. Boyce to W. W. Boyce, April 12, 1862, quoted in *Letters of Warren Akin, Confederate Congressman*, ed. Bell I. Wiley (Athens: University of Georgia Press, 1959), 4–5.

45. Brevard Diary, January 21, 1861, SCL; Lizzie Neblett to Will Neblett, undated letter fragment [1864], Neblett Papers, UTA.

46. Betty Herndon Maury, *The Confederate Diary of Betty Herndon Maury, 1861–1863*, ed. Alice Maury Parmalee (Washington, D.C.: privately printed, 1938), 89.

47. Beale, *Journal*, June 1, 1862, 47; Eliza Kendrick Walker Reminiscences, 117–18, ADAH.

48. Catherine Cochran Reminiscences, March 1862, vol. 1, VHS; Mary Greenhow Lee Diary, June 29, July 15, 1862, HL; Laura Lee Diary, June 13, 1863, August 18, 1864, WM. See also Sarah Fitch Poates Diary, July 6, 8, 23, November 1, 1863, Asa Fitch Papers, CU.

49. Mary Greenhow Lee Diary, March 22, 1862, HL.

50. Emma Mordecai Diary, May 6, 1865, Mordecai Family Papers, SHC; Genovese, *Roll, Jordan, Roll*, 105–6; Robert Manson Myers, ed., *The Children of Pride: A True Story of Georgia and the Civil War* (New Haven: Yale University Press, 1972), 1274, 1287, 1308.

51. Broun Diary, Christmas 1861, RU; Charlotte Ravenel, March 1, 11, 1865, in *Two Diaries from Middle St. John's, Berkeley, South Carolina, February–May 1865: Journals Kept by Susan R. Jervey and Miss Charlotte St. J. Ravenel* (Pinopolis, S.C.: St. John's Hunting Club, 1921), 37; Emma Slade Prescott Reminiscences, vol. 1, p. 10, AHC. See Fox-Genovese, *Within the Plantation Household*, 197.

52. Anne Firor Scott, *The Southern Lady: From Pedestal to Politics, 1830–1930* (Chicago: University of Chicago Press, 1970), 28–32. On this point, see Fox-Genovese, *Within the Plantation Household*, 115, 128. See also Amanda Worthington Diary, April 25, 1863, MDAH.

53. George C. Rable, *Civil Wars: Women and the Crisis of Southern Nationalism* (Urbana: University of Illinois Press, 1989), 255; Kate Foster Diary, November 15, 1863, DU; Susan Dabney Smedes, *Memorials of a Southern Planter*, ed. Fletcher Green (New York: Knopf, 1965), 223; Lizzie Carter to her sister, March 23, 1863, W. Vance Brown Papers, NCDAH; Martha Horne, "War Experiences," in *Reminiscences of the Women of Missouri during the Sixties*, by Missouri Division, United Daughters of the Confederacy (Jefferson City, Mo.: Hugh Stephens, 192-), 43; Worthington Diary, August 13, 1865, MDAH; Malvina Gist Waring, March 8, 1865, in *Heroines of Dixie: Winter of Desperation*, ed. Katharine M. Jones, 2 vols. (1955; rpt., Saint Simons Island, Ga.: Mockingbird Books, 1975), 2:197 (Malvina Black Gist was widowed early in the war and remarried to become a Waring after the end of the conflict.); *The Civil War Diary of Mrs. Henrietta Fitzhugh Barr, 1862–3*, ed. Sally Kiger Winn (Marietta, Ohio: Marietta College Press, 1963), 25. See also Annie Harper Reminiscences, 46, MDAH; Emma Holmes, *The Diary of Miss Emma Holmes, 1861–1866*, ed. John Marszalek

(Baton Rouge: Louisiana State University Press, 1979), 467; and Sarah Anne Grover Strickler Diary, August 12, 1862, UVA.

54. Amelia Barr to My Dear Jenny, March 3, [1866?], Amelia Barr Papers, UTA; Lizzie Neblett to Will Neblett, August 8, 1863, Neblett Papers, UTA; Matthella Page Harrison Diary, April 28, 1863, UVA.

CHAPTER FOUR

1. Maria M. Hubard Diary, September 10, 1861, VHS. Title quotation is from "A Daughter of Old Virginia" in *Richmond Daily Enquirer*, March 7, 1862.

2. I will rely here on what Claudia Goldin calls the "necessary and significant distinction" between "work for one's family for which neither money nor barter is exchanged, and work that is generally compensated within or outside the home." See Goldin, *Understanding the Gender Gap: An Economic History of American Women* (New York: Oxford University Press, 1990), 13. For economists, it is the market nature of this labor that is critical; for our purposes, the distinctions of public versus domestic—labor for family versus labor for others—is crucial as well.

3. See Alice Kessler-Harris, *Out to Work: A History of Wage Earning Women in the United States* (New York: Oxford University Press, 1982); Elizabeth Fox-Genovese, *Within the Plantation Household: Black and White Women of the Old South* (Chapel Hill: University of North Carolina Press, 1988); Suzanne Lebsock, *The Free Women of Petersburg: Status and Culture in a Southern Town, 1784–1860* (New York: Norton, 1984); Jane H. Pease and William H. Pease, *Ladies, Women, and Wenches: Choice and Constraint in Antebellum Charleston and Boston* (Chapel Hill: University of North Carolina Press, 1990); and Victoria E. Bynum, *Unruly Women: The Politics of Social and Sexual Control in the Old South* (Chapel Hill: University of North Carolina Press, 1992), 7–8.

4. Barnwell quoted by Emma Holmes, *The Diary of Miss Emma Holmes, 1861–1866*, ed. John Marszalek (Baton Rouge: Louisiana State University Press, 1979), 102. Lila Chunn to Willie Chunn, March 20, 1862, Willie Chunn Papers, DU.

5. Ella Gertrude Clanton Thomas, *The Secret Eye: The Journal of Ella Gertrude Clanton Thomas, 1848–1889*, ed. Virginia Ingraham Burr (Chapel Hill: University of North Carolina Press, 1990), 237.

6. Subheading quoted from Mary Jane Cook Chadick Diary, September 10, 1864, DU; W. Buck Yearns and John G. Barrett, eds., *North Carolina Civil War Documentary* (Chapel Hill: University of North Carolina Press, 1980), 231, 237; Thomas Woody, *A History of Women's Education in the United States*, 2 vols. (New York: Science Press, 1929), 1:498. Joel Perlman is finding a distinctively lower rate of feminization in southern than northern teaching in this period. Phone conversation, July 5, 1994.

7. Calvin Wiley, "Report of the Superintendent of Common Schools for the Year 1862," in Yearns and Barrett, *North Carolina Civil War Documentary*, 231; *Augusta Daily Constitutionalist*, May 14, 1863.

8. *Central Presbyterian*, September 8, 1864; J. K. Kirkpatrick, "The Duty of Females

in Relation to the Future Educational Interests of Our Country," in Yearns and Barrett, *North Carolina Documentary*, 232; Kirkpatrick, *North Carolina Journal of Education* 7 (July 1864): 88–89. See efforts of North Carolina State Education Association to encourage female teaching, "Proceedings of the 6th Annual Meeting of the State Education Association," *North Carolina Journal of Education* 4 (November 1861): 326.

9. Hollins Institute, *The Education of Teachers in the South . . . To which is Attached A Catalogue of the Institute* (Lynchburg: Virginia Power Press, 1864), 15; "The Education of Southern Women," *De Bow's Review* 31 (October–November 1861): 382–83. See Rachel Bryan Stillman, "Education in the Confederate States of America, 1861–1865" (Ph.D. dissertation, University of Illinois, Champaign-Urbana, 1972).

10. "Education of Southern Women," 382–83, 381, 385. See Christie Anne Farnham, *The Education of the Southern Belle: Higher Education and Student Socialization in the Antebellum South* (New York: New York University Press, 1994).

11. "Education of Southern Women," 384, 385.

12. "Educated Woman—In Peace and War," *Southern Field and Fireside*, April 11, 1863.

13. James G. Ramsey, *An Address Delivered by Hon. James G. Ramsey, before the young ladies of Concord Female College at Statesville, May 29th, 1863* (Statesville, N.C.: Iredell Press, 1863), 16; Hollins Institute, *Education of Teachers*, 13–14, 15.

14. *Annual Catalogue of the Trustees, Officers, and Students of the Tuscaloosa Female College* (Tuscaloosa, Ala.: J. F. Warren, 1861), 8.

15. Chadick Diary, September 10, 1864, DU; *Richmond Enquirer*, July 10, 1863.

16. Virginia Daniel Woodruff Diary, May 1, 1862, HC.

17. Abbie Brooks Diary, January 23, 1865, AHC; Mary Stringfield to W. W. Stringfield, March 27, 1864, W. W. Stringfield Papers, NCDAH; Jennie Pendleton Journal, June 15, 1864, Mary E. W. Shell Papers, MDAH; Emily Perkins to Belle Edmondson, in *A Lost Heroine of the Confederacy: The Diaries and Letters of Belle Edmondson*, ed. William Galbraith and Loretta Galbraith (Jackson: University Press of Mississippi, 1990), 7; Sarah Morgan, *The Civil War Diary of Sarah Morgan*, ed. Charles East (Athens: University of Georgia Press, 1991), 153.

18. Quoted in Fox-Genovese, *Within the Plantation Household*, 46; Holmes, *Diary*, 172; Anais to My Dear Husband, April 29, 1863, Warren Ogden, Collector, Miscellaneous Civil War Letters, TU; Margaret Gillis Diary, July 19, 1863, May 30, 1864, ADAH.

19. Caroline Kean Hill Davis Diary, January 2, 1862, February 28, 1863, VHS; Clara D. MacLean Diary, August 11, 1861, DU; Holmes, *Diary*, 315, 410–11, 418; Emma Slade Prescott Reminiscences, vol. 2, pp. 32–33, AHC.

20. Brooks Diary, February 27, March 6, February 1, 1865, AHC, and Amelia Pinkind to Isabella Woodruff, August 4, 1862, Isabella Ann Woodruff Papers, DU.

21. Subheading quoted from Malvina Gist in *Heroines of Dixie: Winter of Desperation*, ed. Katharine M. Jones, 2 vols. (1955; rpt., Saint Simons Island, Ga.: Mockingbird Books, 1975), 2:199. Elizabeth Richmond to Zebulon Vance, April 5, 1864, Zebulon Vance Papers, NCDAH. See also Delia Jones to Zebulon Vance, January 6, 1863, Vance Papers, NCDAH.

22. Diana Johnston to Jefferson Davis, July 18, 1864, RG 109, Citizens File, NA; Lizzie Yarrington to Jefferson Davis, November 9, 1864, Letters Received, Confederate Secretary of the Treasury, RG 365, NA; Annie Bronaugh to the Secretary of War, March 21, 1863, LRCSW, reel 82, B233, NA; M. H. Sydnor to Jefferson Davis, April 9, 1864, RG 109, Citizens File, NA; Catherine Windle to Jefferson Davis, March 6, 1862, RG 109, Citizens File, NA. See also Kate Rowland Diary, February 5, 1862, MOC.

23. Sue Whiting to Jefferson Davis, April 28, 1864, RG 109, Citizens File, NA.

24. George C. Rable, *Civil Wars: Women and the Crisis of Southern Nationalism* (Urbana: University of Illinois Press, 1989), 131–35, and Janet E. Kaufman, "Treasury Girls," *Civil War Times Illustrated* 25 (May 1986): 32–38.

25. Inspection Report, Quartermaster Department, Richmond, August 26, 1864, Inspection Reports, RG 109, reel 7, 22, M935, NA; *Richmond Enquirer*, November 4, 1862; memorandum, John Whitford Papers, NCDAH; J. C. Compton, "The Selma Arsenal," W file, ADAH; Mary Ann Huff, "The Role of Women in Confederate Georgia" (M.A. thesis, Emory University, 1967), 44; Kaufman, "Treasury Girls," 36; *Richmond Enquirer*, March 17, 1863. There was widespread recognition of the injustice of such low salaries for clothing workers. See *Richmond Daily Enquirer*, November 3, 1863, and "Oppression," *Children's Friend*, December 1862. See also Elizabeth Maxwell et al. to Zebulon Vance, October 8, 1864, Vance Papers, NCDAH.

26. Mary DeTreville, "Extracts from the Letters of a Confederate Girl to a Cousin in Virginia," in *South Carolina Women in the Confederacy*, ed. Mrs. Thomas Taylor, Mrs. A. T. Smythe, Mrs. August Kohn, Miss M. B. Poppenheim, and Miss Martha Washington, 2 vols. (Columbia, S.C.: State Co., 1903), 2:181. See also Julia Morgan, who describes her children working at cartridge making. When offered pay, "The girls were too patriotic to take any money for their services, but the little boys thought they would make a little money for themselves." Julia [Mrs. Irby] Morgan, *How It Was: Four Years among the Rebels* (Nashville: Publishing House of the Methodist Episcopal Church, 1892), 105.

27. MacLean Diary, May 31, 1862, DU; and C. Vann Woodward, ed., *Mary Chesnut's Civil War* (New Haven: Yale University Press, 1981), 350.

28. Adelaide Stuart to her aunt, November 7, September 30, 1864, January 23, 1865, September 30, 1864, John Dimitry Papers, DU.

29. Malvina Gist in Katharine M. Jones, *Heroines of Dixie*, 2:120, 173, 199, 200.

30. Subheading quoted from Mary Chesnut, June 29, 1861, in Woodward, *Mary Chesnut's Civil War*, 85. Susan Reverby, *Ordered to Care: The Dilemma of American Nursing, 1850–1945* (Cambridge: Cambridge University Press, 1987); Charles Rosenberg, *The Care of Strangers* (New York: Basic Books, 1986); Rosenberg, "Florence Nightingale on Contagion: The Hospital as Moral Universe," in *Explaining Epidemics and Other Studies in the History of Medicine* (New York: Cambridge University Press, 1992); Jane E. Schultz, "The Inhospitable Hospital: Gender and Professionalism in Civil War Medicine," *Signs* 17 (Winter 1992): 363–92; Francis B. Simkins and James W. Patton, "The Work of Southern Women among the Sick and Wounded of the Confederate Armies," *Journal of Southern History* 1 (November 1935): 475–96; Ann Douglas Wood, "The War within a War: Women Nurses in the Union Army," *Civil War History*

18 (September 1972): 197–212; Nina Bennett Smith, "The Women Who Went to the War: The Union Army Nurse in the Civil War" (Ph.D. dissertation, Northwestern University, 1981); Evelyn J. Driver, "Confederate Nursing: State of the Art, 1861–1865" (unpublished paper kindly lent by the author); Arlene Keeling, "Supporting the Cause: Nursing Activities of Southern Women during the Civil War" (unpublished paper kindly lent by the author); Sister Mary Denis Maher, *To Bind up the Wounds: Catholic Sister Nurses in the U.S. Civil War* (Westport, Conn.: Greenwood, 1989); Rable, *Civil Wars*, 121–28; H. H. Cunningham, *Doctors in Gray: The Confederate Medical Service* (Baton Rouge: Louisiana State University Press, 1958). On the prevalence of male nursing in the War of 1812, see Victor Robinson, *White Caps: The Story of Nursing* (Philadelphia: Lippincott, 1946), 140–42.

31. Kate Cumming, *Kate: The Journal of a Confederate Nurse*, ed. Richard Barksdale Harwell (Baton Rouge: Louisiana State University Press, 1959), 135; *Mobile Advertiser and Register*, June 11, 1862; *Milledgeville Southern Federal Union*, July 22, 1862.

32. *Confederate Baptist*, October 15, 1862; "Florence Nightingale and Southern Ladies," *Southern Monthly* 2 (May 1862): 6, 7.

33. *Charleston Daily Courier*, August 16, 1861; Ladies Defense Association, June 8, 1861, MOC; *Atlanta Daily Intelligencer*, November 6, 1862, September 27, 1861; *Augusta Weekly Constitutionalist*, September 4, 1861.

34. Mary Rutledge Fogg to Jefferson Davis, September 16, 1861, 5668, LRCSW, RG 109, reel 10, M437, NA; Letitia Tyler Semple to Judah Benjamin, November 19, 1861, 7535, LRCSW, RG 109, reel 15, M437, NA; Letitia Tyler Semple to Edward Joyner, July 17, 1861, 2338, LRCSW, RG 109, reel 5, M437, NA; Mrs. Fielding Lewis Taylor, "Captain Sallie Tompkins," *Confederate Veteran* 24 (November 1916): 521, 524; William Anderson to Juliet Opie Hopkins, September 1, 11, 1861, Alabama Hospital Papers, ADAH; see also Lucille Griffith, "Mrs Juliet Opie Hopkins and Alabama Military Hospitals," *Alabama Review* 6 (April 1953): 99–120; "Florence Nightingale and Southern Ladies," 5–9.

35. W file, ADAH; Greenville Ladies Association Minutes, January 3, 1863, DU; Louise Medway to Jefferson Davis, September 13, 1864, Jefferson Davis Papers, DU; Meta Morris Grimball Diary, October 10, 1862, SHC.

36. J. B. Magruder to Leroy Walker, July 18, 1861, 2686, LRCSW, RG 109, reel 10, NA; Magruder also noted that slave women could be hired for half the cost of a soldier's salary. On African Americans working in hospitals, see Clarence Mohr, *On the Threshold of Freedom: Masters and Slaves in Civil War Georgia* (Athens: University of Georgia Press, 1986), 128–35. Mohr lists statistics of attendants in numerous Georgia hospitals, in Samuel Hollinsworth Stout Papers, UTA; see similar statistics for Montgomery, Ala., December 26, 1864, in W File, Confederate Hospitals, ADAH; *Journal of the Congress of the Confederate States of America*, vol. 1, 1861–65 (Washington, D.C.: Government Printing Office, 1904–5), 726; and U.S. War Department, *The War of the Rebellion: A Compilation of the Official Records of the Union and Confederate Armies*, 127 vols. and index (Washington, D.C.: Government Printing Office, 1880–1901), series 1, 4:883.

37. Cumming, *Kate*, 16.

38. "Journal of the Confederate Congress, First Congress, Second Session," in *Southern Historical Society Papers* (Richmond: Byrd Printers, 1928), 46:237, Senate, September 25, 1862.

39. *Official Records*, series 2, 4:199–200, September 27, 1862. *Confederate Baptist*, October 8, 1862; Rable, *Civil Wars*, 166.

40. Phoebe Yates Pember, *A Southern Woman's Story: Life in Confederate Richmond*, ed. Bell Irvin Wiley (1959; rpt., Saint Simons Island, Ga.: Mockingbird Books, 1974), 16, 115. Pember's name is also spelled Phebe in some sources. I will use only Phoebe in the text but will cite original spelling in the notes.

41. Ibid., 17.

42. Ibid., 15–16; Fannie A. Beers, *Memories: A Record of Personal Experience and Adventure during Four Years of War* (Philadelphia: Lippincott, 1888), 94, 204; Ada Bacot Diary, January 10, 1863, SCL. See also J. Fraise Richard, *The Florence Nightingale of the Southern Army: Experiences of Mrs. Ella K. Newsom, Confederate Nurse in the Great War of 1861–1865* (New York: Broadway, 1914); Emily V. Mason, "Memories of a Hospital Matron," *Atlantic Monthly*, September, October 1902, 305–18, 475–85; Julia Morgan, *How It Was*; and South Carolina Hospital Aid Association, *Report of the South Carolina Hospital Aid Association in Virginia, 1861–2* (Richmond: MacFarlane and Fergusson, 1862).

43. Pember, *Southern Woman's Story*, 19.

44. Ibid., 34.

45. Ibid., 57; Cumming, *Kate*, 65.

46. Cumming, *Kate*, 124, 208.

47. Ibid., 135.

48. Ibid., 198, 113.

49. Emma Crutcher to Will Crutcher, March 20, 21, 1862, Crutcher-Shannon Papers, UTA.

50. Ibid., April 7, 8, 1862.

51. Pember, *Southern Woman's Story*, 21. See Sara Crane Reminiscences, Nicolson Family Papers, AHC; Lila to Uncle Tom, July 1864, Tomlinson Fort Papers, EU; Emma Mordecai Diary, May 25, June 17, 1864, Mordecai Family Papers, SHC; Constance Cary Harrison, "Richmond Scenes in '62," in *Battles and Leaders of the Civil War*, ed. Robert Underwood Johnson and Clarence Clough Buel, 4 vols. (1884; rpt., New York: Castle Books, 1956), 2:445; and Sara Agnes (Mrs. Roger) Pryor, *Reminiscences of Peace and War* (New York: Macmillan, 1904), 182.

52. Pryor, *Reminiscences*, 182–83, 187, 185.

53. Woodward, *Mary Chesnut's Civil War*, 158, 372, 667, 668.

54. Cornelia Peake McDonald, *A Woman's Civil War: A Diary, with Reminiscences of the War, from March 1862*, edited and with an introduction by Minrose C. Gwin (Madison: University of Wisconsin Press, 1992), 38; on amputation, see also Mary Foushee to Juliet Opie Hopkins, August 8, 1861, Alabama Hospitals, ADAH; Cumming, *Kate*, 25; Harriette Cary Diary, May 8, 1862, WM; Mrs. S. E. D. Smith, *The Soldier's Friend* (Memphis, Tenn.: Bulletin, 1867), 53; and Mary Greenhow Lee Diary, November 12, 1862, HL. See also Laurann Figg and Jane Farrell-Beck, "Amputation in

the Civil War: Physical and Social Dimensions," *Journal of the History of Medicine* 48 (October 1993): 454–75.

55. Mary Greenhow Lee Diary, September 25, July 11, 1863, HL; Laura Lee Diary, September 20, 1862, WM.

56. Mary Greenhow Lee Diary, September 27, 1862, August 14, 1863, July 29, 1864, May 28, 1862, HL; Laura Lee Diary, September 20, 1864, WM.

57. Mary Greenhow Lee Diary, April 1, November 12, 1862, November 6, 1863, HL; Laura Lee Diary, April 1, 1862, July 11, 1864, WM; Percy L. Rainwater, ed., "The Civil War Letters of Cordelia Scales," *Journal of Mississippi History* 1 (July 1939): 173; Bacot Diary, January 1, 28, February 14, 1862, SCL. See also Catherine Broun Diary, September 13, 1862, Broun Family Papers, RU.

58. Mary Foushee to Juliet Opie Hopkins, August 6, 1861, Alabama Hospitals, ADAH. On sick nurses, see also Cumming, *Kate*, 75, and 262, where she describes Mrs. Newsom's withdrawal from hospital service because of illness, and South Carolina Hospital Aid Association, *Report*, 15.

59. See Charleston *Courier*, July 16, 1863, and Charleston *Mercury*, July 30, 1863.

60. Laura Lee Diary, September 20, 1864, September 27, 1862, WM; see, for another similar example, Susan Caldwell's description of the influx of wounded after Antietam into Warrenton, Virginia, in *"My Heart Is So Rebellious": The Caldwell Letters, 1861–1865*, ed. J. Michael Welton (Warrenton, Va.: Fauquier National Bank, 1991), 155; on Culpeper, Virginia, as a hospital, see Daniel Sutherland, "Introduction to War: The Civilians of Culpeper County, Virginia," *Civil War History* 37 (June 1991): 134.

61. Cumming, *Kate*, 99; Smith, *Soldier's Friend*, 80.

62. Emma Crutcher to Will Crutcher, February 7, March 21, 1862, Crutcher-Shannon Papers, UTA; Evans quoted in Richard, *Florence Nightingale*, 93; Julia Morgan, *How It Was*, 123–24.

63. Mildred Duckworth to Juliet Opie Hopkins, November 11, 1861, Alabama Hospitals, ADAH.

64. Cumming, *Kate*, 4. See the same sentiments on 191.

65. On destruction of sensibility, see Pember, *Southern Woman's Story*, 114; on limiting compassion, see Cumming, *Kate*, 153; Woodward, *Mary Chesnut's Civil War*, 677, 304; MacLean Diary, March 3, 1862, DU.

66. Woodward, *Mary Chesnut's Civil War*, 85.

67. Cumming, *Kate*, 191; Mohr, *On the Threshold of Freedom*, 130–35; report to George William Brent from R. L. Brodie, Medical Division of the West, December 26, 1864, W File, Confederate Hospitals, Montgomery, ADAH; Consolidated Morning Report, January 14, 1864, Helen Thompson Papers, MDAH. This sense of inadequacy and of what one might label "survivor's guilt" is evident in accounts of other nurses' experiences. See Vera Brittain, *A Testament of Youth* (1933; rpt., New York: Wideview Books, 1978).

68. Holmes, *Diary*, 315; Emma Crutcher to Will Crutcher, March 21, 1862, Crutcher-Shannon Papers, UTA.

69. Woodward, *Mary Chesnut's Civil War*, 350.

1. George Peddy Cuttino, ed., *Saddle Bag and Spinning Wheel: Being the Civil War Letters of George W. Peddy and Kate Featherston Peddy* (Macon, Ga.: Mercer University Press, 1981), 180. For almost identical language, see Minerva to Robert Bone, January 17, 1863, Robert Bone Papers, EU; Ellen to Samuel Moore, January 22, 1863, Samuel J. C. Moore Papers, SHC; and Octavia to Winston Stephens, November 21, 1862, November 6, 1863, Bryant-Stephens Papers, UFL. Title quotation is from Julia to John Davidson, June 29, 1863, Davidson Family Papers, AHC; subheading quoted from A. Grima to Alfred Grima, November 27, 1863, Grima Family Papers, THNOC. French translated by the author.

2. Emma to Will Crutcher, March 6, January 22, 1862, Crutcher-Shannon Papers, UTA. See also Lizzie Neblett to Will Neblett, May 30, 1863, Lizzie Neblett Papers, UTA; Mary Bell to Alfred Bell, May 28, January 30, 1862, Alfred W. Bell Papers, DU; and Mary Curry to Duncan Curry, March 31, 1862, Curry Hill Plantation Papers, GDAH.

3. Emma Crutcher to Will Crutcher, January 22, 1862, Crutcher-Shannon Papers, UTA. On dream interpretation, see also Lizzie Ozburn to Em, February 18, 1861, Katherine Elizabeth Ozburn Papers, GDAH.

4. Emma to Will Crutcher, January 4, 1861 [misdated; correct year is 1862], Crutcher-Shannon Papers, MDAH; Ella Gertrude Clanton Thomas, *The Secret Eye: The Journal of Ella Gertrude Clanton Thomas, 1848–1889*, ed. Virginia Ingraham Burr (Chapel Hill: University of North Carolina Press, 1990), 193; Emma Holmes, *The Diary of Miss Emma Holmes, 1861–1866*, ed. John Marszalek (Baton Rouge: Louisiana State University Press, 1979), 147; Caroline Kean Hill Davis Diary, February 20, 1865, VHS.

5. M. M. Dulany Diary, June 13, 1862, VHS; Lizzie Ozburn to Jimmie Ozburn, September 12, 1861, Ozburn Papers, GDAH. See, on waiting for news, Davis Diary, July 8, 1862, VHS; on bad news as relief, see Margaret Beckwith Reminiscences, June 1, 1862, 2:6, VHS. Margaret Junkin Preston's sister heard of her son's July death in December 1863; see Elizabeth Randolph Allan, ed., *The Life and Letters of Margaret Junkin Preston* (Boston: Houghton Mifflin, 1903), 172. Catherine Cochran observed, "The silence becomes positively appalling," May 15, 1863, in Catherine Cochran Reminiscences, vol. 1, VHS.

6. A. Grima to Alfred Grima, November 27, 1863, Grima Family Papers, THNOC; Richard F. Ridgway, *Self-Sufficiency at All Costs: Confederate Post Office Operations in North Carolina, 1861–1865* (Charlotte: North Carolina Postal History Society, 1988), 50. See also Mary Elizabeth Massey, *Refugee Life in the Confederacy* (Baton Rouge: Louisiana State University Press, 1964), 127. "Separation is always very sad, even with the ability to write freely, but when one is deprived of receiving news from those who are dear, it is horrible to bear." Translation by the author.

7. Emma to Will Crutcher, January 4, 1861 [misdated; correct year is 1862], Crutcher-Shannon Papers, MDAH; Fannie Gordon to General John Gordon, May 15, 1864, Fannie B. Gordon Papers, GDAH; see Ellen to Samuel Moore, March 22, 1863,

Moore Papers, SHC; Lizzie Neblett to Will Neblett, May 29, 1864, Neblett Papers, UTA; *Huntsville Democrat*, August 21, 1861; Mary Bell to Alfred Bell, May 22, 1862, Bell Papers, DU. See also Minerva to Robert Bone, December 23, 1861, Bone Papers, EU. On letters, see Steven M. Stowe, *Intimacy and Power in the Old South: Ritual in the Lives of the Planters* (Baltimore: Johns Hopkins University Press, 1987), esp. 50–121.

8. Lizzie Neblett to Will Neblett, June 9, 1863, May 9, 1864, Neblett Papers, UTA; Emma Crutcher to Will Crutcher, March 13, 1862, Crutcher-Shannon Papers, UTA. See Cornelia Noble Diary, October 8, 1862, UTA.

9. George Peddy to Kate Peddy, April 18, 1862, in Cuttino, *Saddle Bag*, 83; David McRaven to Amanda, December 25, 1864, in "The Correspondence of David Olando McRaven and Amanda Nantz McRaven, 1864–1865," ed. Louis A. Brown, *North Carolina Historical Review* 26 (January 1949): 73; Mary Bell to Alfred Bell, February 11, 1862, Bell Papers, DU.

10. Rose Lewis to her husband, February 22, 1863, Burwell Boykin Lewis Papers, DU; Emma Crutcher to Will Crutcher, February 1, 1862, Crutcher-Shannon Papers, UTA; Emma Crutcher to Will Crutcher, March 14, 1862, Crutcher-Shannon Papers, MDAH; Julia to John Davidson, June 29, 1863, Davidson Family Papers, AHC. See also Jorantha Semmes, February 7, 1864, Benedict Joseph Semmes Papers, SHC.

11. Sarah Kennedy Diary, December 22, 1862, TSL; Susan Caldwell to Lycurgus Caldwell, December 14, 1862, in *"My Heart Is So Rebellious": The Caldwell Letters, 1861–1865*, ed. J. Michael Welton (Warrenton, Va.: Fauquier National Bank, 1991), 162. See also E. P. Petty to My dear Wife, February 12, 1863, in Elijah P. Petty, *Journey to Pleasant Hill: The Civil War Letters of Captain Elijah P. Petty, Walker's Texas Division, CSA*, ed. Norman D. Brown (San Antonio: University of Texas Press, 1982), 140.

12. John Davidson to Julia Davidson, November 3, 1862, Davidson Family Papers, AHC. " 'Seeing the elephant,' " John Phillip Reid has written, meant "to face a particularly severe ordeal . . . to learn the realities of a situation first hand, or to encounter the unbelievable." The term gained currency in the prewar years as a description for crossing the continent on the overland trail. See Reid, *Law for the Elephant: Property and Social Behavior on the Overland Trail* (San Marino, Calif.: Huntington Library, 1980), ix, x. My thanks to Sarah Gordon for this reference.

13. Cuttino, *Saddle Bag*, 197, 203, 51.

14. Mary Bell to Alfred Bell, August 26, January 30, August 30, 1862, Bell Papers, DU.

15. Lizzie Neblett to Will Neblett, April 15, May 13, 1864, Neblett Papers, UTA.

16. Emma Crutcher to Will Crutcher, February 1, April 8, 1862, Crutcher-Shannon Papers, UTA; Emily Harris Diary, November 7, 1863, WC; Lavinia to R. L. Dabney, May 5, 1862, C. W. Dabney Papers, SHC. On shunning responsibility, see "The Diary of Louisa Brown Pearl," ed. James Hoobler, *Tennessee Historical Quarterly* 38 (Fall 1979): 308–21, and Octavia to Winston Stephens, October 1, 1862, Bryant-Stephens Papers, UFL.

17. See Welton, *"My Heart Is So Rebellious."*

18. Petty, *Pleasant Hill*, 103; Morgan Callaway to Leila Callaway, August 28, December 20, 1863, Morgan Callaway Papers, EU.

19. John Davidson to Julia Davidson, August 12, 1863, Davidson Family Papers, AHC.

20. Mary Bell to Alfred Bell, July 27, September 21, 1862, Bell Papers, DU.

21. Octavia to Winston Stephens, October 31, 1862, Bryant-Stephens Papers, UFL; Robert Bullock to Amanda Bullock, November 8, 1863, Robert Bullock Papers, GDAH; James Reed, *The Birth Control Movement and American Society: From Private Vice to Public Virtue* (New York: Basic Books, 1978).

22. Lizzie Neblett to Will Neblett, August 13, December 6, 1863, July 3, May 17, 1864, Neblett Papers, UTA. See also Ellen to Samuel Moore, December 5, 7, 1861, Moore Papers, SHC, and James Turner to Ann Turner, February 8, 1864, Anne Marie Stewart Turner Papers, RU. When Turner comes home, he promises he will "love and admire but keep at a distance" to soothe her fears of pregnancy.

23. John Davidson to Julia Davidson, January 20, 1861, Davidson Family Papers, AHC. See Octavia Stephens's discussion of Winston's sexual frustration, Octavia to Winston Stephens, May 26, 1863, Bryant-Stephens papers, UFL.

24. John Davidson to Julia Davidson, March 5, 1864; see also March 22, 1864, Davidson Family Papers, AHC. See Octavia Stephens's concerns about brothels and her husband's fidelity and his reassurances, Octavia to Winston Stephens, July 27, November 21, 1862, June 19, 1863, January 18, 1864, Bryant-Stephens Papers, UFL.

25. Lizzie Neblett to Will Neblett, July 3, 1864, Neblett Papers, UTA.

26. Cuttino, *Saddle Bag*, 20; Julia Davidson to John Davidson, May 1, 1864, Davidson Family Papers, AHC; Will Neblett to Lizzie Neblett, November 22, 1863, and Lizzie Neblett to Will Neblett, November 29, 1863, Neblett Papers, UTA.

27. Martha Hodes, "Wartime Dialogues on Illicit Sex: White Women and Black Men," in *Divided Houses: Gender and the Civil War*, ed. Catherine Clinton and Nina Silber (New York: Oxford University Press, 1992), 235.

28. Lizzie Neblett to Will Neblett, March 28, 1864, and Will Neblett to Lizzie Neblett, November 23, 1863, Neblett Papers, UTA. See similar tale in Ellen to Samuel Moore, April 10, 1864, Moore Papers, SHC.

29. John Davidson to Julia, March 5, April 1, 1864, and Julia Davidson to John Davidson, April 17, February 25, 1864, Davidson Family Papers, AHC.

30. Lila Chunn to Willie Chunn, March 18, 1863, Willie Chunn Papers, DU; Cuttino, *Saddle Bag*, 255.

31. Lila Chunn to Willie Chunn, May 10, 1863, Chunn Papers, DU; Lizzie Ozburn to Jimmie Ozburn, September 11, 1861, Ozburn Papers, GDAH; Judith Walzer Leavitt, *Brought to Bed: Childbearing in America, 1750–1950* (New York: Oxford University Press, 1986); Richard W. Wertz and Dorothy C. Wertz, *Lying In: A History of Childbirth in America* (New York: Free Press, 1977); Sally G. McMillen, *Motherhood in the Old South: Pregnancy, Childbirth, and Infant Rearing* (Baton Rouge: Louisiana State University Press, 1990); Carroll Smith-Rosenberg, "The Female World of Love and Ritual," *Signs* 1 (Autumn 1975): 1–29.

32. Morgan Callaway to Leila Callaway, May 7, 1862; Leila Callaway to Morgan Callaway, September 30, October 6, 1862; Morgan Callaway to Leila Callaway, October 16, 1862; and Leila Callaway to Morgan Callaway, October 27, November 7, 1862, Callaway Papers, EU.

33. Anais Eustis to Celestine Favrot, March 8, 1865, Henry Favrot Papers, TU; Emma Crutcher to Will Crutcher, December 28, 1861, Crutcher-Shannon Papers, UTA (subheading quoted from this letter). See also Margaret Gillis Diary, May 5, 1861, ADAH, begging to be spared the burden of children, an ironic statement given that she would die in childbirth after the war.

34. Thomas, *Secret Eye*, 187; Allan, *Life and Letters of Margaret Junkin Preston*, 158; Mrs. Thomas Taylor, Mrs. A. T. Smythe, Mrs. August Kohn, Miss M. B. Poppenheim, and Miss Martha Washington, eds., *South Carolina Women in the Confederacy*, 2 vols. (Columbia, S.C.: State Co., 1903), 2:145; Ellen Moore to Samuel Moore, August 12, 1861, Moore Papers, SHC; Kennedy Diary, October 5, 1863, September 10, 1864, TSL.

35. Carrie Berry Diary, August 3, 9, September 10, 4, 1864, AHC.

36. Mary Bell to Alfred Bell, May 22, 1862, Bell Papers, DU; Mary W. M. Bell to her husband, September 1, 1863, Mary Walker Meriwether Bell Papers, TSL; Noble Diary, May 18, 1863, UTA; Ellen Moore to Samuel Moore, July 23, May 1, 1863, Moore Papers, SHC.

37. Susan Caldwell, in Welton, *"My Heart Is So Rebellious,"* 54, 247; Leila Callaway to Morgan Callaway, April 24, 1862, and Morgan Callaway to Leila Callaway, April 24, 1862, Callaway Papers, EU; Mary W. M. Bell to her husband, n.d. [1863], Bell Papers, TSL. See "To Mothers," *Edgefield Advertiser*, March 18, 1863.

38. Lizzie Neblett to Will Neblett, August 13, December 13, October 28, 1863, May 17, March 12, 1864, Neblett Papers, UTA. See also Ellen Moore to Samuel Moore, August 2, 1863, Moore Papers, SHC. Contemporary scholars of family violence emphasize the importance of distinguishing between punishment and abuse. Linda Gordon, in particular, stresses the significance of cultural and historical perspectives in establishing that distinction. I view the disapproval of Lizzie's aunt and the anticipated disapproval of Will as indications that whipping a ten-month-old baby was not generally regarded as acceptable childrearing in white families of nineteenth-century Texas. See Gordon, *Heroes of Their Own Lives: The Politics and History of Family Violence* (New York: Viking Penguin, 1988), 5, 180. See also Bertram Wyatt-Brown, "Child Abuse, Public Policy, and Childrearing: An Historical Approach," in *Governing the Young: Work Papers #2*, ed. Barbara Finkelstein (College Park: University of Maryland School of Education, 1981), 1–34. Historian Philip Greven makes the çase for regarding all physical punishment as abuse in *Spare the Child: The Religious Roots of Punishment and the Psychological Impact of Physical Abuse* (New York: Knopf, 1991). For a view of the repercussions of the violence of slavery within the black family, see Brenda Stevenson, "Distress and Discord in Virginia Slave Families, 1830–1860," in *In Joy and in Sorrow: Women, Family, and Marriage in the Victorian South, 1830–1900*, ed. Carol Bleser (New York: Oxford University Press, 1991).

39. Bertram Wyatt-Brown, *Southern Honor: Ethics and Behavior in the Old South* (New York: Oxford University Press, 1982), 169. See Kate Rowland's ambivalence about physical punishment of her young son, Kate Rowland Diary, November 19, 1864, EU.

40. Grace Elmore Diary, February 11, 1865, SCL. Subheading quoted from this letter.

41. L. Virginia French Diary, September 25, 1864, TSL. See also Herschel Gower, "Beersheba Springs and L. Virginia French: The Novelist as Historian," *Tennessee Historical Quarterly* 42 (Summer 1983): 115–37; and Virginia Lewis Peck, "The Life and Works of L. Virginia French" (Ph.D. dissertation, Vanderbilt University, 1939).

42. French Diary, February 8, 1865, TSL.

43. Ibid., September 25, 1864.

44. Ibid., February 14, May 14, 1865. On Russell Aubrey and *Macaria*, see below, Chapter 7.

45. French Diary, March 27, 1865, May 8, 1864, May 11, 1863, TSL.

46. Julia Davidson to John Davidson, July 21, 1864, Davidson Family Papers, AHC.

47. Catherine Edmondston, *Journal of a Secesh Lady: The Diary of Catherine Ann Devereux Edmondston, 1860–1866*, ed. Beth G. Crabtree and James W. Patton (Raleigh: North Carolina Department of Archives and History, 1979), 166.

48. French Diary, August 20, 1865, TSL; Martha Fort to George Fort, January 29, 1862, Tomlinson Fort Papers, EU.


**CHAPTER SIX**

1. H. R., letter, *Southern Literary Messenger* 38 (February 1864), 125. Title is quoted from Sara Agnes (Mrs. Roger) Pryor, *Reminiscences of Peace and War* (New York: Macmillan, 1904), 25.

2. Lizzie Neblett Diary, May 3, 1852, Lizzie Neblett Papers, UTA; Kate Foster Diary, December 7, 1871, DU. On single women in the early nineteenth century, see Lee Virginia Chambers-Schiller, *Liberty, a Better Husband: Single Women in America: The Generations of 1780–1840* (New Haven: Yale University Press, 1984).

3. Rebecca [?] to Nettie Fondren, May 21, 1863, Mitchell-Fondren Papers, GDAH; Anna Kirtland to Hattie Palmer, May 14, 1862, Palmer Family Papers, SCL; J. J. Delchamps, *Love's Ambuscade* (Mobile: A. G. Horn, 1863), 54; C. Vann Woodward, ed., *Mary Chesnut's Civil War* (New Haven: Yale University Press, 1981), 588, 589.

4. Emma Walton to Abby Slocomb, October 5, 1863, Walton-Glenny Papers, THNOC; Pryor, *Reminiscences*, 259.

5. Sarah Morgan, July 24, 1862, in *The Civil War Diary of Sarah Morgan*, ed. Charles East (Athens: University of Georgia Press, 1991), 175; Ellen Roberts to Ellora Reese, December 4, 1864, Confederate Diaries, 8:209–10, GDAH; Lucy Rebecca Buck, *Sad Earth, Sweet Heaven: The Diary of Lucy Rebecca Buck*, ed. William Pettus Buck (Birmingham, Ala.: Cornerstone, 1973), 34; Margaret Gillis Diary, January 23, 1861, ADAH.

6. Bettie A. Lyell, Valedictory Address, Southern Female College, Petersburg, Va., July 6, 1863, 16, VSL.

7. Rebecca to Nettie Fondren, May 21, April 23, 1863, Mitchell-Fondren Papers, GDAH. On crushes, see Nancy Sahli, "Smashing: Women's Relationships before the Fall," *Chrysalis* 8 (1979): 17–27; Martha Vicinus, "Distance and Desire: English Boarding School Friendships," *Signs* 9 (Summer 1984): 600–622; Carroll Smith-Rosenberg,

"The Female World of Love and Ritual: Relationships between Women in Nineteenth Century America," *Signs* 1 (Autumn 1975): 1–29. For a discussion of romantic friendships in antebellum southern boarding schools, see Christie Anne Farnham, *The Education of the Southern Belle: Higher Education and Student Socialization in the Antebellum South* (New York: New York University Press, 1994), 155–67.

8. Clara Solomon Diary, March 29, 1862, LSU.

9. Ibid., November 21, 1861, April 5, March 25, 1862; Mary Greenhow Lee Diary, October 4, 1862, HL. For a discussion of the emergence of the category of "homosexual" in the late nineteenth century, see Jeffrey Weeks, "The Construction of Homosexuality," in *Sex, Politics, and Society: The Regulation of Sexuality since 1800* (London: Longman, 1981), 96–121; Jonathan Katz, "The Invention of the Homosexual, 1880–1950," in *Gay/Lesbian Almanac: A New Documentary* (New York: Harper and Row, 1983), 137–74; and John D'Emilio and Estelle Freedman, "Toward a New Sexual Order, 1880–1930," in *Intimate Matters: A Social History of Sexuality in America* (New York: Harper and Row, 1988), 171–235.

10. Louise M. Nichols Diary, May 21, 22, 17, 22, September 9, 1863, UTA.

11. Sarah Lois Wadley Diary, December 10, 1863, SHC; see also August 13, December 11, February 26, 1864; Nannie Haskins Diary, May 3, 1863, TSL.

12. Haskins Diary, March 23, 1863, TSL; Lizzie Sawyer to My dear Aunt, December 17, 1861, Sawyer Papers, NCDAH. On southern courtship, see H. E. Sterkx, *Partners in Rebellion: Alabama Women in the Civil War* (Rutherford, N.J.: Fairleigh Dickinson University Press, 1970), 148–67; George C. Rable, *Civil Wars: Women and the Crisis of Southern Nationalism* (Urbana: University of Illinois Press, 1989), 51–54, 193–94; Steven M. Stowe, " 'The *Thing* Not Its Vision': A Woman's Courtship and Her Sphere in the Southern Planter Class," *Feminist Studies* 9 (Spring 1983): 113–30; and generally, Karen Lystra, *Searching the Heart: Women, Men, and Romantic Love in Nineteenth-Century America* (New York: Oxford University Press, 1989).

13. Judith McGuire, *Diary of a Southern Refugee during the War* (1867; rpt., New York: Arno Press, 1974), 329; Amanda Chappelear Diary, September 9, 1862, VHS; Alice Ready Diary, February 13, 1862, SHC; Malvina Waring, March 15, 12, 1865, in *South Carolina Women in the Confederacy*, ed. Mrs. Thomas Taylor, Mrs. A. T. Smythe, Mrs. August Kohn, Miss M. B. Poppenheim, and Miss Martha Washington, 2 vols. (Columbia, S.C.: State Co., 1903), 1:282, 281; Phoebe Pember to Lou Gilmer, February 19, 1864, in Phoebe Yates Pember, *A Southern Woman's Story*, ed. Bell Irvin Wiley (1959; rpt., Saint Simons Island, Ga.: Mockingbird Books, 1990), 137.

14. Amanda Worthington Diary, January 9, February 5, 1862, September 24, 1863, January 19, 1865, MDAH; Kate Cumming, *Kate: The Journal of a Confederate Nurse*, ed. Richard Barksdale Harwell (Baton Rouge: Louisiana State University Press, 1959), 46.

15. Emma Holmes, January 21, June 11, 1863, in *The Diary of Miss Emma Holmes, 1861–1866*, ed. John Marszalek (Baton Rouge: Louisiana State University Press, 1979), 225, 266; Ada Bacot Diary, January 31, 1862, SCL; Thomas B. Hall to Bolling Hall, Jr., June 15, 1863, Bolling Hall Papers, ADAH; Woodward, *Mary Chesnut's Civil War*, 472, 489–90.

16. Alden quoted in Francis Butler Simkins and James Welch Patton, *The Women of the Confederacy* (Richmond: Garrett and Massie, 1936), 188; Gillis Diary, February 7, 1863, ADAH; Jack to C. D. MacLean, August 13, 1863, Clara Dargan MacLean Papers, DU; Louisa Walton to Isabella Woodruff, January 3, 1862, Isabella Ann Woodruff Papers, DU; Isabella Woodruff, "Private Thoughts," December 18, 1864, Woodruff Papers, DU; clipping, "Chance Acquaintances," Mary Early Scrapbook, 7, VHS.

17. Sarah Kennedy to her husband, March 19, 1864, Sarah Kennedy Papers, TSL; Mary W. M. Bell to her husband, September 1, 1863, Mary Walker Meriwether Bell Papers, TSL; Naomi Hayes to Lucy Polk, July 26, 1863, Lucy Williams Polk Papers, NCDAH.

18. *Richmond Enquirer*, December 30, 1862, January 1, 1864.

19. Harriette Cary Diary, May 31, 1862, WM.

CHAPTER SEVEN

1. Alice Ready Diary, April 23, 1861, SHC. Title is quoted from Lucy Rebecca Buck, *Sad Earth, Sweet Heaven: The Diary of Lucy Rebecca Buck*, ed. William Pettus Buck (Birmingham, Ala.: Cornerstone, 1973), 41.

2. *Southern Literary Messenger*, quoted in Nina Baym, *Novels, Readers, and Reviewers: Responses to Fiction in Antebellum America* (Ithaca: Cornell University Press, 1984), 36.

3. Mary Kelley, *Private Woman, Public Stage: Literary Domesticity in Nineteenth Century America* (New York: Oxford University Press, 1984), 7.

4. On women as writers and readers and on the literary marketplace more generally, see Kelley, *Private Woman*; Linda K. Kerber, " 'We Own That Ladies Sometimes Read': Women's Reading in the Early Republic," in *Women of the Republic: Intellect and Ideology in Revolutionary America* (Chapel Hill: University of North Carolina Press, 1980), 233–64; Nina Baym, *Woman's Fiction: A Guide to Novels by and about Women in America, 1820–1870* (Ithaca: Cornell University Press, 1978); Baym, *Novels, Readers, and Reviewers*; Jane Tompkins, *Sensational Designs: The Cultural Work of American Fiction, 1790–1860* (New York: Oxford University Press, 1984); Elizabeth Moss, *Domestic Novelists in the Old South: Defenders of Southern Culture* (Baton Rouge: Louisiana State University Press, 1992); Susan Coultrap-McQuin, *Doing Literary Business: American Women Writers in the Nineteenth Century* (Chapel Hill: University of North Carolina Press, 1990); Michael Warner, *The Letters of the Republic: Publication and the Public Sphere in Eighteenth Century America* (Cambridge, Mass.: Harvard University Press, 1990); and Anne Goodwyn Jones, *Tomorrow Is Another Day: The Woman Writer in the South, 1859–1936* (Baton Rouge: Louisiana State University Press, 1980). On reading in particular, see Cathy N. Davidson, ed., *Reading in America: Literature and Social History* (Baltimore: Johns Hopkins University Press, 1989), and Elizabeth Flynn and Patrocinio P. Schweikart, *Gender and Reading: Essays on Readers, Texts, and Contexts* (Baltimore: Johns Hopkins University Press, 1986). During the antebellum years 40 percent of novels reviewed in journals and newspapers were

by women; by 1872 women wrote 75 percent of novels published in America. See Coultrap-McQuin, *Doing Literary Business*, 2.

5. L. Virginia French Diary, January 1, 1865, TSL; Emma LeConte Diary, January 28, 1865, SHC. See also Abbie Brooks Diary, January 28, 1865, AHC, and Harriette Cary Diary, June 18, 1862, WM. For a similar characterization of reading as drug and as fantasy, see Elizabeth Fox-Genovese, *Within the Plantation Household: Black and White Women of the Old South* (Chapel Hill: University of North Carolina Press, 1988), 261. Fox-Genovese does not deal explicitly with the war years when, I argue, the psychological importance of books to southern women became even more pronounced.

6. Ella Gertrude Clanton Thomas Diary, March 29, 1865, DU; Emma Crutcher to Will Crutcher, January 24, 1862, Crutcher-Shannon Papers, UTA; Caroline Kean Hill Davis Diary, July 21, 1863, VHS; LeConte Diary, February 5, 1865, SHC.

7. Buck, *Sad Earth, Sweet Heaven*, 41.

8. Mary Greenhow Lee Diary, October 11, April 19, 1863, HL; Davis Diary, February 1, 1865, VHS; Buck, *Sad Earth, Sweet Heaven*, 185.

9. Louisa McCord Smythe Recollections, SCL, 50; Anne Shannon Martin Diary, March 11, 1864, MDAH; see also Lizzie Simons Diary, September 12, 1862, UTA; Emma Holmes, *The Diary of Miss Emma Holmes, 1861–1866*, ed. John Marszalek (Baton Rouge: Louisiana State University Press, 1979), 461–62; Emma Mordecai Diary, May 14, 1864, Mordecai Family Papers, SHC; Mrs. Thomas Taylor, Mrs. A. T. Smythe, Mrs. August Kohn, Miss M. B. Poppenheim, and Miss Martha Washington, eds., *South Carolina Women in the Confederacy*, 2 vols. (Columbia, S.C.: State Co., 1903), 1:80; and Margaret Beckwith Reminiscences, 2:8, VHS.

10. Holmes, *Diary*, 202.

11. Sidney Harding Diary, September 29, 1863, LSU; Holmes, *Diary*, 177; C. Vann Woodward, ed., *Mary Chesnut's Civil War* (New Haven: Yale University Press, 1981), 242; *Richmond Enquirer*, February 20, 1863; Kate Stone quoted in Edmund Wilson, *Patriotic Gore* (New York: Farrar, Straus and Giroux, 1962), 260–61; Stone, *Brokenburn: The Journal of Kate Stone, 1861–1868*, ed. John Q. Anderson (Baton Rouge: Louisiana State University Press, 1955), 233; Cary Diary, June 10, 1862, WM; Emily Andrews to Alice Niles Andrews, June 19, 1864, Alice E. Niles Papers, DU. See Ella Gertrude Clanton Thomas, *The Secret Eye: The Journal of Ella Gertrude Clanton Thomas, 1848–1889*, ed. Virginia Ingraham Burr (Chapel Hill: University of North Carolina Press, 1990), 188–89, on the effect of the blockade on the availability of books.

12. Anna Maria Cook, *The Journal of a Milledgeville Girl, 1861–1867*, ed. James C. Bonner (Athens: University of Georgia Press, 1964), 37; Amanda Worthington Diary, February 17, 1862, MDAH; Amanda Chappelear Diary, October 25, 1862, VHS; Holmes, *Diary*, 200–201. See Worthington Diary, January 9, 1865, MDAH; she thinks she ought not to read novels but cannot help it. On a similar sort of attraction to a similar but twentieth-century style of romantic hero, see Janice A. Radway, *Reading the Romance: Women, Patriarchy, and Popular Literature* (Chapel Hill: University of North Carolina Press, 1984).

13. Woodward, *Mary Chesnut's Civil War*, 326.

14. Ibid., 296, 301; Ellen Moore to Samuel Moore, February 7, 1864, Samuel J. C.

Moore Papers, SHC; Elizabeth Pringle Diary, August 27, March 10, 1861, SCHS. See also Sophia Partridge Diary, January 14, 1864, NCDAH, and Catherine Edmondston, *Journal of a Secesh Lady: The Diary of Catherine Ann Devereux Edmondston, 1860–1866*, ed. Beth G. Crabtree and James W. Patton (Raleigh: Division of Archives and History, 1979), 654.

15. Ready Diary, April 8, 1862, SHC; Lise Mitchell Diary, March 1, 1862, TU; Constance Cary Harrison, *Recollections Grave and Gay* (New York: Scribners, 1911), 123; Edmondston, *Journal of a Secesh Lady*, 655.

16. "The Education of Southern Women," *De Bow's Review* 31 (October/November 1861): 390.

17. Subheading paraphrased from Mrs. Thomas Womack to Zebulon Vance, July 23, 1863, Zebulon Vance Papers, NCDAH. There is an important and growing literature on women's autobiographical writings and their significance in the definition of the female self. See Shari Benstock, ed., *The Private Self: Theory and Practice of Women's Autobiographical Writings* (Chapel Hill: University of North Carolina Press, 1988); Judith Gardiner, "On Female Identity: Writing by Women," *Critical Inquiry* 8 (Winter 1981): 347–61; Elizabeth Bruss, *Autobiographical Acts: The Changing Situation of a Literary Genre* (Baltimore: Johns Hopkins University Press, 1976); Estelle C. Jelinek, *The Tradition of Women's Autobiography: From Antiquity to the Present* (Boston: Twayne, 1986); Jelinek, ed., *Women's Autobiography* (Bloomington: Indiana University Press, 1980); Patricia Spacks, *Imagining a Self* (Cambridge, Mass.: Harvard University Press, 1976); and Carolyn Heilbrun, *Writing a Woman's Life* (New York: Norton, 1988); on autobiography more generally, see James Olney, ed., *Autobiography: Essays Theoretical and Critical* (Princeton: Princeton University Press, 1980); Olney, ed., *Studies in Autobiography* (New York: Oxford University Press, 1988); Albert E. Stone, *Autobiographical Occasions and Original Acts* (Philadelphia: University of Pennsylvania Press, 1982); and Janet Varner Gunn, *Autobiography: Toward a Poetics of Experience* (Philadelphia: University of Pennsylvania Press, 1982). On women's writing North and South during the war, see Mary Elizabeth Massey, *Women in the Civil War* (Lincoln: University of Nebraska Press, 1994), 175–96 (originally published as *Bonnet Brigades: American Women and the Civil War* [New York: Knopf, 1966]).

18. Susan Cornwall Diary, March 18, 1857, SHC.

19. Julia Davidson to John Davidson, June 29, 1863, Davidson Family Papers, AHC; Karen Lystra, *Searching the Heart: Women, Men, and Romantic Love in Nineteenth-Century America* (New York: Oxford University Press, 1989), 26–27. See also, on letters, Steven M. Stowe, *Intimacy and Power in the Old South: Ritual in the Lives of the Planters* (Baltimore: Johns Hopkins University Press, 1987).

20. Adelia Etheridge to Jefferson Davis, December 22, 1863, LRCSW, RG 109, reel 126, M437, E4, NA; Lucy White to Jefferson Davis, August 6, 1864, Samuel Richey Papers, MUO; Mrs. Thomas Womack to Zebulon Vance, July 23, 1863, and Mahala Hundley to Zebulon Vance, July 16, 1863, Vance Papers, NCDAH.

21. Sarah Morgan quoted in *Heroines of Dixie: Winter of Desperation*, ed. Katharine M. Jones, 2 vols. (1955; rpt., Saint Simons Island, Ga.: Mockingbird Books, 1975), 1:128; Judith McGuire quoted in ibid., 2:220; Sarah Morgan, *The Civil War Diary of*

*Sarah Morgan*, ed. Charles East (Athens: University of Georgia Press, 1991), 121; Clara Solomon Diary, May 26, 1862, LSU.

22. Mary Greenhow Lee Diary, October 9, February 18, 28, 1863, HL; Edmondston, *Journal of a Secesh Lady*, 272; Holmes, *Diary*, 53.

23. Lise Mitchell Diary, August 1, 1862, TU; Mary Chesnut, in Woodward, *Mary Chesnut's Civil War*, xxii; Elisabeth Muhlenfeld, *Mary Boykin Chesnut: A Biography* (Baton Rouge: Louisiana State University Press, 1981).

24. Rebecca to Nettie Fondren, April 23, 1863, Mitchell-Fondren Papers, GDAH; Virginia Cowdin to Jefferson Davis, March 17, 1861, Jefferson Davis Papers, YU. Coultrap-McQuin finds that writing was a good economic choice for nineteenth-century women; see *Doing Literary Business*, 23. Anne Goodwyn Jones describes writing as "for many years . . . almost the only profession that a Southern lady of good family . . . might pursue without being thought by her society to have in effect 'desexed' herself." See *Tomorrow Is Another Day*, 5.

25. Nannie Haskins Diary, September 24, 1864, TSL.

26. Brooks Diary, October 3, 1865, AHC. Brooks did in fact publish after the war.

27. Holmes, *Diary*, 465; French Diary, February 14, 1864, January 8, 1865, TSL.

28. Edmondston, *Journal of a Secesh Lady*, 282.

29. Mary Greenhow Lee Diary, April 22, 1862, HL; Caroline Gilman quoted in Kelley, *Private Woman*, 180.

30. West and Johnston to Constance Cary, December 26, 1863, Burton Harrison Papers, LC; Harrison, *Recollections*, 213–14; Henry Timrod to Clara Dargan, August 20, 1864, Clara Dargan MacLean Papers, DU.

31. Mary B. Clarke to Macfarlane and Fergusson, September 21, [1861], Macfarlane and Fergusson Papers, VHS.

32. *Augusta Weekly Constitutionalist*, October 16, 1861.

33. Augusta Jane Evans, *Macaria; or, Altars of Sacrifice*, ed. Drew Gilpin Faust (1864; rpt., Baton Rouge: Louisiana State University Press, 1992). Page numbers cited from this edition. Augusta Jane Evans to P. G. T. Beauregard, August 4, 1862, quoted in William Perry Fidler, *Augusta Evans Wilson, 1835–1909: A Biography* (University: University of Alabama Press, 1951), 95.

34. Heilbrun, *Writing a Woman's Life*, 48; Anne Goodwyn Jones, *Tomorrow Is Another Day*, 353. See also Sandra Gilbert and Susan Gubar, *The Madwoman in the Attic: A Study of Women and the Literary Imagination in the Nineteenth Century* (New Haven: Yale University Press, 1978).

35. On single women, see Lee Virginia Chambers-Schiller, *Liberty, a Better Husband: Single Women in America: The Generations of 1780–1840* (New Haven: Yale University Press, 1984).

36. Mary Legg to Harriet Palmer, December 10, 1863, Palmer Family Papers, SCL.

37. Haskins Diary, October 15, 1864, TSL; Mary Greenhow Lee Diary, June 9, 14, 1864, HL; Thomas Diary, June 29, 1864, DU. For other examples, see Anna Maria Green, July 30, 1864, in Cook, *Journal of a Milledgeville Girl*, 52; Holmes, *Diary*, 369; Mary to W. W. Stringfield, March 27, 1864, W. W. Stringfield Papers, NCDAH; Emily Andrews to Alice Niles, June 19, 1864, Niles Papers, DU; French Diary, July 10, 1864,

TSL; Willie to Amanda Worthington, July 25, 1864, Amanda Worthington Papers, MDAH; and Belle Edmondson, *A Lost Heroine of the Confederacy: The Diaries and Letters of Belle Edmondson*, ed. William Galbraith and Loretta Galbraith (Jackson: University Press of Mississippi, 1990), 126.

38. D. K. W., in *Richmond Age* 1 (January 1865): 388, 390, 391, 392; Belle Edmondson Diary, June 17, 20, 1864, SHC.

39. Fidelia in *Mobile Evening News*, August 1, 1864.

40. Augusta Jane Evans to P. G. T. Beauregard, November 20, 1867, Augusta Jane Evans Papers, BU. On her intentions, see Evans to J. L. M. Curry, October 7, 1865 in Curry Papers, DU, and Evans to Alexander Stephens, November 29, 1865, Alexander Stephens Papers, EU.

CHAPTER EIGHT

1. Title quoted from Annie Darden Diary, July 20, 1861, NCDAH; Emma Holmes, *The Diary of Miss Emma Holmes, 1861–1866*, ed. John Marszalek (Baton Rouge: Louisiana State University Press, 1979), 25–26.

2. Stephen Elliott, *Ezra's Dilemna [sic]. A Sermon* (Savannah: George N. Nichols, 1863), 17; Drew Gilpin Faust, *The Creation of Confederate Nationalism: Ideology and Identity in the Civil War South* (Baton Rouge: Louisiana State University Press, 1988), 26–28; see Emma Crutcher to Will Crutcher, January 4, 1862, Crutcher-Shannon Papers, MDAH. See also James Silver, *Confederate Morale and Church Propaganda* (Tuscaloosa, Ala.: Confederate Publishing, Co., 1957); Richard Beringer, Herman Hattaway, Archer Jones, and William N. Still, Jr., *Why the South Lost the Civil War* (Athens: University of Georgia Press, 1986), 82–107; and James Moorhead, *American Apocalypse: Yankee Protestants and the Civil War, 1860–1869* (New Haven: Yale University Press, 1978). Emma Holmes read two of Stephen Elliott's sermons in the *Southern Episcopalian* in the summer of 1861 that showed "how visibly the Hand of God was with us throughout all our struggles for freedom." See Holmes, *Diary*, 90.

3. Subtitle quoted from Laura Nisbet Boykin, *Shinplasters and Homespun: Diary of Laura Nisbet Boykin*, ed. Mary Wright Stock (Rockville, Md.: Printex, 1975), 46. Kate Carney Diary, February 28, 1861, SHC; Keziah Brevard Diary, January 1, 1861, SCL; see also Amanda Worthington Diary, January 5, 1862, MDAH; Lucy Wood Butler to Waddy Butler, November 12, 1861, Lucy Wood Butler Papers, UVA; and Laura A. Haygood, "Every Cloud Has a Silvery Lining," October 24, 1863, Atticus Haygood Papers, EU. See Timrod quoted by Malvina Waring, "A Confederate Girl's Diary, March 9, 1865," in *South Carolina Women in the Confederacy*, ed. Mrs. Thomas Taylor, Mrs. A. T. Smythe, Mrs. August Kohn, Miss M. B. Poppenheim, and Miss Martha Washington, 2 vols. (Columbia, S.C.: State Co., 1903), 1:280.

4. *Christian Observer*, January 23, 1862; Holmes, *Diary*, 57; Faust, *Creation*, 28–29.

5. Nancy Emerson Diary, July 4, 1862, UVA; on Sumter, see J. H. Elliott, *The Bloodless Victory: A Sermon* (Charleston: A. E. Miller, 1861). See Ellen Moore to Samuel Moore, n.d. [1861], for comments on parallels between Manassas and 2 Chron. 20, Samuel J. C. Moore Papers, SHC.

6. Holmes, *Diary*, 111; Sarah Estes Diary, November 14, 1862, TSL; Boykin, *Shin-plasters and Homespun*, 46. On Job, see, for example, Margaret Gwyn Diary, December 2, 1863, DU.

7. Darden Diary, July 20, 1861, NCDAH.

8. Abby Slocomb to J. B. Walton, September 25, 1863, Walton-Glenny Papers, THNOC; Mattie Seward to Nettie Fondren, March 31, 1863, Mitchell-Fondren Papers, GDAH; Julia Davidson to John Davidson, July 17, 1863, Davidson Family Papers, AHC; Kate Foster Diary, July 28, 1863, DU; see Kate Foster on fall of Vicksburg, July 9, 1863, DU; see Annual Meeting of the Congregation of College Church, Oxford, Miss., January 5, 1863, Maud Brown Papers, 105, MDAH. On perception of social ills, see Amelia Rainey to Kate McClure, October 11, 1861, McClure Papers, SCL; Brevard Diary, October 24, 1860, SCL; Emma Mordecai Diary, May 17, 1864, Mordecai Family Papers, SHC; and Sarah Dorsey to Leonidas Polk, February 20, 1862, Leonidas Polk Papers, US. Thanks to Bertram Wyatt-Brown for bringing this citation to my attention. For a more extensive discussion of the South's perception of its sins, see Faust, *Creation*, 41–82.

9. Lizzie Ozburn to Jimmie Ozburn, October 20, 1861, Katherine Elizabeth Ozburn Papers, GDAH; Anais to My Dear Husband, April 29, 1863, Warren Ogden Papers, TU; Myra Smith Diary, August 20, 1861, Eunice Stockwell Papers, MDAH; see also Lizzie Simons Diary, November 30, 1862, UTA; A. Grima to Alfred Grima, July 14, 1863, Grima Family Papers, THNOC; Mary Bryan to her daughter, January 24, 1862, John Heritage Bryan Collection, NCDAH; Mary Legg to Hattie Palmer, December 10, 1863, Palmer Family Papers, SCL; and Mary Jane Cook Chadick Diary, November 27, 1863, DU, for similar language; Jane Howison Beale, *The Journal of Jane Howison Beale of Fredericksburg, Virginia, 1850–1862* (Fredericksburg: Historic Fredericksburg Foundation, 1979), 12; Alice Ready Diary, February 11, 1862, SHC.

10. Laura Haygood to My dear friend, n.d., Atticus Haygood Papers, EU; Sarah Espy Diary, November 29, 1862, ADAH; Mary Hort Diary, April 1865, SCL. See also Maggie Allen to Mrs. John Palmer, August 25, 1864, Palmer Family Papers, SCL, and Beale, *Journal*, 43–44.

11. Subheading is quoted from Julia Davidson to John Davidson, June 26, 1862, Davidson Family Papers, AHC; Annie Harper Reminiscences, 13, MDAH; Ready Diary, February 13, 1862, SHC; *Pray, maiden, pray! a ballad for the times, respectfully dedicated to the women of the South* (Richmond: George Dunn, 1864); Laura Comer Diary, January 4, 1862, SHC.

12. Belle Strickland Diary, January 21, 1865, MDAH; Estes Diary, August 17, 1862, TSL; Mary W. M. Bell to her husband, July 22, 1863, Mary Walker Meriwether Bell Papers, TSL. See Mrs. Calvin Brown, "Lafayette County: 1860–1865: A Narrative," MDAH; Catherine Broun Diary, January 26, 1862, Broun Family Papers, RU; Sarah Lois Wadley Diary, November 15, 1861, SHC; Fannie Page Hume Diary, May 11, 1862, UVA; Emma Crutcher to her mother, June 8, 1862, Crutcher-Shannon Papers, MDAH; Emma Balfour Diary, June 2, 1863, MDAH; Foster Diary, September 20, 1863, DU; Laura Lee Diary, March 17, 1862, December 22, 1864, WM; and Kate Rowland Diary, June 26, July 10, 1864, EU. Denominational divisions diminished in significance as opportunities for choice disappeared. See Rowland Diary, November 1, 1863, EU.

13. *Biblical Recorder*, June 17, 1863; see also *Southern Christian Advocate*, September 8, 1864; *Army and Navy Messenger*, March 1, 1864; and Nettie Fondren to Robert Mitchell, December 16, 1862, Mitchell-Fondren Papers, GDAH. There were some civilian revivals, but commentators remarked on how few in comparison with the army. See Elizabeth J. Beach to Father and Mother, July 29, 1864, Elizabeth Beach Papers, MDAH, and Alice Niles to Dear Cousin, September 19, 1863, Alice E. Niles Papers, DU. On family prayer, see Zillah Brandon Diary, August 7, 1862, ADAH; Sarah Morgan, June 26, 1862, in *The Civil War Diary of Sarah Morgan*, ed. Charles East (Athens: University of Georgia Press, 1991), 137; and Harriette Cary Diary, May 18, 1862, WM. On army revivals, see Drew Gilpin Faust, "Christian Soldiers: The Meaning of Revivalism in the Confederate Army," *Journal of Southern History* 53 (February 1987): 63-90.

14. *Richmond Enquirer*, November 14, 1862; Simons Diary, December 31, 1862, UTA; *Southwest Baptist*, January 15, 1863; Mary Greenhow Lee Diary, May 16, 1862, HL; Holmes, *Diary*, 170; Rowland Diary, March 3, 1862, MOC. See also Comer Diary, January 26, March 21, 1862, SHC, and Octavia Stephens to Winston Stephens, January 7, 1862, Bryant-Stephens Papers, UFL.

15. *Religious Herald*, March 14, 1861. On the preponderance of women in antebellum southern churches, see Donald Mathews, *Religion in the Old South* (Chicago: University of Chicago Press, 1977), and Jean E. Friedman, *The Enclosed Garden: Women and Community in the Evangelical South, 1830-1900* (Chapel Hill: University of North Carolina Press, 1985).

16. Mrs. Frances Blake Brockenbrough, *A Mother's Parting Words to her Soldier Boy* (Petersburg, Va.: Evangelical Tract Society, 186-), 4. On the phenomenal success of this tract, see *Religious Herald*, October 23, 1862.

17. Julia Davidson to John Davidson, September 19, June 26, July 1862, Davidson Family Papers, AHC; Rachel Craighead Diary, September 14, 1862, TSL; Margaret Houston to Sam Houston, Jr., July 1, 1864, Hearne Collection, UTA; Leila Callaway to Morgan Callaway, June 11, 1862, Morgan Callaway Papers, EU. See also Emma Crutcher to Will Crutcher, March 14, 1862, Crutcher-Shannon Papers, MDAH, and Ellen Moore to Samuel Moore, July 11, 1861, Moore Papers, SHC.

18. Subheading is quoted from Nannie Haskins Diary, July 14, 1864, TSL; Mrs. C. A. Slocomb to M. Greenwood, October 2, 1864, M. Greenwood Papers, THNOC. On emerging doubt, see Harper Reminiscences, 24, MDAH.

19. Catherine Edmondston, *Journal of a Secesh Lady: The Diary of Catherine Ann Devereux Edmondston, 1860-1866*, ed. Beth G. Crabtree and James W. Patton (Raleigh: Division of Archives and History, 1979), 461; Kate Stone, *Brokenburn: The Journal of Kate Stone, 1861-1868*, ed. John Q. Anderson (Baton Rouge: Louisiana State University Press, 1955), 264.

20. Patricia R. Loughridge and Edward D. C. Campbell, Jr., *Women in Mourning* (Richmond: Museum of the Confederacy, 1985).

21. For a more extensive discussion of the cultural work of the painting, see Drew Gilpin Faust, "Race, Gender, and Confederate Nationalism: William D. Washington's *Burial of Latané*" in *Southern Stories: Slaveholders in Peace and War* (Columbia: University of Missouri Press, 1992), 148-59.

22. See description of Charleston in Holmes, *Diary*, 69–70, and description of similar treatment for one of the first of New Orleans's slain in Clara Solomon Diary, July 16, 1861, LSU; Constance Cary Harrison, *Recollections Grave and Gay* (New York: Scribners, 1911), 188–89; and Brown, "Lafayette County," MDAH.

23. Fannie A. Beers, *Memories: A Record of Personal Experience and Adventure during Four Years of War* (Philadelphia: Lippincott, 1888), 83; Stone, *Brokenburn*, 277; Carrie Fries to J. Shaffner, January 19, 1863, Shaffner Papers, NCDAH; Stone, *Brokenburn*, 258; Haskins Diary, July 14, 1864, TSL; Foster Diary, November 15, 1863, DU; Mary Greenhow Lee Diary, July 24, 1863, HL.

24. "It is necessary to resign oneself to the will of God and accept the crosses that he sends us—I must submit and pray and hope." A. Grima to Alfred Grima, October 30, 1863; see also November 27, 1863, Grima Family Papers, THNOC; for invocations of Deut. 33:25, see Sarah Jane Sams to Randolph Sams, Sarah J. Sams Papers, SCL; Rhoda Duell to L. J. Duell, November 3, 1864, Point Lookout Letters, NA; Edmondston, *Journal of a Secesh Lady*, 55; Sue Richardson Diary, February 5, 1864, EU; and Comer Diary, January 12, 1862, SHC.

25. Julia Davidson to John Davidson, September 8, 1863, Davidson Family Papers, AHC; J. Michael Welton, ed., *"My Heart Is So Rebellious": The Caldwell Letters, 1861–1865* (Warrenton, Va.: Fauquier National Bank, 1991), 241, 255; Cornelia Noble Diary, November 2, 1862, UTA; Mary Stamps to Jefferson Davis, August 16, 1863, photocopy in Papers of Jefferson Davis, RU; Broun Diary, March 8, 1862, RU; M. E. B., "Lights and Shadows of A Solitary Woman's Thoughts," clipping in M. L. Lawton Scrapbook, 25, AHC.

26. Haskins Diary, February 16, 1863, TSL; Solomon Diary, June 7, 1861, LSU; Ready Diary, March 24, 1862, SHC; Mary Ann Harris Gay, *Life in Dixie during the War* (Atlanta: Constitution Job Office, 1892), 195.

27. Estes Diary, November 14, 1862, TSL; Cornelia Peake McDonald, *A Woman's Civil War: A Diary, with Reminiscences of the War, from March 1862*, edited and with an introduction by Minrose C. Gwin (Madison: University of Wisconsin Press, 1992), 241; Gay, *Life*, 273.

28. Ida Wilkom to Secretary of War, February 7, 1862, 11167, LRCSW, RG 109, reel 27, M437, NA.

29. M. V. Caho to Jefferson Davis, January 28, 1864, LRCSW, RG 109, reel 123, C177, NA; Annie Craig to Secretary of War, September 17, 1861, 5689, LRCSW, RG 109, reel 10, NA; Anna McConnell to Jefferson Davis, January 21, 1865, Jefferson Davis Papers, DU; Henrietta McDonald to Jefferson Davis, September 15, 1861, 5668, LRCSW, RG 109, reel 10, NA.

30. Elizabeth Collier Diary, July 3, 1862, SHC.

31. Grace Elmore Diary, May 10, 1865, SCL; Mary Early Diary, April 10, 1865, VHS; L. Virginia French Diary, May 31, 1865, TSL; Mary Greenhow Lee Diary, April 15, 1865, HL. On women's reactions to defeat, see also Richard M. Weaver, *The Southern Tradition at Bay: A History of Postbellum Thought* (New Rochelle, N.Y.: Arlington House, 1968), 270–73. See also George C. Rable, *Civil Wars: Women and the Crisis of Southern Nationalism* (Urbana: University of Illinois Press, 1989), 223–25.

1. *New York World* quoted in *Mobile Evening News*, April 3, 1862; journalist quoted in Francis Butler Simkins and James Welch Patton, *The Women of the Confederacy* (Richmond: Garrett and Massie, 1936), 42; Laura Lee Diary, June 7, 1862, WM; Reid Mitchell, *The Vacant Chair: The Northern Soldier Leaves Home* (New York: Oxford University Press, 1993), chap. 6, "She Devils."

2. See Nina Silber, "Intemperate Men, Spiteful Women, and Jefferson Davis," in *Divided Houses: Gender and the Civil War*, ed. Catherine Clinton and Nina Silber (New York: Oxford University Press, 1992), 283–305, and George C. Rable, *Civil Wars: Women and the Crisis of Southern Nationalism* (Urbana: University of Illinois Press, 1989), 154–80.

3. Subheading quoted from Mary Greenhow Lee Diary, April 1, 1862, HL; Catherine Cochran Reminiscences, vol. 1, March 1862, VHS; Mary Greenhow Lee Diary, April 21, 1862, HL.

4. Mary Greenhow Lee Diary, March 14, 1862, January 3, March 16, 1863, HL.

5. Alice Ready Diary, March 11, 1862, SHC; George Peddy Cuttino, ed., *Saddle Bag and Spinning Wheel: Being the Civil War Letters of George W. Peddy and Kate Featherston Peddy* (Macon, Ga.: Mercer University Press, 1981), 284; L. Virginia French Diary, April 26, 1863, TSL; Emma LeConte Diary, February 14, 1865, SCL; see also Octavia to Winston Stephens, March 12, 19, 1862, Bryant-Stephens Papers, UFL. See also Belle Edmondson's description of filling her hoops with goods to smuggle through the lines, March 16, 1864, in *A Lost Heroine of the Confederacy: The Diaries and Letters of Belle Edmondson*, ed. William Galbraith and Loretta Galbraith (Jackson: University Press of Mississippi, 1990), 97.

6. On the apparent infrequency of rape of white women, see Simkins and Patton, *Women of the Confederacy*, 48; Mitchell, *Vacant Chair*, 102, 104; Susan Brownmiller, *Against Our Will: Men, Women, and Rape* (1975; rpt., New York: Bantam, 1990), 89; and Michael Fellman, *Inside War: The Guerilla Conflict in Missouri during the American Civil War* (New York: Oxford University Press, 1989), 193–230. On black women, see Mitchell, *Vacant Chair*; Fellman, *Inside War*; and Charles Royster, *The Destructive War* (New York: Knopf, 1991), 23, 342. Rumors of violations of white women appear in both private writings and southern newspapers, but it is difficult to assess the reliability of these reports. See, for example, Emma Holmes, *The Diary of Miss Emma Holmes, 1861–1866*, ed. John Marszalek (Baton Rouge: Louisiana State University Press, 1979), 81–82, 434.

7. Fellman, *Inside War*, 205; Thomas Settle to Zebulon Vance, September 21, 1864, Zebulon Vance Papers, NCDAH.

8. Mary Greenhow Lee Diary, April 1, 1862, HL; "F.F.V.'s" are "First Families of Virginia"; Amanda Chappelear Diary, March 17, 1862, VHS; Missouri woman quoted in Fellman, *Inside War*, 196; Mary Greenhow Lee Diary, March 17, 1862, HL; Kate Carney Diary, July 20, 1862, SHC; Mary Greenhow Lee Diary, April 6, 1863, HL. Some Confederate women behind Union lines, in areas such as Nashville, New Orleans, or Washington, D.C., were arrested by Yankee officials who suspected them of spying.

They were sometimes sent beyond the lines and sometimes imprisoned. See, for example, Eugenia Phillips, who was first returned from Washington to the South and later imprisoned in Mississippi, Eugenia Phillips Diary, Philip Phillips Papers, LC.

9. Mary Greenhow Lee Diary, March 22, 1862, HL; Ready Diary, March 22, 1862, SHC; Catherine Broun Diary, November 6, 1862, RU; Munford quoted in Douglas S. Freeman, *The South to Posterity: An Introduction to the Writings of Confederate History* (New York: Scribners, 1939), 107; Cochran Reminiscences, May 15, 1863, vol. 1, VHS; Holmes, *Diary*, 402.

10. Harriette Cary Diary, May 11, 1862, WM; Carney Diary, July 16, 1862, SHC; for other examples, see Abby Day Slocomb to J. B. Walton, July 17, 1862, Walton-Glenny Papers, THNOC; Janie Smith to Janie Robeson, April 12, 1865, Mrs. Thomas Webb Collection, NCDAH; Sarah Kennedy Diary, February 9, 1863, TSL; and Chappelear Diary, April 14, 1862, VHS. The *Milledgeville Southern Federal Union* tallied—and encouraged—these triumphs in regular reports under headlines such as "A Good Hit," "A Good Shot," or "A Good One." See, for example, August 6, 12, September 2, 1862.

11. Cochran Reminiscences, March 1862, vol. 1, VHS; Sarah Morgan, *The Civil War Diary of Sarah Morgan*, ed. Charles East (Athens: University of Georgia Press, 1991), 160; Ready Diary, March 19, 1862, SHC; officer quoted in Simkins and Patton, *Women of the Confederacy*, 43.

12. Mary Ann Huff, "The Role of Women in Confederate Georgia" (M.A. thesis, Emory University, 1967), 116; Elizabeth McKamy Recollections, 2, TSL; Clara B. Eno, "Activities of the Women of Arkansas during the War between the States," *Arkansas Historical Quarterly* 3 (Spring 1944): 18, 20.

13. Subheading quoted from Annie Samuels, Irene Bell, et al. to James Seddon, December 2, 1864, LRCSW, RG 109, reel 122, M437, B692, NA; *Charleston Mercury*, January 8, 1863; *Milledgeville Southern Federal Union*, August 19, 1862. On women as soldiers, see Loreta Janeta Velazquez, *The Woman in Battle: A Narrative of the Exploits, Adventures and Travels of Madame Loreta Janeta Velazquez, Otherwise Known as Lieutenant Harry T. Buford, Confederate States Army* (Hartford, Conn.: Belknap, 1876), which has been labeled a gross exaggeration, if not a fabrication; Mary Elizabeth Massey, *Women in the Civil War* (Lincoln: University of Nebraska Press, 1994), 78–86 (originally published as *Bonnet Brigades: American Women and the Civil War* [New York: Knopf, 1966]); Janet E. Kaufman, "'Under the Petticoat Flag': Women Soldiers in the Confederate Army," *Southern Studies* 23 (Winter 1984): 363–75; DeAnne Blanton, "Women Soldiers of the Civil War," *Prologue* (Spring 1993): 27–33; Simkins and Patton, *Women of the Confederacy*, 74, 80; Chappelear Diary, July 18, 1861, VHS; J. M. Fain to E. Fain, December 10, 1861, Huldah Briant Papers, DU; French Diary, April 17, 1864, TSL; and *Charleston Mercury*, April 5, 1862.

14. Huff, "Role of Women," 54; Leila Morris, "Personal Recollections of the War: Girl Confederate Soldiers," Crumley Family Papers, AHC; *Charleston Mercury* on women's home guard, July 18, 1861; M. A. C. to Dear Cousin, November 9, 1861, Neves Papers, SCL; Mrs. Forrest T. Morgan, "'Nancy Harts' of the Confederacy," *Confederate Veteran* 30 (December 1922): 465–66. See discussion of female Regulators in North Carolina in Anonymous to Governor Zebulon Vance, February 18, 1863, Vance Papers, NCDAH.

15. Annie Samuels, Irene Bell, et al. to James Seddon, December 2, 1864, LRCSW, RG 109, reel 122, M437, B692, NA.

16. Subheading is from Kate Cumming, April 3, 1865, in *Kate: The Journal of a Confederate Nurse*, ed. Richard Barksdale Harwell (Baton Rouge: Louisiana State University Press, 1959), 268; Mary Greenhow Lee Diary, March 17, April 23, 3, March 16, 1862, HL; on age as a factor in belligerency, see Alice Ready's parents' effort to restrain her hostility, Ready Diary, March 31, 1862, SHC, and Ida Trotter's description of her cousin who "spent her time doing all she could to aggravate the Yankees and kept the older members of the family in a constant state of uneasiness," Ida Barlow Trotter Memoirs, 6, MDAH.

17. Mary Greenhow Lee Diary, December 14, 1864; see also August 5, 1865, HL.

18. Sarah Morgan, *Civil War Diary*, 122. See Mary Lee's use of the same notion of "Billingsgate style," Mary Greenhow Lee Diary, March 17, 1862, HL.

19. Ready Diary, April 21, 1862, SHC; Amanda Worthington Diary, October 11, 1864, MDAH; Ada Bacot Diary, June 14, 1862, SCL; Mary Greenhow Lee Diary, September 4, 1862, HL; Sarah Morgan, *Civil War Diary*, 122-23.

20. Phebe Levy Pember to Eugenia Phillips, September 13, 1863, Philip Phillips Papers, LC.

21. Mary Greenhow Lee Diary, November 9, 1863, January 6, 1865; see also February 8, 1863, HL; Cornelia Peake McDonald, *A Woman's Civil War: A Diary, with Reminiscences of the War, from March 1862*, edited and with an introduction by Minrose C. Gwin (Madison: University of Wisconsin Press, 1992), 123.

22. Mary Brown to John Brown, June 20, 1865, W. Vance Brown Papers, NCDAH; Annie Harper Reminiscences, 28, MDAH; on Natchez, see Michael Wayne, *The Reshaping of Plantation Society: The Natchez District, 1860-1880* (Baton Rouge: Louisiana State University Press, 1983); D. Clayton James, *Antebellum Natchez* (Baton Rouge: Louisiana State University Press, 1968); and William K. Scarborough, "Lords or Capitalists? The Natchez Nabobs in Comparative Perspective," *Journal of Mississippi History* 54 (August 1992): 239-67.

23. Kate Foster Diary, September 20, 1863, DU; Harper Reminiscences, 29, MDAH; on fraternization with the enemy, see, for example, Mary Jane Cook Chadick Diary, January 1864, March 1, 1865, DU. The files of the Southern Claims Commission in the National Archives are replete with reports of southern civilians aiding the enemy.

24. Benjamin F. Butler, *Autobiography and Personal Reminiscences of Major-General Benjamin F. Butler: Butler's Book* (Boston: Thayer, 1892), 378; subheading is quoted from 418. On Butler and the women of New Orleans, see Mary Ryan, *Women in Public: Between Banners and Ballots, 1825-1880* (Baltimore: Johns Hopkins University Press, 1990), 130-71; George C. Rable, " 'Missing in Action': Women of the Confederacy," in Clinton and Silber, *Divided Houses*, 134-46; Hans L. Trefousse, *Ben Butler: The South Called Him Beast!* (New York: Twayne, 1957), 107-21; Gerald M. Capers, *Occupied City: New Orleans under the Federals, 1862-1865* (Lexington: University of Kentucky Press, 1965); and Simkins and Patton, *Women of the Confederacy*, 56-58.

25. Butler, *Autobiography*, 417.

26. Ibid., 418.

27. Ibid., 421, 418.

28. Ibid., 419; Marion Southwood, *"Beauty and Booty": The Watchword of New Orleans* (New York: M. Doolady, 1867), 133–36; *Richmond Enquirer*, October 7, 1862.

29. Southwood, *"Beauty and Booty,"* 136; Missouri woman quoted in Fellman, *Inside War*, 196; C. Vann Woodward, ed., *Mary Chesnut's Civil War* (New Haven: Yale University Press, 1981), 343; Trefousse, *Ben Butler*, 113; *Mobile Advertiser and Register*, June 26, 1862; Trefousse, *Ben Butler*, 112. For other women's reactions, see Sarah Morgan, *Civil War Diary*, 76–77; Holmes, *Diary*, 165; Ella Gertrude Clanton Thomas, *The Secret Eye: The Journal of Ella Gertrude Clanton Thomas, 1848–1889*, ed. Virginia Ingraham Burr (Chapel Hill: University of North Carolina Press, 1990), 206; Clara Solomon Diary, May 17, 1862, LSU; Barbara Love to Dear Sister, June 5, 1862, and to Dear Brother, June 18, 1862, Curry Hill Plantation Papers, GDAH; and Kate Stone, *Brokenburn: The Journal of Kate Stone, 1861–1868*, ed. John Q. Anderson (Baton Rouge: Louisiana State University Press, 1955), 111.

30. On public and private spheres, see Dorothy O. Helly and Susan M. Reverby, eds., *Gendered Domains: Rethinking Public and Private in Women's History* (New York: Cornell University Press, 1992).

31. Southwood, *"Beauty and Booty,"* 279; Adelaide Stuart Dimitry, "The Battle of the Handkerchiefs," *Confederate Veteran* 31 (May 1923): 182–83.

32. Mary Greenhow Lee Diary, May 5, 1865, HL.

33. Subheading quoted from Belle Boyd, *Belle Boyd in Camp and Prison* (New York: Blelock, 1865), 86. See Charleston *Mercury*, February 27, 1864; Simkins and Patton, *Women of the Confederacy*, 53, 77–80; Louis A. Sigaud, *Belle Boyd: Confederate Spy* (Richmond: Dietz, 1944); Oscar A. Kinchen, *Women Who Spied for the Blue and the Gray* (Philadelphia: Dorrance, 1972); and Ruth Scarborough, *Belle Boyd: Siren of the South* (Macon, Ga.: Mercer University Press, 1983). Boyd was the most notorious but hardly the only female Confederate spy. See, for example, Edmondson, *Lost Heroine*, and Rose O'Neal Greenhow, *My Imprisonment and the First Year of Abolition Rule at Washington* (London: R. Bentley, 1863).

34. Boyd, *Belle Boyd*, 73.

35. Ibid., 86.

36. Ibid., 110–11.

37. Ibid., 227, 118.

38. Ibid., 461.

CHAPTER TEN

1. Chapter title is a quote from Emma Crutcher in a letter to Will Crutcher, December 20, 1861, Crutcher-Shannon Papers, UTA; Sarah Morgan, *The Civil War Diary of Sarah Morgan*, ed. Charles East (Athens: University of Georgia Press, 1991), 167. For another discussion of Sarah Morgan's "fantasies of cross-dressing," see Clara Juncker, "Behind Confederate Lines: Sarah Morgan Dawson," *Southern Quarterly* 30 (Fall 1991): 13. Special thanks for help with this chapter to Joan Severa, costume historian,

and to the Seminar on War and Peace at the Rutgers Center for Historical Studies, particularly John W. Chambers and Rebecca Brittenham.

2. On the cultural meaning of clothes, especially as related to gender identity, see Marjorie Garber, *Vested Interests: Cross-Dressing and Cultural Anxiety* (New York: Routledge, 1992); Sandra M. Gilbert and Susan Gubar, "CrossDressing and ReDressing: Transvestism as Metaphor," in *No Man's Land: The Place of the Woman Writer in the Twentieth Century*, vol. 2, *Sexchanges* (New Haven: Yale University Press, 1989), 324–76; Julia Epstein and Kristina Straub, eds., *Body Guards: The Cultural Politics of Gender Ambiguity* (New York: Routledge, 1991); Jane Gaines and Charlotte Herzog, eds., *Fabrications: Costume and the Female Body* (New York: Routledge, 1990); Alison Lurie, *The Language of Clothes* (New York: Random House, 1981); Juliet Ash and Elizabeth Wilson, eds., *Chic Thrills: A Fashion Reader* (Berkeley: University of California Press, 1992); and Justine M. Cordwell and Ronald A. Schwarz, *The Fabrics of Culture: The Anthropology of Clothing and Adornment* (New York: Mouton, 1979). On women's clothing in the Confederacy, see George C. Rable, *Civil Wars: Women and the Crisis of Southern Nationalism* (Urbana: University of Illinois Press, 1989), 92–95, and Francis Butler Simkins and James Welch Patton, *The Women of the Confederacy* (Richmond: Garrett and Massie, 1936), 147–52. On fashion in the prewar South, see Elizabeth Fox-Genovese, *Within the Plantation Household: Black and White Women of the Old South* (Chapel Hill: University of North Carolina Press, 1988), 214–24.

3. Sarah Morgan, *Civil War Diary*, 77.

4. Subheading quoted from Mary Greenhow Lee Diary, October 19, 1863, HL; Parthenia Antoinette Hague, *A Blockaded Family: Life in Southern Alabama during the Civil War* (1888; rpt, Lincoln: University of Nebraska Press, 1991), 39; Emma LeConte Diary, January 23, 1865, SHC. Residents of Mobile were exuberant at procuring European cloth from blockade-runners in August 1862. See Harriet Amos, "All-Absorbing Topics: Food and Clothing in Confederate Mobile," *Atlanta Historical Society Journal* 22 (Fall–Winter 1978): 22. Recent underwater archaeology has discovered that blockade-runners carried an "enormous quantity of luxury goods," including hoopskirts. "The implication is that even under duress people in the South were not always willing to sacrifice standards of living that they appreciated. In truth, the Confederate government was hard-pressed to secure space for military supplies on many of the blockade runners." Gordon P. Watts, "Runners of the Union Blockade," *Archaeology* 42 (September/October 1989): 38. My thanks to Amber Moncure for drawing this work to my attention.

5. Mary Greenhow Lee Diary, October 19, September 23, 1863, HL; Hague, *Blockaded Family*, 67; Kate Stone, *Brokenburn: The Journal of Kate Stone, 1861–1868*, ed. John Q. Anderson (Baton Rouge: Louisiana State University Press, 1955), 207; Margaret Junkin Preston, April 3, 1862, in *The Life and Letters of Margaret Junkin Preston*, ed. Elizabeth Randolph Allan (Boston: Houghton, Mifflin, 1903), 134; Margaret Gillis Diary, February 24, 1867, ADAH; Lizzie Neblett to Will Neblett, May 17, 1864, Lizzie Neblett Papers, UTA; see also Ellen Moore to Samuel Moore, August 21, 1863, Samuel J. C. Moore Papers, SHC, and Rutherford County women to Zebulon Vance, June 15, 1863, Zebulon Vance Papers, NCDAH.

6. Lizzie Neblett to Will, January 9, 1864; see also March 28, 1864, Neblett Papers,

UTA. On Sarah Morgan's reaction to slave women being given her clothes by the Yankees, see *Civil War Diary*, 213, 215: "Fancy my magenta organdie on a dark beauty! Bah! I think the sight would enrage me!" (215). C. Vann Woodward, ed., *Mary Chesnut's Civil War* (New Haven: Yale University Press, 1981), 588. "Ci-devant" might be translated as "formerly." Stone, *Brokenburn*, 209; see also 175.

7. Subheading from Morgan Callaway to Leila Callaway, May 7, 1862, Morgan Callaway Papers, EU; James Laver, *Costume and Fashion: A Concise History* (New York: Oxford University Press, 1983), 179; see also 170–72 on the cultural meaning of hoops, and see Doreen Yarwood, *The Encyclopedia of World Costume* (New York: Scribners, 1978), who described the style as "the feminine status symbol of the 1850s" (125); Douglas Russell, *Costume History and Style* (Englewood Cliffs, N.J.: Prentice Hall, 1983); and Nora Waugh, *Corsets and Crinolines* (New York: Theatre Arts Books, 1954). Costume historian Joan Severa has kindly shared her insights with me, dating the era of the hoop in American fashion from its first appearance in advertisements circa 1855 to its demise about 1867. Her book *Dressed for the Photographer: Ordinary Americans and Fashion* is forthcoming.

8. Morgan Callaway to Leila Callaway, May 7, 1862; see also May 26, 1862, Callaway Papers, EU; Emma Crutcher to Will Crutcher, February 1, 1862, Crutcher-Shannon Papers, UTA; Stone, *Brokenburn*, 225; for examples of rising costs of cloth, see Rable, *Civil Wars*, 93–94. On hoops and Confederate fashion, see also "Revolution in Ladies' Fashions," October 19, 1863; "The Latest Fashions," December 7, 1863; and "A Badge of Female Disloyalty," November 24, 1863, all in *Charleston Mercury*.

9. Amanda Worthington Diary, May 11, 1862, MDAH.

10. Hague, *Blockaded Family*, 113–14; Anne Shannon Martin Diary, February 23, 1864, MDAH; Elizabeth P. Hardin, *The Private War of Lizzie Hardin: A Kentucky Confederate Girl's Diary of the Civil War in Kentucky, Virginia, Tennessee, Alabama, and Georgia*, ed. G. Glenn Clift (Frankfort: Kentucky Historical Society, 1963), 205; Ellen Moore to Samuel Moore, January 3, 1863, Moore Papers, SHC; Catherine Cochran Reminiscences, vol. 1, VHS. Stays for corsets were another manufactured item scarce in the wartime South. Sara Pryor entreated a Confederate captain to have replacements made for her by the company gunsmith. See Sara Agnes (Mrs. Roger) Pryor, *Reminiscences of Peace and War* (New York: Macmillan, 1904).

11. Clara Solomon Diary, June 10, 1862, LSU.

12. Ibid., June 22, 25, 1862, September 28, 1861; subheading quoted from June 25, 1862; Ruth McLaurin, "Some War-Time Incidents of Sumter County, S.C.," in *South Carolina Women in the Confederacy*, ed. Mrs. Thomas Taylor, Mrs. A. T. Smythe, Mrs. August Kohn, Miss M. B. Poppenheim, and Miss Martha Washington, 2 vols. (Columbia, S.C.: State Co., 1903), 2:173; Nannie Haskins Diary, July 24, 1864, TSL; on shingling, also see, for example, Leila Callaway to Morgan Callaway, October 7, 1862, December 22, 1863, Callaway Papers, EU, and Sidney Harding Diary, July 26, August 1, 1863, LSU. A costume historian describes nineteenth-century shingling as follows: "hair cut at the jawline, very thick and straight at the bottom, and simply parted in the middle, though many young women curled it with a curling iron in order to fluff it out and control it." Joan Severa, personal communication, August 28, 1993. For another

instance of war-induced haircutting by women, see Mary Louise Roberts, *Civilization without Sexes: Reconstructing Gender in Postwar France, 1917–1927* (Chicago: University of Chicago Press, 1994), 63–87.

13. Worthington Diary, June 1, 1863, MDAH; Cordelia Scales, in *Heroines of Dixie: Winter of Desperation*, ed. Katharine M. Jones, 2 vols. (1955; rpt., Saint Simons Island, Ga.: Mockingbird Books, 1975), 1:191; Edward Edgeville, *Castine: A Charming Romance* (Raleigh: William B. Smith, 1865). On cross-dressing, see also Victoria E. Bynum, *Unruly Women: The Politics of Social and Sexual Control in the Old South* (Chapel Hill: University of North Carolina Press, 1992), 132.

14. Emma Crutcher to Will Crutcher, December 20, 1861, Crutcher-Shannon Papers, UTA.

15. "Courtship Extraordinary," *Richmond Enquirer*, April 26, 1864.

16. Subheading quoted from Rowena Webster, n.d., Garrett Papers, TSL; Nina Silber, "Intemperate Men, Spiteful Women, and Jefferson Davis," in *Divided Houses: Gender and the Civil War*, ed. Catherine Clinton and Nina Silber (New York: Oxford University Press, 1992), 283–305. See also Mark E. Neely, Jr., Harold Holzer, and Gabor S. Boritt, "The Belle of Richmond," in *The Confederate Image: Prints of the Lost Cause* (Chapel Hill: University of North Carolina Press, 1987), 79–96, which includes fine examples of cartoons and engravings, and Chester D. Bradley, "Was Jefferson Davis Disguised as a Woman When Captured?," *Journal of Mississippi History* 36 (August 1974): 246. Mary Lee, for example, did not question the tale; see Mary Greenhow Lee Diary, May 20, 1865, HL.

17. Rowena Webster, n.d., Garrett Papers, TSL; Helen Garner quoted in United Daughters of the Confederacy, Mississippi Division, Stephen Lee Chapter, *War Reminiscences of Columbus, Mississippi* (West Point, Miss.: Sullivan's, 1961), 15; see memoir of Eliza Ann Lanier in Alanda Timberlake Papers, MDAH, and *Richmond Enquirer*, September 10, 1862.

18. Meta Morris Grimball Diary, January 1, 1863, SHC.

19. Florence Percy, *Rock Me to Sleep, Mother* (Columbia, S.C.: Julian Selby, 1862); Drew Gilpin Faust, *The Creation of Confederate Nationalism: Ideology and Identity in the Civil War South* (Baton Rouge: Louisiana State University Press, 1988), 18–19.

20. Subheading quoted from Sarah Morgan, *Civil War Diary*, 183; Lizzie Neblett to Will Neblett, March 20, 1864, Neblett Papers, UTA; Sarah Morgan, *Civil War Diary*, 182–83; see also Sarah Anne Grover Strickler Diary, May 9, 1865, UVA.

21. Sarah Morgan, *Civil War Diary*, 65; Belle Edmondson, March 5, 1864, in *A Lost Heroine of the Confederacy: The Diaries and Letters of Belle Edmondson*, ed. William Galbraith and Loretta Galbraith (Jackson: University Press of Mississippi, 1990), 91; Elizabeth Collier Diary, April 11, 1862, SHC; Emma Walton to J. B. Walton, May 12, 1863, Walton-Glenny Papers, THNOC; Sallie Munford quoted in Douglas S. Freeman, *The South to Posterity: An Introduction to the Writings of Confederate History* (New York: Scribners, 1939), 109. See also Octavia Stephens to Winston Stephens, December 11, 1863, Bryant-Stephens Papers, UFL; Worthington Diary, February 11, 25, 1862, MDAH; Lizzie Neblett to Will Neblett, April 27, 1864, Neblett Papers, UTA; Abby Slocomb to J. B. Walton, October 23, 1862, Walton-Glenny Papers, THNOC; Bragg

quoted in Rable, *Civil Wars*, 150; Mary Ann Loughborough quoted in Katharine M. Jones, *Heroines of Dixie*, 2:7; *Richmond Enquirer*, October 4, 1864.

22. Sarah Morgan, *Civil War Diary*, 156.

23. *Countryman*, May 3, 1864. For a twentieth-century example of this ideological strategy, see Margaret Randolph Higonnet, Jane Jenson, Sonya Michel, and Margaret Collins Weitz, eds., *Behind the Lines: Gender and the Two World Wars* (New Haven: Yale University Press, 1987), 7.

24. Maria M. Hubard Diary, June 25, 1861, VHS; Clara MacLean Diary, March 3, 1862, DU; Woodward, *Mary Chesnut's Civil War*, 677.

25. Ella Gertrude Clanton Thomas, *The Secret Eye: The Journal of Ella Gertrude Clanton Thomas, 1848–1889*, ed. Virginia Ingraham Burr (Chapel Hill: University of North Carolina Press, 1990), 204; Catherine Edmondston, *Journal of a Secesh Lady: The Diary of Catherine Ann Devereux Edmondston, 1860–1866*, ed. Beth G. Crabtree and James W. Patton (Raleigh: Division of Archives and History, 1979), 64.


CHAPTER ELEVEN

1. Title is quoted from Mary Bryan to My dear Daughter, May 20, 1863, John Heritage Bryan Collection, NCDAH.

2. See my discussion of combat stress in Civil War soldiers in Faust, "Christian Soldiers: The Meaning of Revivalism in the Confederate Army," in *Southern Stories: Slaveholders in Peace and War* (Columbia: University of Missouri Press, 1992), 88–109. See also Herbert Hendin and Ann Pollinger Haas, *Wounds of War: The Psychological Aftermath of Combat* (New York: Basic Books, 1984); Robert Jay Lifton, *Home from the War* (New York: Simon and Schuster, 1973); and Richard Severo and Lewis Milford, *The Wages of War: When America's Soldiers Came Home: From Valley Forge to Vietnam* (New York: Simon and Schuster, 1989).

3. Mary Jane Cook Chadick Diary, January 1, 1865, DU; L. Virginia French Diary, March 26, 1863, TSL; Emma Dobson to James Seddon, January 3, 1865, LRCSW, RG 109, reel 147, M437, D4, NA; Annie Upshur to Jefferson Davis, January 3, 1865, LRCSW, RG 109, reel 114, U2, NA.

4. Mary Greenhow Lee Diary, May 21, June 2, 1865, HL; Catherine Cooper Diary, April 6, 1863, TSL; Emily Harris Diary, February 17, 1865, November 23, 1862, October 9, November 21, 1864, WC.

5. Cornelia Peake McDonald, *A Woman's Civil War: A Diary, with Reminiscences of the War, from March 1862*, edited and with an introduction by Minrose C. Gwin (Madison: University of Wisconsin Press, 1992), 99; Mary Legg to Hattie Palmer, July 3, 1863, Palmer Family Papers, SCL. For an almost identical remark, see Ella Gertrude Clanton Thomas, *The Secret Eye: The Journal of Ella Gertrude Clanton Thomas, 1848–1889*, ed. Virginia Ingraham Burr (Chapel Hill: University of North Carolina Press, 1990), 257.

6. Abbie Brooks Diary, April 4, 1865, AHC; Myrta Lockett Avary, ed., *A Virginia Girl in the Civil War, 1861–1865* (New York: Appleton, 1903), 41; Sara Agnes (Mrs.

Roger) Pryor, *Reminiscences of Peace and War* (New York: Macmillan, 1904), 372; Lizzie Neblett to Will Neblett, August 11, 1863, Lizzie Neblett Papers, UTA. For uses of the term *callous*, see Amelia Pinkind to Isabella Woodruff, September 15, 1861, Isabella Woodruff Papers, DU; Mary Greenhow Lee Diary, August 9, 1862, HL; and Emma LeConte Diary, January 18, 1865, SCL.

7. Belle Edmondson Diary, April 17, 1864, SHC; M. A. Parkman to Jefferson Davis, March 25, 1863, LRCSW, RG 109, reel 106, M437, P130, NA; French Diary, August 9, 1863, TSL; Emily Harris Diary, November 18, 1864, WC.

8. Julia Davidson to John Davidson, August 1863, Davidson Family Papers, AHC; Thomas, *Secret Eye*, 250; A. Grima to Alfred Grima, November 27, 1863, January 4, 1864, Grima Family Papers, THNOC; Constance Cary Harrison, *Recollections Grave and Gay* (New York: Scribners, 1911), 83; Elizabeth Randolph Allan, ed., *The Life and Letters of Margaret Junkin Preston* (Boston: Houghton, Mifflin, 1903), 148; Sarah Jane Sams to Randolph Sams, February 10, 1865, Sams Family Papers, SCL; Julia Le Grand, *The Journal of Julia Le Grand, New Orleans, 1862–1863*, ed. Kate Mason Rowland and Mrs. Morris L. Croxall (Richmond: Everett Waddey, 1911), 44–45. "I see only sacrifices, victims, ruin, misery, nothing to gain . . . massacres without result." French translated by the author.

9. Marinda Branson Moore, *The Dixie Speller* (Raleigh: Branson and Farrar, 1864), 23. On World War I as the birth of the modern, see Paul Fussell, *The Great War and Modern Memory* (New York: Oxford University Press, 1975).

10. Betty Herndon Maury, *The Confederate Diary of Betty Herndon Maury, 1861–1863*, ed. Alice Maury Parmalee (Washington, D.C.: privately printed, 1938), 60; Sal to Robert Mabry, October 25, 1864, Robert C. Mabry Papers, NCDAH; Margaret Crawford, "Tales of a Grandmother," in *South Carolina Women in the Confederacy*, ed. Mrs. Thomas Taylor, Mrs. A. T. Smythe, Mrs. August Kohn, Miss M. B. Poppenheim, and Miss Martha Washington, 2 vols. (Columbia, S.C.: State Co., 1903), 1:210.

11. On extortion in the Confederacy, see Drew Gilpin Faust, "'Sliding into the World': The Sin of Extortion and the Dynamic of Confederate Identity," in *The Creation of Confederate Nationalism: Ideology and Identity in the Civil War South* (Baton Rouge: Louisiana State University Press, 1988), 41–57.

12. Mary Bell to Alfred Bell, July 20, 1862, Alfred W. Bell Papers, DU; Louisa Rice to Zachariah Rice, December 29, 1862, Zachariah Rice Papers, AHC; Mary Pugh to Richard Pugh, November 9, 1862, Richard Pugh Papers, LSU; Octavia Stephens to Winston Stephens, March 19, 1862, Bryant-Stephens Papers, UFL.

13. Avary, *Virginia Girl*, 302; Harris Diary, March 31, 1864, WC; Margaret Easterling to Jefferson Davis, December 3, 1862, LRCSW, RG 109, reel 45, M437, E227, NA; Mary L. Scales to the Confederate Secretary of War, September 8, 1862, LRCSW, RG 109, reel 72, S890, NA.

14. Mary Chichester to Arthur Chichester, May 2, 1864, Point Lookout Letters, NA;. Thomas, *Secret Eye*, 240.

15. See C. B. Macpherson, *The Political Theory of Possessive Individualism: Hobbes to Locke* (New York: Oxford University Press, 1962), for a discussion of this transformation, and see Carole Pateman, *The Sexual Contract* (Stanford: Stanford University Press, 1988), for a perspective on these issues that includes gender.

16. On the shift from republicanism to liberalism, see, for example, Steven Watts, *The Republic Reborn: War and the Making of Liberal America, 1790–1820* (Baltimore: Johns Hopkins University Press, 1987); Joyce Appleby, *Capitalism and a New Social Order: The Republican Vision of the 1790s* (New York: New York University Press, 1983); Gordon Wood, *The Creation of the American Republic, 1776–1787* (Chapel Hill: University of North Carolina Press, 1969); Drew R. McCoy, *The Elusive Republic: Political Economy in Jeffersonian America* (Chapel Hill: University of North Carolina Press, 1980); and Gordon Wood, *The Radicalism of the American Revolution* (New York: Knopf, 1992). The literature on republicanism is voluminous. See, for overviews, Daniel T. Rodgers, "Republicanism: The Career of a Concept," *Journal of American History* 79 (June 1992): 11–38, and Robert E. Shalhope, "Republicanism and Early American Historiography," *William and Mary Quarterly* 39 (April 1982): 334–56.

17. For a classic statement of the liberation of women by war, see William Chafe, *The American Woman: Her Changing Social, Economic, and Political Roles, 1920–1970* (New York: Oxford University Press, 1972). For examples of Confederate women speaking of necessity as the mother of invention, see Clara Solomon Diary, May 18, 1862, LSU, and Amelia Pinkind to Isabella Woodruff, August 4, 1862, Woodruff Papers, DU. Julia Davidson to John Davidson, September 8, 1863, Davidson Family Papers, AHC.

18. On women encouraging men to desert, see, for example, remarks of Kate Cumming, in *Kate: The Journal of a Confederate Nurse*, ed. Richard Barksdale Harwell (Baton Rouge: Louisiana State University Press, 1959), 296, and R. E. Lee to Zebulon Vance, February 24, 1865, and J. Johnston Pettigrew to Vance, May 22, 1863, Vance Papers, NCDAH. Quotations are from B. M. Edney to James Seddon, August 18, 1863, LRCSW, RG 109, reel 90, M437, E106, NA, and Charles Fenton James to Dear Sister, February 13, 1864, Charles Fenton James Papers, SHC. See Ella Lonn, *Desertion during the Civil War* (New York: Century, 1928), and Richard Bardolph, " 'Inconstant Rebels': Desertion of North Carolina Troops in the Civil War," *North Carolina Historical Review* 41 (Spring 1964): 163–89. Those women who clung to their patriotism demonstrated their exceptionality in their complaints about the contrasting sentiments around them. See Kate Stone, *Brokenburn: The Journal of Kate Stone, 1861–1868*, ed. John Q. Anderson (Baton Rouge: Louisiana State University Press, 1955), 344, and Mary Greenhow Lee Diary, April 19, 1865, HL.

19. *Montgomery Daily Advertiser*, June 15, 1864.

20. Augusta Jane Evans, "Women of the Confederacy," clipping in M. L. Lawton Scrapbook, 66, AHC.

21. Tombeckbee Presbytery of Alabama, Minutes, April 8, 1865, HFPC; Pryor, *Reminiscences*, 326; Grace Elmore Diary, February 7, 1865, SCL; Thomas, *Secret Eye*, 220; C. Vann Woodward, ed., *Mary Chesnut's Civil War* (New Haven: Yale University Press, 1981), 430; Mary Early Diary, January 19, 1865, VHS; George C. Rable, *Civil Wars: Women and the Crisis of Southern Nationalism* (Urbana: University of Illinois Press, 1989), 200. See also Phoebe Yates Pember, *A Southern Woman's Story: Life in Confederate Richmond*, ed. Bell Irvin Wiley (1959; rpt., Saint Simons Island, Ga.: Mockingbird Books, 1974), 127, and Judith McGuire, *Diary of a Southern Refugee, during the War* (New York: E. J. Hale, 1867), 328–29.

22. *Richmond Enquirer*, February 12, 1864; Will Neblett to Lizzie Neblett, March 12, 1864, Neblett Papers, UTA.

23. On bread riots and female violence, see Michael Chesson, "Harlots or Heroines? A New Look at the Richmond Bread Riot," *Virginia Magazine of History and Biography* 92 (April 1984): 131–75; Victoria E. Bynum, *Unruly Women: The Politics of Social and Sexual Control in the Old South* (Chapel Hill: University of North Carolina Press, 1992); Paul Escott, *Many Excellent People: Power and Privilege in North Carolina, 1850–1900* (Chapel Hill: University of North Carolina Press, 1986), 23, 67; J. A. Richardson to Zebulon Vance, April 18, 1864, Vance Papers, NCDAH; and A. L. W. Stroud to Jefferson Davis, May 6, 1864, in U.S. War Department, *The War of the Rebellion: A Compilation of the Official Records of the Union and Confederate Armies*, 127 vols. and index (Washington, D.C.: Government Printing Office, 1880–1901), series 1, 52(2): 667–68.

24. Elizabeth Fix to Jefferson Davis, February 21, 1865, RG 109, Citizens Files, NA; Thomas, *Secret Eye*, 252; Almira Acors to Jefferson Davis, March 23, 1862, LRCSW, RG 109, reel 29, M437, A62, NA.

25. McDonald, *Woman's Civil War*, 224.

26. Gaines M. Foster, *Ghosts of the Confederacy: Defeat, the Lost Cause, and the Emergence of the New South* (New York: Oxford University Press, 1987).


EPILOGUE

1. Mary Greenhow Lee Diary, September 13, 1865, HL; Garland R. Quarles, *Occupied Winchester, 1861–1865* (Winchester, Va.: Winchester-Frederick County Historical Society, 1991), 16. Title is quoted from Lucy Rebecca Buck, *Sad Earth, Sweet Heaven: The Diary of Lucy Rebecca Buck*, ed. William Pettus Buck (Birmingham, Ala.: Cornerstone, 1973), 50.

2. Ninth Census of the United States, Population Schedules and Agricultural Schedules, Grimes County, Tex., NA; Lizzie Neblett Reminiscence, May 25, 1912, UTA.

3. Margaret Gillis Diary, June 6, 1866, ADAH.

4. See Nell Irvin Painter, "Introduction: The Journal of Ella Gertrude Clanton Thomas: An Educated White Woman in the Eras of Slavery, War, and Reconstruction," in *The Secret Eye: The Journal of Ella Gertrude Clanton Thomas, 1848–1889*, ed. Virginia Ingraham Burr (Chapel Hill: University of North Carolina Press, 1990), 1–67; Mary Elizabeth Massey, "The Making of a Feminist," *Journal of Southern History* 39 (February 1973): 3–22; Virginia Ingraham Burr, "A Woman Made to Suffer and Be Strong: Ella Gertrude Clanton Thomas, 1834–1907," in *In Joy and in Sorrow: Women, Family, and Marriage in the Victorian South, 1830–1900*, ed. Carol Bleser (New York: Oxford University Press, 1991), 215–32.

5. Lucy Rebecca Buck, April 18, 1862, in *Sad Earth, Sweet Heaven*, 50; Emma Mordecai Diary, May 20, 1865, SHC; Wilbur Fisk Tillett, "Southern Womanhood as Affected by the War," *Century* 43 (November 1891): 12, 13.

6. Marjorie Stratford Mendenhall, "Southern Women of a 'Lost Generation,'" *South*

*Atlantic Quarterly* 33 (October 1934): 345; Tillett, "Southern Womanhood," 15. On women's education in the postwar era, see also Anne Firor Scott, *The Southern Lady: From Pedestal to Politics, 1830–1930* (Chicago: University of Chicago Press, 1970), 114–15.

7. See Kathleen Berkeley, "Elizabeth Avery Meriwether, 'An Advocate for Her Sex': Feminism and Conservatism in the Post Civil War South," *Tennessee Historical Quarterly* 43 (Winter 1984): 390–407; Marjorie Spruill Wheeler, *New Women of the New South: The Leaders of the Woman Suffrage Movement in the Southern States* (New York: Oxford University Press, 1993), 80–81; and Suzanne Lebsock, "Radical Reconstruction and the Property Rights of Southern Women," *Journal of Southern History* 43 (May 1977): 195–216.

8. Lebsock, "Radical Reconstruction," 215.

9. Amanda Sims to Harriet Palmer, February 9, 1867, Palmer Family Papers, SCL; Kate Stone, *Brokenburn: The Journal of Kate Stone, 1861–1868*, ed. John Q. Anderson (Baton Rouge: Louisiana State University Press, 1955), 363, 364. On posttraumatic stress in Confederate soldiers, see Drew Gilpin Faust, "Christian Soldiers: The Meaning of Revivalism in the Confederate Army," in *Southern Stories: Slaveholders in Peace and War* (Columbia: University of Missouri Press, 1992), 88–109.

10. See Gaines M. Foster, *Ghosts of the Confederacy: Defeat, the Lost Cause, and the Emergence of the New South* (New York: Oxford University Press, 1987), and Charles Reagan Wilson, *Baptized in Blood: The Religion of the Lost Cause, 1865–1920* (Athens: University of Georgia Press, 1980).

11. Emily Harris Diary, November 7, 1863, WC; Drew Gilpin Faust, " 'Trying to Do a Man's Business': Gender, Violence, and Slave Management in Civil War Texas," in Faust, *Southern Stories*, 174–92. For examples of other women who shared Thomas's configuration of postwar commitments, see Berkeley, "Elizabeth Avery Meriwether," and Carol Bleser and Frederick Heath, "The Clays of Alabama: The Impact of the Civil War on a Southern Marriage," in Bleser, *In Joy and in Sorrow*, 135–53.

12. Wheeler, *New Women of the New South*, 18; Scott, *Southern Lady*, 163. See also Cita Cook, "Public Daughters of the New South: Young White Women in Civic Ceremonies, 1877–1917" (paper delivered at the Organization of American Historians Annual Meeting, Atlanta, 1994).

13. Lizzie Neblett to Will Neblett, undated letter fragment [1864], Lizzie Neblett Papers, UTA; Wheeler, *New Women of the New South*, 112, 118. Many scholars before me have remarked on how divisions of race undermined feminism in the postwar South. For an elegantly stated example, see Suzanne Lebsock, *The Free Women of Petersburg: Status and Culture in a Southern Town, 1784–1860* (New York: Norton, 1984), 237–49. See also Jacquelyn Dowd Hall, *Revolt against Chivalry: Jessie Daniel Ames and the Women's Campaign against Lynching* (New York: Columbia University Press, 1979), and Grace Elizabeth Hale, " 'Some Women Have Never Been Reconstructed': Mildred Lewis Rutherford, Lucy M. Stanton, and the Racial Politics of White Southern Womanhood, 1900–1930" (unpublished paper kindly lent by the author).

1. C. Vann Woodward, *The Burden of Southern History* (Baton Rouge: Louisiana State University Press, 1960); revised editions published in 1968 and 1993. Quotation is from the 1968 edition, p. 19.

2. See William Faulkner, *Requiem for a Nun* (New York: Random House, 1950), 92, and Faulkner, *Intruder in the Dust* (New York: Random House, 1948).

3. For an overview of the historical literature, see Darlene Clark Hine, ed., *The State of Afro-American History: Past, Present, and Future* (Baton Rouge: Louisiana State University Press, 1986); for a literary example, see Toni Morrison, *Beloved* (New York: Knopf, 1987).

4. On disdain, see Marjorie Spruill Wheeler, *New Women of the New South: The Leaders of the Woman Suffrage Movement in the Southern States* (New York: Oxford University Press, 1993), 40. Susan B. Anthony quoted in Elaine Partnow, *The Quotable Woman* (New York: Meridian, 1993), 189.

# BIBLIOGRAPHIC NOTE

## PRIMARY SOURCES
*Manuscripts and Printed and Iconographic Materials*

The most significant sources for this book have been the manuscript letters and diaries of Confederate women and their families located at the more than two dozen libraries and repositories listed at the beginning of the Notes. Diaries often provide a more introspective view of the writer than letters, which are from the outset explicitly fashioned for a particular audience. But so many Civil War diarists wrote in hopes of eventual publication or with an eye to posterity that a scholar must carefully define the writers' larger purposes before evaluating these works as well. Just as I have argued that there was little space for private lives in the wartorn South, so I would suggest that few manuscripts can really be considered "private" papers. Confederate women knew they lived in an important historic moment, and they often wrote to exert their influence over that history. Postwar reminiscences raise even more significant problems, for the scholar must evaluate the role of hindsight and the influence of late nineteenth-century contexts and concerns. Although such reminiscences abound, in both manuscript and published forms, I have been both cautious and sparing in my use of them. Far more valuable to me have been the women's letters that appear in the surviving records of Confederate national and state governments. I have found collections of letters to the governors of Georgia, Mississippi, and North Carolina, housed in the archives of each state, especially useful. The Letters Received by the Confederate Secretary of War and other correspondence from civilians located in the Confederate government records at the National Archives offer unparalleled insight into the lives of white women of all classes—from the wealthiest slave mistresses to illiterate farm wives, who asked their more educated neighbors to forward their dictated concerns to Richmond. Manuscript records of nongovernmental institutions proved less helpful to me, partly because record keeping was often so incomplete during the war years. Nevertheless, I found some church and denominational records useful, most notably those at the Historical Foundation of the Presbyterian Church at Montreat, North Carolina. Archives of women's educational institutions were difficult to locate and, with the exception of those of long-lived Hollins College of Roanoke, Virginia, less revealing than I had hoped. Minutes of women's voluntary and soldiers' aid organizations tend to be fragmentary but usually list officers and activities and enumerate goods produced for the front.

The popularity of Civil War history has combined with expanding interest in the past experience of women to encourage editors and publishers to reprint growing numbers of wartime diaries and letters. As a result, many primary materials are now readily available in bookstores and public libraries. These are an invaluable resource for scholars and teachers and permit even a general reader the opportunity to engage these women directly. More than a dozen such editions are cited in my notes. Perhaps the best known of these is C. Vann Woodward's Pulitzer Prize–winning edition of *Mary Chesnut's Civil War* (New Haven: Yale University Press, 1981), but the interested reader can, for example, also readily locate recent new editions of the diaries of Cornelia Peake McDonald, Ella Gertrude Clanton Thomas, Kate Stone, Sarah Morgan, Emma Holmes, Ada Bacot, and Keziah Brevard. Editions of family letters are abundant as well. Here the classic is Robert Manson Myers's edition of *The Children of Pride: A True Story of Georgia and the Civil War* (New Haven: Yale University Press, 1972), the letters of the devoutly Presbyterian Jones family.

For my purposes, material printed during the war years themselves has proved indispensable as a source of insight into the wider cultural and social context and discourse in which Confederate women operated. Shortages of paper and of printing machinery inhibited Confederate publishing, but an influential newspaper and periodical press nevertheless survived until the last days of the war. The endnotes demonstrate how useful I have found local and denominational newspapers, for discussion of women's roles and duties was a staple of cultural commentary. The lengthier disquisitions of the periodical press are perhaps even more revealing on subjects such as nursing, women's education, and women authors. The interaction between these cultural voices and women's own experiences were critical to women's redefinitions of themselves in the war era.

Two bibliographies of Confederate imprints, intended to be exhaustive, together with a microfilmed edition of their contents make the great bulk of published Confederate literature readily available to the researcher: Marjorie Lyle Crandall, *Confederate Imprints: A Check List* (Boston: Boston Athenaeum, 1955), vols. 1 and 2; Richard Harwell, *More Confederate Imprints* (Richmond: Virginia State Library, 1957), vols. 1 and 2; and *Confederate Imprints, 1861–1865* (143 reels of microfilm) (New Haven: Research Publications, 1974). I have found printed songs, sermons, novels, and poetry essential to my effort to understand Confederate popular culture and women's place within it. Published state and national government laws and records, also included in these bibliographies, proved essential to my analysis of relevant legislation, particularly in regard to nursing and conscription.

Iconographic materials have posed a special challenge, in part because historians have not tended in the past to treat them as seriously and rigorously as other sorts of evidence. Identifications and attributions of photographs have been made casually and often without attention to the standards historians would apply to the documentary record. In my search for illustrations for this book, I have been appalled to find photographs seemingly randomly captioned by an author or editor, as if the accuracy of their titles somehow did not matter as much as the accuracy of the accompanying text. Just to give one example: a widely reprinted photograph captioned "Southern Women and their Slaves" is in fact a picture of northern abolitionist teachers and their recently emancipated pupils.

Another challenge to the scholar wishing to use visual materials about white southern women is their scarcity. I would contend they are in fact the least photographed and most literally invisible group, black or white, North or South. Soldiers attract overwhelming attention from photographers and engravers; slaves and recently freed people are also of great interest to Civil War artists and photographers and appear not infrequently in the visual record, although black men are certainly more often represented than black women. Photography was widespread enough in the North that pictures of white northern women are available in numbers that are simply not paralleled in the South, where photographers were less numerous and engraving was technologically underdeveloped. As a result, images of white southern women are quite rare, and many of those we do have come, like the oft-reprinted engravings in *Harper's Weekly* and *Frank Leslie's Illustrated Newspaper*, from northern sources. I would hope that historians could begin to attend more closely and carefully to photographic sources. We need as well to work with the objects—hair sculptures, socks, homespun dresses, and so forth—that represent the material record of southern women during the war.

### SECONDARY SOURCES ON CONFEDERATE WOMEN

Because the literature on the Civil War is voluminous—it is the most written-about subject in American history—I will confine my remarks here to works explicitly focused on white southern women. Traditional Civil War historiography has not entirely neglected the experience of white southern women, although treatments have tended to focus on celebrating women's contributions to men's military efforts. Francis Butler Simkins and James Welch Patton's *Women of the Confederacy* (Richmond: Garrett and Massie, 1936) remains useful for its extensive research into the lives of mostly elite white women. Mary Elizabeth Massey's *Bonnet Brigades: American Women and the Civil War* (New York: Knopf, 1966), written at the time of the Civil War centennial and recently reprinted as *Women in the Civil War* (Lincoln: University of Nebraska Press, 1994), is a learned consideration of women North and South that is less dated than its original title would lead one to expect. H. E. Sterkx has written a state study, *Partners in Rebellion: Alabama Women in the Civil War* (Rutherford, N.J.: Fairleigh Dickinson University Press, 1970), that contains some nuggets of local history. The value of Bell Irvin Wiley's *Confederate Women* (Westport, Conn.: Greenwood Press, 1975) is limited by its biographical approach. Far more useful than any of these for the contemporary reader is George Rable's *Civil Wars: Women and the Crisis of Southern Nationalism* (Urbana: University of Illinois Press, 1989), which has been enriched by the outpouring of work in women's history that occurred in the decade and a half prior to its appearance. Rable's extensive research and his judicious insights have been invaluable to me, although I have chosen to place more emphasis on concepts of class and gender in shaping my analytic framework and on cultural materials in contextualizing my analysis. Rable has been unfailingly generous as I have mucked about on what he might understandably have regarded as his turf.

The evolution of women's history toward the broader study of gender is exerting an important influence on the growing numbers of studies of Civil War women. An early example of this is *Divided Houses: Gender and the Civil War* (New York: Oxford

University Press, 1992), edited by Catherine Clinton and Nina Silber. This volume is particularly valuable because it contains essays by a number of scholars who have larger works in progress, many of which should be available in the very near future.

Careful attention to my extensive endnotes will reward the reader interested in more detailed information about both primary and secondary sources.

# INDEX

Adolescent girls, 38; friendships between, 143–44, 151–52
African Americans, 112, 256. *See also* Blacks; Slaves
Agriculture, 31–32, 54
Aiken, S.C., Ladies Relief Association, 93
Alabama: ladies' aid associations in, 24
Alden, Esther, 148
Alexander (captain), 198
American Freedman's Inquiry Commission, 126
American Revolution, 5
Amputation, 106–7
Andrews, Emily, 158
Ann (slave), 71
Anthony, Susan B., 256–57
Antietam, battle of, 96, 107, 182
Arp, Bill, 43
Asheville, N.C., 207
Athens, Ga., 25
Atkinson, Bishop Thomas, 182
Atlanta, Ga., Union occupation of, 40–41, 43, 130
Atlanta Hospital Association, 93–94
Augusta, Ga., 44
*Augusta Daily Constitutionalist*, 83
Augusta *Southern Field and Fireside*, 22, 84, 167
*Augusta Weekly Constitutionalist*, 22, 168
Authors, women as, 154, 161, 165, 166–68, 169, 288–89 (n. 4)

Bacon, Francis, 160
Bacot, Ada, 26, 148; on secession, 11; on Civil War, 21–22; and slaves, 57, 58, 62, 63; as volunteer nurse, 99–100, 108, 110, 206
Bagby, Lucy, 11
Banks, Nathaniel, 212–13

Baptist Female College of Southwest Georgia, 39
Barnwell, Rev. Robert, 81
Barr, Amelia, 78
Barr, Henrietta, 78
Barton, Clara, 111
Beale, Jane Howison, 73, 182
Beckwith, Margaret, 44
Beers, Fannie, 99, 189
Bell, Alfred, 118, 121
Bell, Irene, 204
Bell, Mary (of Franklin, N.C.): and slaves, 71–72; correspondence with husband, 118, 121, 123, 241; on children, 130
Bell, Mary W. M. (of Tennessee), 130–31, 132, 149–50, 185
Berry, Carrie, 130
Betty (slave), 76
*Biblical Recorder*, 185
Bill (slave), 127
Birth control, 124
Blackford, Mary, 22
Blacks, 256; as Union soldiers, 60; women, sexual vulnerability, 73, 200; and clothing, 222–23; emancipated, white women and, 253–54. *See also* Slaves
Blockade, 45, 46–47, 48–49, 158
Blockade-runners, 221, 300 (n. 4)
Blunt, Annie, 168
Boarding schools, 39, 57, 142
Books, 153–57, 158, 178
Botts, John Minor, 38
Boyce, Mrs. W. W., 73–74
Boyd, Belle: killing of Yankee soldier, 202, 215; spying career, 214–19
Boykin, Charlotte, 157
Boykin, Laura Nisbet, 181
Bragg, Elsie, 231

{ 313 }

women's fashion and, 223; Confederate collapse and, 245–47

Clinton, Catherine, 273 (n. 21)

Clothing: homespun, 46, 47–48, 49, 51, 221–22, 269 (n. 28), 269–70 (n. 29); economic conditions and, 48–49, 222–23; government seamstresses, 89–90; cross-dressing, 220, 226–30; shortages, 220–21; hoopskirts, 223–26, 300 (n. 4), 301 (n. 7); theatrical costumes, 227–28

Clothing Bureau, 89

Coastal defense, 28–29

Cobb, Mary Ann, 25

Cochran, Catherine, 75–76, 197, 201, 225

Coleman (overseer), 67, 68

Colleges, 251

Collier, Elizabeth, 194, 231

Columbia *Daily Southern Guardian*, 43

Columbus, Miss., 29

Comer, Laura, 184

Concord (N.C.) Female College, 84

Confederacy: female patriotism and, 13–14, 15, 16–17, 25, 243–44; women's disillusionment with, 28, 238, 239–41, 242, 243–44, 245, 246–47; naval defenses, 28–29; role of slavery in, 30, 53–54, 55; conscription, 30–31, 32, 55–56, 241; military mobilization, 30–31, 45, 81, 109; household structures, 34–35; Union blockade of, 45, 46–47, 48–49, 158; economic conditions in, 45, 51, 221; military clothing bureaus, 50, 89; slave uprisings in, 58, 59; Lost Cause iconography, 60, 247, 252–53, 254; women's employment in, 81, 82, 84, 88–89, 97, 109; military hospitals, 95–96, 97–98; postal service, 115–16; *Macaria* and, 168–69, 172; nationalism, 172, 180, 192, 195; religion and, 179–82, 192–93, 194, 195; surrender of, 194, 228; Union occupa-

tion in, 197; social frivolity in, 244–45; constitution of, 262 (n. 3). *See also* South

Confederate army, 120; conscription and, 30, 204; salaries, 89; prostitution and, 125; religion in, 185, 186; women's frustration with, 204, 240–41; desertion in, 243

*Confederate Baptist*, 93

Confederate Congress, 32, 55, 96, 97–98

Confederate Memorial Society, 247

Confederate navy, 28

Confederate Post Office, 116

Conscription: enactment of, 30, 32, 54; effects on women and households, 32, 51, 54–56, 98; exemption for slave managers, 55; women's opposition to, 204, 241

Constitutional law, 4–5

Cook, Minerva Marie Louise Hynes, 269 (n. 28)

Cooper, Catherine, 236

Cooper, Samuel, 89

Cornwall, Susan, 12

Cotton cards, 48

Courtship: disruptions of war and, 38, 148, 151, 161; and female friendships, 144; military camps and, 146; widows and, 148, 149–50

Craighead, Rachel, 186

Craven, Elizabeth, 273 (n. 21)

Creasy, Edward: *Fifteen Decisive Battles of the World*, 160

Crime, 240

Crocker, Marcellus (general), 207

Crossley, Martha Jane, 47

Crutcher, Emma: on tableaux vivants, 28; as refugee, 36–37, 249; as hospital volunteer, 102–4, 110, 113; correspondence with husband, 114–15, 117, 118, 121; on children, 129, 130; on reading, 155; and clothing fashions, 224, 225, 227, 233; as teacher, 249, 250–51

Farmville (Va.) Female College, 39

Fashion: and women's identity, 220–21, 223, 233; homespun textiles and, 221–22; hoopskirts, 223–26, 300 (n. 4), 301 (n. 7); hairstyles, 226, 301–2 (n. 12)

Faulkner, William, 255–56

Fellman, Michael, 200

Female dependence: and subordination of women, 59, 211; upon slaves, 61–62, 77–78, 226; use of violence and, 63, 70; employment and, 82; religion and, 194, 195; wartime experience and, 251

Female-headed households, 33, 34

Female identity: wartime disruptions and, 6–7, 23–24, 137; "ladyhood," 7, 27, 110, 113, 247, 253; desire to escape from, 20, 221, 231–33; wealth and, 43; use of violence and, 70, 232; employment and, 112–13; relation to men and marriage, 139–40, 141, 151; politicization and, 211; clothing fashions and, 220–21, 223, 233

Female self-sacrifice, 17, 138, 166, 178, 234–35

Female subordination, 122; plantation hierarchy and, 32; sexual vulnerability and, 59, 211; disillusionment with men and, 137, 138, 242, 247; religion and, 193, 194, 195; clothing and, 221

Female vulnerability, 57, 63; sexual, 59, 73, 200, 211, 272–73 (n. 13)

Feminism, 5, 254, 256–57

Fillebrowne (colonel), 217

Fitzhugh, George, 5–6

Floyd County, Ga., 25

Fogg, Mary Rutledge, 94

Fondren, Nettie, 31, 143

Ford, Lacy, 269 (n. 28)

Fort, Martha, 56, 138

Foster, Kate, 140, 182; on household labor, 78; and brother's death, 190–91; on Union occupation troops, 207

Foucault, Michel, 264 (n. 17)

Fox-Genovese, Elizabeth, 265 (n. 32), 273 (n. 21), 274 (n. 42), 289 (n. 5)

*Frank Leslie's Illustrated Newspaper*, 228

French, Johns Hopkins, 134–35

French, Lucy Virginia Smith: as author and editor, 134, 166; disenchantment with husband and men, 134–35, 136, 138, 159; on reading, 154–55; and religion, 195; and Union occupation troops, 199; frustration with war, 235, 238

Friendships between women, 142–45, 151–52

Fries, Carrie, 190

Front Royal, battle of, 217

Galveston, Tex., 245

Garner, Helen, 229

Gay, Mary, 49, 193

Gender roles, 260 (n. 2); social hierarchy and, 3–4, 5–6, 32; effects of Civil War on, 4, 5, 6, 7, 135–37, 247; women's right to protection, 6, 59, 247; prerogatives of womanhood, 7, 199–201; and women's self-sacrifice, 17–18, 166; women and escape from, 20, 231–33; and master-slave relations, 54, 63–64, 69, 70; conscription and, 55–56; ideology of female dependence, 59, 63, 78, 82, 211, 251; and use of violence, 63, 69, 70; and women's employment, 82, 90, 92, 98, 110, 112–13; and women's education, 84; and female friendships, 144; women authors and, 166, 177; Union occupation troops and, 197, 199–200, 201, 205, 210, 211; politicization of women and, 210, 211–12, 213–14; women's wartime exploitation of, 215, 218–19; women's fashion and, 221, 223; cross-dressing and, 227, 228, 229–30; racial prerogatives and, 253–54

General Order No. 28, 209–12

teers and, 93–94, 101–12; Confederate government and, 96, 97–98; matrons, 97, 98–101; visiting, 102–4

Households: economy of, 31–32; diversity of, 34–35, 37; home manufacturing, 45–48, 49, 50–51, 221–22, 269 (n. 28), 269–70 (n. 29); domestic labor, 49, 72, 77–78, 130

Houston, Margaret, 187

Hubard, Lucy, 232

Hubard, Maria, 27, 28, 80

Hughes, Sarah, 74–75

Hundley, Mahala, 163

Inflation, 44, 88

Ingraham, Mrs. A., 59

Interracial relationships, 126–27

Ironclad warships, 28, 29

"I've Kissed Him and Let Him Go," 18

"I Would Like to Change My Name," 17

Jackson, Thomas J. ("Stonewall"), 215, 217

*Jacksonville Standard*, 11

Jeff (slave), 61

*Jeff Petticoats*, 229

Jett, Nancy Mae, 41

Joe (slave), 64

Johnston, Diana, 88–89

Jones, Anne Goodwyn, 171

Jones, Eva, 76

Jones, Mary, 76–77

Joynes, Edward, 85

Kate (slave), 69

Kelley, Mary, 154

Kemble, Fanny, 176–77

Kennedy, Jimmy, 130

Kennedy, Mary, 130

Kennedy, Sally, 130

Kennedy, Sarah, 73, 120, 121, 130, 149

Kerber, Linda, 263 (n. 7)

Kirkpatrick, J. K., 83

Kirtland, Anna, 140

Knitting, 25, 49, 50

Labor shortages, 81, 88, 92

Ladies Memorial Associations, 252

"Ladyhood," 7, 27, 110, 113, 247, 253

LaGrange, Ga., 203

Latané, William, 188

Laura (slave), 74

Lawton, Sarah, 14–15

Lebsock, Suzanne, 252

LeConte, Emma, 50, 155, 156, 199, 221

Lee, Laura, 58, 76, 109

Lee, Mary Greenhow, 31, 215; as displaced person, 40, 41, 214, 248; household of, 40, 156; and household labor, 49, 76; home textile production, 50; on black soldiers, 60; and slaves, 76, 77; as hospital volunteer, 107–8, 110, 206, 214; on wartime friendships, 144; on reading, 156–57, 175; as writer, 164, 166, 175; and religion, 185, 188–89, 198; frustration with war, 191, 195, 236; hostility toward Yankee soldiers, 197–98, 200, 201, 205, 206, 214, 219; on clothing fashions, 222; on reconstruction, 248, 254

Legg, Mary, 26–27, 47, 175, 236

Le Grand, Julia, 20, 239

Letters: between husbands and wives, 115–20, 162, 243; cost of mail service, 116; to government officials, 162–63, 193–94; censorship of, 243

Lewis, Rose, 118

Liberalism, 171–72, 243

Lincoln, Abraham, 58, 154, 185

Literature, 153–54, 158, 165, 255

Liza (slave), 71

Lost Cause iconography, 60, 247, 252–53, 254

Love, Mrs. C., 28–29

*Love's Ambuscade* (Delchamps), 140

Lucy (slave), 226

Lucy Cobb Institute, 143
Lystra, Karen, 162

Mabry, Sal, 240
McClellan, George B., 159, 201
McClure, Kate, 61
McConnell, Anna, 194
McCord, Louisa, 106, 110, 111, 112, 232, 233
McCurry, Stephanie, 269 (n. 28)
McDonald, Cornelia, 246; as nurse, 106, 107; and religion, 193; and Union occupation troops, 200, 206; difficulties providing for children, 206, 236
McDonald, Harry, 200
McDonald, Henrietta, 194
McGuire, Judith, 146, 163
McKamy, Elizabeth, 202
McKee, Eliza, 111–12, 232
MacLean, Clara Dargan, 27, 232–33; as teacher, 87, 90–91; on women's employment, 91, 111–12; on wartime marriages, 148; as author, 167
*Macon Daily Telegraph*, 55
McRaven, David, 118
Magruder, J. B., 96
Mail service, 115–16, 243
Manassas, first battle of, 181, 189
Manufacturing, 45, 80–81; household production, 45–48, 49, 50–51, 221–22, 269 (n. 28), 269–70 (n. 29)
Marriage: northern customs and, 6; preferences for soldiers, 17, 140, 146; disruption of gender roles in, 136–37; and women's identity, 139–40, 151; single women's preoccupation with, 140, 145–46, 150, 151; women's cynicism toward, 141; sexual relations and, 147–48; widows and, 148, 150
Martha (slave), 135
Martin, Anne, 157, 225
Mason, Emily, 99
Maury, Betty, 59–60

Medway, Louise, 96
Men: in social hierarchy, 4, 32, 193; and protection of women, 6, 59, 121, 247, 251; military expectations of, 13–15, 30; women's envy of, 20, 111, 221, 231, 232; absence from homefront, 31, 32, 36, 51, 63–64, 115; and women's employment, 47, 123; management of slaves, 53, 54–55, 63, 70; and violence, 63, 65, 70; as nurses, 92, 97; slaves on homefront, 126–27, 266 (n. 1); and birth and rearing of children, 128, 132–34; women's disillusionment and anger with, 134, 137, 138, 204, 231–32, 251, 253, 256; women's identity and, 139–40, 141; women and clothing of, 220, 221, 227–28, 233; cross-dressing, 228–29; effects of war on, 252–53
Meyers (overseer), 66–67, 68, 69–70
Middle-class women, 154
Middleton, Susan, 52
Militarism, 239
Military camps, 146, 185
Military companies, 203
Military mobilization, 30–31, 45, 81, 109
Milledgeville, Ga., 27
*Milledgeville Confederate Union*, 6, 27, 46, 96
*Milledgeville Southern Federal Union*, 93, 203
Milroy, Robert (general), 198
Minor, John B., 22, 23
Mississippi, textile production in, 48
*Mississippi Homespun* (Lohrenz and Stamper), 48
Missouri, guerrilla warfare in, 200
Mitchell, Lise, 28, 44, 160, 164
Mobile, Ala., 124
*Mobile Advertiser and Register*, 58, 93, 210
*Mobile Evening News*, 176
*Mobile Register*, 244
*Monitor* and *Merrimac*, battle of, 28

15, 37, 116, 128; on ladies' aid societies, 25; on religion, 182

Pacifism, 239
Palmer, Harriet, 11, 47, 175, 236
*Palmetto State*, C.S.S., 29
Patriarchy and paternalism: Civil War and, 4; in plantation hierarchy, 32; men's departure for war and, 35, 121–23, 133–34; and protection of women, 59, 121; and slavery, 62–63, 70; women's employment and, 90, 110–11; and childrearing, 132–34; Confederate collapse and, 245, 247; Lost Cause mythology and, 247, 252–53; black emancipation and, 247, 253
Patriotism: conflict with family life, 13, 15, 16–17; and female self-sacrifice, 17, 234–35, 244; and anger toward Yankees, 21, 206; and women's employment, 22, 83; religion and, 180; erosion of, 238, 242, 243–44, 246, 247
Patsy (slave), 72
Peddy, George, 47, 114, 118, 120, 126, 128, 199
Peddy, Kate, 47, 114, 120–21, 128, 199
Pember, Phoebe Yates Levy, 110; as hospital matron, 98–99, 100–101, 102, 109, 111, 113; on wartime marriages, 146; on religion, 206
Pendleton, Jennie, 86
Peninsula campaign, 201
Perkins, Emily, 64, 86
Petersburg, Va., 43, 227–28
Pettus, John, 56
Petty, E. P., 123
Physicians, 100
Pickett's Charge, 256
Pinkind, Amelia, 88
Plantations, 31–32, 45; slave management, 55, 60; household labor, 77–78; women's raids on, 245
Poetry, 167

Politics, 243; women and, 10–12, 13, 54, 193–94, 262 (n. 4); religion and, 180, 193, 195; politicization of women, 210, 211–12, 213–14
Portsmouth, Va., 93
Poverty, 42
Prayer groups, 185
Pregnancy, fear of, 123–24, 126, 127–28
Prescott, Emma Slade, 77, 87
Preston, Mrs. John, 91
Preston, Margaret Junkin, 31, 129, 222, 238
Pringle, Elizabeth, 160
Propaganda, 48
Property laws, 251–52
Prostitution, 124–25, 212
Protection of women: male responsibility for, 6, 7, 59, 121, 247, 251; fear of blacks and, 59, 253
Pryor, Sara Agnes, 23, 104–6, 237, 244
Publishing industry, 154, 158
Pugh, Mary Williams, 241

Race, 260 (n. 2), 261–62 (n. 1); social hierarchy and, 3–4, 7, 223, 253–54; and protection of women, 59, 253
Racism, 73; in suffrage movement, 254
*Raleigh Standard*, 167
Ramsey, James D., 84–85
Randolph, Mrs. George, 98
Randolph County, Ala., 31
Rape, 200
Ravenel, Charlotte, 77
Reading, 154–61, 168, 175, 178
Ready, Alice: on frustration of being female, 20, 21; on availability of soldiers, 146; on reading, 153, 160; and religion, 182–83, 184, 192; and Union occupation troops, 198–99, 201, 202, 205–6
Reconstruction, 248
Refugees, 40–41, 42–45, 71, 161
Reid, John Phillip, 283 (n. 12)

Religion: *Macaria* and, 174; role in Confederacy, 179–82, 192–93, 194, 195; in politics, 180, 193, 195; and wartime suffering, 181–84, 187, 188–89, 191–92, 193; disruptions of war to, 184–86, 192–93, 195; soldiers and, 185, 186–87

*Religious Herald*, 186

Republicanism, 243

Revolutionary War, 5

Rhoda (slave), 61

Rice, Louisa, 241

Richmond, Elizabeth, 88

Richmond, Va.: women's employment in, 91; social opportunities in, 91–92, 146, 245; wartime marriages in, 150; Union invasion of, 159–60, 167; casualties in, 189; clothing trade in, 222–23

*Richmond Age*, 176, 178

Richmond *Christian Observer*, 180

*Richmond Enquirer*, 86, 167; on homespun fabrics, 46; on slave insurrection, 58; on wartime marriages, 150, 228; on book smuggling, 158; on social frivolity, 245

*Richmond Record*, 18

Roberts, Ellen, 141

"Rock Me to Sleep, Mother," 230

Rome, Ga., 202

Rosa (slave), 72

Rowland, Charlie, 13

Rowland, Kate (of Georgia), 13

Rowland, Kate (of Virginia), 185–86

Rutherford County, N.C., 222

Sam (slave), 66–69

Sams, Sarah Jane, 239

Samuels, Annie, 204

Sandy (slave), 71

Sarah (slave), 67, 69, 274 (n. 34)

Saxon, Elizabeth, 60

Scales, Cordelia, 108, 175, 227

Scales, Mary, 241–42

Scott, Anne Firor, 77, 253, 265 (n. 32)

Scott, Susan, 64

Scott, Walter, 157

Seamstresses, 89–90

Secession, 9–10, 11–13

Semmes, Jorantha, 37

Semmes, Thomas Jenkins (senator), 97

Semple, Letitia Tyler, 94

Separate spheres, 230, 263 (n. 7); and politics, 12; and women's employment, 82, 85; and women's self-sacrifice, 138; and women's fashion, 223, 225–26

"Servant problem," 250, 254

Seven Days battles, 39–40

Seven Pines, battle of, 238

Severa, Joan, 301 (n. 7)

Seward, Mattie, 182

Sewing, 24–25

Sexuality: husbands' absence and, 123, 124, 126; fear of pregnancy and, 123–24, 126, 127; soldiers and, 124–26; interracial relations, 126–27; and female friendships, 144; and wartime marriages, 147–48; women's fashion and, 223

Sexual vulnerability, 59, 211, 272–73 (n. 13); of black women, 73, 200

Sharkey, William, 133

Shelby, N.C., 28

Shelby County, Ala., 31

Shenandoah Valley, 197

Sheridan, Philip H., 214

Sherman, William T., 91; invasion of Georgia, 36, 40–41, 45, 130; and civilian population, 197

Shiloh, battle of, 96–97

Shorter, John Gill, 31, 32, 48

Sigaud, Louis, 214

Silber, Nina, 228

Simms, William, 97

Sims, Amanda, 11, 252

Single women, 139; preoccupation with marriage, 140, 145–46, 150, 151; cyni-

alry, Company D, 16; home defense in, 28; and slave trade, 262 (n. 3); women's political activism in, 262 (n. 4)

Virginia Insane Asylum, 236

Volunteer work, 90, 109

Wadley, Sarah, 43, 47, 145

Walker, Eliza, 74

Walton, Emma, 140, 231

Walton, Louisa, 31

Warner, Susan, 154

War production, 25, 45

Washington, William D.: *The Burial of Latané*, 188–89

Webster, Rowena, 228–29

Wesleyan Female College, 203

West, George, 45

West, Josephine, 45

Whipping: of slaves, 63, 64, 69, 273 (n. 21); of children, 132, 285 (n. 38)

White, Lucy, 163

Whiteness, 4, 254

White supremacy, 254

Widows, 110, 148, 149–50

Wiley, Calvin, 82–83

Wilkom, Ida, 193

William (slave), 62

Wilmington, N.C., Soldiers' Aid Society, 96

Winchester, Va., 31, 231; hospitals in, 107, 109; Union occupation of, 205, 206

*Winchester Virginian*, 14

Windle, Catherine, 89, 90

Witherspoon, Betsey, 57

Womack, Mrs. Thomas, 163

Women's organizations, 23–24, 265 (n. 32); production of troop supplies, 24–25; and hospitals, 93–94, 95–96; postwar, 253

Women's rights movement, 5, 6, 256

Women's schools, 39–40, 83–84, 142–43

Wood, Lucy, 9–10, 11, 24

Woodruff, Isabella, 31, 148–49

Woodruff, Virginia Daniel, 86

Woodward, C. Vann, 164, 255, 256

Working classes, 41, 50, 90

World War I, 239

Worthington, Amanda: and household labor, 78; and availability of soldiers, 146–47, 148; on reading, 158; hostility toward Yankee soldiers, 206; and clothing fashions, 225, 226–27

Writing, 161–68, 178, 291 (n. 24)

Wyatt-Brown, Bertram, 132

Yarrington, Lizzie, 89

Yeadon, Richard, 29

ALONE OF ALL HER SEX
*The Myth and the Cult of the Virgin Mary*
by Marina Warner

Exploring the various roles Mary has assumed—Virgin, Queen, Bride, Mother, Intercessor—and drawing on various disciplines, Marina Warner shows how the figure of Mary has shaped and been shaped by changing social and historical circumstances from the first century to the present day.

History/0-394-71155-6

BLACK WOMEN IN WHITE AMERICA
*A Documentary History*
edited by Gerda Lerner

Slaves and school teachers, political activists and domestic servants, factory workers and philanthropic club women relate their own histories and the larger experience of their race and gender in this brilliantly researched and moving anthology.

Women's Studies/African-American Studies/0-679-74314-6

THE DEVIL IN THE SHAPE OF A WOMAN
*Witchcraft in Colonial New England*
by Carol F. Karlsen

In this provocative study, Carol F. Karlsen examines a society in which fears of witchery and witch hunts helped reinforce the status quo and reflected deeper sexual, religious, and economic tensions.

History/Women's Studies/0-679-72184-3

FEMINISM
*The Essential Historical Writings*
edited by Miriam Schneir

This richly diverse collection traces the path of women's struggle for freedom from the time of the American Revolution to the years after World War I. This seminal work includes excerpts from authors ranging from Mary Wollstonecraft to Virginia Woolf.

Women's Studies/History/0-679-75381-8

FEMINISM IN OUR TIME
*The Essential Writings
from World War II to the Present*
edited by Miriam Schneir

Here are the writings that inspired and continue to shape contemporary feminism as the source of the most profound social change in the
world today. Beginning with the trailblazing works of Simone de
Beauvoir, Doris Lessing, and Betty Friedan, *Feminism in Our Time*
charts the women's movement to the present day.

Women's Studies/History/0-679-74508-4


LABOR OF LOVE, LABOR OF SORROW
*Black Women, Work and the Family,
from Slavery to the Present*
by Jacqueline Jones

"A seminal work of scholarship, which has no rival."
—Henry Louis Gates, Jr.

*Labor of Love, Labor of Sorrow* offers a powerful account of the
changing role of American black women, in the labor force and in
the family.

*Winner of the Bancroft Prize*
Social History/0-394-74536-1


A MIDWIFE'S TALE
*The Life of Martha Ballard,
Based on Her Diary, 1785–1812*
by Laurel Thatcher Ulrich

*A Midwife's Tale* tells the story of midwife and healer Martha
Ballard, who kept a diary that recorded her arduous work as well as
her domestic life in eighteenth-century Maine.

*Winner of the Pulitzer Prize
and the Bancroft Prize*
American History/Women's Studies/0-679-73376-0

ALSO AVAILABLE:
*Good Wives*/0-679-73257-8

REFUGE

*An Unnatural History of Family and Place*

by Terry Tempest Williams

Through tragedies both personal and environmental, Utah-born naturalist Terry Tempest Williams creates a document of renewal and spiritual grace that is a moving meditation on nature, women, and grieving.

Women's Studies/Nature/0-679-74024-4

THE ROAD FROM COORAIN

by Jill Ker Conway

A remarkable woman's clear-sighted memoir of growing up Australian: from the vastness of a sheep station in the outback to the stifling propriety of postwar Sydney; from an untutored childhood to a life in academia; and from the shelter of a protective family to the lessons of independence.

Autobiography/0-679-72436-2

THE SECOND SEX

by Simone de Beauvoir

Drawing on extensive interviews with women of every age and station of life, masterfully synthesizing research about women's historic and economic roles, *The Second Sex* is an encyclopedic and brilliantly argued document of inequality and enforced "otherness."

Women's Studies/0-679-72451-6

SISTERHOOD IS POWERFUL

*An Anthology of Writings*
*From the Liberation Movement*

Edited by Robin Morgan

This anthology is a comprehensive collection of writings from the women's liberation movement, including articles, poems, photographs, and manifestos.

Current Events/0-394-70539-4

Available from your local bookstore, or call toll-free to order:
1-800-793-2665 (credit cards only)